Women, Families, and Communities

READINGS IN AMERICAN HISTORY

Volume II

FROM 1865

Women, Families, and Communities

READINGS IN AMERICAN HISTORY

SECOND EDITION

NANCY HEWITT

KIRSTEN DELEGARD

PEARSON
Longman

New York   San Francisco   Boston
London   Toronto   Sydney   Tokyo   Singapore   Madrid
Mexico City   Munich   Paris   Cape Town   Hong Kong   Montreal

Vice President and Publisher: Priscilla McGeehon
Executive Editor: Michael Boezi
Executive Marketing Manager: Sue Westmoreland
Editorial Assistant: Vanessa Gennarelli
Production Manager: Savoula Amanatidis
Project Coordination and Text Design: Elm Street Publishing Services, Inc.
Electronic Page Makeup: Integra Software Services, Pvt. Ltd.
Cover Design Manager: Wendy Ann Fredericks
Cover Designer: Susan Koski Zucker
Cover Photo: Lewis Wickes Hine/NYPL Digital Gallery
Photo Researcher: Anita Dickhuth
Manufacturing Buyer: Lucy Hebard
Printer and Binder: Courier Corporation—Stoughton
Cover Printer: Courier Corporation—Stoughton

For permission to use copyrighted material, grateful acknowledgement is made to the
copyright holders on p. 323, which are hereby made part of this copyright page.

Library of Congress Cataloging-in-Publication Data

Women, families, and communities: readings in American history, volume 2 from
    1365/[edited by] Nancy Hewitt, Kirsten Delegard.—2nd ed.
      p. cm.
    ISBN–13: 978-0-321-41487-8 (alk. paper)
    1. Women—United States—History.   2. United States—Social conditions.   I. Hewitt,
    Nancy A.   II. Delegard, Kirsten.
    HQ1410.W646 2008
    306.85082'0973—dc22   2007019733

Please visit us at www.ablongman.com

ISBN 13: 978-0-321-41486-1
ISBN 10: 0-321-41486-1

1 2 3 4 5 6 7 8 9 10—CRS—10 09 08 07

To my brother, Will, and in memory of Tom.
N. H.

To my mother, Dorothy Delegard,
who taught me the importance of women,
families, and communities.
K. D.

Contents

Part IV Mobilizing Communities   186

Part V Families in Transition   248

Appendix   295

Good research and good teaching go hand in hand. The first edition of *Women, Families, and Communities: Readings in American History* grew directly out of the connection between these two activities in Nancy Hewitt's own work. As a student of women's history—and more specifically of women's activism and women's work in Rochester, New York, and Tampa, Florida—Hewitt traced the ways that ordinary mothers, wives, and daughters contributed to the development of their families and communities. At the same time, as a teacher of introductory American history, she focused on the ways that the major events in our nation's past—wars, elections, depressions, and technological revolutions—shaped and were shaped by the lives and actions of common women and men.

The articles collected here provide an introduction for students and instructors to the rich historical literature on women, families, and communities as well as a means for integrating the insights of this research into the story of North America's past. Most students come to college with a limited knowledge of the diverse experiences of American women across time and place. Fortunately, many college textbooks in American history now incorporate substantial information on women and family life, but given the vast amount of material to be covered, they can generally offer only brief attention to these topics in any one period. Women's history textbooks provide a much richer array of materials on a more diverse range of women. Still, it is difficult in a textbook or in lectures to cover both the broad sweep of American or women's history and the particular experiences and actions of a wide array of historical actors. By combining the readings from this anthology with texts, lectures, and other monographs, students will learn how ordinary individuals, like themselves, participated in the shaping of America's past.

What is clear in looking at the table of contents in this volume and in works on women's history in general is the diversity of American experiences. Although it is impossible to capture this diversity in a single collection, it is possible to encourage students to think about the range and richness of the American past. How did American Indians respond to European colonization? How did Africans respond to slavery? How did the experiences and meanings of industrialization, World War I, or the Great Depression differ by region, race, class, ethnic background, and gender? How and when did groups generally viewed as oppressed—American Indians, African Americans, workers, women, immigrants—find the means to organize and protest on their own behalf? How did age shape individual experiences of and responses to colonization, war, industrialization, urbanization, and other historical developments? Each of these questions and the many others raised by the authors of the articles included here challenges us to see how everyday life and the "great events" of history intersect.

It is precisely at such intersections that women's historians most often are struck by the impossibility of separating women's experiences from those of men. In teaching American history, many of us have now integrated research on female activists and female workers into the larger stories of social reform and agricultural and industrial development. Even if we focus on seemingly more masculine historical endeavors such as war, we quickly see how the activities and experiences of women and men are intertwined. We cannot fully understand the causes of wars, their short-term consequences or long-term significance, the means by which one side wins and the other loses, or even the particular strategies and tactics employed, without examining women's as well as men's participation.

In the earliest wars studied in an American history survey course—the French and Indian War, the Revolutionary War, the Civil War—the boundaries between the battlefield and the home front were blurred and always changing. During such conflicts, although women and men were expected to carry out different tasks, either sex might find itself called upon to nurse, cook, sew, spy, or fight. In later periods, when North Americans fought their wars overseas—in Cuba, the Philippines, Europe, and Asia—women's and men's roles were more distinct. Still, as men left for training camp and foreign combat, women expanded their activities on the home front to encompass many traditionally male jobs within the family, community, industries, government, and professions. In the most recent conflicts involving the United States—in Afghanistan and Iraq, for example—women have served in a much wider array of roles within the military and more have joined men on the battlefront. In whichever time period, whether men alone or men and women are serving on the frontlines, and whatever the location or duration of battles, family and community members find their normal relations disrupted and transformed—sometimes temporarily, sometimes forever.

Developing links between women's history and history that has traditionally emphasized men and masculine activities is one of the goals of this work. Thus, the readings included here, most of which were written by women's historians, were selected because they chronicle local as well as national history; social as well as political and economic development; and women's as well as men's experiences and actions.

These articles provide case studies of individuals, families, and communities that illustrate broader historical themes. The introductions to each of the chronological parts, the headnotes to each of the articles, and the Suggested Readings and Web Sites and Questions for Study and Review at the end of each article place the individual essays in a wider context. At the same time, this material suggests how larger historical developments were themselves shaped by the events that occurred in particular families and communities. For each article, the study and review questions require students to relate the material presented to major issues of the time period and to other articles in the reader.

As researchers, scholars generally approach history as a complex process in which a wide range of individuals, experiences, and institutions come into play. As teachers, we often find it difficult to convey such complexities to our students. This volume is an attempt to introduce into the American history and women's history survey course more of the process of studying history. By asking students to connect political events with social forces and great affairs of state with common occurrences such as birth, marriage, housework, childrearing, sex, sharecropping, and washing clothes, we can help students understand what was involved in forming, sustaining, and transforming the people, families, and communities that built our nation.

This second edition of *Women, Families, and Communities* reflects many of the changes in American history and American women's history that have occurred since 1990. It also reflects the insights of the co-editor, Kirsten Delegard, an independent historian whose work focuses on revising understandings of women's activism by examining how conservative women shaped politics in the twentieth century. Thus, this edition not only incorporates an even wider range of racial, ethnic, and regional perspectives than the first edition but also incorporates a wider range of ideological perspectives. This edition also explores more fully the gendered character of the American past. Interactions between women and men—whether in the midst of colonial conquest, plantation households, social activism, or military ventures—are highlighted throughout the volumes. In addition, men's relation to other men is also examined in particular contexts, including the California Gold Rush, post-Civil War politics, and the civil rights movement. Finally, since the first edition was published, studies of sexuality have reshaped understandings of women's and gender history. New work in this field appears in this volume, demonstrating the intimate connections among sexuality, family, and community life and local and regional political and social developments.

The selection of articles and images has been an intense learning experience. We have been constantly amazed, and often frustrated, in making hard choices among the profusion of wonderful books, articles, prints, and photographs. We hope that the revisions and additions to this edition of *Women, Families, and Communities* will make the volumes as intellectually engaging and challenging to students as the work has been to us.

For their thoughtful evaluations and constructive suggestions, we wish to thank our reviewers: Kathryn Abbott, Western Kentucky University; Linda Alkana, California State University–Long Beach; Jacqueline Cavalier, Community College of Allegheny County; Stephanie Cole, University of Texas–Arlington; Kate M. Dierenfield, Canisius College; Christine Erickson, Indiana–Purdue University, Fort Wayne; Laura Fishman, York College; Jackie Flowers, Clackamas Community College; Anne Klejment, University of St. Thomas; Wendy Kline, University of Cincinnati; Peter Levy, York College; Alison M. Parker, State University of New York–Brockport; Linda Pitelka, Maryville University; Lelia Roeckell, Molloy College; Catherine Tobin, Central Michigan University; Shirley Teresa Wajda, Kent State University; and Nancy Zens, Central Oregon Community College.

Nancy Hewitt
Kirsten Delegard

History has a dual meaning: It refers both to the events of the past and to interpretations of those events. The events that make up American history involved all kinds of people and took place in every type of setting. Rich, middling, and poor; white, brown, and black; native-born and immigrant; young and old; female and male; in cities and on farms; in metropolitan centers and in small villages; in long-settled communities and on the move; North and South; East and West—all Americans shaped the nation's history. Indians, blacks, and Hispanics as well as Europeans populated the North American continent; immigrant and farm families as well as "first families" produced its citizens; workers and grassroots activists as well as entrepreneurs and political leaders shaped its development.

Yet for a long time, scholars' interpretations of the past concentrated on Western Europeans and their American-born descendants, especially the men who served as business, political, or military leaders. These figures received far more attention than any other group, often more than all other groups combined. Such interpretations directed our eyes to a narrow segment of the continent's rich history. Like viewfinders at the Grand Canyon, they focused our gaze on the most spectacular peaks and valleys but failed to reveal the more mundane materials and processes that helped forge these vistas.

Historians are less like viewfinders than photographers. They actively select the angle of vision and the subject that they think will best reflect or illuminate a particular moment. A photographer covering a presidential campaign rally may stand in the crowd, but he or she will use a telephoto lens to zoom in on the candidate. In the morning paper, then, one will see only blurred, background images of the women and men who will vote in the election but a detailed, larger-than-life portrait of the man or woman who seeks to represent them. If we think of history textbooks as providing snapshots of significant moments in America's past, then this volume is an attempt to bring the blurred backgrounds into focus—indeed, to bring those background figures momentarily to the forefront.

Since the first edition of *Women, Families, and Communities* was published in 1990, much has changed in the world of photography as well as in women's history. Digital cameras, scanners, camera phones, computers, and similar technologies make it easier for ordinary people to capture images and events and to disseminate them electronically to a wide and varied audience. Still, it is important to remember that earlier changes in technology also transformed American society and women's and men's relationships to visual culture. In 1839, for example, Louis Daguerre perfected the first practical method for taking photographs, and daguerreotypes (early photographs) became popular among urban residents who sat for pictures at local studios and rural folk who were introduced to the technique by traveling daguerreotypists. The Civil War greatly increased the demand for daguerreotypes as soldiers sent home pictures of themselves in uniform and commercial photographers like Mathew Brady chronicled the conflict on the battlefield. Such images—or engravings and lithographs based on them—were widely circulated due to advances in print technology in the early and mid-nineteenth century, which led to inexpensive illustrated newspapers and magazines. Some women used the new technology to advance their views on the social issues of the day. Abolitionist and women's rights advocate Sojourner Truth sold portraits of herself, known as *cartes de visite,* to help support herself and her reform activities. A host of later inventions, from the first inexpensive handheld camera (marketed as the Kodak) to the movie camera, television, video, computers, and camera phones, continued to democratize the creation and circulation of visual images.

Each of these new technologies transformed the way we see the world and whom we see in the world. Today television stations increasingly employ pictures or videos shot by individuals who happen to be present when a newsworthy event occurs. Indeed, those individuals sometimes help to determine what is newsworthy. Video clips produced by amateurs, for instance, might reveal a grainy underside of life—police beating an unarmed suspect—or a heroic moment—neighbors catching a baby thrown from the window of a burning home—that would otherwise be missed. Such images are no more easily interpreted than those created by professional camera crews, but they do provide a different perspective, and they frequently illuminate figures that might otherwise have remained hidden from history. At the same time, digital cameras, camera phones, and Web sites offer ordinary women and men new opportunities to shape and circulate their own images and those of others. Our familiarity today with the means by which images can be manipulated, for better or worse, should sensitize us as we examine earlier representations of women, and men, in American history. And the pictures and video clips themselves will provide future generations with new ways to investigate at least some of those background figures in American history.

To focus on a wide range of American experiences, we can draw on the voluminous work produced in the last three decades by social historians.

Social history emphasizes the experiences of common women and men, allowing us to hear the voices of those rendered "inarticulate" by traditional interpretations. Viewing the past as a dynamic process in which all Americans participated, these scholars have revealed the ways that American Indians, African Americans, immigrants, workers, and women shaped their worlds and our history. Other types of historians have now embraced the questions raised by social historians. Political historians investigate the role of race, class, and gender in voting and campaigning. Cultural historians trace the rise of the market economy and consumer culture or the ways African Americans and women shape and are shaped by music, literature, art, and film.

These historians have been especially concerned to discover the ways that those with only limited resources influenced the course of economic, social, and political development. By focusing on individual forms of resistance to exploitation (such as a slave feigning illness or purposely setting a slow pace of work) as well as collective acts of protest (such as boycotts, demonstrations, and organized social movements), historians have illuminated an entirely new historical terrain. This terrain is one on which ordinary women and men—regardless of their wealth, status, or formal political power—become active agents of change, affecting critical historical developments.

To uncover the activities and ideas of less powerful groups, historians often search out evidence on individual families and communities as a means of exploring the occurrences of everyday life. These events are then placed beside those we conventionally think of as important in America's past to illuminate the relations between ordinary people and extraordinary events. The present volume will draw on this rich body of research to bring these background figures into focus.

The purpose of focusing on more common people and their daily routines, of moving apparently peripheral figures to center stage, is not simply to replace one angle of vision with another. While we are examining seemingly unremarkable women and men in their families and communities, we will often discover their remarkable qualities—courage, persistence, strength, ingenuity. We will find that common folk performed uncommon feats when social upheaval, economic crisis, wartime mobilization, or personal necessity demanded that they do so. Yet at the same time, we will find women and men prevented from acting in their own interests or those of their neighbors by poverty, prejudice, and other disabling factors. Finally, we will explore how some members of less powerful groups—wealthy women, for example—used their access to education, financial resources, or political influence to shape (or constrain) the lives and life choices of others.

This volume, then, will examine how ordinary people both shaped and were shaped by the persons and events traditionally considered central to the nation's development. Ultimately, a new vision of our history will appear, one that brings into simultaneous focus national events and leaders and ordinary people in local communities. In this way, relationships between common folk in their everyday lives (people like most of you reading this book) and individual leaders of states, armies, corporations, and social movements will be made clearer.

Photographs are not only selective images of persons and events. They are also often idealized versions, simple images that reflect complex realities. The portrait of a former slave holding a white child (previous page) can carry many captions, none of which will fully capture the intimate and ambiguous relations between black women and their white charges. The look in this unnamed woman's eyes may be resignation or defiance. Her employment as a nanny after the Civil War may be a sign of new opportunities or renewed bondage. The baby may grow up to be a member of the Ku Klux Klan or of the National Association for the Advancement of Colored People.

We all develop images of the kinds of people who make up the population— of women and men, blacks and whites, workers and bosses, rural southerners and cosmopolitan northerners. Our perceptions range from accurate to stereotypical to fanciful. These images emerge from newspapers, television, schoolrooms, novels, films, advertising, Web sites, community and family attitudes, and a host of other sources. In past centuries, sermons, paintings, magazines, lectures, traveling museums, cartoons, folktales, and songs were even more important in shaping Americans' views of the world around them and, perhaps more markedly, of people and places far distant. Such images, regardless of their accuracy, affected the ways that any one group of Americans responded to others—Europeans to American Indians, whites to blacks, country folk to city dwellers, southerners to northerners, women to men.

Depictions of women, families, and communities have changed dramatically over the years, but in each era dominant images have provided ideals to be either emulated or defied. Indian princesses, submissive wives, hardy pioneers, black nannies, Victorian ladies, flamboyant flappers, wartime riveters, happy homemakers, women's libbers—each presented a portrait with which or against which women were measured and measured themselves. Since most such figures were based on a single class or race of women, it is only by examining a variety of individuals from a range of families and communities that we can begin to understand how such ideal types arose and what their effects were on women and men of particular times and places.

Family and community are also idealized notions. Leading commentators from every generation of American citizens have lamented the decline of the "traditional" family and the loss of the "close-knit" community. Puritan clergy and born-again Christians, female moral reformers of the mid-nineteenth century and political candidates of the twenty-first, eighteenth-century diarists and contemporary bloggers have all bemoaned the failure of real-life families and communities to live up to the models we carry in our minds. We should not let the similarity of these laments obscure real differences in the changing forms of family and community life over time and across region, race, ethnicity, and class.

Yet commonalities in these laments can tell us something important about people's shared desire for a sense of place and of belonging, regardless of how big or developed or powerful the nation as a whole becomes. Again, only by examining a variety of settings and situations over the course of American history can we begin to understand the multiple forms family and community have taken and their effects on regional, racial, ethnic, and class relations and on national development.

Women's historians have devoted particular attention to these dimensions of our American heritage: common folk, daily life, dominant cultural symbols and images, definitions of family and community, popular forms of protest, and differences in each of these rooted in race, class, ethnicity, and region. Women's historians, focusing initially on the differences in women's and men's experiences in the past, have asked new questions, introduced new sources, offered new interpretations of the roles that women played in America, and suggested new ways of marking major transitions and turning points in our nation's history.

Emerging from the women's movement of the 1960s and 1970s, these scholars initially applied the feminist rubric—"the personal is political"—to examinations of history. Thus, they focused on the relations between public and private spheres, home and work, domesticity and politics. They considered whether changes in household technology and birth control methods might be as important as presidential elections and wars in determining how to divide American history into meaningful units of study. To probe these and other issues, researchers examined diaries and letters, census data and wills, sermons and novels, clothing and advertisements, and other artifacts left by those whose words and actions were not purposely recorded for posterity.

This research provides portraits of women as mothers, daughters, and wives; as servants, slaves, and free women; as wage earners, housewives, and volunteers; as immigrants, migrants, and settlers; and the whole range of roles that formed the female half of society. Some scholars focus on notable women—Abigail Adams, Elizabeth Cady Stanton, Ida B. Wells, Eleanor Roosevelt, Rosa Parks—demonstrating their right to be set alongside their male counterparts in the pantheon of American heroes. Others study all-female organizations and institutions—women's colleges and prisons, suffrage associations, literary societies, or single-sex reform groups—arguing for women's vital contributions to every phase of the nation's development. Some examine women's work, in and outside the family, and analyze its contributions to farming, commerce, slavery, industry, and the ever expanding service sector. Many follow the lives of ordinary women, as individuals and in groups, from birth to death, seeking to understand the parameters of female lives and how they have changed over time and place.

Yet researchers were not interested in looking at women only as a separate group, as important as that dimension of our history is. Rather, they also studied women in relations to men, to communities, and to the larger society. From this dual perspective—women's own experiences as women and their relationships with men—women's historians began rewriting American history to reflect the contributions and activities of the whole population. In doing so, they introduced gender—the cultural prescriptions and social roles assigned to individuals on the basis of their sex—as a critical category of analysis.

Since the 1980s, many scholars of women's and gender history have highlighted differences among women and the conflicts and challenges such differences spark. Scholars in the field have long sought to analyze women's agency, but more of them now recognize the ways that women wield power, and not only for progressive causes and ideals. Some women, for example, express racist beliefs and work to have them enshrined in law or enacted through violence in local communities. Throughout the past, women have disagreed with each other over fundamental political and social issues, and some have had a greater chance than others to put their ideas into practice. Given such disparities, it remains critical to trace the histories of women with few resources who have acted on behalf of themselves and their families and communities, confronting individuals and institutions that have more power and resources. Whether focusing on women with abundant or limited resources, it is also important to analyze women's relations with men as they pursue social and political agendas. When do women organize alongside other women, and when do they ally themselves with men? And how does each choice shape their public efforts and private relationships?

A renewed emphasis on culture has also transformed women's and gender history in recent years. For example, scholars have focused on how cultural differences among Indians, Europeans, and Africans shaped contact and conflict in the Americas during the colonial period and beyond. They have explored images and ideals of women and men from various races, regions, nationalities, religions, classes, and ages, exploring the ways that such representations shape, and distort, their interactions across time and place. Finally, cultural historians have joined with social and political historians to demonstrate the intertwined character of public and private life by examining such topics as the militarization of women and society in wartime; women's use of patriotic, moralistic, or racist rhetoric and icons to advance their own rights; and changes in patterns of consumption and consumer culture.

In expanding the reach of women's and gender history, scholars continue to frame their studies in different ways. Some use a wide-angle lens, emphasizing national or international developments; others focus in more closely on regional developments; and still others hone in on local histories or individual biographies.

This volume highlights the work of those who analyze women in the context of their families and communities. In such studies, the new scholarship on women is integrated with that on men, and the lives of native-born white women and men are set beside those of American Indians, African Americans, and immigrants. The particular communities examined here cover various regions of the country and include members of a wide range of races, classes, and ethnic groups. Using gender as a key category of analysis, each study illuminates some important aspect of our nation's development. Collectively, these readings reveal the changing nature of women's and men's roles and of family and community across the course of American history and analyze how these changes shaped and were shaped by larger social, economic, and political forces.

The articles in this book will provide evidence that can be used in combination with information from other readings, lectures, and discussions to draw a new portrait of our national past. Imagine for a moment what the slave trade, the American Revolution, the Gold Rush, the Great Depression, or the civil rights movement would look like if viewed for the first time through the lens of a video camera held by a woman standing in her local community. Imagine the Pocahontas legend if it had been recorded and embellished by Indian women rather than English men. Think for a moment of the way Sherman's March to the Sea during the Civil War would have been portrayed by a house slave in Atlanta. How might the breaking waves of the Atlantic Ocean or the overland trail to the West have been seen by a young wife with a child in tow and another on the way? Consider what a document listing the advantages of technological progress might contain if it were compiled by a young woman factory worker in the 1840s or the owner of a new wringer washer in the 1920s.

Contemplate what Pearl Harbor meant to a black domestic servant in Texas or a Japanese-American girl completing her senior year of high school. Speculate on the way organized black women in Montgomery, Alabama, would remember Martin Luther King, Jr., whom they had to persuade to lead the city's bus boycott in 1955.

How might these portraits of the past vary if in each situation the woman recording or recalling the moment was replaced by her brother? How would they differ if history were recorded not from the perspective of their family and community, but from yours? By combining the rich documentation of ordinary women's and men's lives collected by historians with traditional interpretations of significant events and with our own understanding of how change occurs, we can begin to focus on a more complete picture of the past. This picture brings into view diverse groups of Americans and a wide range of issues, individuals, and events. If we could make it move, we would have something like a videotape of the past, perhaps the closest we could come to making the events of history and our interpretations of them converge. Even then, however, we might not agree with another person's idea of American history, for each person's view of historical events is unique. That uniqueness reflects in part America's heritage of diversity.

From the moment when American Indians, Europeans, and Africans first encountered one another in the New World, diversity characterized the continent's development. In the present, diversity—and the creativity and conflict it nurtures—continues to define the American nation. Differences in race and region, ethnicity and class, wealth and power, sex and social status shaped the nation's history as they shape the lives, culture, economic opportunities, and political choices of those who live in the United States. By capturing that half of history that occurred in local communities, among ordinary families composed of common women and men, we reveal this diversity and thus more fully illuminate both the past and the present. The readings in this book will remind us that everyone—presidents, generals, corporate leaders, students, wage earners, and housewives—helps to create history.

Volume II

FROM 1865

Women, Families, and Communities

READINGS IN AMERICAN HISTORY

PART I

The New American Order

Lewis Hine illuminated the hardships of early twentieth century immigrant workers through photographs like this, which shows a woman and children performing industrial piecework on their tenement kitchen table.

The Civil War and the Reconstruction that followed were turning points in American history. As the nation was ripped apart and then reunited, economic, social, and political systems were transformed. Constitutional amendments granted citizenship to African Americans newly freed from slavery and voting rights to African American men; industrial development in the North, spurred by the necessities of war, continued to expand while southern lands and agriculture lay shattered; western settlement once again boomed as railroads traversed the mountain states and American Indians were forced onto reservations; and new forms of education, communication, and transportation forged closer connections among the nation's diverse regions.

These stories of U.S. development were played out not just on the terrain of high politics and national economies, however, but also in the everyday lives of women, families, and communities. The experiences of women in the South are especially revealing. More than a quarter of the one million men who served in the Confederate Army died during the Civil War. The South was thus filled with widows and with single women who had little hope of finding a husband. Even white women whose husbands returned home might end up caring for invalids and supporting their households financially. To meet the needs of their families, white women in the post–Civil War South advocated better schools, higher education for women, and state support of hospitals, orphan asylums, almshouses, and other forms of social welfare. By the late nineteenth century, these women had formed women's clubs, temperance societies, and even suffrage associations. Some also established organizations like the United Daughters of the Confederacy to commemorate Civil War battles and cemeteries and to memorialize what they viewed as the righteousness of the Confederate cause.

African American women in the South faced quite different challenges in reconstructing their families and communities. Although they were freed from bondage, many had been long separated from parents, children, and husbands. Since marriage did not legally exist for slaves, even couples who had been together for years had no formal recognition of their marital status. Moreover, newly freed blacks had to reconstitute their families in a period of enormous economic and political upheaval, at a time when transportation and communication systems had been shattered by war. Of course, African Americans also had to find work in a devastated economy and gain at least a minimal education, in part to keep from being cheated by hostile white employers. Most freedwomen and men did not have the resources to establish a new life on their own, and thus many invested in building community institutions like schools and churches to improve their chances collectively. Finally, as black women and men struggled to create new lives, they faced the wrath of former Confederates who were embittered by defeat and ready to lash out at any southerners, especially black southerners, whom they saw as benefiting from the Union victory.

The Ku Klux Klan, founded in 1866 by Confederate veterans, was one of several white supremacist organizations established in direct response to the efforts of African

Americans to make their freedom count. The Klan was especially vicious in its attacks on black families who had purchased land, opened businesses, or participated in electoral politics. At the same time, black women continued to face sexual abuse at the hands of white men, who had grown used to exploiting enslaved women without fear of legal reprisal and who harbored even greater hostility toward freedwomen. The Memphis riot of 1866, analyzed in Chapter One by Hannah Rosen, offers a vivid portrait of the brutality faced by African Americans across the South immediately following emancipation. Rosen highlights the ways that sexual violence was wielded to beat down freedwomen and men who sought to claim first-class citizenship. Yet freedwomen testified to this violence before a congressional committee established to investigate the riot, demonstrating their courage and their refusal to be silenced by beatings, rapes, and other forms of abuse.

In the North, it was industrial development, the growth of cities, and the rapid increase in immigration in the late nineteenth century that most dramatically transformed the lives of women, families, and communities. These developments were accelerated by the completion of the transcontinental railroad in 1869, which sped people and goods across the nation just as telegraphs and telephones sped communications. The U.S. government had gained control over vast lands in the West before the Civil War, but significant areas of the Great Plains, the Rocky Mountain region, and the Pacific coast only experienced mass migration of Americans from the East and Asian immigrants from the West in the postwar period. At the same time, the U.S. Army shifted its focus from the South to the West, battling American Indians for control of territories and resources. A series of Indian defeats, ending with the Battle of Wounded Knee in 1890, ensured U.S. domination of the West. By this time, tribal life had already been disrupted by federal policies, like the Dawes Severalty Act (1887), that assigned Indians individual plots of land in exchange for what proved to be the limited benefits of U.S. citizenship. Western expansion for whites meant not only the decimation of Indian lands, lives, and customs, however, but also access to more natural resources—like coal and timber—to fuel urban and industrial development back east.

Western migration surged in the 1880s and 1890s, and so too did immigration to the United States and the migration of rural Americans to cities across the nation. Between 1860 and 1890, some ten million immigrants entered the United States, mostly from Ireland, Germany, and Scandinavia. This number was nearly double the number of immigrants who had entered the nation in the previous half century. From 1890 to 1920, the rate of immigration increased at an even faster rate with more and more newcomers arriving from Italy, Poland, Russia, and other southern and eastern European countries. Cities like New York, Philadelphia, Buffalo, Atlanta, Cleveland, St. Louis, and Chicago grew rapidly as new immigrants and rural migrants swelled urban populations.

Chicago was among the fastest growing cities in the nation in the late nineteenth century. A burgeoning town of thirty thousand in 1850, it was the world's sixth largest city by 1890, with nearly one million residents. Such rapid growth, including waves of immigrants from all over Europe, fueled urban and industrial growth. But it also led to dramatic increases in disease and crime, demands for schools and hospitals, shortages of clean water and safe food, new dangers from industrial accidents and crowded tenement houses, and tens of thousands of new residents who did not speak or read English or understand American laws and customs. Such problems inspired hundreds of native-born women to organize on behalf of urban reform.

Most of these female reformers were the daughters of affluent white families who took advantage of the new educational opportunities offered women in the late nineteenth century. By the 1870s, women could attend state colleges and universities in the Midwest and West that had been established as part of a federal program of educational land grants approved during the Civil War. In the same period, private women's colleges flourished in the Midwest and Northeast. The establishment of Vassar, Mt. Holyoke, Wellesley, Barnard, Bryn Mawr, Smith, and Radcliffe colleges between 1865 and 1894 ensured affluent young women the right to an education as rigorous as that offered by Ivy League universities for men. Private and public women's colleges also opened in the South, offering important though often limited educational opportunities for well-to-do white women. The opportunities for African American, working-class, and immigrant women were always far more limited, by either outright discrimination or cost. Still, the expansion of women's colleges began to change attitudes toward education for all women in the late nineteenth and early twentieth centuries.

The well-educated women who took up the banner of urban reform in the 1880s and 1890s often placed education near the top of their agenda. One of the most renowned of these women was Jane Addams. In 1882, she graduated from Rockford College in Illinois, where she met Ellen Gates Starr. The two women rejected the pleasures and responsibilities of marriage and family, hoping instead to find meaningful work that would improve the larger society. In 1889, Addams and Starr founded Hull House, a women-run settlement house in Chicago modeled on male-led institutions they had visited a year earlier in London. Hull House, in turn, served as a model for numerous other settlement houses in cities throughout the Northeast and Midwest. Although U.S. settlement houses did not exclude men from their activities, most were built around vibrant communities of women activists who viewed each other as members of an extended family. Indeed, settlement houses (and women's colleges) provided some female reformers with the chance to choose other women as their life partners, establishing an alternative to heterosexual marriage.

In Chapter Two, Kathryn Kish Sklar traces the evolution of Hull House and the relations among the women reformers who found a home there. The founders of the settlement initially offered assistance and education in American ways to immigrant women and their families, but they soon came to appreciate the diverse cultural traditions that immigrants brought to the city. Settlement house reformers also learned a good deal about impoverished neighborhoods, factory life, and urban politics; and many began to advocate for laws that would protect immigrants at home and at work. In turn, these experiences in local and state politics led settlement house residents like Jane Addams to become firm supporters of women's suffrage. At the same time, settlement workers established strong bonds among themselves and offered financial and emotional support to female reformers who found themselves in need.

The women who founded Hull House were in the vanguard of a wave of reform that swept across the United States between roughly 1890 and 1920, a period that became known as the Progressive Era. Some progressive reformers advocated state intervention, such as laws to protect workers or to regulate the manufacture and sale of alcohol; others favored community-based efforts that relied on persuasion rather than legal enforcement. Some worked to ensure racial and sexual equality; others believed that racial and sexual hierarchies were natural and could not be changed. Some reformers worked within the nation's two major political parties; others formed third parties, such as the Progressive Party or the Socialist Party. Still others rejected partisan politics altogether, seeking change instead through voluntary associations, churches, and similar institutions. Some thought that prohibiting the sale and consumption of alcohol would solve many of the nation's problems; others believed that women's suffrage would eliminate political corruption and ensure better treatment of workers, children, and families; and still others advocated changes in city, state, and national government as the key to improving society. Clearly, progressive reformers and organizations formed no united front. Instead, clusters of associations competed to advance their own social vision and political agenda. One common feature of these multiple movements, however, was the significant involvement of women.

Still, even among women reformers, the goals and styles of activism varied by race, class, ethnicity, and region. Among middle-class women, one common thread was the assumption that women's public efforts were directly linked to their familial roles. Even reformers who remained single throughout their lives, such as Jane Addams or Susan B. Anthony, employed domestic analogies to promote and justify women's involvement in the public arena. As suffragist Rheta Childe Dorr proclaimed in the early 1900s:

> Women's place is in the Home, but Home is not contained within the four walls of the individual house. Home is the community. The city full of people is the Family. The public school is the real Nursery. And badly do Home and Family need their "mother."

Dorr captured the sentiments of a broad spectrum of female progressives. This included the reformers at Hull House and other settlement houses. The Hull House women used names like "Sister Kelley" to emphasize their familial spirit. Though many of these women were attracted to socialist and other radical doctrines, they rooted their political efforts in the protection of home and family. These concerns also motivated women to enter male-dominated professions, such as medicine and law, or to forge careers in the new helping professions, like social work and library science.

Middle-class African American women embraced similar issues in their own communities. They came together in women's clubs, settlement houses, and temperance and suffrage societies "for the purpose of encouraging habits of cleanliness and industry, promoting child welfare, and bringing about culture and efficiency in general homemaking." Here, too, growing numbers sought entrance into the professions, including law and journalism as well as teaching and nursing. Yet, for black women like Ida B. Wells, Lugenia Burns Hope, Charlotte Hawkins Brown, and others, the protection of home and family could not be achieved until and unless racial segregation and racist violence was eradicated.

Despite common concerns and shared strategies, many women's organizations remained segregated during the Progressive Era. For community-based groups, race and ethnic organizations echoed the patterns of residential segregation with African American families living in some areas of a city, immigrants in another neighborhood, and native-born whites in their own sections. But even national organizations like the General Federation of Women's Clubs, the Women's Christian Temperance Union, the National American Women's Suffrage Association, and the Young Women's Christian Association either formally excluded African American women or established separate black branches at the state and local levels. African American women did not wait for admission to these white women's organizations, however. Instead, they established state and national associations on their own, culminating in the founding of the National Association of Colored Women in 1896. The number of national organizations of women reformers that emerged in the 1880s and 1890s reflected the growing clout that female reformers wielded during the Progressive Era. Yet most of the hands-on work of these associations was carried out on a day-to-day basis by members who participated in the thousands of local societies scattered across the country.

For some women, especially working-class and immigrant women, community-based organizations were often more important than national associations as vehicles for reform. Although many working-class women shared the concerns of their more well-to-do sisters, they usually approached social reform in distinctive ways and were more likely to organize locally in the late nineteenth and early twentieth centuries. Their organizations grew as the number of working women increased. Between 1890 and 1900, the proportion of working women, as well as the number of working-class women, increased significantly. The number of women in the paid labor force climbed from 4 to 5.3 million in that single decade, with African American and immigrant women leading the way. Though domestic service and the sewing trades remained the largest employers of women, clerical and sales jobs as well as positions as telephone and telegraph operators and as waitresses also swelled the ranks of working women.

Immigrant women flooded into factories at the turn of the twentieth century, particularly in the garment industry. There, young Italian and Russian Jewish women contributed to the family finances despite the low wages they were paid by employers. To do so, they worked twelve- to fourteen-hour days in dirty, noisy factories with few safety precautions and no safety net for those who took ill or were injured on the job. In Chapter Three, Annelise Orleck examines the working lives of these immigrant women and analyzes the decisions of some to organize on their own behalf. Focusing on activists like Fannia Cohn, Clara Lemlich, Pauline Newman, and Rose Schneiderman, Orleck shows how they embraced the radical political traditions carried to America by Jewish immigrants and wielded them to improve the lives of both immigrant families and individual women workers. At the same time, they sought to educate themselves in American ways of life and to provide at least informal instruction for those they organized in the economics of wage labor and corporate wealth, the legal rights of workers, and the possibilities for political action.

To achieve their goals, female labor organizers made common cause with middle-class reformers based in settlement houses and joined forces with affluent allies in the Women's Trade Union League. They also worked alongside working-class men in labor unions, whom they depended on for financial support and advice on tactics and strategies. Still, in the final analysis, immigrant women workers often had to depend on each other to ensure that their interests as women and as workers gained recognition. Like many other women in the United States during the late nineteenth and early twentieth centuries, immigrants found that their own families and communities were often the last safety net in times of trouble and the best allies in moments of collective action.

As the United States expanded and changed during the late nineteenth and early twentieth centuries, women faced new challenges and developed new strategies for improving their own lives and that of their families, their communities, and the nation.

Confronted with racist violence, economic and geographic dislocations, class and racial injustices, and urban and industrial hazards as well as gender discrimination, women—individually and collectively—forged a wide range of movements, organizations, and agendas that became part of the new American order.

Suggested Readings and Web Sites

Marilyn Mayer Culpepper, *All Things Altered: Women in the Wake of Civil War and Reconstruction* (2002)

Ellen Fitzpatrick, *Endless Crusade: Women Social Scientists and Progressive Reform* (1990)

Donna Gabaccia, *From the Other Side: Women, Gender and Immigrant Life in the U.S., 1820–1990* (1994)

Glenda E. Gilmore, *Gender and Jim Crow: Women and the Politics of White Supremacy in North Carolina, 1896–1920* (1996)

Susan A. Glenn, *Daughters of the Shtetl: Life and Labor in the Immigrant Generation* (1990)

Seth Koven and Sonya Michel, *Mothers of a New World: Maternalist Politics and the Origins of Welfare States* (1993)

Robyn Muncy, *Creating a Female Dominion in American Reform, 1890–1935* (1991)

Anne Firor Scott, *Natural Allies: Women's Associations in American History* (1991)

Deborah Gray White, *Too Heavy a Load: Black Women in Defense of Themselves: 1894–1994* (1999)

Urban Experience in Chicago: Hull House and its Neighborhoods, 1889–1963
http://www.uic.edu/jaddams/hull/urbanexp/index.htm

African American Odyssey
http://memory.loc.gov/ammem/aaohtml/exhibit/aointro.html

Emma Goldman Papers Project
http://sunsite.berkeley.edu/Goldman/

"Devastated, demoralized, and destitute" is how one historian described the post–Civil War South. As the primary battlefield during both the war and the peace that followed, this region experienced more dramatic and traumatic changes than any other section of the country. In the decade and a half of upheaval, plantation mistresses sought to maintain their families' estates, often as sole managers in the absence of male kin, while slave women and men struggled to expand their freedom and to sustain or re-create black family and community life. While northern women joined local soldiers' aid societies, the products of which were channeled into the massive U.S. Sanitary Commission, southern women labored individually or through informal associations. The Confederate government provided no assistance in dispensing relief.

African American women found the war years especially difficult. Black men were hauled off to war alongside planters and their sons or forced into munitions factories, or became convinced that flight across Union lines was the best hope for freedom. Many joined the Union Army. African American women were often left behind on plantations to support for themselves and their children. Women also frequently seized any opportunity to flee increasingly desperate conditions, seeking to escape slavery behind Union Army lines. But this wartime flight was dangerous. Union military policies left women and children to fend for themselves in the chaos of conflict; many of these camp followers battled violence, starvation, and disease. Those lucky enough to land work with the Union Army faced new drudgery as the servants of soldiers, whose lives were eased by freedmen and women eager to cook, launder, drive horses, and assume responsibility for some of the most backbreaking labors of military life.

The Union victory guaranteed the emancipation of the men and women who had sacrificed so much. Yet what did freedom mean in the face of hunger, homelessness, and racial violence? For most African Americans, it guaranteed their right to move freely for the first time. To the chagrin of white southerners, newly emancipated slaves took to the road in their quest to reshape their relationships with one another and with white society. They crisscrossed the South in search of family members lost to slavery and war. They fled the virtual slavery of the countryside in search of a decent wage, a good piece of land, or lost property. They sought relief from physical violence and tried to track down those government agents who they heard would supply them with forty acres and a mule. These journeys were critical to their efforts to simply survive while the federal government worked to erect a legal framework for reconstructing the nation.

Memphis—a city renowned for its antebellum slave markets—became a magnet for ambitious African Americans in the aftermath of the Civil War. They sought legal support from the city's Union Army troops and the newly established Freedmen's Bureau in their quest for full citizenship. They immediately laid claim to the city, constructing institutions and communities that supported their aspirations as free people. The city offered the promise of true emancipation: the right to move without hindrance in public spaces, earn decent wages, and live peacefully with their families. But these efforts to transform Memphis infuriated whites, who rampaged against newly emancipated men and women in 1866. Terror reigned as rioters burned and looted buildings, using beatings, murder, and rape to punish anyone viewed in violation of antebellum racial codes.

Hannah Rosen focuses her analysis on the sexual violence that erupted during this riot, highlighting the systematic and ritualized nature of these rapes. Reconstruction battles over race and citizenship were waged on the bodies of African American women determined to be free from sexual abuse. Victims of the Memphis attacks testified to the brutality they had experienced, triggering additional federal protection for newly emancipated African Americans. This was a brave challenge to white men who were determined to re-establish the racial hierarchies of slavery through sexual violence. Yet this resistance did little to deter rapists in the years that followed; the sexual abuse of African American women continued to be a source of great danger and great pain. It was a burden borne largely in silence. Lynchings of African American men became the iconic symbol of racial oppression in these years; rape would not emerge as a central issue in the African American freedom struggle until almost a century after the Memphis riots.

"Not That Sort of Women": Race, Gender and Sexual Violence during the Memphis Riot of 1866
HANNAH ROSEN

On June 1, 1866, in the Gayoso House hotel in downtown Memphis, Tennessee, a former slave named Frances Thompson spoke before a congressional committee investigating the riot that had occurred in that city one month earlier. Thompson informed the committee that seven white rioters broke into the house that she shared with another former slave, Lucy Smith. Thompson recounted her efforts to

---

Hannah Rosen, "'Not the Sort of Women': Race, Gender and Sexual Violence During the Memphis Riot of 1866" from *Sex, Love, Race:* Crossing Boundaries in North American History Martha Hodes, ed. Copyright © 1999 by New York University Press. Used by permission of the publisher.

All over the South in the aftermath of the Civil War, white men terrorized freedmen and freedwomen in an effort to reassert slave-era race hierarchies. This lithograph from a popular illustrated magazine depicts how whites used arson and murder in May 1866 to punish African Americans who were asserting their new freedoms in Memphis, Tennessee. This episode garnered national publicity, thanks in part to the bravery of freedwomen willing to provide public testimony about the sexual violence they endured during the carnage.

resist the demand for "some woman to sleep with" made by these men. "I said that we were not that sort of women, and they must go." Yet her refusal to have sex proved unacceptable to the intruders. Thompson described to the committee how both she and Lucy Smith were raped.

Frances Thompson was among five freedwomen who recounted being subject to sexual violence during what became known as the Memphis Riot. This attack on recently emancipated slaves commenced in the late afternoon of May 1, 1866, and persisted for three days. It took place primarily in the neighborhood of South Memphis, where the freed community of the city was concentrated. The assailants were mostly city police and other lower-middle-class white men, many of whom lived in the same neighborhood with the riot's victims. The riot represented the culmination of increasing tensions between a growing freed community and white Memphians, above all between African American Union soldiers stationed at the federal army's Fort Pickering in South Memphis and the city's white police force. During the riot at least forty-eight African Americans were killed and between seventy and eighty were wounded. Rioters set fire to ninety-one houses and cabins, four churches, and twelve schools, robbed one hundred freedpeople, and destroyed approximately $127,000 worth of property. Rioters also raped at least five freedwomen. Freedwomen's testimony about these sexual attacks reveals the ways that gender and sexuality became key sites for waging battles over race after emancipation, as rioters struggled to reclaim privileges as white men, and black women struggled to be free.

For African American women to testify in a legal forum about sexual violence was itself a dramatic political act in the battles of Reconstruction. Prior to emancipation, one demonstration of white male dominance of southern society had been the virtual legal impunity with which white men sexually abused African American women. Antebellum laws in the southern states generally excluded female slaves from the legal definition of those who could be raped, and did not recognize their abuse as a crime. This exclusion was justified in the law by the absence of legal sanction for marriage between slaves and thus the lack of patriarchal rights that could be violated by coerced sexual intercourse outside marriage. This logic dovetailed with widespread imagery representing black women as sexually indiscriminate, consenting to and even pursuing sexual activity with white men, and thus lacking feminine "virtue." It was this quality of "virtue," along with patriarchal rights, that was imagined to be injured in the crime of rape. Thus freedwomen declaring publicly that the violence they had suffered constituted rape, that they were the "sort of women" who could be violated and who deserved legal protection from sexual abuse, represented a radical reversal of both antebellum legal notions and white constructions of black womanhood.

Historians of the Memphis Riot have often pointed to the occurrence of rape to highlight the atrocities and terror that freedpeople suffered over those tumultuous three days. Yet the significance of the specifically sexual form of this violence has not been explored. Sexual violence in the midst of a race riot reveals more than simply extreme brutality. The instances where rioters raped freedwomen reflect the nexus of race, gender, and sexuality within the overall power struggles gripping the post–Civil War South. I will explore this nexus by examining the ways in which post-emancipation struggles over racial relations and identities in Memphis were fought out on the ground of gender and sexuality. Gendered constructions of race emerged in the everyday political conflicts in Memphis in the time leading up to the riot, particularly in contests over the meaning and significance of race transpiring in various arenas of the city's public space. Strikingly similar gendered constructions of race were invoked by rioters when they sexually assaulted black women. This discursive convergence sheds light on the historical meaning of the sexual violence that occurred during the Memphis Riot. As white southern men struggled to reclaim the power and privilege that white manhood had signified in a slave society, they turned to black women's gender and sexuality as a site for reenacting and reproducing racial inequality and subordination. This politicization of gender and sexuality shaped the perilous terrain upon which freedwomen struggled to render freedom meaningful for themselves and their communities.

Complicating a reading of the sexual violence that occurred during the Memphis Riot is the riot's unexpected postscript. Ten years after testifying before the congressional committee about having been raped, Frances Thompson was arrested for being a man dressed in women's clothing. Thompson's transvestism raises important questions about the form and meaning of the sexual violence that occurred during the Memphis Riot, the full implications of which cannot be explored within the confines of this article. I will, though, discuss the propagandistic use made of Frances Thompson's cross-dressing by conservatives in their efforts to discredit all the women who testified that they had been raped and in general to oppose Reconstruction in Memphis. The newspaper coverage that followed Thompson's exposure as a cross-dresser reveals again the central role that gender and sexuality played in contests over race in the post-emancipation South.

Prior to the Civil War, Memphis's black population had been relatively small: 3,882 people, or 17 percent of the city's inhabitants in 1860. Ninety-five percent of this group were slaves whose public conduct was strictly regulated by city ordinances. Although laws prohibiting slaves' travel through the city without a pass, hiring out their own time, residing away from their owner, or congregating for social or political activities were never fully enforced, city police were empowered to interfere with and constrain the actions of African Americans in the city at all times. Moving about the streets of antebellum Memphis, white and black people observed and experienced racial difference in their everyday lives in part through inequalities in the power to utilize the city's public spaces.

The Civil War permanently altered these racial dynamics in Memphis, where public space was transformed by the resultant change in status and dramatic increase in number of African Americans. The occupation of the city by the Union army in June 1862 brought thousands of African American migrants to the city. Regiments of black troops were stationed at Fort Pickering, located at the southern edge of the city. Following these troops came their family members and other fugitive slaves seeking the protection of the Union forces. By 1865 these migrants together with African Americans already living in Memphis constituted 40 percent of the city's total population, or just under eleven thousand people, an increase to the antebellum black population of 275 percent. The significance of this migration for social relations and public activity in Memphis lay not only in its size. In the past, African Americans had been brought to Memphis by force, to be sold in slave markets and to labor in white-owned businesses and homes; after the Union occupation, they entered Memphis as a "city of refuge," a space in which they would be free.

During the Civil War and Reconstruction years, refugees from slavery forcefully entered public spaces in Memphis—the streets, markets, saloons, and other visible spaces of labor and leisure; public sites of legal authority, such as police stations, the Freedmen's Bureau, and courtrooms; civil institutions such as schools, churches, and benevolent societies; and realms of public discourse such as speaking events, parades, and the Republican press—in anticipation of new rights and freedoms. The political status of these new public actors in Memphis was uncertain. They were no longer slaves, yet they had no formal political rights. Until the Civil Rights Act was passed in April 1866, African Americans were denied even the most nominal legal recognition as citizens. Nonetheless, freedpeople made use of the limited power available to them to claim many aspects of citizenship. They began their lives in Memphis with expectations for freedom that included the ability to enjoy free movement, social life, and family in an urban community of their own choosing, to be compensated for their labor, and to have these rights protected by law in the form of the Freedmen's Bureau and the police power of the occupying Union army. They expected to be citizens of the city. The reaction of many whites illustrates how powerfully African Americans' public activities in Memphis disrupted whites' previous norms of racial difference rooted in slavery and adumbrated a new nonracialized citizenship. A conflict over public space ensued, as white Memphians sought therein to redraw racial boundaries, delegitimate black people's public presence, and oppose the new power differentials embodied in what they observed around them.

African American women were central actors in the process of laying claim to a new urban citizenship in ways that dramatically transformed public life in Memphis. Women constituted a sizable proportion of those former slaves who made their way to Memphis both during and after the Civil War. White Memphians quickly experienced the reality of emancipation and the changed meaning of race through these women's movement through public space and their use of public authority in the form of the Freedmen's Bureau Court and the police protection of the Union army. Some whites responded by attempting to cast black women's new public presence in a disparaging light. Both white police officers and newspaper editors from the city's conservative press, in their conduct toward and representation of freedwomen in the city's public spaces, enlisted gendered constructions of race, specifically a discourse representing all black women as "unvirtuous" or "bad," and often as prostitutes, to depict black women as unworthy of citizenship. These representations were echoed in the words and actions of rioters who raped black women during the Memphis Riot, suggesting how this violence reflected the confluence of race, gender, and sexuality that structured everyday political conflict in the post-emancipation South.

It was specifically to realize their freedom that African American women migrated to Memphis after the end of the Civil War. Freedwomen fled conditions reminiscent of slavery in the countryside—physical violence, work with no pay, forced separation from family—and came to the city to seek assistance and protection made available by the power of African American Union soldiers and the federal authority of the Bureau. Some came specifically to join, and seek support from, male family members in the Union army. Many women enlisted the aid of soldiers in order to claim possessions, children, and compensation owed them for past labor from abusive employers on the plantations from which they had fled. Thus black women came to Memphis to assert new rights of citizenship—motherhood, property ownership, rights as free laborers—that were guaranteed by state power in the hands of armed black men.

In the city, black women secured other profound, if less tangible, liberties previously reserved for whites. For instance, they fashioned social lives and urban communities that revolved around the grocery-saloons and street corners of South Memphis. In these spaces, freedwomen gathered, danced, and drank with black soldiers, often into the morning hours. Freedwomen also helped build independent black churches in Memphis, such as the Methodist Episcopal Church and various Baptist churches. Former slave women were the backbone of these institutions. They sponsored picnics, fairs, and other public events to raise funds for new church buildings and organized mutual aid societies for the support of church members.

Black women further undermined whites' prior monopoly on public life, and exclusive claims to citizenship, by utilizing the Freedmen's Bureau Court to secure their rights. Freedwomen pressed charges against whites to claim unpaid wages and to protest violent assaults. The impact of legal action at times spilled over from the court into the streets, when whites resisted verdicts and clashed with soldiers making arrests, collecting fines, and confiscating property. Even when cases did not lead to convictions, freedwomen's actions brought charges of white abuse against blacks, and evidence of the new rights and powers of former slaves, prominently into the public eye. Overall, black women's actions after emancipation left indelible marks on Memphis's landscape, changing the city materially and redrawing the racial boundaries around citizenship and freedom symbolized by activities in its public space.

When the presence of freedwomen in Memphis was noted by the conservative press of the city, it was never in reference to victims or opponents of exploitation and abuse. Nor were black women represented as "respectable" church women or "ladies" participating in the civic life of their community. Rather, the rhetoric of newspaper editors and the focus of most reporting suggest efforts to denigrate the public activities of freedwomen in the city by insinuating connections between their presence and an alleged increase in crime and disorder, specifically of "lewd women" or prostitutes, supposedly threatening white Memphians in the city's streets and alleys. Onto the real activities of women in public, in all their variety and unpredictability, was imposed a bifurcated concept of womanhood. As was common in nineteenth-century depictions of urban life in the United States in general, women were represented as inhabiting one of two opposing realities: the delicate, chaste, and virtuous "lady" or the vicious, rude "public woman," or prostitute, the former being the woman whom society must protect, the latter by whom society was threatened. In post-emancipation Memphis, this binary imagery operated along racial lines. Representations of African American women in the conservative press implied their essential relation to the latter category. Depictions were not consistent; the negative characteristics associated with freedwomen were presented at times as menacing and at other times as comical. Together these images appearing throughout commentary on local affairs elaborated the racial power and privilege of whites in Memphis by gendering black women as "bad" women, and often as sexually "dangerous." Newspaper reports labeled black women's presence in the city's public spaces illegitimate and thus challenged their claim to identities as citizens.

For instance, Neely Hunt, a freedwoman, with the assistance of a squad of black Union soldiers, forcibly entered and searched the house of a white family where she believed her child was being held. For this action she was punished not only by the Freedmen's Bureau, which had her arrested, but also by negative characterizations of her in the *Memphis Daily Appeal.* This paper described Hunt as a "negress," who was "enraged," "raving," "threatening," and "us[ing] very abusive and insulting language," in contrast to "the ladies of the house," whose delicate constitutions were allegedly unsettled by this confrontation. The *Appeal* labeled Hunt a liar and suggested that her deceitful and disreputable character was generalizable to all freedwomen. By identifying assertive black women acting in the public of Memphis with terms such as "negress," the press avoided describing them as "women," distancing them from images of respectable womanhood and associating them with disrepute. Newspaper editors often combined this strategy with other insulting labels, such as when the *Appeal* reported the charge of theft of a pistol made against "an ugly looking negress." Another news item repeatedly used "wench," a term meaning "young female" that also had implications of servitude and sexual wantonness, to describe a black woman charged with drunk and disorderly conduct. Another reported the arrest of five "female roughs of African descent" for disorderly conduct and speculated about the origins of black women's alleged misbehavior: "Freedom seems to have an intoxicating effect on colored females." And the report of a robbery by three black men who supposedly stole a number of hoopskirts editorialized that the skirts were intended as gifts for "some of their dark paramours." Through an assertion of both theft and illicit sexual relations, this report questioned the legitimacy and honor of freedwomen appearing in public in fine clothes.

Images associating black women in Memphis with disrepute and sexual promiscuity circulating in the city's conservative press were reinforced by police action against freedwomen, such as frequent arrests for "lewdness," "vagrancy," and "drunk and disorderly conduct." These arrests, often under false charges and amounting to harassment of black women by police, were then highlighted and exaggerated in newspaper accounts. Some reports implied that a specific incident indicated an epidemic of black prostitution, such as the following: "Six more negro prostitutes were yesterday arrested and brought before the officers of the Freedmen's Bureau, who sent them out to work on different farms in the country." Others used arrests of black women for charges that may or may not have been associated with prostitution simply to assert that those arrested were prostitutes: "Three colored prostitutes were arrested, charged with vagrancy, and were hired out to contractors to go into the country and work," and "Viney Springer, Mary Jane Springer, and Sarah Parker, colored nymphs *du pave*, were arrested for disorderly conduct and incarcerated." These reports make clear the high price freedwomen paid for these arrests, being either imprisoned in the city jail or forced to leave the city and labor on plantations. Although some black women may have been engaged in prostitution or criminal activity, there is evidence that many of these arrests were fraudulent and abusive. A "prominent citizen" reported one such case to the city's Republican newspaper. He had witnessed a white man "kicking a colored woman, who was calling loudly for a 'watch.' Soon a well known officer came running to the rescue, and without asking her for explanations, seized the woman, threw her down, slapped her in the face, dragged her on the ground and finally took her to the station-house and locked her up for disorderly conduct." Other officers, similarly "well known," made a practice of harassing, insulting, and abusing freedwomen. These same officers would be recognized by freedpeople among the Memphis rioters.

One such policeman harassed Amanda Olden, a freedwoman living in South Memphis, with a false charge related to prostitution just days before the riot. Olden was not intimidated by this officer's particular extortion scheme and took her charges to the Freedmen's Bureau. There she recounted that "one Carol or Carrol, a city policeman, came to my house, and compelled me to give him twenty-two dollars at the same time falsely charging me with keeping a house of ill-fame." Carroll told Olden that this money would cover her fine for the charged offense. However, when she went to the Recorder of the Police Court the next morning, "ready for an investigation of these false charges . . . this policeman did not appear, nor had he made any report of this action in my case to his proper officer." Through false charges against African American women, city police not only contributed to the representation of freedwomen as "unvirtuous" in Memphis's public, they also attempted to use those representations to exploit individual women in ways that could be hidden from the public under the cloak of that same imagery.

The actions of Officers Welch and Sweatt, the latter of whom was also later identified among the rioters, offer further evidence of police using arrests to denigrate the activities of black women in the public spaces of Memphis rather than to punish real offenders. According to a complaint filed with the Freedmen's Bureau by three black men who had attended a "negro ball," the two police officers intruded into the party and "proceeded to arrest some two or three of the ladies" in attendance. These policemen thus imputed a disreputable character to black women enjoying the privileges of "ladies" in public. Men from the party intervened and forcibly prevented the police from taking the women away. Welch and Sweatt retreated, but soon returned with several armed white firemen, who "cocking their weapons demanded a surrender" and "behaved in a very rough and boisterous manner, crying 'shoot the damned niggers.'" That the men and women attending this ball were apparently members of the city's small African American elite seems to have prevented violent incident and allowed the African Americans involved to reassert respectable gender identities as ladies and gentlemen. They received an apology from the firemen, who explained that Welch and Sweatt had "misrepresented the affair," and from the mayor, responding to the provost marshal's complaint that such incidents were "becoming so frequent as to demand attention."

Although most freedwomen did not receive apologies for police misconduct, they did pursue retribution through the courts of the Bureau to defend, and to construct, their rights to enjoy free movement, work, and leisure in the public spaces of Memphis. Certain whites, such as police and newspaper editors, contested those rights as they sought to reassert their control over public space, and over the meanings of race signified by a free black presence in public. The conduct of the Memphis Riot suggests that those three days of violence represented a similar attempt to eviscerate the meaning of African American citizenship and freedom.

It was not surprising that the Memphis Riot began as a clash between black Union soldiers and city police. Since the initial occupation of the city by the federal army, the police force and black troops had been the front lines in an ongoing battle between civilian and military authorities over governance of the city. When their paths crossed in the streets, they often taunted each other, using "very hard language . . . daring each other to fight," concluding at times in serious physical violence. Many observers believed that the police were often the instigators, insulting, shoving, and threatening black men in uniform, and often arresting soldiers under unspecified or fabricated charges and beating soldiers in custody. In the days before the riot, two cases of severe beatings by police led to calls from soldiers for vengeance if such practices were repeated. Given escalating tensions, it would seem not to be a coincidence that several policemen waited until May 1, 1866, the day after most black soldiers had been mustered out of service and forced to turn in their army weapons, to provoke the conflict that began the riot. On this day, the police knew that they now had the upper hand.

Nor was it surprising that the riot began as a clash over freedpeople's activities in public space, in this case a visible and festive gathering of African Americans on a main thoroughfare of South Memphis. On Tuesday afternoon a group of police officers interrupted an impromptu street party on South Street, in which freedwomen, children, and soldiers were "laughing and shouting and making considerable noise." "Some of them [were] hallooing 'Hurrah for Abe Lincoln,' and so on," recalled Tony Cherry, a discharged soldier and participant. "A policeman came along and told them to hush, and not to be hallooing in that way, and another policeman said, 'Your old father, Abe Lincoln, is dead and damned.'" The police sought to silence this defiant tribute to emancipation by arresting some of the soldiers. As the police began to retreat with two soldiers in custody, other soldiers fired pistols in the air or perhaps at the police. On hearing these gunshots and seeing one police officer fall (he apparently slipped and shot himself in the leg with his own gun), the police turned and began shooting indiscriminately into the crowd. Although those few soldiers with weapons fired back, they were overpowered; few white men were injured in the fighting.

Rumors of an uprising of African American soldiers spread through the city, bringing other white men from South Memphis and surrounding areas into the riot. After several hours of what was termed by one observer "an indiscriminate slaughter" of freedpeople by police and white civilians, Union army officers from Fort Pickering arrived to quell the disturbance, forcibly dispersing the crowds and marshaling most black soldiers into the fort. Here soldiers were held over the next few days against their will and despite the efforts of many to leave, rendered powerless to protect their families from the violence that ensued. Around ten o'clock that night, a large crowd of police and white civilians spread throughout South Memphis. Under the pretense of searching for weapons to stop the alleged uprising, rioters intruded into freedpeople's houses and brutalized residents, beginning the looting, assault, murder, arson, and rape that would continue until Thursday evening.

The Memphis Riot was one episode in an ongoing battle over race, citizenship, and rule in the post-emancipation public of Memphis. The riot was a protest among certain lower-middle-class white men against the power freedpeople exercised in public space, and the nonracialized citizenship this power signified. In that sense it was a violent continuation of the efforts of many white Memphians to reclaim privileges for whiteness and to counter new identities and powers for African Americans that challenged white dominance. The freedwoman Hannah Robinson remembered hearing one rioter declare, "It is white man's day now." Throughout the process of reclaiming the "day" for white men, rioters would employ constructions of gender as weapons in efforts to resignify racial difference and inequality.

Rioters acted out meanings of white manhood and insisted on "unworthy" gender identities for African Americans through violence against black women. This can be seen, first, in how certain black women became targets of rioters' violence. Ann Freeman recounted that the party of white men who broke into her home declared that "they were going to kill all the women they caught with soldiers or with soldiers' things." Directing violence against black women because of their relationship to black Union soldiers was made particularly evident in the case of rape. Four of the survivors of rape during the riot were connected to soldiers in ways that figured prominently in the women's recollections of what they had suffered.

Lucy Tibbs was about twenty-one when she came to Memphis from Arkansas soon after the Civil War broke out. She came to the city with her husband, who by 1866 had found work on a streamboat and was away from home much of the time. She lived in South Memphis with her two small children, and was nearly five months pregnant with her third. On May 1 she was outside when the fighting began. She screamed in outrage as "they broke and run in every direction, boys and men, with pistols, firing at every black man and boy they could see." After observing the shooting death of two soldiers and seeing rioters "going from house to house," she understood that all black soldiers were in danger. She thus encouraged her older brother, Bob Taylor, who had been a member of the Fifty-ninth U.S. Colored Infantry stationed in Memphis, to flee. He ran, but was found dead the next morning near the bayou in back of Tibbs's house. Later that night, a crowd of men broke into her home and stole three hundred dollars. One of these men raped her while "the other men were plundering the house." She later speculated that her home had not been randomly chosen for attack: "I think they were folks who knew all about me, who knew that my brother had not long been out of the army and had money."

Harriet Armour came to Memphis as a slave before the Civil War began. Later she married an African American Union soldier, who was in Fort Pickering during the riots. She lived around the corner from Lucy Tibbs, and she too watched the initial clashes and killings of Tuesday evening. Early Wednesday morning, two men carrying revolvers came to her room. Molly Hayes, a white woman who lived in the adjacent house, overheard these men confronting Armour: "There were two men who came there and asked her where her husband was. She said he was in the fort. They said, 'Is he a soldier?' She said, 'Yes.' . . . The last word I heard him say was, 'Shut the door.'" Armour testified that after they barred her door shut, they both raped her: "[One of the men] had to do with me twice and the other man once, which was the same as three."

Sixteen-year-old Lucy Smith had been raised in slavery in Memphis. Frances Thompson, who was somewhat older, had been a slave in Maryland. At the time of the riot, Smith and Thompson shared a South Memphis home, supporting themselves by taking in sewing, washing, and ironing. Late Tuesday night, seven white men, two of whom were police officers, came to their house and stayed for close to four hours, during which time they robbed Smith and Thompson of many of their possessions and all of their money and food. The rioters threatened to shoot them and set fire to their house. Smith testified that one of these men also choked and then raped her, and that another attempted to rape her. Thompson recounted being beaten by one of the rioters and raped by four. Thompson and Smith also both remembered that the rioters demanded to know why there were red, white, and blue quilts in the house. Thompson later testified, "When we told them we made them for the soldiers they swore at us, and said the soldiers would never have them on their beds, and they took them away with the rest of things." They also noticed pictures of Union army officers in the room, and as Smith later remembered, "they said they would not have hurt us so bad if it had not been for these pictures."

By raping women associated with black Union soldiers, white men reclaimed their power over representatives of black masculinity, of freedpeople's power and protection in public space, and of federal and military power in Memphis. Rioters demonstrated that black soldiers, now decommissioned, disarmed, and absent, were unable to protect freedwomen from violence. Yet it was not only as women related to soldiers that freedwomen were attacked. Equally important to understanding the sexual form of violence during the Memphis Riot is an analysis of the ways in which rioters enacted particular relations with freedwomen themselves. Through acts of rape, rioters physically overpowered black women. In the process, they also used language and acted in a manner that identified these women as "unvirtuous" or "lewd," in ways reminiscent of the representations of African American womanhood circulating in the conservative press in Memphis prior to the riot. That discourse had offered all white men identities as superior and worthy of power through the denigration of African American women. However, these identities were not necessarily realized in the lives of many white men, whose power was frequently challenged in their everyday interactions with freedpeople. The language rioters used and the scenes they staged around rape reveal how white men attempted to realize that discourse in a tangible way in their own conflicts with freedwomen, and thus attempted to experience for themselves a white manhood that rested on the dishonor of black women.

During the riot, men initiated rape with casual requests for sex and other patterns of behavior that invoked imagery of black women as sexually available to white men. Recall the dialogue described to the congressional investigating committee by Frances Thompson. The seven men who broke into her and Lucy Smith's home in the middle of the night treated their residence as if it were a brothel and demanded that Thompson and Smith act out roles as servants and prostitutes. The men first insisted that they be served supper. Thompson remembered the rioters saying, "they must have some eggs, and ham, and biscuit. I made them some biscuit and strong coffee, and they all sat down and ate." Lucy Smith similarly testified, "They told us to get up and get some supper for them. We got up, and made a fire and got them supper." When finished eating, the intruders announced that "they wanted some woman to sleep with." Thompson recounted that it was when she insisted that she and Smith "were not that sort of women" that the men physically attacked her, asserting that Thompson's claim "didn't make a damned bit of difference." Smith also refused the rioters' demand and the identity they imputed to her. She testified that when "they tried to take advantage of me . . . I told them that I did not do such things, and would not." In response, one of the men "choked me by the neck" and "said he would make me." It was then that these men "drew their pistols and said they would shoot us and fire the house if we did not let them have their way with us."

On the night of May 2, the words and actions of the rioters who assaulted two freedwomen living in adjoining rooms similarly identified these women as "unvirtuous" and sexually available to white men. Elvira Walker described to the congressional committee the following scene: "I was entirely alone; some men came and knocked at my door. They came in, and said they were hunting for weapons. . . . One of them put his hands into my bosom. I tried to stop him, and he knocked down my hands with his pistol, and did it again." This man forcibly touched Walker's body in ways that implied that in his eyes she was not a respectable woman. He then further insulted her. "He . . . said there was $5 forfeit money, and that I must come to the station-house with him." This demand for cash was strikingly similar to Officer Carroll's attempted extortion from Amanda Olden a few days earlier. It suggests that this man was a member of the police force and that he intended to identify Walker with illicit sexual activity.

This theme was continued when the same group of rioters entered the room next door, where Peter and Rebecca Ann Bloom were sleeping. The rioters forcibly removed Peter Bloom from the room, demanding that he obtain the five dollars needed to avoid Walker's arrest. One rioter remained behind. As Rebecca Ann Bloom recounted, "He wanted to know if I had anything to do with white men. I said no. He held a knife in his hand, and said that he would kill me if I did not let him do as he wanted to. I refused. He said, 'By God, you must,' and then he got into bed with me, and violated my person, him still holding the knife." The man who raped Bloom, like those who attacked Thompson and Smith, first solicited her for sex and then employed force when his request was rejected. "Having to do with," a phrase also repeated by Harriet Armour and Frances Thompson in their testimony, referred to sexual intercourse. By asking Bloom whether she had intercourse with white men, this rioter forced her to engage in a dialogue that positioned her as an "unvirtuous" woman. In drawing attention to his whiteness, his words identified her blackness. He simultaneously refused to recognize her identity as a wife, though her husband had just been dragged from the bed in which she still lay. Instead of the respect in theory attributed to married women, the rioter invoked myths of black women seeking sexual relations with white men. When Bloom refused to participate in his fantasy, he forced her under threat of deadly violence.

These sexual assaults, then, were not spontaneous acts of sexual aggression released from "normal" restraints in the pandemonium of a riot. They were, rather, elaborate and, in a sense, "scripted" enactments of fantasies of racial superiority and domination that operated around gendered constructions of racial difference and concluded in rape. In lengthy encounters, assailants employed words and violence to position freedwomen in previously constructed "scripts" that placed them in the role of being "that sort of women" who could not or would not refuse the sexual advances of a white man. In these "scripts," white men demanded sex, black women acquiesced, and white men experienced their dominance and superiority through black women's subservience. In this sense, these men attempted to make meaningful to themselves and their audience of other rioters the racist discourses on black women's gender and sexuality circulating in Memphis at the time. Through rape, rioters acted out identities as superior and powerful white men by refusing any recognition of "virtue" and rights to "protection" for African American women. In freedwomen's testimony, there is evidence of their refusal of rioters' "scripts," of their articulation of a gendered identity different from the one white men were attempting to impose. When freedwomen rejected the scenes set up by the attackers, the men imposed them with threats or physical force. With their violence, rapists struggled to stage events that "proved"—in a type of causally backward logic—freedwomen's lack of "virtue" by forcing their participation in "dishonorable" acts.

There was a contradiction inherent in these scenes: black women were not in fact consenting, and thus proving their own lack of "virtue" rather, white men were engaging in extremely "unvirtuous" conduct, forcing women to participate in sexual acts against their will. Rioters contained this contradiction through conduct that erased black women's agency and cloaked white men's force. Through their demands for food followed by sex, or inquiries about freedwomen's sexual partners, rioters invoked antebellum racist imagery of black women as sexually promiscuous and always available for sexual relations with white men, simulating an air of everyday, casual, and consensual sex that belied the terror and violent coercion involved in their actions. Other aspects of assailants' language further denied that they acted against the will of the women they attacked. Harriet Armour remembered as particularly painful that one of the men who raped her questioned her reason for crying. This man tried to force her to perform fellatio. "Then [he] tried to make me suck him. I cried. He asked what I was crying about, and tried to make me suck it." This rioter's question dismissed the possibility that his actions could cause Armour pain, that she had will or "virtue" that could be violated by such an act. In Lucy Tibbs's case, one of the rioters objected to the conduct of the man who raped her on the grounds of Tibbs's pregnancy. Yet this man's words only further denied the possibility of committing rape against a black woman. Tibbs remembered his saying, "Let that woman alone—that she was not in any situation to be doing that." Although this suggests the perhaps common contradiction between white imagery of black women as sexually "loose" and the reality of white men's interactions with specific black women, his words also implied that had she not been pregnant, she would have been available for sex. As well, his choice of the active voice to describe Tibbs in this moment—"*She* was not in any situation to be *doing* that"—shows a refusal to recognize her lack of consent to sexual intercourse.

That some of the rapes that occurred during the riot took place within a discourse simulating scenes of promiscuous black women willingly engaging in sex with white men did not prevent the attackers from inflicting extreme violence. For instance, Lucy Smith described the violence she suffered:

> One of them . . . choked me by the neck. My neck was swollen up next day, and for two weeks I could not talk to anyone. After the first man had connexion with me, another got hold of me and tried to violate me, but I was so bad he did not. He gave me a lick with his first and said I was so damned near dead he would not have anything to do with me. . . . I bled from what the first man had done to me. I was injured right smart. . . . They were in the house a good while after they hurt me, but I lay down on the bed, for I thought they had killed me. . . . I was in bed two weeks after.

The women surviving rape during the Memphis Riot experienced prolonged physical pain and terror. Each rape was ultimately carried out through violence or threats of death that belied the casual scenes that the perpetrators sought to stage.

Placing this reading of sexual violence in the context of the conflicts over public space leading up to the Memphis Riot reveals another layer to the political meaning of rioters' rape "scripts." By dishonoring black women, white men contested the power these women exercised in the public spaces of Memphis. To identify black women as "loose" women or prostitutes was to imply that they were the "sort of women" who endangered the community if free and unrestrained in public. Through their violence, rioters attacked the citizenship freedwomen had exercised in public by attacking their identities as respectable women. This is not to suggest that this was a consciously designed strategy. The relationship between gendered constructions of racial difference and contests over citizenship was deeply embedded in the discourse circulating among white opponents of Reconstruction in Memphis. The white men who raped freedwomen during the Memphis Riot enacted a fantasy of social subordination that drew on an existing gendered discourse of racial inequality, one that had already politicized gender identities in contests over race, power, and citizenship in post-emancipation Memphis.

The Memphis Riot came to an end on Thursday, May 3, when federal troops spread throughout the city. By that time the murderous events of the past three days had drawn the attention of Republicans in Washington, D.C. On May 14, 1866 Congressman Thaddeus Stevens proposed that a congressional committee travel to Memphis to investigate "the recent bloody riots in that city." Radical Republicans looked to this investigation to provide support for their position that stronger federal intervention into the affairs of southern states was necessary to protect the rights and lives of freedpeople.

Stevens's plan was adopted. A House select committee composed of three congressmen—Ellihu B. Washburne of Illinois and John M. Broomall of Pennsylvania, both Republicans, and George S. Shanklin of Kentucky, a Democrat—arrived in Memphis on May 22. Sixty-six African Americans came before the committee to testify. For the freedwomen who testified about sexual violence, the committee created a forum of unprecedented state power in which they articulated new public identities as citizens and contested racist constructions of black womanhood. For African American women, to testify that they had been raped was a radical act in the context of southern state law and tradition. A legal and cultural refusal to recognize black women's accounts of rape had served a dominant white discourse of racial inequality that bolstered slavery in the antebellum South. Post-emancipation imagery of freedwomen as "unvirtuous" drew on this pre-war exclusion of black women from the category of "women" who could be raped. The rioters who raped freedwomen had expressed these same meanings to contest the power that freedwomen were exercising as citizens of Memphis. When black women represented their experience of coerced sexual intercourse with white men as a violation of their will, they asserted a claim to the status of "woman" and "citizen." In the process, they would also counter conventional discourses on womanhood, rape, and "virtue."

Freedwomen employed language of violation and harm in order to identify assailants' actions as rape rather than illicit sex. Rebecca Ann Bloom maintained before the Freedmen's Bureau that the man who got into bed with her had "violated my person, by having connexion with me." Before the congressional committee, Frances Thompson affirmed that she and Lucy Smith were "violated" by the men who intruded into their home. Lucy Smith chose similar words to describe rioters' actions: they "tried to violate me . . . [and] they hurt me." When asked by

Congressman Washburne whether the men who plundered her home had hurt her, Lucy Tibbs responded, "they done a very bad act," and then confirmed Washburne's assumption that by this she meant they had "ravish[ed]" her. Stressing that rioters's actions were imposed against their will, freedwomen refuted the contrary image that rioters had sought to create in the scenes surrounding the actual rapes, namely that the women's experiences were evidence of their own lack of "virtue." Freedwomen further confuted rioters' "scripts" that had denied black women's agency and suffering by recounting the terror they had experienced. Harriet Armour recalled how she cried but was too terrified to call for help. Lucy Smith believed that there were seven men who came into her house on the night she was raped, but "I was so scared I could not be certain." Lucy Tibbs recounted that "I was so scared I could not tell whether they were policemen or not," and described begging her assailants to leave her and her children in peace. This testimony resisted the meanings that assailants had attempted to stage during the riot.

Some of the women who testified had to defend their honor in the face of hostile and insinuating questioning from members of the committee. After answering in the affirmative the chair's question, "Did they ravish you?," Lucy Tibbs still had to contend with the commitee's apparent doubt. Washburne continued, "Did they violate your person against your consent?" to which Tibbs again insisted, "Yes Sir. I had just to give up to them. They said they would kill me if I did not." Washburne again suggested the possibility that the attack was somehow a product of Tibbs's own conduct: "Were you dressed or undressed when these men came to you?" She stated that she was dressed. "Did you make any resistance?" the chair then asked. Tibbs responded by sharing with him the information she had used to calculate her safest course of action: "No sir; the house was full of men. I thought they would kill me; they had stabbed a woman near by the night before." Tibbs had heard others report that this same woman had also been raped. Believing that resistance might result in her own death, Tibbs surrendered to the assailant physically. But here, in the committee's hearing room, she resisted both the rioters' and the congressmen's implications that what had happened in some way reflected shame on herself.

Harriet Armour also came under challenging questioning from the committee. She recounted that she had seen no possibility of escape from the men who attacked her, because one of them had barred her door shut. Washburne then asked, "What did he do with the window?" Armour explained that she could not have fled through the window because two slats were nailed across it. "And you made no resistance?" he asked. "No," she answered, repeating that "they had barred the door. I could not get out, and I could not help myself." Yet the suspicions persisted. "Did I understand you that you did not try to prevent them from doing these things to you?" Congressman Broomall asked in disbelief. "Could not the people outside have come to help you?" Armour tried again to explain her strategy to survive the attack:

> No, sir; I did not know what to do. I was there alone, was weak and sick, and thought I would rather let them do it than to be hurt or punished. . . . I should have been afraid to call [for help]. . . . I thought I had just better give up freely; I did not like to do it, but I thought it would be best for me.

Both Armour and Tibbs had yielded to the rioters' demands in order to prevent further violence, and in the case of Tibbs perhaps to protect her children. Yet their judgment of what to do in such a situation did not conform to the patriarchal framework within which the elite white men on the committee appear to have imagined rape. The congressmen's questioning implied that even under the threat of potentially deadly force, anything but ceaseless resistance to sexual violation raised questions about a woman's "virtue."

Washburne and Broomall may have sincerely doubted Armour's and Tibbs's testimony that they had been raped, because it seemed to these men that the women had not resisted enough. It is also possible that the Republican congressmen's questions were intended to elicit further details so as to shape the testimony in ways that would best represent the women's claims before a national audience. In either case, when faced with the congressmen's apparent uneasiness about their testimony, Armour and Tibbs defended their actions. They made clear that, as much as they had suffered from the rapes they experienced, they did not share the assumption that rape would damage them in ways worth risking death to prevent. Nor did they accept the implications of the rioters, that their submission implied that they were "unvirtuous" women. Armour and Tibbs both firmly maintained that despite physical acquiescence, the sex occurred against their will. To defend their honor and represent the events as violation, the women struggled to make intelligible to the committee a perspective that grew out of their experiences during the riot, and perhaps out of their experiences as slaves. They had recently lived under a system of slavery in which many women faced the grim choice between submitting to forced sexual intercourse with white men or risking other physical harm to themselves and their loved ones. These women's testimony then implicitly shifted the parameters of patriarchal discourse on rape. By inserting black women's experiences and perspectives into a public discussion of sexual violence, they presented alternative constructions of honorable womanhood. To them, in this context, honor depended more on surviving and protesting injustice than on privileging and protecting a patriarchal notion of women's sexual "virtue."

Perhaps Armour's persistence in demonstrating, under a barrage of hostile insinuation, that her strategy for survival in no way reflected her own dishonor stemmed from the fact that she had already suffered from another's sense that she was less valuable as a woman because of the attack. Cynthia Townsend, a freedwoman and neighbor of Armour, testified that "When [Armour's husband] came out of the fort, and found what had been done, he said he would not have anything to do with her any more." It was clear that Armour suffered enormously from her husband's rejection. "She has sometimes been a little deranged since then," Townsend explained. In her testimony, Armour moved from subject to subject quickly, suggesting that recounting these stories may have been particularly difficult for her, more so than was apparent in other freedwomen's accounts. She segued directly from her description of one man's efforts to force her to perform fellatio to, "I have not got well since my husband went away," thereby connecting the attack with her husband's departure. Armour was the only woman testifying to indicate any ostracism by a member of her community as a result of rape. It is possible that Armour's experience was exacerbated by the fact that she was attacked in daylight and thus suspected that others were aware of what was being done to her ("It was an open shanty, and they could see right in"). Any observers were doubtless powerless to stop the attack. Nonetheless, the fact that she understood her ordeal to have been a public spectacle of sorts may have been a factor in her devastation; it may have alienated her from her community, and contributed to her husband's rejection.

What is striking, then, is Armour's courage in coming forward to tell this story again in another public setting, that of the congressional hearing. There was no practical need for Armour or other women to discuss sexual assaults in order to condemn the rioters. When Armour, Lucy Tibbs, Lucy Smith, and Frances Thompson testified before this committee, they all reported other crimes and forms of violence in addition to rape, namely, theft and battery. That they chose to recount having suffered sexual violence, despite the risks involved, suggests that this testimony served ends important to them: the public condemnation of and protest against these acts as violation, and the implicit affirmation of their identities as free women with the will to choose or refuse sexual relations and with the right to be protected by law. Given the conservative pre-riot discourse that imputed dishonorable gendered identities of African American women, and the police harassment of black women in Memphis, both of which were efforts to limit black women's power as citizens, these women's portrayals of themselves as survivors of rape appear as important political acts in African Americans' overall struggle to realize their freedom.

The courage the freedwomen showed in making their suffering public garnered the support of the Republican majority of the congressional investigating committee. Despite the committee's hostile questioning, freedwomen's narratives served Republican interests in representing southern white men as "unreconstructed" and thus unprepared for self-rule. The committee majority's final report highlighted the rape of African American women to depict the white rioters as uncivilized and dishonorable men. Eleven thousand copies of the report were printed, and it was excerpted in newspapers across the country. Describing the riot as "an organized and bloody massacre of the colored people of Memphis," this report stated,

> The crowning acts of atrocity and diabolism committed during these terrible nights were the ravishing of five different colored women by these fiends in human shape. . . . It is a singular fact, that while this mob was breathing vengeance against the negroes and shooting them down like dogs, yet when they found unprotected colored women they at once "conquered their prejudices," and proceeded to violate them under circumstances of the most licentious brutality.

To bolster this representation of the rape of black women as the ultimate atrocity of the riot, the authors assured readers that Lucy Smith was "a girl of modest demeanor and highly respectable in appearance." They similarly noted that both Harriet Armour and Lucy Tibbs were married—and thus legitimate—women, and that Tibbs had two young children and was pregnant with her third. Through these images of female respectability, the committee's majority sought to preempt accusations of the "dishonorable" character of the women and therefore doubts about their legitimacy as victims of sexual assault.

Images of feminine "virtue" rooted in modesty and submission within marriage had not been part of freedwomen's self-representations when they defended their honor before the congressional committee. In general, freedwomen in Memphis had not shown their definitions of womanhood to depend upon notions of "proper" and submissive femininity. Rather, through their own forceful presence in the city's public spaces, they had claimed identities as women who were active, outspoken, and assertive with regard to their own and their community's rights to live freely as citizens. Yet once freedwomen's narratives concerning rape entered into the arena of national politics, their words were forced into a discourse of womanhood and "virtue" not of their own making. When the congressional committee portrayed freedwomen as victims of rape, they drew on the same opposition between "virtuous" and "unvirtuous" women that conservatives had manipulated prior to the riot in order to reject black women's claims to full citizenship. And, as we will see, this same binary discourse of "virtue" and "vice" would ultimately help conservatives to discredit black women's testimony on sexual violence.

After the congressional investigation, no rioters were arrested or charged with any crimes. Freedwomen's testimony, though, did help to promote several state and national measures that extended greater protection and political power to African Americans during Reconstruction. And the conservative press in Memphis was silenced by the overwhelming evidence of violence enacted by white men presented by the committee's report. The conservative *Appeal*, earlier full of condemnations of black women as deceitful, disreputable, and depraved, offered no immediate critique of the freedwomen who testified that they had been raped.

Ten years later, however, conservatives in Memphis stumbled upon their chance to vindicate white men from charges made in the congressional report and to dismiss the freedwomen's testimony about rape. In 1876 Frances Thompson was arrested for "being a man and wearing women's clothing." Because Thompson's testimony had occupied a prominent place in the congressional committee's report, her arrest for cross-dressing—an incident that might have received only passing mention in the local press under different circumstances—filled the city columns for days. Her arrest also served the interests of conservatives-turned-Democrats in the 1876 presidential election campaign, which would ultimately mark the end of Reconstruction at the national level and return control over the southern states to white southerners. In this context, the conservative newspapers contended that Thompson's transvestism proved her testimony about rape to have been a lie.

Thompson herself paid dearly for her supposed crime. After her arrest she was placed on the city's chain gang, where she was forced to wear men's clothing and suffered constant ridicule and harassment from crowds drawn to the scene by mocking press reports. Soon after she completed her prison term of one hundred days, she was discovered alone and seriously ill in a cabin in North Memphis. Members of the freed community moved her to the city hospital, where she died on November 1, 1876. The coroner's report of her death recorded that she was indeed anatomically male.

What can we make of the fact that Thompson—with a woman's identity and a male body—testified that she had been raped during the Memphis Riot? Was she drawing on Lucy Smith's experience of rape to perform for the committee that she too was a woman? Or had she in fact been raped? Had the rioters been shocked when they discovered the "truth" about her anatomy? Or were they aware in advance that she was anatomically male? Did they attack her because of that fact? Was the materiality of bodies irrelevant, superseded by a "script" of black women's sexual wantonness that mattered most? Unfortunately, there are no sources with which to answer these questions.

There is evidence, though, of a campaign of vilification against Thompson in the conservative press, one designed to refute charges of white southern brutality against African Americans and to oppose Reconstruction policies supported by Republicans. Similar to the disparagement of black women prior to the riot, newspaper editors described Thompson as "lewd," associated her with prostitution, and portrayed her as the epitome of "unvirtuous" gender and sexuality. They attributed to her "vile habits and corruptions," decried her "utter depravity," and accused her of using her "guise" as a woman to facilitate her supposed role as "wholesale debaucher" and "procuress" of numberless young women for prostitution. The papers then used these charges to condemn their Republican opponents, reminding their readers that the Republican Party—now referred to as "the Frances Thompson Radical party"—had relied upon Thompson's "perjurous evidence" to condemn white men in Memphis for violence and brutality.

The conservative press alleged that Thompson's testimony was merely a charade to discredit the words of all the black women who testified that they had been raped during the Memphis Riot. The *Memphis Daily Appeal* criticized Lucy Smith for her corroboration of Thompson's testimony, which was now dismissed as "utterly at variance with the truth." The paper also mocked Smith's claim that she herself had been "violated." The *Appeal* insinuated that Smith did not possess the "virtue" supposedly needed for a woman to protest rape, because—and this they asserted with no evidence—Smith had been "occupying the same bed with Thompson" prior to the riot. The other women who testified were not mentioned by name, but the conservative papers implied that Thompson's transvestism exposed the entire congressional report as "vile slander," manufactured by Republicans solely for political gain. With no new information other than Thomson's cross-dressing, one conservative paper denounced the report: "The evidence of the vilest wretches was received and worded in smooth phrase and published to the world to prove that the Southern people were a set of barbarians and assassins." The *Appeal* went further, enlisting Thompason's image to vindicate all white southerners from accusations of racist violence during Reconstruction:

> Whenever you hear Radicals talking of the persecutions of the black race in the south, ask them what they think of Frances Thompson and the outrages committed on her by the Irish of this city during the celebrated riots. These pretended outrages in the south are all of a piece with this Frances Thompson affair. It is out of such material as this that all their blood-and-thunder stories are manufactured.

Critics of Reconstruction attempted to supplant recognition of African American women's experiences of sexual violence—now mere "pretended outrages"—with the image of Thompson's allegedly "deviant" and "depraved," cross-dressing male body. Ultimately, Thompson's transvestism was such a powerful tool for conservatives not because Thompson was represented as bizarre or unique, but rather because her image resonated so strongly with the pre-existing conservative discourse attributing dishonorable gender and sexuality to all African American women. It was but a small step from images of women who were "unvirtuous" to images of women who were so "unvirtuous" that they were not women at all.

This postscript to the history of freedwomen's testimony about rape during the Memphis Riot suggests once again how discourses of gender and sexuality played a central role in political struggles over race, following emancipation. Former slaves in Memphis had insisted on their right as citizens to move, live, and work freely in the public spaces of the city. Their actions adumbrated a new social order that challenged the racial hierarchy of the antebellum South. White city police and conservative newspaper editors responded to African Americans' entry into public life in Memphis, among other ways, by condemning black women in public as prostitutes and by depicting them overall as the "sort of women" who were not "virtuous" and therefore not worthy of citizenship. In this way, gender served as a metaphor for racial difference. When emancipation threatened to efface racial inequality, racial difference was reinscribed through the misrepresentation and stigmatization of black women's gender and sexuality.

I have tried to show how the rapes that occurred during the Memphis Riot formed part of this same discourse of racialized gender. Rioters who raped freedwomen sought to reassert racial inequality and the privileges of white manhood by enacting antebellum fantasies of black women's sexual subservience and lack of feminine "virtue." During the rapes themselves, and indeed simply by testifying to having been raped, African American women rejected these scripts. Political contests over African American citizenship and freedom following emancipation were partly fought out through battles over gendered constructions of racial difference, battles that included elaborate and contested scenes of horrific sexual domination and violence. Analyzing incidents of rape, particularly in moments of violent political conflict, as part of discourse allows us to begin to understand the multiple historical forces and ideas that have given shape to this form of violence.

Questions for Study and Review

1. What were the conflicts that led to the Memphis Riot of 1866, and who did the rioters target and why?

2. Almost fifty African Americans were killed during these riots, but Rosen focuses on the five rape cases that came out of the violence. Why are these rapes important to study, and what makes sexual violence significant in this context?

3. Why was it revolutionary to hear an African American woman's voice in a legal forum, and what assumptions and stereotypes did these witnesses challenge through their testimony?

4. What were the long-term implications of this violence and the investigations that followed?

Suggested Readings and Web Sites

Elsa Barkley Brown, "Negotiating and Transforming the Public Sphere: African American Political Life in the Transition from Slavery to Freedom," In *Jumpin' Jim Crow: Southern Politics from Civil War to Civil Rights* (2000)

Tera Hunter, *To 'joy My Freedom: Southern Black Women's Lives and Labors After the Civil War* (1997)

Jacqueline Jones Royster, ed., *Southern Horrors and Other Writings: The Anti-Lynching Campaign of Ida B. Wells, 1892–1900* (1997)

Patricia Schechter, *Ida B. Wells-Barnett and American Reform, 1880–1930* (2001)

Freedmen and Southern Society Project
   http://www.history.umd.edu/Freedmen/

Library of Congress American Memory Project
   http://memory.loc.gov/ammem/aapchtml/aapchome.html

African Americans and whites in the South sought to remake their lives in the aftermath of the Civil War. The lives of Americans in the North and Midwest were also dramatically transformed in the late nineteenth century, but changes there were linked more closely to urban industrial and technological developments. As the result of improved transportation and communication and the demand for industrial labor, young women and men from rural areas and immigrants from eastern and southern Europe flooded cities from New York to Chicago.

While cities offered new opportunities for many Americans, cities' rapid growth also fostered new problems. Increased demands for housing, sanitation, running water, public transportation, and medical care arose alongside growing concerns about rising rates of poverty, crime, prostitution, and industrial injuries and accidents. For most immigrants these difficulties were exacerbated by differences of language and culture. Immigrant women and children seemed especially vulnerable to the dangers of city life. In response, more privileged women, most of them born and raised in the United States, sought new ways to address and help shape the forces of social change.

In the 1890s—a decade of economic crisis and partisan political realignments— a generation of female college graduates forged a new institutional base from which to launch their reform programs. Young idealists established settlement houses in New York, Boston, Philadelphia, Chicago, and dozens of other cities, in the hope that their efforts could lessen the ills produced by inner-city life and massive immigration.

Both women and men joined the settlement house movement, though most houses were sex-segregated in accommodating their full-time residents. Men, however, had numerous other vehicles for pursuing social change and did so while leading independent lives. Women had few alternatives if they wished to maintain their respectability while living outside the traditional family circle and dedicating themselves to public activism. Also, in the decades before the vote was won nationally, women relied more heavily than men on scientific studies and collective lobbying efforts to make their influence felt.

For Jane Addams, Florence Kelley, Lillian Wald, and hundreds of women like them, the all-female communities created in the settlement houses provided emotional and economic support, afforded contacts with other women's organizations and with male allies, and increased female activists' social and political clout. Sklar's examination of one of the most influential settlement communities—Chicago's Hull House—reveals how sisterly bonds were forged from common family backgrounds and then mobilized in the service of a shared social vision. At the same time, Hull House functioned as part of the complex network of alliances and organizations that rendered the settlement so effective in the political arena.

Using the example of antisweatshop legislation, Sklar demonstrates the capacity of settlement women to affect practical change and recognizes the complex implications of that single piece of legislation for the lives of Chicago's working-class and immigrant women and families. As settlement women and other mostly middle-class females gained access to the formal political arena, they began to determine what types of legislation were most beneficial not only for themselves but for women of all ethnic, race, and class backgrounds. The efforts of Hull House leaders illustrates both the benefits and the dangers of that situation.

Hull House in the 1890s: A Community of Women Reformers
KATHRYN KISH SKLAR

What were the sources of women's political power in the United States in the decades before they could vote? How did women use the political power they were able to muster? This essay attempts to answer these questions by examining one of the most politically effective groups of women reformers in U.S. history—those who assembled in Chicago in the early 1890s at Hull House, one of the nation's first social settlements, founded in 1889 by Jane Addams and Ellen Gates Starr. Within that group, this study focuses on the reformer Florence Kelley (1859–1932). Kelley joined Hull House in 1891 and remained until 1899, when she moved to Lillian Wald's Henry Street Settlement on the Lower East Side of New York, where she lived for the next twenty-seven years. According to Felix Frankfurter, Kelley "had probably the largest single share in shaping the social history of the United States during the first thirty years of this century," for she played "a powerful if not decisive role in securing legislation for the removal of the most glaring abuses of our hectic industrialization following the Civil War." It was in the 1890s that Kelley and her colleagues at Hull House developed the patterns of living and thinking that guided them throughout their lives of reform, leaving an indelible imprint on U.S. politics. This essay attempts to determine the extent to which their political power and activities flowed from their collective life as coresidents and friends and the degree to which this power was attributable to their close affiliation with male reformers and male institutions.

The effects of both factors can be seen in one of the first political campaigns conducted by Hull House residents—the 1893 passage and subsequent enforcement of pathbreaking antisweatshop legislation mandating an eight-hour day for women

Kathryn Kish Sklar, "Hull House in the 1890s: A Community of Reformers," *Signs* 10:4 (1985): pp. 657–677. Copyright © by the University of Chicago Press. Reprinted by permission of the University of Chicago Press and the author.

and children employed in Illinois manufacturing. This important episode reveals a great deal about the sources of this group's political power, including their own collective initiative, the support of other women's groups, and the support of men and men's groups. Finally, it shows how women reformers and the gender-specific issues they championed helped advance class-specific issues during a time of fundamental social, economic, and political transition.

• • •

The community of women at Hull House made it possible for Florence Kelley to step from the apprenticeship to the journeyman stage in her reform career. A study of the 1893 antisweatshop campaign shows that the community provided four fundamental sources of support for her growth as a reformer. First, it supplied an emotional and economic substitute for traditional family life, linking her with other talented women of her own class and educational and political background and thereby greatly increasing her political and social power. Second, the community at Hull House provided Kelley with effective ties to other women's organizations. Third, it enabled cooperation with men reformers and their organizations, allowing her to draw on their support without submitting to their control. Finally, it provided a creative setting for her to pursue and develop a reform strategy she had already initiated in New York—the advancement of the rights and interests of working people in general by strengthening the rights and interests of working women and children.

As a community of women, Hull House provided its members with a lifelong substitute for family life. In that sense it resembled a religious order, supplying women with a radical degree of independence from the claims of family life and inviting them to commit their energies elsewhere. When she first crossed the snowy threshold of Hull House "sometime between Christmas and New Year's," 1891, Florence Kelley Wischnewetzky was fleeing from her husband and seeking refuge for herself and her three children, ages six, five, and four. "We were welcomed as though we had been invited," she wrote thirty-five years later in her memoirs. The way in which Kelley's family dilemma was solved reveals a great deal about the sources of support for the political activity of women reformers in the progressive era: help came first and foremost from women's institutions but also from the recruited support of powerful men reformers. Jane Addams supplied Kelley with room, board, and employment and soon after she arrived introduced her to Henry Demarest Lloyd, a leading critic of American labor policies who lived with his wife Jessie and their young children in nearby Winnetka. The Lloyds readily agreed to add Kelley's children to their large nursery, an arrangement that began a lifelong relationship between the two families. A sign of the extent to which responsibility for Kelley's children was later assumed by members of the Hull House community, even after her departure, was the fact that Jane Addams's closest personal friend, Mary Rozet Smith, regularly and quietly helped Kelley pay for their school and college tuition.

A bit stunned by her good fortune, the young mother wrote her own mother a summary of her circumstances a few weeks after reaching Hull House: "We are all well, and the chicks are happy. I have fifty dollars a month and my board and shall have more soon as I can collect my wits enough to write. I have charge of the Bureau of Labor of Hull House here and am working in the lines which I have

Residents of Hull House lived in apartments within the building and took their meals together in the common dining room. This photograph from 1930 shows settlement house founder Jane Addams seated at the head of the middle table, flanked by fellow activist Alice Hamilton. Settlement houses provided women like Addams, Hamilton, and Florence Kelley with an invaluable blend of personal and professional support as they worked to achieve social, economic, and political reform.

always loved. I do not know what more to tell you except this, that in the few weeks of my stay here I have won for the children and myself many and dear friends whose generous hospitality astonishes me." This combination of loving friendship and economic support served as a substitute for the family life from which she had just departed. "It is understood that I am to resume the maiden name," she continued to her mother, "and that the children are to have it." It did not take Kelley long to decide to join this supportive community of women. As she wrote Friedrich Engels in April 1892, "I have cast in my lot with Misses Addams and Starr for as long as they will have me." To her mother she emphasized the personal gains Hull House brought her, writing, "I am better off than I have been since I landed in New York since I am now responsible *myself* for what I do." Gained at great personal cost, Kelley's independence was her most basic measure of well-being. Somewhat paradoxically, perhaps, her autonomy was the product of her affiliation with a community.

One significant feature of Hull House life was the respect that residents expressed for one another's autonomy. Although each had a "room of her own," in

Kelley's case this room was sometimes shared with other residents, and the collective space was far more important than their small private chambers. Nevertheless, this intimate proximity was accompanied by a strong expression of personal individuation, reflected in the formality of address used at Hull House. By the world at large Kelley was called Mrs. Kelley, but to her close colleagues she was "Sister Kelley," or "Dearest F. K.," never Florence. Miss Addams and Miss Lathrop were never called Jane or Julia, even by their close friends, although Kelley occasionally took the liberty of calling Addams "gentle Jane." It was not that Hull House was bleak and business-like, as one resident once described male settlements in New York, but rather that the colleagues recognized and appreciated one another's individuality. These were superb conditions for social innovation since the residents could draw on mutual support at the same time that they were encouraged to pursue their own distinct goals.

This respect for individuality did not prevent early Hull House residents from expressing their love for one another. Kelley's letters to Jane Addams often began "Beloved Lady," and she frequently addressed Mary Rozet Smith as "Dearly Beloved," referring perhaps to Smith's special status in Addam's life. Kelley's regard for Addams and Addams's for her were revealed in their correspondence after Kelley left in 1899. Addams wrote her, "I have had blows before in connection with Hull House but nothing like this"; and Mary Rozet Smith added, "I have had many pangs for the dear presiding lady." Later that year Addams wrote, "Hull House sometimes seems a howling wilderness without you." Kelley seems to have found the separation difficult since she protested when her name was removed from the list of residents in the *Hull House Bulletin*. Addams replied, "You overestimate the importance of the humble Bulletin," but she promised to restore Kelley's name, explaining that it was only removed to "stop people asking for her." Fourteen years later in 1913 Addams wrote "Sister Kelley," "It is curious that I have never gotten used to you being away from [Hull House], even after all these years!"

One source of the basic trust established among the three major reformers at Hull House in the 1890s—Jane Addams, Julia Lathrop, and Florence Kelley—was similarity of family background. Not only were they all of the upper middle class, but their fathers were politically active men who helped Abraham Lincoln found and develop the Republican Party in the 1860s. John Addams served eight terms as a state senator in Illinois, William Lathrop served in Congress as well as in the Illinois legislature, and William Kelley served fifteen consecutive terms in Congress. All were vigorous abolitionists, and all encouraged their daughters' interests in public affairs. As Judge Alexander Bruce remarked at the joint memorial services held for Julia Lathrop and Florence Kelley after their deaths in 1932, "Both of them had the inspiration of great and cultured mothers and both had great souled fathers who, to use the beautiful language of Jane Addams in speaking of her own lineage, 'Wrapped their little daughters in the large men's doublets, careless did they fit or no.'"

These three remarkable women were participating in a political tradition that their fathers had helped create. While they were growing up in the 1860s and 1870s, they gained awareness through their fathers' experience of the mainstream of American political processes, thereby learning a great deal about its currents—particularly that its power could be harnessed to fulfill the purposes of well-organized interest groups.

Although Hull House residents have generally been interpreted as reformers with a religious motivation, it now seems clear that they were instead motivated by political goals. In that regard they resembled a large proportion of other women social settlement leaders, including those associated with Hull House after 1900, such as Grace and Edith Abbot, whose father was Nebraska's first lieutenant governor, or Sophonisba Breckinridge, daughter of a Kentucky congressman. Women leaders in the social settlement movement seem to have differed in this respect from their male counterparts, who were seeking alternatives to more orthodox religious, rather than political, careers. In, but not of, the Social Gospel movement, the women at Hull House were a political boat on a religious stream, advancing political solutions to social problems that were fundamentally ethical or moral, such as the right of workers to a fair return for their labor or the right of children to schooling.

Another source of the immediate solidarity among Addams, Lathrop, and Kelley was their shared experience of higher education. Among the first generation of American college women, they graduated from Rockford College, Vassar College, and Cornell University, respectively, in the early 1880s and then spent the rest of the decade searching for work and for a social identity commensurate with their talents. Addams tried medical school; Lathrop worked in her father's law office; Kelley, after being denied admission to graduate study at the University of Pennsylvania, studied law and government at the University of Zurich, where she received a much more radical education than she would have had she remained in Philadelphia. In the late 1880s and early 1890s, the social settlement movement was the right movement at the right time for this first generation of college-educated women, who were able to gain only limited entry to the male-dominated professions of law, politics, or academics.

While talented college women of religious backgrounds and inclinations were energetically recruited into the missionary empires of American churches, those seeking secular outlets for their talents chose a path that could be as daunting as that of a missionary outpost. Except for the field of medicine, where women's institutions served the needs of women physicians and students, talented women were blocked from entering legal, political, and academic professions by male-dominated institutions and networks. In the 1890s the social settlement movement supplied a perfect structure for women seeking secular means of influencing society because it collectivized their talents, it placed and protected them among the working-class immigrants whose lives demanded amelioration, and it provided them with access to the male political arena while preserving their independence from male dominated institutions.

Since Hull House drew on local sources of funding, often family funds supplied by wealthy women, Jane Addams found it possible to finance the settlement's activities without the assistance or control of established religious or educational institutions. In 1895 she wrote that Hull House was modeled after Toynbee Hall in London, where "a group of University men . . . reside in the poorer quarter of London for the sake of influencing the people there toward better local government and wider social and intellectual life." Substituting "college-trained women" for "University men," Hull House also placed a greater emphasis on economic factors. As Addams continued, "The original residents came to Hull House with a conviction that social intercourse could best express the growing sense of the economic unity of society." She also emphasized their political autonomy, writing that the first residents "wished the social spirit to be the undercurrent of the life of Hull-House, whatever direction the stream might take." Under Kelley's influence in 1892, the social spirit at Hull House turned decisively toward social reform, bringing the community's formidable energy and talents to bear on a historic campaign on behalf of labor legislation for women and children.

The settlement did play a critical leadership role in this venture, but it was never alone. Indeed it was part of a complex network of women's associations in Chicago in the 1890s. About thirty women's organizations combined forces and entered into local politics in 1888 through the Illinois Women's Alliance, organized that year by Elizabeth Morgan and other members of the Ladies Federal Union no. 2073 in response to a crusading woman journalist's stories in the *Chicago Times* about "City Slave Girls" in the garment industry. The alliance's political goals were clearly stated in their constitution: "The objects of the Alliance are to agitate for the enforcement of all existing laws and ordinances that have been enacted for the protection of women and children—as the factory ordinances and the compulsory education law. To secure the enactment of such laws as shall be found necessary. To investigate all business establishments and factories where women and children are employed and public institutions where women and children are maintained. To procure the appointment of women, as inspectors and as members of boards of education, and to serve on boards of management of public institutions." Adopting the motto "Justice to Children, Loyalty to Women," the alliance acted as a vanguard for the entrance of women's interests into municipal and state politics, focusing chiefly on the passage and enforcement of compulsory education laws. One of its main accomplishments was the agreement of the city council in 1889 "to appoint five lady inspectors" to enforce city health codes.

The diversity of politically active women's associations in Chicago in the late 1880s was reflected in a list of organizations associated with the alliance. Eight bore names indicating a religious or ethical affiliation, such as the Woodlawn branch of the Women's Christian Temperance Union and the Ladies Union of the Ethical Society. Five were affiliated with working women or were trade unions, such as the Working Women's Protective Association, the Ladies Federal Union no. 2703, and (the only predominantly male organization on the list) the Chicago Trades and Labor Assembly. Another five had an intellectual or cultural focus, such as the Hopkins Metaphysical Association or the Vincent Chatauqua Association. Three were women's professional groups, including the Women's Press Association and the Women's Homeopathic Medical Society. Another three were female auxiliaries of male social organizations, such as the Lady Washington Masonic Chapter and the Ladies of the Grand Army of the Republic. Two were suffrage associations, including the Cook County Suffrage Association; another two were clubs interested in general economic reform, the Single Tax Club and the Land Labor Club no. 1; and one was educational, the Drexel Kindergarten Association.

Florence Kelley's 1892 entrance into this lively political scene was eased by her previous knowledge of and appreciation for the work of the alliance. Soon after its founding she had written the leaders a letter that was quoted extensively in a newspaper account of an alliance meeting, declaring, "The child labor question can be solved by legislation, backed by solid organization, and by women cooperating with the labor organizations, which have done all that has thus far been done for the protection of working children." In Chicago Kelley was perceived as a friend of the alliance because in 1889 and 1890 she had helped to organize the New York Working Women's Society's campaign "to add women as officials in the office for factory inspection." According to Kelley, the Society, "a small group of women from both the wealthy and influential class and the working class, . . . circulated petitions, composed resolutions, and was supported finally in the years 1889 and 1890 in bringing their proposal concerning the naming of women to factory inspectorships to the legislature, philanthropic groups and unions." As a result in 1890 the New York legislature passed laws creating eight new positions for women as state factory inspectors. This was quite an innovation since no woman factory inspector had yet been appointed in Great Britain or Germany, where factory inspection began, and the only four previously appointed in the United States had been named within the last two years in Pennsylvania. Writing in 1897 about this event, Kelley emphasized the political autonomy of the New York Working Women's Society: "Their proposal to add women as officials in the office for factory inspection was made for humanitarian reasons; in no way did it belong to the goals of the general workers' movement, although it found support among the unions." Thus when Kelley arrived at Hull House, she had already been affiliated with women's associations that were independent of trade unions even though cooperating with them.

For Kelley on that chilly December morning the question was not whether she would pursue a career in social reform but how, not whether she would champion what she saw as the rights and interests of working women and children but how she would do that. The question of means was critical in 1891 since her husband was unable to establish a stable medical practice, even though she had spent the small legacy inherited on her father's death the year before on new equipment for his practice. Indeed so acute were Kelley's financial worries that, when she decided to flee with her children to Chicago, she borrowed train fare from an English governess, Mary Forster, whom she had probably befriended at a neighborhood park. Chicago was a natural choice for Kelley since Illinois divorce laws were more equitable, and within its large population of reform-minded and politically active women she doubtlessly hoped to find employment that would allow her to support herself and her children. Although the historical record is incomplete, it seems likely that she headed first to a different community of women—that at the national headquarters of the Women's Christian Temperance Union (WCTU). She had been well paid for articles written for their national newspaper, the *Union Signal*— the largest women's newspaper in the world, with a circulation in 1890 of almost 100,000—and the WCTU was at the height of its institutional development in Chicago at that time, sponsoring "two day nurseries, two Sunday schools, an industrial school, a mission that sheltered four thousand homeless or destitute women in a twelve-month period, a free medical dispensary that treated over sixteen hundred patients a year, a lodging house for men that had . . . provided temporary housing for over fifty thousand men, and a low-cost restaurant." Just after Kelley arrived, the WCTU opened its Women's Temple, a twelve-story office building and hotel. Very likely it was someone there who told Kelley about Hull House.

The close relationship between Hull House and other groups of women in Chicago was exemplified in Kelley's interaction with the Chicago Women's Club. The minutes of the club's first meeting after Kelley's arrival in Chicago show that on January 25, 1892, she spoke under the sponsorship of Jane Addams on the sweating system and urged that a committee be created on the problem. Although a Reform Department was not created until 1894, minutes of March 23, 1892, show that the club's Home Department "decided upon cooperating with Mrs. Kelly [sic] of Hull House in establishing a Bureau of Women's Labor." Thus the club took over part of the funding and the responsibility for the counseling service Kelley had been providing at Hull House since February. (Initially Kelley's salary for this service was funded by the settlement, possibly with emergency monies given by Mary Rozet Smith.) In this way middle- and upper-middle-class clubwomen were drawn into the settlement's activities. In 1893 Jane Addams successfully solicited the support of wealthy clubwomen to lobby for the antisweatshop legislation: "We insisted that well-known Chicago women should accompany this first little group of Settlement folk who with trade-unionists moved upon the state capital in behalf of factory legislation." Addams also described the lobbying Hull House residents conducted with other voluntary associations: "Before the passage of the law could be secured, it was necessary to appeal to all elements of the community, and a little group of us addressed the open meetings of trades-unions and of benefit societies, church organizations, and social clubs literally every evening for three months." Thus Hull House was part of a larger social universe of voluntary organizations, and one important feature of its political effectiveness was its ability to gain the support of middle-class and working-class women.

In 1893 the cross-class coalition of the Illinois Women's Alliance began to dissolve under the pressure of the economic depression of that year, and in 1894 its leaders disbanded the group. Hull House reformers inherited the fruits of the alliance's five years of agitation, and they continued its example of combining working-class and middle-class forces. In 1891 Mary Kenney, a self-supporting typesetter who later became the first woman organizer to be employed by the American Federation of Labor, established the Jane Club adjacent to the settlement, a cooperative boardinghouse for young working women. In the early 1890s Kenney was a key figure in the settlement's efforts to promote union organizing among working women, especially bookbinders. Thus the combination of middle-class and working-class women at Hull House in 1892–93 was an elite version of the type of cross-class association represented by the Illinois Women's Alliance of the late 1880s—elite because it was smaller and because its middle-class members had greater social resources, familiarity with American political processes, and exposure to higher than average levels of education, while its working-class members (Mary Kenney and Alzina Stevens) were members of occupational and organizational elites.

By collectivizing talents and energies, this community made possible the exercise of greater and more effective political power by its members. A comparison of Florence Kelley's antisweatshop legislation, submitted to the Illinois investigative committee in February 1893, with that presented by Elizabeth Morgan dramatically illustrates this political advantage. The obvious differences in approach indicate that the chief energy for campaigning on behalf of working women and children had passed from working-class to middle-class social reformers. Both legislative drafts prohibited work in tenement dwellings, Morgan's prohibiting all manufacturing, Kelley's all garment making. Both prohibited the labor of children under fourteen and regulated the labor of children aged fourteen to sixteen. Kelley's went beyond Morgan's in two essential respects, however. Hers mandated an eight-hour day for women in manufacturing, and it provided for enforcement by calling for a state factory inspector with a staff of twelve, five of whom were to be women. The reasons for Kelley's greater success as an innovator are far from clear, but one important advantage in addition to her greater education and familiarity with the American political system was the larger community on which she could rely for the law's passage and enforcement.

Although Elizabeth Morgan could draw on her experience as her husband's assistant in his work as an attorney and on the support of women unionists, both resources were problematic. Thomas Morgan was erratic and self-centered, and Elizabeth Morgan's relationship with organized women workers was marred by sectarian disputes originating within the male power structure of the Chicago Trades and Labor Assembly. For example, in January 1892, when she accused members of the Shirtwaist Union of being controlled by her husband's opposition within the assembly, "a half dozen women surrounded [her] seat in the meeting and demanded an explanation. She refused to give any and notice was served that charges would be preferred against her at the next meeting of the Ladies' Federation of Labor." Perhaps Morgan's inability to count on a supportive community explains her failure to provide for adequate enforcement and to include measures for workers over the age of sixteen in her legislative draft. Compared to Kelley's, Morgan's bill was politically impotent. It could not enforce what it endorsed, and it did not affect adults.

Kelley's draft was passed by the Illinois legislature in June 1893, providing for a new office of enforcement and for an eight-hour day for women workers of all ages. After Henry Demarest Lloyd declined an invitation to serve as the state's first factory inspector, reform governor John Peter Altgeld followed Lloyd's recommendations and appointed Kelley. Thus eighteen months after her arrival in Chicago, she found herself in charge of a dedicated and well-paid staff of twelve mandated to see that prohibitions against tenement workshops and child labor were observed and to enforce a pathbreaking article restricting the working hours of women and children.

Hull House provided Kelley and other women reformers with a social vehicle for independent political action and a means of bypassing the control of male associations and institutions, such as labor unions and political parties; at the same time they had a strong institutional framework in which they could meet with other reformers, both men and women. The drafting of the antisweatshop legislation revealed how this process worked. In his autobiography, Abraham Bisno, pioneer organizer in the garment industry in Chicago and New York, described how he became a regular participant in public discussions of contemporary social issues at Hull House. He joined "a group . . . composed of Henry D. Lloyd, a prominent physician named Bayard Holmes, Florence Kelley, and Ellen G. [Starr] to engage in a campaign for legislation to abolish sweatshops, and to have a law passed prohibiting the employment of women more than eight hours a day." Answering a question about the author of the bill he endorsed at the 1893 hearings, Bisno said, "Mrs. Florence Kelly [*sic*] wrote that up with the legal advice of myself, Henry Lloyd, and a number of prominent attorneys in Chicago." Thus as the chief author of the legislation, Florence Kelley drew on the expertise of Bisno, one of the most dedicated and talented union organizers; of Lloyd, one of the most able elite reformers in the United States; and, surely among the "prominent attorneys," of Clarence Darrow, one of the country's most able reform lawyers. It is difficult to imagine this cooperative effort between Bisno, Kelley, and Lloyd without the existence of the larger Hull House group of which they were a part. Their effective collaboration exemplified the process by which members of this remarkable community of women reformers moved into the vanguard of contemporary reform activity, for they did so in alliance with other groups and individuals.

What part did the Hull House community, essential to the drafting and passage of the act, have in the statute's enforcement? Who benefited and who lost from the law's enforcement? Answers to these questions help us view the community more completely in the context of its time.

During the four years that Kelley served as chief factory inspector of Illinois, her office and Hull House were institutionally so close as to be almost indistinguishable. Kelley rented rooms for her office across the street from the settlement, with which she and her three most able deputies were closely affiliated. Alzina Stevens moved into Hull House soon after Altgeld appointed her as Kelley's chief assistant. Mary Kenney lived at the Jane Club, and Abraham Bisno was a familiar figure at Hull House evening gatherings. Jane Addams described the protection that the settlement gave to the first factory inspection office in Illinois, the only such office headed by a woman in her lifetime: "The inception of the law had already become associated with Hull House, and when its ministration was also centered there, we inevitably received all the odium which these first efforts entailed. . . . Both Mrs. Kelley and her assistant, Mrs. Stevens, lived at Hull-House; . . . and one of the most vigorous deputies was the President of the Jane Club. In addition, one of the early men residents, since dean of a state law school, acted as prosecutor in the cases brought against the violators of the law." Thus the law's enforcement was just as collective an undertaking as was its drafting and passage. Florence Kelley and Alzina Stevens were usually the first customers at the Hull House Coffee Shop, arriving at 7:30 for a breakfast conference to plan their strategy for the day ahead. Doubtlessly these discussions continued at the end of the day in the settlement's dining hall.

One important aspect of the collective strength of Kelley's staff was the socialist beliefs shared by its most dedicated members. As Kelley wrote to Engels in November 1893, "I find my work as inspector most interesting; and as Governor Altgeld places no restrictions whatever upon our freedom of speech, and the English etiquette of silence while in the civil service is unknown here, we are not hampered by our position and three of my deputies and my assistant are outspoken Socialists and active in agitation." In his autobiography Bisno described the "fanatical" commitment that he, Florence Kelley, and most of the "radical group" brought to their work as factory inspectors. For him it was the perfect job since his salary allowed him for the first time to support his wife and children and his work involved direct action against unfair competition within his trade. "In those years labor legislation was looked on as a joke; few took it seriously," he later wrote. "Inspectors normally . . . were appointed from the view point of political interest. . . . There were very few, almost no, court cases heard of, and it was left to our department to set the example of rigid enforcement of labor laws." Although they were replaced with "political interests" after the election of 1896, this group of inspectors showed what could be accomplished by the enactment of reform legislation and its vigorous enforcement. They demonstrated that women could use the power of the state to achieve social and economic goals.

Kelley and her staff began to take violators of the law to court in October 1893. She wrote Lloyd, "I have engaged counsel and am gathering testimony and hope to begin a series of justice court cases this week." She soon completed a law degree at Northwestern University and began to prosecute her own cases. Kelley found her work enormously creative. She saw potential innovations in social reform all around her. For example, she thought that the medical chapter of her annual report would "start a new line of activity for medical men and factory inspectors both." True to her prediction, the field of industrial medicine later was launched at Hull House by Alice Hamilton, who arrived at the settlement in 1897. Thus the effects of this small band of inspectors continued long after their dispersal. The community of women at Hull House gave them their start, but their impact extended far beyond that fellowship, thanks in part to the settlement's effective alliance with other groups of women and men.

● ● ●

Historians of women have tended to assume that protective labor legislation was imposed on women workers by hostile forces beyond their control—especially by men seeking to eliminate job competition. To some degree this was true of the 1893 legislation since, by closing tenement dwellings to garment manufacture and by depriving sweatshop contractors of the labor of children under fourteen, the law reduced the number of sweatshops, where women and children predominated, and increased the number of garment workers in factories, where men prevailed. Abraham Bisno was well aware of the widespread opposition to the law and took time to talk with offenders, "to educate the parents who sent their children to work, and the employers of these children, the women who were employed longer than eight hours a day, and their employers." Jane Addams also tried to help those who were deprived of work by the new law: "The sense that the passage of the child labor law would in many cases work hardship, was never absent from my mind during the earliest years of its operation. I addressed as many mother's meetings and clubs among working women as I could, in order to make clear the objective of the law and the ultimate benefit to themselves as well as to their children."

Did the children benefit? While further research is needed on this question, recent scholarship pointing to the importance of working-class support for the schooling of working-class children has revised earlier estimates that children and their families did not benefit. At best the law was a halfway measure that encouraged but could not force parents to place their children in school. Nevertheless, Florence Kelley was pleased with the compliance of parents and school officials. As she wrote Henry Demarest Lloyd, "Out of sixty-five names of children sent to the Board of Education in our first month of notifying it when we turned children under 14 yrs. of age out of factories, twenty-one were immediately returned to school and several others are known to be employed as nursegirls and cashgirls i.e. in non-prohibited occupations. This is good co-operation." While schools were inadequate and their teachers frequently prejudiced against immigrants, education was also an important route out of the grinding poverty that characterized immigrant neighborhoods. Thus it is not surprising that a large minority of parents complied with the law by enrolling their children in school.

The chief beneficiaries of the law, apart from those children who gained from schooling, were garment workers employed in factories. Most of these were men, but about one in four were women. The 1893 law was designed to prevent the erosion of this factory labor force and its replacement by sweatshop labor. Bisno described that erosion in his testimony before the state investigating committee early in 1893, stating, "Joseph Beifeld & Company have had three hundred and fifty employees some eleven or twelve years ago inside, and they have only eighty now to my knowledge, and they have increased their business about six times as much as it was eleven years ago." This decline of the factory population inevitably caused a decline of union membership since it was much more difficult to organize sweatshop workers. Thus as a union official Bisno was defending his own interests, but these were not inimical to all women workers.

Demonstrating the support of women unionists for the law's enforcement, members of the Women's Shoemakers Union chastised the Chicago Trades and Labor Assembly in February 1894 for their lukewarm support of the by-then-beleaguered eight-hour restriction. They "introduced resolutions, strongly condemning the manufacturers of this City for combining to nullify the state laws. . . . The resolutions further set forth that the members of the Women's Shoemakers Union effected as they were by the operation of the Eight hour Law unanimously approved the Law and for the benefit of themselves, for their sister wage workers and the little children, they pleaded for its maintenance and Enforcement." Although some women workers—particularly those who headed households with small children—must have opposed the law's enforcement, others, especially single women and mothers able to arrange child care, stood to gain from the benefits of factory employment. In a study completed for the Illinois Bureau of Labor Statistics in 1892, Florence Kelley found that 48 percent of Chicago working women lacked the "natural protectors" of fathers, or husbands. Viewing them as a permanent feature of the paid labor force, she pointed to the importance of their wages to their families, thereby refuting the notion that all working women were supported by male wage earners. Although the historical evidence does not reveal how many, some young women who had formerly worked in sweatshops and whose families relied heavily on their wages doubtlessly benefited from the legislation by moving into larger factories with better working conditions.

The 1893 statute made it possible for women as well as men to move from exploitative, low-paying sweatshops into larger shops and factories with power machinery, unions, and higher wages. While the law's prohibition of tenement manufacturing obviously enabled such mobility, its eight-hour clause was no less instrumental since it attacked the basic principles of the sweating system—long hours and low wages. The average working day in the garment industry was about ten hours, but in some sweatshops it could be as long as twelve, thirteen, or fourteen hours. Reducing the working day from ten to eight hours did not significantly decrease production in factories with electric or steam-powered machinery since productivity could be raised by increasing a machine's speed or a worker's skill level. However, the eight-hour law drove many subcontractors or "sweaters" out of business since it eliminated the margin of profit created by workers' long hours at foot-powered sewing machines. From the sweatshop workers' perspective, it reduced wages even further since they were paid by the piece and could finish a much smaller amount of goods in eight hours. The wages of factory workers, by contrast, were likely to remain the same since negotiations between employers and employees customarily included a consideration of what it cost to sustain life, a factor absent from the sweaters' calculations.

Another group who benefited indirectly from this "antisweating" legislation were the men who worked in industries employing large numbers of women workers. Historians of protective labor legislation in England and the United States have noticed the tendency of male co-workers to benefit from legislation passed to protect women. This was true as early as the 1870s in Massachusetts and as late as the 1930s, when many states had laws limiting the hours of women but not the hours of men. The strategy of extending the legislation de facto to men seems to have been a deliberate intent of Kelley and her staff in the mid-1890s. At a high point in her experience as a factory inspector, Kelley wrote Engels on New Year's Eve, 1894: "We have at last won a victory for our 8 hours law. The Supreme Court has handed down no decision sustaining it, but the Stockyards magnates having been arrested until they are tired of it, have instituted the 8 hours day for 10,000 employees, men, women and children. We have 18 suits pending to enforce the 8 hours law and we think we shall establish it permanently before Easter. It has been a painful struggle of eighteen months and the Supreme Court may annul the law. But I have great hopes that the popular interest may prove too strong." When the eight-hour clause of the law was declared unconstitutional in 1895, therefore, it was beginning to affect industry wide changes in Chicago's largest employers, extending far beyond the garment district.

The biggest losers from the enforcement of the 1893 legislation, as measured by the volume of their protest, were Chicago's manufacturers. Formed for the explicit purpose of obtaining a court ruling against the constitutionality of the eight-hour law, the Illinois Manufacturer's Association (IMA) became a model for other state associations and for the National Association of Manufacturers, formed in 1895. After 1899, when Kelley embarked on a thirty year campaign for state laws protecting women and children, the National Association of Manufacturers was her constant nemesis and the chief rallying point of her opposition. Given the radical ideas and values behind the passage and enforcement of the 1893 legislation, it is no surprise that, at this stage of her career, Kelley's success inspired an opposition that remained her lifelong foe.

After the court decision the *Chicago Tribune* reported, "In far reaching results the decision is most important. It is the first decision in the United States against the eight-hour law and presents a new obstacle in the path of the movement for shorter hours." An editorial the next day declared: "Labor is property and an interference with the sale of it by contract or otherwise is an infringement of a constitutional right to dispose of property. . . . The property rights of women, says the court, are the same as those of men." For the first but not the last time in her reform career Florence Kelley encountered opponents who claimed the banner of "women's rights." In 1921 with the introduction of the Equal Rights Amendment by Alice Paul and the National Women's Party, the potential conflict between women's rights and the protection of women workers became actual. Nearly a generation earlier in 1895 the opposition was clearly a facade for the economic interests of the manufacturers.

What conclusions can be drawn about the Hull House community from this review of their activities on behalf of antisweatshop legislation? First, and foremost, it attests to the capacity of women to sustain their own institutions. Second, it shows that this community's internal dynamics promoted a creative mixture of mutual support and individual expression. Third, these talented women reformers used their institution as a means of allying with male reformers and entering the mainstream of the American political process. In the tradition of earlier women's associations in the United States, they focused on the concerns of women and children, but these concerns were never divorced from those of men and of the society as a whole. Under the leadership of Florence Kelley, they pursued gender-specific reforms that served class-specific goals.

In these respects the Hull House community serves as a paradigm for women's participation in Progressive reform. Strengthened by the support of women's separate institutions, women reformers were able to develop their capacity for political leadership free from many if not all of the constraints that otherwise might have been imposed on their power by the male-dominated parties or groups with which they cooperated. Building on one of the strengths of the nineteenth-century notion of "women's sphere"—its social activism on behalf of the rights and interests of women and children—they represented those rights and interests innovatively and effectively. Ultimately, however, their power encountered limits imposed by the male-dominated political system, limits created more in response to their class-specific than to their gender-specific reform efforts.

Questions for Study and Review

1. How did the residents of Hull House become such effective advocates for progressive reform? How did the institution nurture and amplify the activism of its residents?

2. What does settlement life tell us of the changing relations of educated, middle-class women to their families and communities at the turn of the twentieth century?

3. To what extent did Hull House residents represent the wishes and concerns of working-class and immigrant women and families?

4. Why did the settlement house movement attract so many women at the turn of the twentieth century, and how did this movement differ from earlier forms of female activism?

Suggested Readings and Web Sites

Victoria Bissell Brown, *The Education of Jane Addams* (2004)

Victoria Bissell Brown, ed., Jane Addams, *Twenty Years at Hull House* (1999)

Estelle Freedman, "Separatism as Strategy: Female Institution Building and American Feminism, 1870–1930," *Feminist Studies* (Fall 1979)

Louise A. Knight, *Citizen: Jane Addams and the Struggle for American Democracy* (2005)

Molly Ladd-Taylor, *Mother-work: Women, Child Welfare, and the State, 1890–1930* (1994)

Kathryn Kish Sklar, *Florence Kelley and the Nation's Work* (1995)

Deborah A. Skok, *A Boost From Below: Chicago's Catholic Settlement Houses and Day Nurseries, 1893–1930* (2007)

Hull House and Its Neighborhoods, 1889–1963

http://www.uic.edu/jaddams/hull/urbanexp/

Harvard University's Open Collections Program

http://ocp.hul.harvard.edu/ww/people_kelley.html

Women and Social Movements in the United States, 1600–2000

http://www.binghamton.edu/womhist/projectmap.htm

Settlement house residents focused much of their attention on the millions of immigrants, most from southern and eastern Europe, who entered the United States in the thirty years after 1890. Italian and Slavic, Catholic and Jewish families dominated this wave of migration, pouring into seaboard cities and then spreading out into industrial centers across the Northeast and Midwest. They provided not only a challenge for middle-class reformers but also a labor force to fuel industrial growth. Immigrant men laid the railroad track, mined the coal, and manned the blast furnaces that made the United States the world's leading industrial power at the turn of the twentieth century. Yet the wages of male heads of household were not enough to support a working-class family in this new industrial order. Most families turned to sons and daughters to supplement the earnings of fathers, leaving mothers to see to childcare and domestic labors.

While young women had always worked, they had traditionally labored within their own homes or as domestic servants in the homes of others. By the turn of the twentieth century, however, young working-class women streamed into offices, department stores, and the burgeoning garment industry. The textile mills that had recruited women into the nation's first industrial revolution in the early nineteenth century were dwarfed by the garment industry that fueled the second industrial revolution. This new wave of industrialization made family members even more dependent on one another for survival. At the same time, it created a sharper division between household work and wage work.

The invention of the sewing machine sparked the modern garment industry. The production of clothing was now broken into discrete tasks that could be repeated endlessly by the same worker. Immigrant women largely provided the hands required by this new system of production. Even though it was grueling, dangerous, miserably paid, and often regarded as morally suspect, most young women still preferred it to the isolation and even lower wages of domestic service.

At the turn of the twentieth century, the United States was the most dangerous country in the world in which to labor; conditions deteriorated as demands for profits escalated. New technology and long working hours combined with a complete absence of regulatory oversight to create a deadly mix for the thousands of American workers killed on the job each year. Orleck explores how four young women who came of age on the shop floor of the early twentieth-century garment industry became determined to change these conditions. They led thousands of workers in legendary labor protests that highlighted many of the problems surrounding industrial development in the late nineteenth century. These young women built powerful unions and organized work stoppages that forced the industry to curb some of its worst abuses.

The leaders profiled by Orleck entered garment factories at a young age. These workplaces were dirty, degrading, and frequently life-threatening, but they offered immigrant women like Pauline Newman, Rose Schneiderman, Fannia Cohn, and Clara Lemlich intense comradeship. Nurtured by radical political traditions within the immigrant Jewish community and by older workers conversant in Socialism, these young women embraced militant trade unionism and received an education more intense than any they could have received in school.

These women had to overcome the indifference of male union officials, who assumed that young women in the garment industry could never match men's labor solidarity. Veteran male activists had focused their attention on winning a family wage that would allow the wives of working men to abstain from wage work. Young women activists had a different vision for the labor movement and were driven by the belief that working women should be fairly compensated for their labor. They sustained this vision in the face of male hostility by drawing on the economic and political support provided by middle- and upper-class women allies like those associated with the Women's Trade Union League. Female labor activists welcomed this support, both the favorable publicity these politically connected women could provide during strikes and the improved government oversight of factories that they demanded. Yet there were limits to this alliance. Working-class organizers frequently faced condescension and ambivalence from their middle-class sisters, who were often uncomfortable with the most radical strains of trade unionism.

During the winter of 1909–1910, the labor activists profiled by Orleck led tens of thousands of young co-workers to victory in a dramatic strike against the shirtwaist industry. This action won important wage and hour concessions from manufacturers; more importantly, it demonstrated the capacity of young garment workers to maintain the solidarity necessary to sustain a strike. Little more than a year after this important triumph, however, the death of 146 workers in a disastrous fire at the Triangle Shirtwaist Company illuminated how much work remained for labor leaders like Lemlich and Schneiderman. After a fire broke out in the building, young women perished in the flames or jumped to their death from the roof. The company had trapped the workers inside when it locked the front doors, a practice designed to keep workers at their machines and labor organizers off the premises.

Ultimately, women's shop floor militancy transformed the garment industry, the trade union movement, and the lives of many women workers. By 1919, 40 percent of women garment workers were members of unions that gave them the bargaining power to shape their working conditions. None of these women could rely on the vote to advance their political agendas until well after their most important union victories had been achieved. But their success in reshaping American factories demonstrates how women throughout history have wielded powerful political influence without ever entering voting booths or legislative chambers.

Coming of Age: The Shock of the Shops and the Dawning of Working Women's Political Consciousness

ANNELISE ORLECK

The 1907 rent strike made headlines in all the New York newspapers and transformed its petite and pugnacious leader, Pauline Newman, into a Lower East Side celebrity. Lauded in the press, courted by radical leaders in the community, the dark-eyed, dark-haired sixteen-year-old found that she liked the spotlight: "The press gave us front page publicity and my own photo was carried under the caption 'leader of the strike.' . . . I became 'famous.' I was invited to speak at meetings which provided an opportunity for self-expression and the art of speaking in public. As my 'fame' grew so did my interest in all things concerning working and living conditions of my fellow workers."

Newman was keenly interested in labor issues well before the 1907 rent strike. Indeed, many of the techniques she used in the strike—such as assembling a core group to mobilize an entire community, and forming local housewives' committees to manage each block—were adapted from union-building strategies she'd observed on the shop floor. Though only sixteen in 1907, Newman was already a seasoned worker; like so many immigrant Jewish women of her generation, including Rose Schneiderman and Clara Lemlich, she had spent her childhood as a laborer in the sweatshops of lower Manhattan. Fannia Cohn did not enter a garment shop until the age of twenty, but she too was profoundly shaped by the experience.

Coming of age in New York's early-twentieth-century garment shops, the four would become determined organizers of their fellow "working girls." Their political commitment was fueled primarily by anger at the filthy and dangerous conditions under which they were forced to work. But it was sustained by affection and loyalty to their fellow workers and guided by the tutelage of more seasoned political hands. The four found emotional support in factory-floor friendships and late-night study groups. And as they began to organize, they were introduced to mentors: older workers, Socialist Party activists, and Progressive reformers. All of these influences helped to create, by the end of the century's first decade, a critical mass of radicalized young women garment workers. Schneiderman, Newman, Lemlich, and Cohn were among the most highly regarded of these. By the time they reached their mid-twenties, the four had distinguished themselves by their eloquence, spirit, and tenacity in fighting to improve not only their own lives but also those of their sister workers.

Pauline Newman first began working in a hairbrush factory in 1901, at the age of ten. Two years later, a relative found her a better-paying job at the most famous of early-twentieth-century garment factories, the Triangle Shirtwaist Factory on

Lewis Hine put photography to the service of social change, documenting the lives of turn-of-the-twentieth-century immigrants in New York. He photographed sweatshops and tenements in the hopes that images like this one could persuade politicians to enact regulations that would protect laborers, particularly women and children. This image shows the dark and crowded working conditions of a 1908 New York sweatshop.

Washington Square. Newman spent her girlhood at a sewing machine stitching women's shirtwaists—the contemporary name for man-tailored blouses and dresses.

At an age when most girls in the United States were still in grade school, immigrant working girls like Newman spent twelve- to fourteen-hour days in the harshest of atmospheres. Their bodies and minds reeled from the shock of the shops: the deafening noise, the brutal pace, and the rebukes of foremen. Some children were able to slough off the hardship with jokes and games. Others, realizing that they were destined to spend their youth in dank factories rather than in classrooms or schoolyards, grew sullen and withdrawn.

Newman fought depression by recording what she saw around her. She kept detailed notebooks and submitted poems and articles to the Yiddish language press. Later, she penned descriptions of the shops that she hoped would convince others of the urgent need to regulate factory conditions. Her vivid prose evokes the gloom that many children must have felt:

> Most of the so-called factories were located in old wooden walkups with rickety stairs, splintered and sagging floors. The few windows were never washed and their broken panes were mended with cardboard. . . . In the winter a stove stood in the middle of

the floor, a concession to the need for heat, but its warmth rarely reached the workers seated near the windows. During the summer months the constant burning of gas jets added their unwelcome heat and smell to an atmosphere already intolerably humid and oppressive. . . . There was no drinking water available. . . . Dirt, smells and vermin were as much a part of the surroundings as were the machines and the workers.

Rose Schneiderman and Clara Lemlich also spent their youth in factories. Schneiderman began working at age thirteen in a department store, but, lured by higher wages, she became a capmaker at sixteen. Lemlich was a twelve-year-old seamstress in her small Ukrainian village; by sixteen she was a dressmaker in New York. As teenagers, all three hoped to rise to skilled positions in the garment trades. They had heard that garment work offered opportunity for advancement, and they believed that Jewish shop owners and supervisors would be kind and fatherly toward young Jewish workers.

Clara Lemlich, like so many others, was quickly disillusioned by her first job in a New York garment shop: "I went to work two weeks after landing in this country. We worked from sunrise to set seven days a week. . . . Those who worked on machines had to carry the machines on their back both to and from work. . . . The shop we worked in had no central heating, no electric power. . . . The hissing of the machines, the yelling of the foreman, made life unbearable."

The conditions Lemlich described had deteriorated since the turn of the century. With the invention and refinement of the industrial sewing machine, operators were forced to speed up their work: A 1905 garment worker was expected to sew twice as fast as her 1900 counterpart. By the end of the century's first decade, one study of factory conditions in women's trades reported that the "high rate of speed . . . leaves its impression on even the most robust worker." In shop after shop, researcher Annie MacLean found that workers' nerves were noticeably strained: "It appears in heavy eyes with deep dark rings, in wrinkled skin, and old young faces. The high rate of speed that must be maintained through so many successive hours is undermining the health of thousands of girls in this industry."

Among all the torments of the shop, what workers hated most were the petty humiliations imposed by foremen and "foreladies." Without time to think or permission to speak, they felt that they had been turned into machines. Clara Lemlich was furious about being so dehumanized. "And the bosses! They hire such people to drive you!," she wrote bitterly. "It is a regular slave factory. Not only your hands and your time but your mind is sold." In another article, she explained: "For talking, shop girls were immediately fired. . . . At the conclusion of the day's work, the girls were searched like thieves."

Anger drove young women workers like Lemlich and Newman to band together. Untrained and largely unschooled, these young women were drawn to Socialism and trade unionism not because they felt an ideological affinity but because they had a desperate need to improve their working conditions. "I knew very little about Socialism," Lemlich recalled. "[But] the girls, whether Socialist or not, had many stoppages and strikes." Newman too found that for most young women workers, political understanding followed action rather than precipitating it: "We of the 1909 vintage knew nothing about the economics of . . . industry or for that matter about economics in general. All we knew was the bitter fact that, after working seventy and eighty hours in a seven day week, we did not earn enough to keep body and soul together." These assertions reveal much about the political development of the tens of thousands of women garment workers who would soon amaze New York and the nation with their militancy.

Shop-floor culture fed the young women's emerging sense of political identity. Working alongside older men and women who discussed Socialism daily, they began to feel a sense of belonging to a distinct class of people in the world: workers. This allegiance would soon become as important to them as their Judaism. The shops also provided an opportunity for bonding with other women. Slowly, out of their workplace experiences, they began to develop a complex political identity in which class, gender, and ethnicity overlapped. Because most of their fellow garment workers were Jewish *and* female, Newman, Lemlich, Schneiderman, and Cohn felt loyalty not simply to the working class but particularly to the Jewish female working class. Jewish identity would play a less prominent role in their politics in later years, when they branched out and organized many different kinds of women workers. But for the rest of their lives they would remain committed to the melding of gender and class they had first experienced among their fellow garment workers.

Political sophistication was not uncommon among Jewish immigrant girls of their generation. Many had encountered Socialist ideas as children in Eastern Europe, in the Yiddish newspapers of New York's Lower East Side, and at the family dinner table. Still, it took shop work to give those ideas life and urgency. Faced with the harsh realities of factory labor, young women workers began to think and talk about how they could use Socialism and unionism to improve their daily lives.

In Progressive Era New York, they quickly found that they had other potential allies besides working men: middle-class suffragists and reformers who held out the seductive promise of cross-class sisterhood. These educated women flattered the young immigrants with attention and praise and provided money, protection from police brutality, and assistance in gaining positive press coverage. Such women gave Schneiderman, Newman, Lemlich, and Cohn their first real insights into the U.S. upper classes and helped the young leaders broaden their political understanding beyond the bounds of Jewish immigrant culture.

Just as important, they sharpened the young women's consciousness of gender, clarifying the differences between their political vision and that of their Socialist brothers. Each in her own way, Newman, Schneiderman, Lemlich, and Cohn all embraced the ideology of sisterhood propounded by such feminists and suffragists. Each woman's organizing, writing, and thinking over the next half century reflected her own struggle to adapt and apply the insights of feminism to the lives of working-class women. Awareness of gender discrimination, more than anything else in their political education, would set them apart from the Jewish Socialist men who led the emerging garment unions.

Young women workers were moved by the idea of sisterhood. It meshed with the bonding they saw at the marketplaces and in their neighborhoods. Even more profoundly, it captured their own experiences in the sex-segregated shops where they worked. The majority of New York's garment workers were little more than girls, and the relationships they forged with factory friends were similar to those of schoolgirls—intense, melodramatic, and deeply loyal. They were teenage confidantes as well as fellow workers, and they relied on shop-floor rapport to soften the harshness of factory life.

Shared dreams of revolution also intensified their bonds. With her dashing, bespectacled bravado, Pauline Newman captured the imagination of many young co-workers. Sometimes, as this letter from Triangle worker. J. A. H. Dahme to the sixteen-year-old Newman illustrates, the lines between political commitment and personal infatuation blurred: "Yes, I understand you—understand you to that depth of thoroughness as only one who has long suffered can. . . . From the deepest deepest place of my bosom let me utter the words, 'We shall be friends in joy and sorrow!' What is there sweeter in life than the sympathy between woman and woman—what purer than the sincerity of hearts—what greater than the harmony of minds? . . . Yours in friendship and socialist comradeship."

Highly emotional herself, Newman did not always know how to respond to such adulation, but she thrived in the loving atmosphere of her shop. The community of young women at the Triangle Shirtwaist Factory was so important to her, in fact, that she stayed there long after she could have found higher-paying work elsewhere. With friends who have worked together for years, Newman later wrote, "you are no longer a stranger and alone." For young immigrant women trying to build lives in a new land, such bonds were powerful and lasting. From these shop-floor friendships would soon evolve the ties of union sisterhood.

Shop Floor Life and "The School of Solidarity," 1898–1906

Pauline Newman and her co-workers at the Triangle Shirtwaist Factory literally grew up together. Only twelve when she first came to Triangle, Newman was assigned to a corner known as "the kindergarten," where workers as young as eight, nine, or ten years old trimmed threads from finished garments. They labored, Newman later recalled, "from 7:30 A.M to 6:30 at night when it wasn't busy. When the season was on we worked till 9 o'clock. No overtime pay." Their only taste of a normal childhood came through the songs and games they invented to help pass the time, the stories they told and the secrets they shared.

By the early twentieth century, New York State had passed laws prohibiting night work for children. But little attempt was made to enforce them. On the rare occasions when an inspector showed up at her factory, Newman remembered, "the employers were always tipped off. . . . 'Quick,' they'd say, 'Into the boxes!' And we children would climb into the big box the finished shirts were stored in. Then some shirts were piled on top of us and when the inspector came—No children." In a way it was fun, Newman remembered. They thought they were playing a game like hide and seek.

But it wasn't really a game. Children who had to help support their parents grew up quickly. Rose Schneiderman was thirteen when her mother begged United Hebrew Charities, an organization run by middle-class German Jews, to find her daughter a "respectable job" at a department store. Retail jobs were deemed more respectable than factory work because the environment was more pleasant and sexual harassment was thought to be less common. Deborah Schneiderman worried that factory work would sully Rose's reputation and make her less marriageable. A job as a fashionable salesgirl, she hoped, would usher Rose into the middle class. The single mother who had fed her children on charity food baskets and had been forced to place them in orphanages was grimly determined to help them escape poverty. Perhaps self-conscious about a childhood that was poor even by Lower East Side standards, Schneiderman latched onto her mother's obsession with respectability. That preoccupation lasted throughout her life, shaping and limiting her political and personal choices.

But then as now, pink-collar jobs paid significantly less than industrial work. Anxious to free her mother from the rigors of maintaining their tenement building, Schneiderman left her job in Ridley's department store for the harsher and more morally suspect conditions of an industrial shop. Making linings for caps and hats, she immediately raised her weekly income from $2.75 to $6. As the sole supporter of her family, the sixteen-year-old hoped to work her way up quickly to a skilled job in the cap trade.

Clara Lemlich's family also relied on her wages, particularly because her father was unemployed. She aspired to the skilled position of draper, one of the highest-paid positions a woman could attain in the dressmaking trade. Despite terrible working conditions, many ambitious young women chose garment work over other jobs because it seemed to offer their greatest chance to acquire skills and command high wages. When these hopes were dashed, some young workers grew angry. That anger was fanned and channeled by older women in the shops who were itching to challenge the authority of the bosses.

That is what happened to Rose Schneiderman, who, like many skilled women garment workers, was blocked from advancement by the unofficial gender hierarchy at her factory. Finding that all the highest-paid jobs in her capmaking shop were reserved for men, Schneiderman asked around about ways to break through those barriers. When she approached fellow worker Bessie Braut with her concerns, Schneiderman was initiated simultaneously into trade unionism, Socialism, and feminism. Schneiderman recalled, "Bessie was an unusual person. Her beautiful eyes shone out of a badly pockmarked face and the effect was startling. An outspoken anarchist, she made a strong impression on us. She wasted no time in giving us the facts of life—that the men in our trade belonged to a union and were, therefore, able to better their conditions. She added pointedly that it would be a good thing for the lining-makers to join a union along with the trimmers, who were all women."

Schneiderman, Braut, and several other workers called on the secretary-treasurer of the United Cloth Hat and Cap Makers to request union recognition for their fledgling local of trimmers and lining makers. Skeptical of young women's ability to organize, the official told them to gather twenty-five signatures from women working at other factories. Schneiderman and her comrades stationed themselves at factory doors with membership blanks in hand and approached women as they came off their shifts. Within a few days they had enough signatures to win a charter for their local, and Schneiderman was elected secretary.

Surprising even herself, the once-shy redhead soon found she could be an eloquent and fierce advocate for her fellow workers. In recognition of her growing reputation, the capmakers elected her to the Central Labor Union of New York. Deborah Schneiderman was disturbed by the turn Rose's life was taking. She warned Rose that if she pursued a public life she would never find a husband. No man wants a woman with a big mouth, her mother said.

In the flush of excitement at the praise and warmth suddenly coming her way, young Rose did not stop to worry. In organizing, she had found both a calling and a world of friends. She had no intention of turning back. "It was such an exciting time," she wrote later. "A new life opened up for me. All of a sudden I was not lonely anymore. . . . It was the beginning of a period that molded all my subsequent life."

Fannia Cohn, too, chose garment work as her path to a career. And like Schneiderman, Lemlich, and Newman, she found a community there. Unlike the others, however, she did not enter a garment factory looking for work that paid well. She was a comfortable middle-class woman in search of a trade ripe for unionizing.

Cohn arrived in New York in 1904 and moved in with her affluent cousins. There was little about her early days in the United States that was comparable to the hard-pressed scrambling for a living that the Schneidermans, Lemlichs, and Newmans experienced. Her cousins offered to support her while she studied, but the independent nineteen-year-old wanted to pay her own way. She soon found a job with the American Jewish Women's Committee, providing aid and information to new arrivals at Ellis Island. Though it was an appropriate job for a middle-class woman of some education, Cohn quickly grew restless and quit after only a few weeks. "It was too much of a charitable nature," she explained to a friend. For a time she toyed with the idea of going to college. But soon, to the chagrin of the cousins who had paid her passage from Russia, Cohn decided that she had only one ambition: to join the working class in its struggle for a better life. "My family suggested that I complete my studies and then join the labor movement but I rejected this as I did not want to come into it from 'without' but from 'within.' I realized then that if I wanted to really understand the mind, the aspirations of the workers, I should experience the life of the worker in a shop." In 1905, Fannia Cohn became a sleevemaker. For a year she moved from shop to shop until, in the "white goods" trade, she found the organizing challenge she was looking for.

Shops that manufactured white goods—underwear, kimonos, and robes—were considered particularly hard to organize. Production took place in tiny sweatshops, not large factories, and the manufacturing process had been broken down into small tasks that required little skill. The majority of white goods workers were immigrant girls under the age of fifteen. And because they came from a wide range of backgrounds—Jewish, Italian, Syrian, Turkish, and Greek—it was difficult for them to communicate with each other, let alone organize. As a result, these workers were among the lowest paid in the garment trades.

At twenty, Cohn was an elder in the trade. With her high school education and fluency in three languages, she was seen as a mother figure by many of the adolescents in the shops. She and a handful of older women workers began to operate as mentors, meeting with the girls in each shop and identifying potential leaders. Cohn taught her co-workers to read, write, and speak in public, hoping they would channel those skills into the union struggle. Cohn had already created the role that she would play throughout her career: an educator of younger workers.

Education was a primary driving force in the metamorphosis of all four young women from shop workers to union organizers. From the isolated towns and restive cities of Eastern Europe, where gender, class, and ethnicity stymied Jewish girls' hopes for education, the lure of free public schooling in the United States beckoned powerfully. Having to drop out of school to work was more than a disappointment for many Jewish immigrant girls; it was their first great disillusionment with the dream of America. And they did not give that dream up easily.

"When I went to work," Rose Schneiderman remembered, "I was determined to continue my studies." Her only option was to attend one of the many night schools then open to immigrant workers in New York. Having carried with her from Poland the ideal of education as an exalted, liberating process, she was disgusted by the mediocre instruction she encountered and felt betrayed by teachers who seemed to be patronizing her. "I enrolled and went faithfully every evening for about four weeks. But I found that . . . the instructor seemed more interested in getting one-hundred-percent attendance than in giving one-hundred-percent instruction. He would joke and tell silly stories. . . . I soon realized I was wasting my time." Schneiderman left the evening school but did not stop studying. She asked older co-workers if she could borrow books that she had discussed with them in the shop. In the evenings, she read with her mother at home. Serializations of Emile Zola's *J'Accuse* and other contemporary writings in the Yiddish evening paper *Abendblatt* gave Rose a taste for literature. "I devoured everything I could get my hands on."

Clara Lemlich was an equally avid reader. At the end of each twelve-hour day stitching shirtwaists, she would walk from her factory to the East Broadway branch of the New York Public Library. There she read the library's entire collection of Russian classics. "I was so eager to learn things," she later recalled. When she tired of solitary study, Lemlich joined a free night school on Grand Street. She returned home late each night, ate the dinner her mother had kept warm for her, then slept for just a few hours before rising again for work.

That zest for learning was typical of Jewish immigrant working girls. In one contemporary study of working women, 12.5 percent of the Jewish women listed reading as their favorite pastime, even though it was not one of the choices presented. A study called "Working Girls in Evening Schools" found that, in New York City, 40 percent of those enrolled were Jewish.

Frustration with the limited and patronizing quality of night school education was also typical. Popular author Anzia Yezierska captured that impatience in a story called "Crazy to Learn," in which an immigrant girl, admonished repeatedly by her night school principal to study something useful, finally cries out in anguish, "Ain't thoughts useful? . . . Does America only want the work from my body?" Night school English classes must have confirmed those fears. While men were taught to identify political leaders, women were taught the names of kitchen utensils. While men were asked to translate the sentence "I read the book," women translated "I wash the dishes."

Not surprisingly, young women like Schneiderman, Newman, and Lemlich turned to radical politics to fulfill their desire for a life of the mind. If no other school was available, then what Pauline Newman called "the school of solidarity" would have to do. Membership in the Socialist Party and in unions, tenant organizations, and benevolent societies provided immigrant women with an opportunity to learn and study that most would never have gotten otherwise. And as Newman put it, "Because they were hitherto deprived of any tutorship, they at once became ardent students."

Pauline Newman was just fifteen when she first knocked on the doors of the Socialist Literary Society. Although women were not yet allowed to join, she was permitted to attend classes. The Literary Society was a revelation to the young worker. There she was introduced to the writings of Shakespeare, George Eliot, and Thomas Hardy and personally met writers like Jack London and Charlotte Perkins Gilman, who came to speak there. Gratitude, however, didn't stop her from joining a successful petition drive to admit women to the society.

For Newman—as for Clara Lemlich, who attended Marxist theory classes at the Socialist Party's Rand School—studying was more than a distraction from work. The "desire to get out of the shop," Newman wrote later, "to learn, to understand, became the dominant force in my life." But unlike many immigrants, who saw schooling as a ladder out of the working class, both she and Lemlich were committed to helping others rise with them. So Newman and Lemlich formed study groups that met during lunch hours and after work to share what they were learning with their friends.

"We tried to educate ourselves," Newman remembered of her co-workers at the Triangle Shirtwaist Factory. "I would invite the girls to my room and we took turns reading poetry in English to improve our understanding of the language." In another interview, she elaborated on these reading lessons:

> We read Dickens, George Eliot, the poets. I remember when we first heard Thomas Hood's "Song of the Shirt" I figured that it was written for us. You know, because it told the long hours of stitch, stitch, stitch. I remember one of the girls said, "He didn't know us. Did he?" And I said, "No he didn't." But it had an impact on us. Later on . . . we got to know Shelley. . . . Very few people know his poem dealing with slavery called "The Masque of Anarchy." He appealed to us . . . because it was a time when we were ready to rise.

Like Newman's Zionist sisters back in Kovno, young women garment workers found that their groups nourished a spirit of rebellion. Reveling in beautiful language and debating difficult ideas made them feel that they had defeated those who would reduce them to machines. Because they had to steal the time to study, the young women approached everything they read with a heightened sensitivity. And when something they were reading struck a chord of recognition, seemed to reflect on their own lives, the catharsis was not only emotional; it was political.

The evolution of Lemlich's study group illustrates how study often led to union activity. Older workers, who were teaching Lemlich the craft of draping, invited her to join their lunchtime discussion groups to learn more about trade unionism. Soon Lemlich and a group of young women waistmakers formed their own study group. Discussion quickly escalated to action, and they decided to form a union.

Skilled male workers in the shirtwaist trade had been trying to establish a union since 1900. But after five years the union had managed to attract only ten members. The problem, Lemlich told her male colleagues, was that women workers had to be approached by an organizer who understood their particular needs as women. They bristled at the suggestion that this young girl might know more about their business than they did. But years later, one conceded that the failure of the first waistmakers' union was due at least in part to their ham-fisted tactics: "We would issue a circular reading somewhat as follows: 'Murder the exploiters, the blood-suckers, the manufacturers. . . . Pay your dues. . . . Down with the Capitalists!'" Few women or men showed up at their meetings.

During the spring of 1905 the union disbanded and reorganized as Local 25 of the ILGWU, with Clara Lemlich and a group of six young women from her waistmaking shop on the executive board. Taking their cue from Lemlich, the new union used women organizers to attract women workers. Lemilch addressed street-corner meetings in English and Yiddish and found Italian women to address the Italian workers. Soon, like Schneiderman, Newman, and Cohn, she realized that she had found a calling.

Socialists, Reformers, and New York Shop Girls, 1905–1909

In the progressive atmosphere of early-twentieth-century New York City, influential people quickly noticed the militant young working women. Older Socialists, trade unionists, and middle-class reformers offered their assistance. These benefactors helped the young organizers sharpen their arguments, provided financial assistance, and introduced them to politicians and public officials. The protégés recognized the importance of this informal mentoring and would later work to recreate such networks in the unions, schools, and training programs they built for young women workers. Schneiderman, Newman, Lemlich, and Cohn were keenly aware that young working women needed help from more experienced and more powerful allies. But they also worried that the voices of women workers might be outshouted in the clamorous process of building alliances. From these early days, they battled to preserve the integrity of their vision.

Pauline Newman found her first mentors in the Socialist Party, which she joined in 1906 at the age of fifteen. Older women, including former garment worker Theresa Serber Malkiel, took her on as a protégé. Newman quickly blossomed under their tutelage. Before long she was running street-corner meetings. Armed with a sonorous voice and the certitude of youth, she would take "an American flag and a soapbox and go from corner to corner," exhorting the gospel of Socialism in Yiddish and English. "I, like many of my friends and comrades, thought that socialism and socialism alone could and would someday fill the gap between rich and poor," Newman recalled. In a neighborhood crowded with sidewalk proselytizers, this child evangelist became one of the party's most popular street-corner attractions.

In 1908, nine years before New York State gave women the vote, seventeen-year-old Newman was nominated by the Socialist Party to run for New York's Secretary of State. Newman used her campaign as a platform for suffrage. Her speeches were heckled by some Socialist men, and her candidacy provoked amused commentaries in New York City newspapers; some writers snickered at the prospect of a "skirted Secretary of State." It was a largely symbolic crusade, but Newman felt that she got people talking about the idea of women in government. The highlight of the campaign was her whistlestop tour with presidential candidate and Socialist leader Eugene V. Debs on his "Red Special" train.

The Socialist Party opened up a new world to Newman, who, after all, had never graduated from elementary school. Along with Debs, she met future Congressmen Meyer Berger and Morris Hillquit and leading Socialist intellectuals. Newman later wrote about the excitement of discussions that carried over from meetings and went into the night as she and her friends walked through Central Park, arguing till the sun came up. Those nights made her feel part of a historic moment.

While Newman was being nurtured by the Socialist Party, Rose Schneiderman found her mentors in the United Cloth Hat and Cap Makers. At the union's 1904 convention she was elected to the General Executive Board; she was the first woman to win such a high-level post in the American labor movement. During the winter of 1904–5, Schneiderman's leadership skills were tested when owners tried to open up union shops to nonunion workers. The largely immigrant capmaker's union called for a general strike. The 1905 strike was a watershed event in Schneiderman's emerging career. Her role as the only woman leader in the union won attention from the press and lasting respect from male capmakers, including the future president of the union, Max Zaritsky, who became a lifelong friend and admirer.

It also brought her to the attention of the newly formed Women's Trade Union League (WTUL), an organization of progressive middle- and upper-class women reformers founded in 1903 to help working women organize. Schneiderman had misgivings about the group because she "could not believe that men and women who were not wage earners themselves understood the problems that workers faced." But she trusted the League's best-known working-class member, Irish shirtmaker Leonora O'Reilly. And she could not ignore the favorable publicity that the WTUL won for the strikers. By March 1905, Schneiderman had been elected to the executive board of the New York WTUL. In 1906, the group elected her vice president.

Schneiderman's entrance into the New York WTUL was an important turning point for both her and the organization. Three years after its founding, the WTUL remained dominated by affluent reformers who had dubbed themselves "allies" of the working class. Despite their genuine commitment to trade unionism, League leaders had credibility problems among women workers. Representatives from most of New York's major unions were on its executive board, but they rarely attended the meetings. Schneiderman had joined the League recognizing that working women lacked the education, the money, and the political clout to organize effectively without powerful allies. Still, she remained ambivalent for a variety of reasons.

The progressive reformers who dominated the League tried to steer workers away from radical influences, particularly the Socialist Party. Yet Schneiderman and O'Reilly, the League's leading working-class organizers, were Socialist Party members and saw unionism as a potentially revolutionary tool. As a result, the pair often felt torn by competing loyalties. Socialists distrusted their work with upper-crust women reformers. Union men were either indifferent or openly hostile to working women's attempts to become leaders in the labor movement. And the League women often seemed to Schneiderman and O'Reilly to act out of a patronizing benevolence that had little to do with real coalition building. The two grew angry at what they saw as attempts by wealthy allies to manipulate them. In January 1906, Leonora O'Reilly announced the first of her many resignations from the League, claiming "an overdose of allies."

There were a few deep friendships between affluent WTUL leaders and working women like Schneiderman, O'Reilly, and Pauline Newman, who joined the League in 1909. Mary Dreier, a reformer who was then president of the New York WTUL, was very close to Newman, Schneiderman, and O'Reilly. Her friendship with O'Reilly was particularly strong and over the years would come to include financial support. Such bonds created hope that intimacy was possible between women of different classes; but cross-class friendships were the exception rather than the rule. Newman later said of Dreier, "Mary was loved, deeply loved by everybody." However, the same could not be said of her sister Margaret Dreier Robins, president of the national WTUL. "Margaret was respected," Newman said, "and admired, but there was no love." Working women like Newman never lost sight of the ways their class background separated them from wealthy reformers. Sisterhood was exhilarating, but outside the WTUL, their lives and political agendas diverged sharply.

This political and social tension heightened working-class activists' emotional dependence upon one another. Schneiderman, Newman, and O'Reilly were a tight trio. After heart disease and an invalid mother confined O'Reilly to her home in Brooklyn, Newman and Schneiderman visited her every Saturday for years. When they weren't in New York, they wrote weekly. Letters between the three are filled with political advice, affectionate banter, and expressions of gratitude. Such relationships were not easy to come by for women whose lives violated the gender norms of both contemporary U.S. society and the immigrant communities from which they came. Pauline Newman continued to mourn O'Reilly for decades after the older woman's death in 1927. As late as 1984, when she was ninety-four years old, Newman could not talk about O'Reilly without tears.

By contrast, these women's relations with most wealthy League supporters were marked by deep ambivalence. Schneiderman's confusion about WTUL beneficence first came to a head in 1908, when League supporter Irene Lewisohn offered to pay both her salary as an organizer and her expenses toward a college degree. It was not an uncommon practice for Progressive Era philanthropists to offer exceptional working women the chance at an education. Historians Charles and Mary Beard would offer the same opportunity to Clara Lemlich in 1911 and Fannia Cohn in 1914. Though it must have been sorely tempting, the three women turned down the offer with much the same argument; they could not attend college while the vast majority of working women were denied a basic education. Schneiderman did, however, accept Lewisohn's offer of a salary so that she could work full-time as the League's chief organizer.

Lewisohn's crucial support of Schneiderman during those early years highlights a tension in the League that was never completely resolved. If Lewisohn had not paid her salary, Schneiderman would never have been able to cover as much ground, speak to as many women, or unionize as many trades as she did over the next few years. But WTUL backers forced leaders to distance the League from radical working-class activism and to stake out a decidedly middle ground in the struggle for women's rights that was then gathering steam.

Schneiderman tried to counterbalance such influences by encouraging male union leaders to play a more active role in the League, but she had little success. She told them that the WTUL could help the labor movement by successfully organizing women workers, whose low wages might otherwise exert a downward pressure on unionized male wages. A *women's* trade union league was needed, she insisted, because women workers responded to different arguments than did men workers. The League could focus on the particular concerns of women, such as the double shift—having to perform household chores after coming home from long days in the factory. Her suggestions were greeted with indifference. Most male labor leaders believed that women were, at worst, unorganizable and, at best, temporary members of the workforce who would soon marry and stop working. In their view women weren't worth expending energy or resources on because they weren't real workers.

Addressing the First Convention of American Women Trade Unionists, held in New York on July 14, 1907, Schneiderman reported that she "was very much surprised and not a little disappointed that the attention of men unionists was so small." She recalled the shocked expressions on the faces of union leaders when she strode into their meetings to ask for field organizers and strike funds to support her attempts at unionizing working women in New York. "They evidently believed a woman would not attend their meetings," she said. She usually came away empty-handed but continued her work without their help, depending instead on the contributions of League supporters. "I would go through barrooms or anything else," she said, alluding to the union men's preference for holding meetings in bars, "to do my duty by the women who are struggling to secure their rights." The truth is, she told her audience, working women needed more than unions. They needed political power. "The time has come," she said firmly, "when working women of the State of New York must be enfranchised and so secure political power to shape their own labor conditions." The convention passed a suffrage resolution, one of the first prosuffrage statements by any organization representing American working-class women.

Schneiderman confronted middle- and upper-class allies with equal frankness. She told the NYWTUL executive board that they were having little success organizing women workers because they approached their task like scholars, not trade unionists. They surveyed conditions in the women's trades, noting which had the lowest salaries, the longest hours, and the worst hygienic conditions. Then they established committees to study the possibilities for unionizing each trade. Finally they went into the shops to explain their findings to the working women. Schneiderman suggested a simpler alternative: Take their lead from women workers and respond to requests for aid from women workers who were already trying to organize. It was something they had never thought to do.

Before long, requests for help were pouring in, mostly from immigrant Jewish women. In the dress trade, where Clara Lemlich was working, and in the white goods trade, where Fannia Cohn was organizing, women workers had launched a series of wildcat strikes. "It was not unusual for unorganized workers to walk out without having any direct union affiliation," Schneiderman later recalled.

In April 1907, long-simmering anger over speedups, wage cuts, and the requirement that employees pay for their own thread reached a boiling point. The first sign came when a group of women's underwear makers at the Milgrim shop on Grand Street staged a spontaneous walkout. Schneiderman rushed in to guide the strike. She set up picket lines and initiated negotiations between strike leaders and management. The women won almost all of their demands, including the creation of a permanent grievance committee. Warning them that they would lose these benefits unless they formed a union, Schneiderman urged the strikers to sign up. They did, but they had to affiliate with the League rather than with the ILGWU. The union refused to recognize them, explaining that women had not yet proven themselves capable of organizing. It was a line that Schneiderman, Newman, Cohn, and Lemlich would hear many times over the next twenty-five years.

Foreshadowing its role in the decades to come, the Women's Trade Union League decided to champion women workers ignored by the male-led unions. An underwear makers' union built slowly, claiming three hundred members by the end of the first year. League secretary Helen Marot saw evidence of increasing confidence in the young women. Marot noted at the end of 1907 that finally, after months of allowing a male union representative to run their affairs, "they have one of their own girls who they have elected president."

Schneiderman believed that the Milgrim strike reflected a growing cohesion among young women workers on the East Side. She later described "how different things had been . . . before the strike. The women looked upon each other as enemies because one might get a better bundle of work done than the other. But now, since they had organized and had fought together, there was a kinship among them."

That feeling of militant solidarity spread to Brooklyn, where for two years Fannia Cohn had been struggling against male union leaders' indifference to her campaign to organize white goods workers. Initially the women of Cohn's shop had approached the United Garment Workers (UGW) for help forming a union. UGW officers agreed; however, they insisted that the young women not conduct union meetings unless a male union representative was present, and they never sent one. So when three hundred workers in one shop decided to strike in 1908, they bypassed the UGW and called for help from Schneiderman and the WTUL.

Schneiderman cultivated leadership by placing the workers themselves in charge of their strike. Marot commented, "We have insisted on their managing their own meetings and their strike themselves. . . . This was in marked comparison to the advice of the men who had come to help them. They had started the idea among the girls that they must have a leader. It was interesting to see how the girls took up the idea of being their own leaders and how their interest increased."

The Brooklyn white goods strike raised a new challenge for Schneiderman: how to forge a sense of solidarity between working-class women of many religions and nationalities. The ethnic makeup of the white goods trade was far more diverse than either Schneiderman's cap trade or Lemlich and Newman's shirtwaist trade. Some organizers believed that underwear manufacturers intentionally hired women from many different immigrant groups, figuring that if the workers couldn't talk to each other, they wouldn't be able to organize. Whether or not that was true, Schneiderman decided that the best way to reach immigrant workers was through organizers who literally spoke their language.

She decided to focus first on Italian workers because, after Jews, they comprised the single largest ethnic group in the garment trades. Recognizing the cultural as well as linguistic differences that separated her from Italian immigrant women,

Schneiderman tried a strategy she would employ many times over the years to come; to identify and cultivate a leader from within the ranks of the workers. She began working with a Brooklyn priest on ways to approach young Italian women. She also got the League to hire an Italian-speaking organizer who assembled a committee of progressive New York Italians—including prominent women professionals and the editor of a popular evening paper *Bolatino de la Sera*—to popularize trade unionism among Italian women workers.

The strategy proved successful. By 1909 enough workers had enlisted that the ILGWU finally recognized the Brooklyn white goods workers' union. The vast majority of its members were teenage girls; these young women elected their mentor, Fannia Cohn, then twenty-four, to the union's first executive board. Cohn, who stepped off the shop floor to a policy-making position, would remain a paid union official for the rest of her life.

In 1909, Clara Lemlich—then in her twenties and on the executive board of ILGWU Local 25—enlisted Schneiderman's aid in her drive to organize shirtwaist makers. For the past three years, Lemlich had been zigzagging between small shops, stirring up trouble. Her first full-scale strike was at Weisen and Goldstein's Manhattan factory. Like the Triangle Shirtwaist Factory, where Newman worked, Weisen and Goldstein's was considered a model shop. The workrooms were modern and airy—a pleasant contrast to the dark basement rooms where most white goods workers labored. However, the advantages of working in a clean, new factory were offset by the strains of mechanization. In 1907 the workers at Weisen and Goldstein's went on strike to protest speedups.

Older male strikers proved critical to Lemlich's political education. Confused by an argument between workers at a strike meeting, Lemlich asked one to explain the difference between Socialist unionism and the "pure and simple trade unionism" of the American Federation of Labor (AFL). When the meeting ended, the man took Lemlich for a long walk. He explained Socialism in terms she could use with her fellow workers. "He started with a bottle of milk—how it was made, who made the money from it through every stage of its production. Not only did the boss take the profits, he said, but not a drop of that milk did you drink unless he allowed you to. It was funny, you know, because I'd been saying things like that to the girls before. But now I understood it better and I began to use it more often—only with shirtwaists."

Lemlich returned to the picket line with a more sophisticated view of organizing. She became a regular at Socialist Party meetings and began attending classes at the Rand School. Through the Socialist Party she became friends with Rose Schneiderman, Pauline Newman, and other young women organizers. Both individually and in tandem, this group of radical young women organized strikes across the Lower East Side.

In 1909, after being fired from two more shops for leading strikes, Lemlich began working at the Leiserson shop. Brazenly, she marched uninvited into a strike meeting that had been called by the shop's older male elite—the skilled cutters and drapers. Warning them that they would lose if they attempted to strike without organizing the shop's unskilled women, Lemlich demanded their help in organizing women workers. They bridled at her nerve, but ultimately they helped her unionize the women.

These young women were the labor militants behind the 1909 shirtwaist makers' strike in New York. The female strikers defied both employers and fellow union organizers, who assumed that young women could never maintain the solidarity necessary for a difficult labor protest. The strikers won broad sympathy, attracting a diverse base of support that included middle-class female reformers and political radicals. Here the strikers are raising money by selling copies of the *New York Call*, the city's Socialist newspaper.

Lemlich, who enjoyed the company of men, saw herself marching side by side with them into a better future for the working class. Still, this unusually self-possessed young woman did not hesitate to challenge even much older men if they expressed indifference or opposition to the idea of organizing women. Her political intensity was offset by great warmth and vitality. Curly-haired, dark-eyed, and flirtatious, Lemlich was a popular entertainer at East Side gatherings; she had a vast repertoire of revolutionary songs. But she also had an iron will and an uncanny certainty about what was right and what was wrong. This gave her a personal power that drew both men and women toward her but sometimes exasperated those she was closest to.

Lemlich's reputation as a leader grew rapidly during the fall of 1909 as stories of her bravery spread. During the Leiserson strike, which began that September, she was arrested seventeen times and had six ribs broken by club-wielding police and company guards. Without complaint, she tended to her bruises and returned to the line. By November 1909, when she stepped onto the stage in Cooper Union's Great Hall of the People to deliver the speech that would spark the largest women's strike the nation had yet seen, Lemlich was not the anonymous "wisp of a girl" that news accounts described. She was a battle-scarred veteran of the labor movement, well known among her fellow workers.

Still, it is worth remembering that in this period, the four women activists were just barely adults. Newman, Schneiderman, and Lemlich still lived with their parents. During the Leiserson strike, Lemlich was so fearful that her parents would try to keep her home if they knew about her injuries that she hid her escapades and bruises from them. Later she explained the events to her grandson: "Like rain the blows fell on me.

The gangsters hit me. . . . The boys and girls invented themselves how to give back what they got from the scabs, with stones and whatnot, with sticks. . . . Sometimes when I came home I wouldn't tell because if I would tell they wouldn't want me to go anymore. Yes, my boy, it's not easy. Unions aren't built easy."

The first decade of the century was vital both to the political maturation of the four young organizers and to the development of a political movement of immigrant working women. Coming of age in the garment trades, Schneiderman, Newman, Lemlich, and Cohn had to negotiate a confusing array of conflicting pulls to forge individual adult identities. Each handled those conflicts differently. But all four were deeply influenced by their experiences on the shop floor; those years would shape the way they organized and thought for the rest of their lives. Between 1900 and 1909, the four set the foundations for their activist careers, refusing to accept any definition of class struggle that did not include the active participation of women, or any definition of feminism that excluded the working class. Over the next ten years they would demonstrate not only what working women could do for themselves but also what they had to offer the trade union, Socialist, and women's suffrage movements.

Questions for Study and Review

1. What were working conditions like in turn-of-the-century garment factories, and what kind of job protections could workers expect in their jobs?

2. Why did young women seek out jobs in the American garment industry, and how did these jobs compare to other occupations open to women?

3. How did these young workers seek to change working conditions? What strategies for change were most successful, and what were the greatest challenges involved in organizing young garment workers?

4. How did alliances between working-class and middle-class activists, such as settlement house residents, alternately further and limit laboring women's activities and agendas?

Suggested Readings and Web Sites

Rosalyn Baxandall and Linda Gordon, eds., *America's Working Women: A Documentary History, 1600 to the Present* (1995)
Ardis Cameron, *Radicals of the Worst Sort: Laboring Women in Lawrence, Massachusetts, 1860–1912* (1993)
Rose Cohen, *Out of the Shadow: A Russian Jewish Girlhood on the Lower East Side* (1995)
Vicki Ruiz, *From Out of the Shadows: Mexican Women in Twentieth-century America* (1998)
The 1911 Triangle Shirtwaist Factory Fire
    http://www.ilr.cornell.edu/TriangleFire/
Working for the Triangle Shirtwaist Factory
    http://historymatters.gmu.edu/d/178
Women Working, 1800–1930
    http://ocp.hul.harvard.edu/ww/
The American Social History Project
    http://www.ashp.cuny.edu/video/heaven/docs.html

PART II

Modern Women

The only self-made female millionaire of the early twentieth century was Madam C. J. Walker, who built her business fortune on modern women's demand for hair care and cosmetic products.

The Progressive Era had not yet come to a close when new issues and new social visions began to emerge. Fostered by World War I, by the rise of consumer culture and commercial entertainment, and by a growing population of young, single city dwellers, social and economic forces began to reshape families and communities in the United States. At the same time, they transformed relations between foreign-born and native-born Americans, blacks and whites, wealthy and poor, parents and children, and women and men. Yet what at first appeared to be a revolution in social and sexual relations turned out to be a less radical transformation in attitudes and behaviors. Still, a more modern notion of womanhood emerged that propelled some women to grasp new opportunities and convinced others to reclaim traditional ways.

Especially in the 1910s and 1920s, the culture of progressive reform, modern notions of race and gender relations, and a resurgence of reactionary politics overlapped. Chicago's Hull House residents were still pursuing their municipal housekeeping chores, for instance, when young working women began pursuing economic autonomy and sexual excitement in the city's factory and rooming house districts. In the South as well, the women reformers who had embraced temperance, suffrage, and municipal housekeeping in the late nineteenth century now faced new challenges as textile factories moved South. Urban factories and mill towns quickly sprang up in the Carolinas, Tennessee, and Georgia, bringing the industrial problems that plagued the North below the Mason-Dixon line and introducing southern working girls to the delights of consumer culture.

For African American women in particular, the forces of progress and reaction converged in dramatic ways. In 1896, the Supreme Court's ruling in *Plessy v. Ferguson* gave constitutional sanction to state laws imposing segregation and requiring the races to be separated in public accommodations, such as parks, playgrounds, and schools, and on public transportation. Yet the demands that blacks live in separate neighborhoods, attend separate schools, and shop in separate stores ensured the continued development of black communities, educational institutions, and businesses in the twentieth century. These changes coincided with a resurgence of the Ku Klux Klan and anti-black violence, but also with the rise of consumer-oriented black businesses and products that offered new economic opportunities for African American women.

The tensions created by overlapping and conflicting customs and laws, ideas and agendas were evident in families and communities across the country. Progressive reformers and women wage earners had often differed about the best ways to improve working-class communities. But these disagreements intensified as young wage-earning women embraced new opportunities for economic autonomy and new forms of consumption and entertainment in the early twentieth century. In Chapter Four, Kathy Peiss explores the lives of young working-class women who spent growing amounts of leisure time away from their families. Joining co-workers in dance halls, movie theaters, amusement parks, and picnic grounds, many single wage-earning women delighted in the new patterns of heterosexual sociability and courtship. Eager to wear the right styles and enjoy the lively entertainments available to working-class youth, these women sought to gain greater control over the money they earned and greater independence from family rules and regulations. At the same time, they were less likely to embrace the social agendas of progressive reformers or the pleas of labor organizers to postpone consumer gratification in order to walk the picket line. Still, union membership increased among working women in the first decades of the twentieth century, and many working girls walked the picket line dressed in handmade fashions they had first glimpsed at the picture show.

African American women, too, combined elements of the new consumer culture with efforts to improve their own lives. Yet most black women were denied employment in factories and were excluded from the unions founded by white working women. They were thus more dependent on their families to make ends meet and less likely or able to abandon the protection and resources offered by close-knit communities. The largest number of black women continued to be employed in agriculture and domestic service, two occupations that were notoriously hard to organize because of the isolated nature of the individual farms and homes where women were employed. Although domestic servants and farm workers did try to unionize, it was self-employed black women—such as laundresses and beauticians—who often had the best chance of improving themselves and their communities.

In Chapter Five, Tiffany Gill explores the opportunities offered to African American women by the expanding business of beauty culture in the early twentieth century. Women who entered the beauty business in this period were faced with difficult choices. Who should define what was beautiful for black women? Were products that straightened hair or lightened skin necessary for African Americans to be considered beautiful, or were they another indication of the power of whites to control black bodies? Whatever choices black businesswomen made regarding beauty standards for African American women, many wielded the profits from beauty culture to benefit the larger community. They did so in part by using the autonomous space offered by beauty shops to advance African American political agendas.

The social and political agendas of African Americans, women, and workers were both enhanced and complicated when the United States entered World War I in 1917. The war served as a catalyst that reinforced ongoing transformations in race relations, sex roles, consumption habits, technological developments, and political realignments. Moreover, the war offered blacks and immigrants opportunities to improve their economic status while proving their loyalty to country and community. Despite President Woodrow Wilson's order to maintain segregated eating facilities and restrooms in the armed services and a nationwide upsurge in anti-German and anti-Semitic attacks, large numbers of African Americans and immigrants volunteered their services to aid the American cause. On the home front, black women and men headed north seeking industrial jobs opened up by the preparations for war. Meanwhile Mexicans crossed the border to fill the demand for agricultural workers. These and other groups excluded from the American mainstream purchased millions of dollars in Liberty Bonds and stamps, often encouraged to do so by women-led campaigns.

Despite these wartime developments, the postwar period was marked by agricultural depression, labor unrest, immigration restriction, and conflicts between black migrants and white residents of northern cities. Lynching and other forms of racial violence, which had continued during the war, escalated thereafter as native-born whites closed ranks against broadening democracy at home after the Allied victory abroad. Nativist sentiments that emerged prior to the outbreak of hostilities in Europe were also heightened by the war. Deeply held fears of foreigners expressed during the war were further fueled by the Bolshevik Revolution, which brought Communists to power in Russia in 1917. An anti-communist Red Scare then erupted in the United States that resulted in deportations of suspected radicals, restrictive quotas on immigration from southern and eastern Europe, and the exclusion of Asian immigrants.

Those seeking to ferret out Communists, socialists, and other radicals focused on native-born female activists as well as foreigners. In 1924, the Chemical Warfare Department of the federal government released a Spider-Web Chart that linked twenty-nine women leaders and fifteen women's organizations to "the Socialist-Pacifist movement in the United States" and "to International Socialism." The chart included not only the Women's International League for Peace and Freedom and other overtly pacifist organizations, but also the National Federation of Business and Professional Women's Clubs, the Young Women's Christian Association, the National Consumers' League, the Women's Christian Temperance Union, the General Federation of Women's Clubs, the National League of Women Voters, the National Council of Jewish Women, and the American Home Economics Association. Ironically, women in some of the targeted organizations had voiced their own concerns about the dangers lurking in immigrant communities and had launched campaigns to "Americanize" foreign-born men, women, and children.

Still, for many Americans, the war offered escape from the prejudices and prohibitions of rural life, from domestic strife, or from racial violence. Young women and men especially were on the move well before war erupted, but increased job opportunities and wartime mobilization intensified this trend. By 1920, according to the U.S. census, the majority of Americans lived in cities for the first time in the nation's history. That same year, American women finally gained the right to vote nationwide with the passage of the Nineteenth Amendment to the U.S. Constitution. Although women in many western states had won voting rights in earlier decades and Illinois and New York State had approved women suffrage immediately following the war, the ratification of the Nineteenth Amendment finally enshrined women as first-class citizens in the nation at large.

The changes that occurred in the early 1900s affected the most intimate aspects of American life. Sexual experimentation in urban centers, increased awareness of birth control, and the emergence of sexual subcultures that rejected traditional definitions of family—such as gay and lesbian circles and bohemians' opposition to monogamy—inspired a new wave of feminist activism. But such challenges to traditional ideals also fueled efforts to revitalize heterosexual marriage and motherhood. Promoted by groups as diverse as ministers, advertising executives, cosmetic companies, movie producers, and beauty pageant sponsors, the "heterosexual imperative" was proclaimed far and wide. Sermons, magazine articles, and popular lectures as well as billboards, radio programs, and theater marquees encouraged Americans to court the opposite sex, fall in love, marry, and bear children. Yet even these "traditional" practices took on new meaning for women who entered marriage with experiences of economic independence, higher education, and voting rights or who had enjoyed the freedom gained in theaters and dance halls or who understood the benefits of birth control.

While many women embraced modern values, new consumer products, and the promise of greater equality between the sexes, others found these changes disorienting and even dangerous. Not satisfied with reasserting traditional views of women and families through advertising, movies, and beauty pageants, some Americans organized more militant movements to oppose social and cultural transformations that they considered un-American and immoral. Many of these groups combined attacks on modern notions of gender and sexuality with efforts to reinvigorate white supremacy. The Ku Klux Klan was one such group. It re-emerged in the 1920s and developed strong followings not only in the South but also in northern states like New Jersey and Indiana.

In Chapter Six, Kathleen Blee traces the Klan's activities in Indiana during the 1920s, noting the KKK's efforts to recruit women to its ranks. Such recruitment efforts and the enthusiastic response of thousands of women raise complicated questions. The importance of women to the Klan in this period suggests that women's roles had indeed been transformed in the preceding decades. Yet Klan women used their newfound rights and freedoms to denounce progressive conceptions of gender relations and modern sexual mores and to deny Catholics and Jews as well as African Americans equal rights in law and custom.

The histories of women in the streets and dance halls of New York City, in the beauty shops run by African American businesswomen, and in Klan meetings in Indiana suggest the complicated forces transforming women's lives and notions of womanhood in the 1910s and 1920s. Taken together, these stories raise critical questions about women's relationships to the family, the community, and the nation. How did modern womanhood differ in major metropolitan areas like New York and Chicago and in the small towns of rural Indiana? Did the ties to family and community among African American beauty culturists distinguish them from the independent working girls "puttin' on style" in New York City? Or did the two groups' shared interest in fashion and heterosexual sociability create common ways of thinking and acting? How did these diverse groups of women imagine their relations to their class, race, and nation?

As modern notions of womanhood emerged in the early twentieth century, small numbers of women made great strides in education, the professions, business, and politics. Most, however, struggled to make sense of the opportunities and dangers offered by an increasingly diverse society in which cities and industries, consumer culture and sexuality, and warring notions of tradition and modernity shaped women, families, and communities.

Suggested Readings and Web Sites

Jean H. Baker, *Sisters: The Lives of America's Suffragists* (2006)

Hazel V. Carby, "'It Jus' Be's Dat Way Sometime': The Sexual Politics of Women's Blues," *Radical America* 20, no. 4 (1986)

Linda Gordon, *The Moral Property of Women: A History of Birth Control Politics in America* (2002)

Jacquelyn Dowd Hall et al., *Like a Family: The Making of a Southern Cotton Mill World* (1987)

Alice Kessler-Harris, *Out to Work: A History of Wage-Earning Women in the United States,* 2nd edition (2003)

Nancy MacLean, *Behind the Mask of Chivalry: The Making of the Second Ku Klux Klan* (1994)

Mary E. Odem, *Delinquent Daughters: Protecting and Policing Adolescent Sexuality in the United States, 1885–1920* (1995)

Clash of Cultures in the 1910s and 1920s
http://www.history.ohio-state.edu/projects/clash

Margaret Sanger Papers Project
http://www.nyu.edu/projects/sanger

Chapter 4

After grueling factory shifts, most young women had limited interest in study circles, settlement house classes, union meetings, and political oratory. All wage earners undoubtedly shared a desire to improve their lives and working conditions. But the labor leaders described by Orleck in the previous article were extraordinary in their commitment to self-betterment and political militancy. For most young women, the excitement of political organizing paled next to the urban pleasures of early twentieth-century New York. After laboring for long hours, young wage earners found the streets, social clubs, and dance halls irresistible. "Putting on style"—dressing flamboyantly to attract attention on the avenue—brought more immediate pleasure than planning for the revolution.

The "rowdy girls" described by Peiss in this article were growing to womanhood as cities came to dominate American life. Cities offered a radically new environment that transformed families and communities as well as expectations for female behavior. Industrialization had concentrated economic opportunities in urban areas that drew young men and women from small towns and rural areas both North and South. The quest for jobs and adventure threw native-born youth together with the immigrants who poured into American cities in the early twentieth century. Explosive growth meant that cities struggled to meet the housing and social services needs of their citizens; most municipalities were ill-equipped to provide even basic services like street paving, sewers, and waste removal. City dwellers had migrated in search of a better life. Yet reform-minded writers, scholars, and activists noted that new urban residents more typically encountered economic hardships, unexpected illness, and squalid living conditions.

Most newcomers to New York City could afford only the cheapest housing. Many families settled in tenements, a word that became synonymous with urban squalor. Tenements were five-to seven-story buildings renowned for their poor lighting, bad ventilation, and terrible sanitary conditions. Each floor of the building was divided into four apartments, and shared toilets were located on the hall or in the backyard. The structures were designed so that only a few rooms received sunlight or fresh air from the street. And the largely windowless buildings were perpetually overcrowded. Boarders—usually young men or women alone in the city—frequently joined large families in the tiny three-room apartments.

Those single migrants who were unwilling to sleep on a makeshift mattress in a tenement kitchen sought more privacy by renting accommodations in one of the city's many rooming houses. Furnished rooms allowed their residents more autonomy than shared tenement quarters but were hardly luxurious. Crowded, noisy, and uncomfortable living conditions made young urbanites eager to escape onto the streets, which teemed with life and excitement.

Once outside, most young women could not resist the consumer culture of the city. Advertisements in newspapers and magazines and displays in store windows ignited a desire for stylish clothes. Young women had to "put on style" if they wanted to participate in the youth culture of the streets, social clubs, and dance halls. Women skipped meals to afford new outfits, devoting some portion of their meager wages to cheap but fashionable ready-made clothing. Many women assembled homemade versions of the latest fashions, copying patterns and sewing the clothes themselves. Attired for fun, girls stepped out. Cautious girls limited themselves to relatively sedate window-shopping expeditions with friends. More daring young women followed the siren song of restaurants, dance halls, and movie palaces. Anxious parents were acutely aware of the dangers of the streets. Once free from adult supervision, many girls engaged in sexual experimentation that ran the danger of turning them into moral outcasts. Yet parents found it almost impossible to counteract the influence of novels, movies, and co-workers who encouraged girls to take advantage of the pleasures of urban life.

Initially young women took jobs to meet the material needs of their families. Wage earning, however, immersed many girls in a youth culture that ultimately set them on a collision course with their parents. As they explored the new commercial amusements of the early twentieth-century American city, "rowdy girls" set in motion a cultural revolution quite different from the one envisioned by Pauline Newman, Rose Schneiderman, Fannia Cohn, and Clara Lemlich. Though differing by race, sexual preference, and neighborhood, working-class women collectively created new sexual standards that were then imitated by middle-class rebels. In the decades that followed, the "flapper"—bold, emancipated, and carefree—came to personify the modern urban woman. But flappers were simply middle-class rebels and bohemians who had adopted the sexual mores and behaviors of "rowdy girls." Working-class girls looking for fun and adventure in the new urban environment had instigated a social transformation that fundamentally changed expectations of behavior for women from all backgrounds.

Putting on Style: Working Women and Consumer Culture in Turn-of-the-Century New York
KATHY PEISS

In the twentieth century, youth is regarded as a distinctive stage of life, a time of self-expression and experimentation before the experience of marriage, children, and work. Clearly applicable to middle-class teen-agers, who can nurture a separate culture in high schools and colleges, this notion of youth may not seem relevant to the working-class adolescents of 1900, who felt the pinch of financial responsibility

Shop windows like these along Division Street in New York City were some of the urban pleasures enjoyed by early twentieth-century working women. This display featured inexpensive versions of high-fashion designs, piquing the desires of young women who saved their paltry wages to splurge on this type of fashionable clothing. Girls wanting to explore any other aspect of the city's youth culture needed nice clothes.

at an early age and subordinated individual desires to the family's survival. Nevertheless, working-class youth spent much of their leisure apart from their families and enjoyed greater social freedom than their parents or married siblings, especially married women. Despite maternal efforts to make the home a place of recreation, they fled the tenements for the streets, dance halls, and theaters, generally bypassing their fathers' saloons and lodges. Adolescents formed social clubs, organized entertainments, and patronized new commercial amusements, shaping, in effect, a working-class youth culture expressed through leisure activity.

Young working-class men had a long history of creating organizations for their own sociability. Militias and volunteer fire companies, for example, provided a structure for the bachelor subcultures of the mid-nineteenth century. By the 1890s, gangs and social clubs had taken over this function. Certain forms of commercial recreation in the nineteenth century, such as pool halls, billiard parlors, and dime museums, were also identified with unmarried men, particularly the lodging-house population. The pattern of age segregation among men continued after 1900; George Bevans found that young workingmen went chiefly to theaters, dances, pool-rooms, and clubs while their fathers sought the camaraderie of saloons and lodges.

Single women in New York also pursued a social life distinct from their working-class parents', but their search for pleasure in public forms of recreation was shaped not only by long-standing patterns of culture and social organization but by new conditions of family life, work, and commercialized leisure in the city. The alluring world of urban amusements drew young women away from the ugliness of tenement life and the treadmill of work. Not content with quiet recreation in the home, they sought adventure in dance halls, cheap theaters, amusement parks, excursion boats, and picnic grounds. Putting on finery, promenading the streets, and staying late at amusement resorts became an important cultural style for many working women. Entrepreneurs sought ways to increase female participation in commercialized recreation, encouraging women's fancy dress, slangy speech, and provocative public behavior. . . . These cultural forms were not simply imposed on working-class female consumers by the emergent entertainment industry, however, but were developed and articulated as well by the young women themselves. Without doubt, amusement entrepreneurs capitalized on female fads and fancies, constructing desires as well as responding to them. Nevertheless, working women and men created their own forms of activity that broadly structured their social rela-tionships and expressed a distinctive constellation of values and concerns. This process is most apparent in two noncommercial forms of recreation, the streets and social clubs, which working-class youth colonized as their own social spaces.

Social Life in the Streets

The city streets were public conduits of sociability and free expression for all working-class people, avenues for protest, celebration, and amusement. Still, children and young people claimed ownership of the streets, despite intensified efforts by police and reformers to eradicate unruly revelry and unsanctioned behavior from the mid-century onward. Young working-class women throughout the nineteenth century were among those who flocked to the streets in pursuit of pleasure and amusement, using public spaces for flamboyant assertion. Although such "rowdy girls" had long been targets of public commentary for their supposed immorality and wanton behav-ior, young women continued to seek the streets to search for men, have a good time, and display their clothes and style in a public arena.

Working-class girls were more supervised than boys, whose choice of activities was seemingly endless: exploring the neighborhoods, scavenging in alleys, shooting craps, playing baseball, masterminding petty robberies, lighting election night bon-fires, chasing ambulances, harassing peddlars. Gang organizations were rampant throughout the working-class districts of the city, where groups of boys held sway over specific blocks, fighting interlopers and rival gangs. Although girls did not enjoy this level of activity and organization, the streets offered countless diversions. As Sophie Ruskay recalled, "We shared the life of the street unhampered by our par-ents who were too busy to try to mold us into a more respectable pattern." Even when saddled with minding a younger sibling, girls could still play sidewalk games, chat with friends, revel in the city's sights and sounds, or gather around itinerant musicians to try out their dancing skill. Girls did not form their own gangs, but some of the more adventurous joined in the boys' fun, roaming the streets and playing tricks on passers-by. As one study noted, "individual girls are frequently attached to boys' gangs and are sometimes real factors in the gang-government." More important, the streets were alternative environments that taught children a repertoire of manners and mores they did not learn in school. Attitudes toward sexuality, marriage, and women's work were conveyed in street games and rhymes.

In their teens, young women and men used the streets as a place to meet the other sex, to explore nascent sexual feelings, and carry on flirtations, all outside the watchful eyes and admonitions of parents. "Doing nothing"—small talk, scuffling, joking, and carrying on—was infused with meaning for working-class youth. With no supervision but the cop on the beat, young women could be unladylike and unrestrained on street corners and in doorways. To Maureen Connelly, an Irish immigrant to the Yorkville section of Manhattan, "fun was standing at the door with boys and girls and kidding around—this was a big thing in our life—until the policeman came and chased us." Some adolescent girls, whom parents and reformers labelled "tough," spent their evenings on street corners and in alleys and gang hangouts until late at night. More respectable young women might promenade the local commercial streets or parks in a group or with a gentleman friend, enjoying the walk, window-shopping, and chatting. Each working-class neighborhood had its place to be seen: Eighth Avenue, with its gaudy movie houses and flashing lights drew crowds of West Side Irish, German, and native-born youth; the Bowery, Grand Street, and 14th Street attracted the inhabitants of the lower East Side; and First Avenue near 72nd Street was known as the Czech Broadway to its promenaders.

Social Clubs

The streets offered uninhibited space for youth activity; social clubs and amusement societies offered an organizational structure. Social clubs evolved from several traditions of associational life, including the lodge, political club, and gang. By the late nineteenth century, street gangs were increasingly being transformed into social or pleasure clubs throughout the working-class neighborhoods of Manhattan, as police and reformers cracked down on gang activity. Social clubs often had the patronage of political associations like Tammany and were places where budding politicos learned to become part of the party machinery. As the *Civic Journal* observed, "To move into public life under local conditions a man must 'play monkey' to the political hand-organ of his party, and it is a *club* that turns the crank."

With names like the Go-Aheads, the East Side Crashers, the Round-Back Rangers, and the Limburger Roarers, the clubs ranged from the respectable to the marginally criminal. University Settlement observed that the social instinct in the lower East Side "[found] its gratification in countless 'Pleasure Clubs,' the height of whose ambitions is a chowder party in summer and a ball in winter." Clubs contained approximately twenty-five to fifty members, youths fifteen to eighteen years of age who attended school or worked in factories and offices. These clubs usually met once a week in a rented hall, saloon, or tenement basement to discuss business and organize dances and entertainments. Other nights club members might gather in a cigar store or cafe to drink, smoke, play cards, and gamble.

Young women's involvement in social and pleasure clubs varied. Some joined clubs that functioned like the lodges and associations of older working-class men. The Roumanian Young Folks' Social Club and the Independent Bukowmaer Young Men's and Young Ladies' Benefit Society were typical *landsmanschaft* organizations of the lower East Side. These proffered mutual assistance, sick benefits, and burial plots while encouraging immigrant youth to remain close to their traditional cultures through sociable gatherings. "We had a social club from our city," recalled Ruth Kaminsky. "We used to go to meetings every second week or meet in our house." However, most young women did not join mutual benefit societies to the same degree as their fathers and brothers. Only saleswomen joined in large numbers, but these associations were usually sponsored by the department stores. The five to ten cents a week other wage-earners customarily spent on insurance and death benefits was often paid into a private insurance company whose function was entirely commercial rather than recreational and communal.

More often, youth organizations tended to be oriented toward amusement and mixed-sex sociability rather than mutual aid, education, or political action. Significantly, social clubs were often called "pleasure clubs" by their patrons, to differentiate them from the more serious-minded lodges and benefit societies. As one investigator testified, women's organizations "seem to be largely social; they belong to little societies; they tell me they belong to a 'Heart and Hand Club,' a social club; nothing for the study of their own wage conditions at all." Women were admitted to auxiliaries of young men's pleasure clubs or formed their own, adopting such outrageous names as the Lady Flashers, the Lady Millionaires, and the Lady Liberties of the Fourth Ward. Organizing social clubs was a simple task. "You get together a number of people, you know, youngsters, . . . in the neighborhood and you just open up a social club," recalled Rachel Levin, who lived in the lower East Side. "We set . . . up our own programs," observed Ida Schwartz, a Russian-born milliner who joined a club when she was seventeen. "We made an organization, and we had a little dues, and then we used to make affairs and you made dances and met people, like young people do." Her club was typical of these organizations; its primary aim was to sponsor elaborate social gatherings for itself and rival clubs, hold dances in rented halls, and congregate at the city's picnic parks and beaches.

These single-sex and mixed-sex clubs structured social interaction by engineering the introduction and rendezvous of working-class youth. Schwartz noted that her club was comprised of men and women from school and work, whose friendship often led to marriage: "We were about twenty couples, and then of course when we got older, we were married . . . among the girls." To parents, allowing a daughter to step out with the crowd was more acceptable than permitting her to go out alone on a date. Young women too sought safety in numbers. Around the time that she graduated eighth grade and entered the workforce, Maureen Connelly joined the Friends of Irish Freedom, an ostensibly political organization, but one which, she noted, "was more social than anything else." The group had meetings every Friday night, followed by a dance, which was "the highlight of our lives." She had little interest in what they did for Ireland, but "most of the girls joined—and of course you didn't go with a boy when you were seventeen. They were there and we danced with them and laughed about them, but you didn't take them serious."

The importance of social clubs as mediators of urban courtship may also be seen in a short story, "Schadchen's Luck," written by a member of the Henry Street Settlement, Samuel Lewenkrohn. In this story, a matchmaker tries unsuccessfully to bring together two young East Siders, who resist his efforts and demand the freedom to seek a mate of their own choosing. The young man's social club runs a ball, and the woman attends with her girl friends to represent their club. The two meet, he asks her to dance, true love triumphs—and the relieved matchmaker claims to have fulfilled his end of the bargain.

The activities that young working-class women pursued in their leisure were largely heterosocial in orientation, directed toward meeting men, dating, romance, and fun. Reformer Belle Israels summed up the attitude of many working girls when she noted, "No amusement is complete in which *he* is not a factor." At the same time, it would be misleading to view the consciousness of most young women solely in terms of a desire for marriage and to argue that their leisure activities simply affirmed the world of their fathers, a traditional patriarchal order.

Ambiguously, young women marked out their leisure time not only as an opportunity for romantic entanglement but also as a sphere of autonomy and assertion. The Bachelor Girls Social Club, composed of female mail order clerks at Siegel-Cooper, addressed this paradox when they were accused by several male co-workers of being "manhaters" and of "celebrat[ing] Washington's Birthday without even thinking of a man." The club heatedly responded: "No, we are not married, neither are we men haters, but we believe in woman's rights, and we enjoy our independence and freedom, notwithstanding the fact that if a fair offer came our way we might not [sic] consider it." Young women's desire for social freedom and its identification with leisure activities spilled over into behavior unsanctioned by parents and neighbors, as well as middle-class reformers. Clubs, for example, could be gathering places for sexual experimentation. A club member familiar with the organizational life of young East Siders reported to the University Settlement that "in all [clubs] 'they have kissing all through pleasure time, and use slang language,' while in some they 'don't behave nice between young ladies.'" Similarly the street corners and doorways were spaces for kissing, hugging, and fondling, free and easy sexual behavior "which seem[s] quite improper to the 'up-towner,'" but was casually accepted by working-class youth.

Clothing, Style, and Leisure

Streets and social clubs, as well as such commercial forms of amusement as dance halls and theaters, became the spaces in which young women could carve out a cultural style expressing these complex and often contradictory values. It was in leisure that women played with identity, trying on new images and roles, appropriating the cultural forms around them—clothing, music, language—to push at the boundaries of immigrant, working-class life. This public presentation of self was one way to comment upon and mediate the dynamics of urban life and labor—poverty and the magnet of upward mobility, sexual assertion and the maintenance of respectability, daughterly submission and the attractions of autonomy and romance, the grinding workday and the glittering appeal of urban nightlife.

Promenading the streets and going places with the crowd, young working-class women "put on style." Dress was a particularly potent way to display and play with notions of respectability, allure, independence, and status and to assert a distinctive identity and presence. Genteel reformers noted with concern the tendency of young working women to present an appearance fraught with questionable moral and social connotations. Mary Augusta LaSelle lamented the use of low decolletage, gauze stockings, high-heeled shoes, freakish hats, and hair dressed with "rats" and "puffs," or artificial hair pieces—"in too many cases a fantastic imitation of the costly costumes of women of large incomes." To such middle-class observers, working women were seeking upward mobility, dressing like their betters in order to marry into a higher class. This interpretation, while not without foundation, obscures the more complex role of fashion and style in the social life of working women.

Proper clothing in working-class culture traditionally helped to define respectability. As Lillian Betts observed of the workingman, "He, with the mother, has one standard—clothes." Among laboring families hard pressed for income, dress divided itself into two types, work clothes and Sunday clothes. Work clothing necessarily varied with the requirements of job and employer, from the crisp white aprons and caps of waitresses to the hand-me-down garments worn by factory hands. Sunday clothes, however, were visible displays of social standing and self-respect in the rituals of churchgoing, promenading, and visiting. Appropriate attire was a requirement of social participation. Elena and Gerda Nakov, two impoverished needlewomen, considered "their clothing [to be] so poor that they were ashamed to go out on Sunday—when everybody else put on 'best dresses'—and would sit in their room all day." For newly arrived immigrants, changing one's clothes was the first step in securing a new status as an American. When Rose Pasternak landed at Castle Garden, her brother took her directly to a hat store: "They said in this country you don't go to work without a hat."

Clothing was only the palpable aspect of competing cultural styles among young working-class women. Patterns of speech, manners, levels of schooling, attitudes toward self-improvement, and class consciousness differentiated groups of women beyond the obvious divisions of ethnicity and religion. In workshops, stores, clubs, and dance halls, observers noted the cliquishness of adolescent girls around these considerations. In the moralistic language of one reform committee, "The several floors of a large factory often mean as many degrees of respectability or demoralization" among working women. Journalist Mary Gay Humphreys described the New York girls of the 1890's who took themselves seriously as independent and thoughtful workers, and reflected this view in their public style. Women strikers in a thread-mill, for example, linked fashion—wearing bonnets—to their sense of American identity and class consciousness, contrasting their militancy to Scottish scabs who wore shawls on their heads. Believing in the labor movement's ideology of self-improvement, organization, and workers' dignity, these women devoted their leisure to lectures, evening school, political meetings, and union dances. While they sewed their own ball gowns and loved display, they also agreed that ribbons were a "foolish extravagance."

For other young women, dress became a cultural terrain of pleasure, expressiveness, romance, and autonomy. "A girl must have clothes if she is to go into high society at Ulmer Park or Coney Island or the theatre," explained Sadie Frowne, a sixteen-year-old garment worker. "A girl who does not dress well is stuck in a corner, even if she is pretty." Similarly, Minnie saved her earnings in order to "'blow herself' to an enormous bunch of new hair, which had transformed her from what she called 'a back number' to 'something dead swell.'" As another working woman succinctly put it, "If you want to get any notion took of you, you gotta have some style about you."

Stylish clothing—a chinchilla coat, a beaded wedding dress, a straw hat with a willow plume—was an aspect of popular culture that particularly tugged at women's desires. Maria Cichetti lovingly remembers hats and the sense of being "dressed": "They were so beautiful, those hats. . . . They were so rich. A woman looked so dressed, you know, in the back, with the bustle. . . . I wanted to grow up to wear earrings and hats and high heels." The demands of fashion caused Rose Pasternak to be docked for lateness:

> That time they wear the big puffs on the hair, you know, like wigs. Until I put on the girdle—my brother and my cousin used to pull the laces for me, you know—until I fix the hair, till I walked to the place to work. . . . I was ten minutes late, five minutes late. . . . On four dollars a week, I never had a full pay.

Many department store clerks, observed a saleswoman, were restrained and sensible in their clothing, but "there are others of us who powder and paint, who bleach our hair, whose bodies suffer for food because every penny goes for clothes." Even newsgirls who could ill afford a presentable shirtwaist might splurge on an outrageous hat. To be stunningly attired at the movies, balls, or entertainments often counted more in the working woman's calculations than having comfortable clothes and shoes for the daily round of toil.

The fashions such young women wore often displayed aristocratic pretensions. Grand Street clothing stores cheaply produced the styles found in exclusive establishments. Working women read the fashion columns, and many could observe wealthy women in department stores and the streets for inspiration in their dressmaking. This seems to have been one manifestation of a broader pattern whereby working-class youth played with the culture of the elite. Etiquette demanded, for example, that they refer to their closest comrades as "lady friends" and "gentleman friends." Jacob Riis even reported the organization of a boys' club which called itself the Gentlemen's Sons' Association. Similarly, romance novels such as *Woven on Fate's Loom,* in which wealthy heroes and long-suffering young heroines underwent the turns of fortune, were popular reading. The female box-makers whom Dorothy Richardson observed even adopted storybook names that connoted wealth and romance, such as Henrietta Manners and Rose Fortune.

Working women's identification with the rich seems to have been more playful and mediated than direct and calculated, as much a commentary on the rigors of working-class life as a plan for the future. Significantly, women did not imitate *haute couture* directly, but adapted and transformed such fashion in creating their own style. While they could ill afford the fine cloth or exquisite decorations of the wealthy woman's dress, there was no purely economic reason why they chose to wear flashy colors, gaudy hats, and cosmetics. Indeed, imitation of "ladies of leisure" might involve admiring the style of prostitutes as well as socialites. As Ruth Rosen has argued, much of the appearance of twentieth-century women, including their use of make-up and wigs, was common among prostitutes before becoming accepted by "respectable" females. In the promiscuous spaces of the streets, the-aters, and dance halls, prostitutes provided a cultural model both fascinating and forbidden to other young working-class women. Tantalized by the fine dress, easy life, sexual expressiveness, and apparent independence, while carefully marking the boundary between the fallen and respectable, a working woman might appro-priate parts of the prostitute's style as her own. So-called "tough girls," as Lillian Wald described the assertive and rowdy working girls of her community, played with the subculture of prostitution: "Pronounced lack of modesty in dress was one of several signs; . . . their dancing, their talk, their freedom of manner, all combined to render them conspicuous."

The complex dynamics of working women's self-definition is suggested in Rose Schneiderman's recollections of her adolescence. The future labor leader and activist voraciously read the romance literature so popular among young working women, and, internalizing its messages, worried that her hair and figure did not fit the fashion of the day: "All the romantic novels I consumed made me a most romantic young woman, and when I looked at myself in a full-length mirror I was very unhappy." Popular culture also helped define ideals of masculinity, although this was mediated by the realities of working-class experiences and expectations: "From the books I read I had also developed a special taste in men. Among other traits, I wanted them well-read and cultured. I never dreamed of marrying a rich man. That was entirely out of my ken." Personal pleasure in dancing outweighed her interest in romance and courtship: "My idea of what a man should be didn't quite match up with the boys Ann Cypress and I were meeting at the Saturday night dances in the neighborhood. . . . I didn't enjoy their company, but I did love to dance and was pretty good at it, so I put up with them."

Putting on style seemed to fly in the face of the daily round of toil and family obligation—an assertive flash of color and form that belied some of the realities of everyday life. Yet this mode of cultural expression, linked to the pleasures of the streets, clubs, and dance halls, was closely shaped by the economic and social relations of working-class life. Maintaining style on the streets, at dance halls, or at club functions was an achievement won at other costs—going without food, sewing into the night to embellish a hat or dress, buying on installment, leaving school early to enter the workforce, and forcing confrontations within the working-class family.

The Family Economy and Conflict Over Leisure

No investigation on the order of George Bevans' *How Workingmen Spend Their Spare Time* provides the detailed information necessary to correlate working women's leisure activities with their family situation, ethnic background, residence, or occupation. Government surveys and reformers' reports provide ample statistical data on women's work, but comparable sources on leisure do not exist. However, the evidence of reformers, observers, journalists, and working women themselves does allow us to explore the parameters within which different young women made choices about their amusements and social life. Cultural practices rooted in religious, ethnic, and class traditions suggest the varying definitions of appropriate behavior for unmarried women in Manhattan's working-class communities. Whether one lived in a family or alone in a boardinghouse were important determinants of social freedom. Relations within the family, too, shaped the choices women could make, as did their access to money and other resources.

Most young women negotiated leisure within the dynamics of the family economy, which was both a strategy for survival and a working-class cultural idea. In an industrial system dominated by low-paying unskilled and semiskilled jobs, the inadequacy of men's wages necessitated the economic contribution of daughters, sons, and wives, thus reinforcing the interdependency of family members. In a 1914 study, for example, the typical working-class family of five contained three wage-earners. Such economic strategies were supported by cultural traditions within working-class communities that legitimated and reinforced notions of mutual obligation, filial responsibility, self-sacrifice, and family unity. The impact of these expectations could be profound, as Lucy, a twenty-three-year-old Italian box-maker supporting her mother and brother, discovered: "The other week my mother turned away a good offer of marriage because she said I must work until my brother is old enough to work." Custom demanded that daughters contribute all or a substantial part of their earnings to the family. In 1888, 72 percent of female factory workers interviewed gave all their earnings, and this figure remained relatively unchanged into the 1910's, when three-quarters to four-fifths handed their pay envelopes over to their parents unopened.

Parents made a distinction between the contributions—and independence—of sons and daughters. Boys were less pressured to contribute all their earnings, often paying half for board and keeping the rest for themselves. Before the 1920's, girls under twenty-one could not make the same arrangement without risking family conflict. Flower-maker Theresa Albino, the daughter of Italian parents, gave all her earnings to her mother, while her eighteen-year-old brother contributed three or four dollars a week. "But you know how it is with a boy," she explained. "He wants things for himself." Similarly Maureen Connelly, an Irish-born saleswoman, observed that her brother paid only board, but "I gave all, I'd be afraid to say I'd give board. The idea never even entered my mind."

Mothers also expected their daughters to help them with housework or tend their younger siblings, an expectation not placed on sons, who had more freedom to roam the streets, play sports, and seek adventures with their gangs or clubs. In an 1888 survey of three thousand female factory workers in Manhattan, for example, three-quarters assisted with the housework after their day of wage labor.

The degree to which parents permitted daughters an independent social life in the public sphere varied among different immigrant groups. Chaperonage remained an important institution among East Side Jews, but parents considered it appropriate for their daughter to go for walks and to dances with men, as long as the parents knew about the excursion beforehand and had met the young man. Young Jewish women often attended theaters, clubs, and dances weekly and, according to one investigator, had greater freedom in spending their income than German or Italian girls. A survey of the favorite amusements of fifteen hundred wage-earning women conducted by sociologist Annie MacLean also suggests ethnic differences. She found that over 50 percent of Jewish girls preferred theaters, concerts, or dances to other forms of entertainment, while a somewhat lesser number of Americans and Germans, approximately 40 percent, did so. Irish women, according to this study, did not attend musical entertainments, but 35 percent preferred theater trips or dancing. In contrast, Italian girls were most likely to engage in home-centered amusements or to state no preference at all; fewer than 30 percent listed a commercial form of leisure as their preference.

More than other working-class youth, unmarried Italian women found their social participation curtailed by conservative cultural traditions regulating women's familial roles and affirming patriarchal authority. Parents ordered daughters to come home directly from their places of employment, turn in their pay envelopes unopened, and help with the housework. Chaperones usually accompanied young women who went out in the evening, and the modern concept of dating was alien to most Italian parents. The requirements of courtship assumed that a woman went out only with the man she would ultimately marry. Rather than attending dances and theaters, the couple would visit at her home several times a week until the courting year had ended. Even when a young woman was permitted to go out, and exceptions were allowed especially for movies, an early curfew was set. These practices reflected the common belief tersely expressed by two Italian parents: "The daughter has [a] better chance at marriage by staying away from public amusements." In the case of Italian girls at least, parental control and daughterly submission extended far beyond the need to ensure the family's economic survival.

Yet this notion of the family economy as the determining structure of young women's experience simplifies the dramas of control, resistance, acquiescence, and subterfuge that occurred within many working-class families. While daughters may have accepted the family claim to their wages and work, struggles often ensued over their access to and use of leisure time. Participation in social life, parental supervision, spending money, and clothing were common issues of conflict. As wage-earners and contributors to the family, they sought to parlay their new-found status toward greater autonomy in their personal lives.

In an example of this familial drama, Louisa, a young woman living in a West Side Irish neighborhood around 1910, discovered that working in a candy factory for five dollars a week gave her power within the family. Her economic contribution enabled her to claim the privilege of going to dance halls, staying out late with men, and purchasing extravagant suits and hats. Social investigator Ruth True observed of Louisa that "the costume in which she steps out so triumphantly has cost many bitter moments at home. She has gotten it by force, with the threat of throwing up her job." Her distraught mother decried such undutiful behavior: "She stands up and answers me back. An' she's comin' in at 2 o'clock, me not knowin' where she has been. Folks will talk, you know, an' it ain't right fer a girl." Indeed, a bargain was struck in many families, with daughters bartering their obedience in turning over wages for the freedom to come and go as they pleased. Reformer Lillian Betts found that the American-born girls she studied viewed independence not as a privilege but a right: "Beyond the fact that some of them must be at home at ten or half-past, there was no law but their own will." Indeed, Maureen Connelly threw caution to the wind when she violated her parents' curfew: "If I went out and I knew I'd get hit if I came in at twelve, so I'd stay out till one."

Even in Italian families, young women carved out spaces in their lives for privacy, independence, and unsupervised social interaction. When parents forbade a young man's visit, a daughter might slip out into the streets to meet him. Antoinette Paluzzi, who came to New York from Sicily in 1920 when she was thirteen, was not allowed by her father to date. Her mother, however, permitted her to walk with a girl friend to the local park, where she would meet her beau, being careful to obey the stipulation that she return home before her father's workday ended. Similarly, Angela Defina and her fiance were chaperoned whenever they went out, but occasionally they took an afternoon off from work to visit the Hippodrome, despite Angela's fears that her father would find out. Some adolescent Italian women even defied cultural tradition by frequenting commercial dance halls. Observing women on the balcony of the Excelsior, a cafe and dance house, a Committee of Fourteen investigator noted that "2 appeared to be respectable Italian girls."

Attitudes toward autonomy differed even between sisters. In the early 1920's, Sophia Margolis dutifully stayed close to home, turning over her pay envelope and sharing her leisure with her mother. In contrast, her sister would take a few dollars of her own wages to spend on clothing and entertainment, and eventually demanded and received the right to pay only board. More independent than Sophia, she stayed out late at Roseland Ballroom's costume parties, risking the neighbors' gossip about her notorious behavior. "My sister would have a good time," recalled Sophia, "going out dancing, going bathing, going to Coney Island by herself."

At its extreme, young women's rebelliousness was expressed in the subculture of "tough girls." At the Lexington Cafe, a saloon on the corner of East 116th Street and Lexington Avenue, a vice investigator observed an eighteen-year-old "Italian street corner tough" conversing with an intoxicated man:

> The girl had no hat on and had probably just left her house to go on an errand when she met this man[.] I heard her say, my mother will think I got lost I was supposed to go to the drug store she wouldn't know what became of me. The man was under the influence of liquor and was trying to put his hands under her skirts, she resisted at first but afterwards let him go as far as he liked.

Although the investigator does not describe this incident and its participants in great detail, the vignette suggests the powerful allure of leisure as a realm of assertion, sexual experimentation, and escape from parental demands.

Family controversy over young women's leisure was compounded by the problem of space and privacy in tenement apartments, where the "parlor" served as kitchen, dining room, and bedroom. New York housing ranged from abysmal rear tenements to "new law" apartments with indoor plumbing and adequate ventilation, but overcrowding remained a dominant characteristic of working-class neighborhoods. Dumb-bell tenements, the prevailing housing type between 1879 and 1901, usually contained several apartments per floor, in a five- to seven-story walk-up. In 1900, an average of eight families lived in each tenement house, and the mean size of households was 4.3 individuals, usually crowded into two or three rooms. Although housing conditions improved after 1900 with the construction of new law tenements, families still had to contend with small rooms and, often, the presence of boarders. Consequently, "privacy could be had only in public," and young people sought the streets, clubs, and halls in order to nurture intimate relationships.

Contention over leisure, social freedom, and dating was also heightened by the inevitable cultural conflicts between the American-born or educated youth and their immigrant parents, who clung to Old World traditions. Lillian Wald noted that the Americanized wage-earning daughter "willingly gave her earnings and paid tribute to her mother's devotion and housekeeping skill, [but] said she felt irritated and mortified every time she returned to her home." Sadie Frowne, a young garment worker, observed that immigrant women criticized her for spending her income on fashionable clothes: "Those who blame me are the old country people who have old-fashioned notions, but the people who have been here a long time know better."

The emergent consumer culture, with its beguiling modernity, challenged parental authority over manners and mores. Women attentively read the advertisements and commentary about personal appearance printed in the working-class dailies, even in the socialist press: the *Jewish Daily Forward* noted in 1915, for example, that facial hair "makes a bad impression"; to eliminate it, women should "go immediately to your druggist and for one dollar buy Wonderstone." Some women apparently pondered such counsel carefully; one young East Sider asked the *Forwards's* "Bintel Brief," an advice column: "Is it a sin to use face powder? Shouldn't a girl look beautiful? My father does not want me to use face powder. Is it a sin?" Increasingly, as young people chose forms of entertainment identified with American culture, parents who had previously decried cheap dance halls and theaters slowly acquiesced to them.

Recreation and the "Woman Adrift"

Although most adolescent working-class women lived at home, a sizable number—as many as sixty-eight thousand in 1910—lived alone, lodging in boardinghouses or renting rooms. Style and amusement were important aspects of their lives as well, but the "woman adrift," as she was called, experienced the culture of the streets, clubs, and dance halls in a different context from those who resided at home. Women who lived outside families trod a fine line between asserting independence and guarding respectability in their everyday lives. Many chose to live with relatives or board in the houses of strangers rather than risk their reputations living alone. Foreign-born women especially tended to seek a room with a "Missus," occupying a passageway or sharing a folding bed in the parlor at night. Among the Italian women whom Louise Odencrantz studied, only one-eighth were not living at home,

Strolling with friends was one of the tamer pastimes for young New Yorkers who "put on style" in the early twentieth century. These young working women had undoubtedly escaped crowded living quarters to enjoy the bustle of the urban scene from the vantage point of a park bench. While they were enjoying each other's company, their fashionable dress was calculated to win admiring glances from passersby.

and of these, the majority resided with kinfolk. This arrangement often created a surrogate family for young women, a necessity for those in low-paying or seasonal jobs. As "daughters," they might help out with cooking or child care and in turn would receive the family's assistance when in need. Since living alone spelled immorality among many immigrants, this strategy also ensured that a woman's respectability would be maintained.

For these women, familial and cultural norms often affected leisure as much as they did women living with their parents. Old World tradition kept most Italian women off the streets and out of public amusements at night, whether they lived at home or not; visiting friends, attending church, going to movies and occasional balls or theatrical events comprised the bulk of their amusements. For one Italian living on her own, decorating a small tenement apartment was her major form of entertainment:

> The room was decorated with several shelves of gay dishes. The images of 18 different saints adorned the head of the bed, bright pictures of the rulers of Italy, advertising calendars and panels, an alarm clock, and a guitar hung on the wall. The care of her room was a daily joy and her only recreation.

Other "women adrift" found housing in noncommercial boarding homes organized by churches and philanthropic agencies, which usually established house rules for recreation and sociability and occasionally organized their own leisure activities. Their residents came mainly from American and "old immigrant" stock, especially English, German, and Irish backgrounds, who were more often employed as office workers, servants, teachers, and nurses than as factory workers or salesclerks. The gentility and bourgeois standards of such homes may well have attracted migrants from small American towns or girls who were otherwise exposed to dominant middle-class notions of domesticity and womanhood.

Still, by 1915, many boarders complained heartily about the regulations on social life enforced in the homes. Women's sense of self-respect was eroded not only by taking charity but by the restrictions imposed on their time and leisure—the enforced quiet, prohibitions on dancing and popular music, limited space to entertain friends, and evening curfews. Locking the doors at ten or eleven o'clock, for example, hampered young women's leisure in a city "where the theatre rarely is over until eleven, and where parties seldom begin until nine."

Many refused to live in the homes, citing their opposition to charity, forced sociability, and a stultifying female culture. "A place like that should have a strictly hotel basis; no Christian stuff; and a decent name," observed one Irish girl. Freedom, to such women, meant such simple acts as choosing one's dinner at a restaurant rather than eating the planned meals of the home, and seeing male faces instead of a roomful of women: "Now I live in a furnished room house and I go into Childs' and I'm as good as the next fellow," said one former resident. Heterosocial relationships were of utmost concern to them. "I don't want to live in a place with a lot of hens," said several women, explaining:

> Everybody calls those Homes the "Old Maids' Retreat" and they're just about right. It's not that I'm crazy about men, that I don't want to live there, but just because I'm normal. If you live in a furnished room house you meet men sometimes and if you don't meet them, at least you see them going in and out, which is something. It must be awful depressing to live with a bunch of gossipy women all the time.

Many young women sought lodging in commercial rooming houses and apartments for greater social freedom, in order to come and go as they pleased. In the 1890's, many New York dwellings were converted into boardinghouses; Mary Gay Humphreys estimated that there were fifteen thousand furnished rooms for rent from Washington Square to Central Park in the blocks between Fifth and Sixth Avenues. "For a young man or young woman whose expenses must be kept within $10 a week, there seemed to be no other mode of existence." Young women pooled their resources to live together in apartments, in "a new order of feminine friendship" that combined autonomy, sociability, and mutual aid. It was often difficult for women to find such rooms, since landladies preferred renting to men, who had larger incomes and smaller reputations to preserve. Still, lodging houses offered a woman the advantages of having her own place and, as a Czechoslovakian domestic servant observed, the opportunity to go out dancing evenings and Saturdays without parental restraint.

Living conditions in these furnished room apartments often drove women into the commercial amusements of the city. Rooms were small, bleak, and cold, and houses usually lacked public parlors or reception rooms where women could socialize with their friends. Moreover, women entertaining men ran the gauntlet between landladies' disapproving stares and the knowing glances of male boarders. For boardinghouse keepers concerned with decency, "the most commonly used device is the rule that one may entertain only 'steadies' in one's room. . . . The working girl who numbers among her acquaintances more than one man is looked upon askance." Thus women combatted the loneliness of the furnished room by seeking out the movie houses, dance halls, cafes, and even saloons as places of rendezvous, diversion, conviviality, and courtship.

Whether they lived at home or alone, young women's notion of a "good time" was intimately linked to the public spaces of the streets, clubs, and commercial amusement resorts. Clearly not all women could pursue these forms of leisure activities. With tiring labor and few resources, many had little opportunity to enter the social whirl. "When the girls get home they're too tired to do anything," observed one bookbinder, a statement confirmed by female workers in restaurants, garment shops, and other businesses. Family responsibilities kept others at home. Investigator Mary Van Kleeck, for example, interviewed Katie, a twenty-two-year-old machine operator in a bindery, who was washing the dishes as her younger sister dressed for a wedding: "Katie said that she used to go to dances and weddings when she was young, but she is too tired to go now."

Other women held strict notions of respectability that limited their participation. Two poor but genteel working sisters defended their reputations when it came to social activities: "Evening amusements we cannot go to for want of clothes and beaux, and in fact we do not care for the company of that class of young men who we *can* know." The demands of the family economy often left women dependent on unsavory men for amusements, an arrangement many rejected. Commented a working girl who gave her weekly wages to her mother, "We have not the money for pretty clothes to attract the boys who would really care for us and of course we have no money to pay for our own amusement, and as a result we stay at home." Some obviously craved the world of popular amusements to which they could not belong. "Never have I been to a moving picture show or taken out," lamented Celia, a young immigrant. "The excursions that leave the pier make me jealous sometimes. . . . Only to be out like everybody else!" Within the varieties of working-class cultural experience, Celia's words suggest that those who could indulge in the city's cheap amusements stood out as a model for other young working women.

Questions for Study and Review

1. How did the demands of urban life change family relations in the United States at the beginning of the twentieth century? What did these changes mean for young women in particular?

2. What do you think young labor leaders like Pauline Newman, Rose Schneiderman, Fannia Cohn, and Clara Lemlich thought about the "rowdy girls" who spent their leisure hours "putting on style" and bantering with boys? Do you think that these labor leaders enjoyed nice clothes and evenings at a dance hall as much as the other girls in their neighborhoods and workplaces?

3. New York City policemen routinely broke up the efforts of "rowdy girls" to socialize on the streets, just as mobs of white men attacked African American women in Memphis in 1866 when they attempted to claim public spaces for their own use. Do you think the "rowdy girls" depicted by Peiss would have been sympathetic to the Memphis women described by Rosen, and why was the presence of women in public perceived to be threatening in such contexts?

4. How do turn-of-the-century campaigns to police the public behavior of young people compare to contemporary efforts to limit teenagers' access to shopping malls, city streets, and other public spaces?

Suggested Readings and Web Sites

Nan Enstad, *Ladies of Labor, Girls of Adventure: Working Women, Popular Culture and Labor Politics at the Turn of the Twentieth Century* (1999)

Pippa Holloway, *Sexuality, Politics and Social Control in Virginia, 1920–1945* (2006)

Christine Stansell, *American Moderns: Bohemian New York and the Creation of a New Century* (2000)

Victoria Wolcott, *Remaking Respectability: African American Women in Interwar Detroit* (2001)

Famous Flappers
www.geocities.com/flapper_culture

New York City Tenement House Museum
http://www.thirteen.org/tenement/eagle.html

Chapter 5

A s white women took jobs in department stores, offices, and garment factories at the end of the nineteenth century, the domestic positions they left behind became the main occupations of African American women, outside of agriculture. The race and sex segregation of the American labor market meant that African American women were restricted to jobs even more grueling and miserably paid than those held by the young labor leaders profiled by Orleck in Chapter Three. While a tiny number of African American women became teachers or businesspeople, the vast majority were relegated to the lowest paid and least prestigious occupations. And even as labor activism transformed working conditions for some women workers at the beginning of the twentieth century, African American women were slow to feel its effects. In fact, the opportunities and hopes of African Americans in the immediate post–Civil War period had withered under the reassertion of white supremacy in the 1890s. Contacts between the races, which had been in a state of flux during Reconstruction, now became tightly regulated and restricted as states all over the South legislated legal discrimination by passing what were known as Jim Crow laws.

In the midst of this intensifying political and economic repression, African American women built a haven for themselves: a beauty industry that gave them the economic autonomy necessary for political mobilization. Beauty culture spawned enterprises that allowed African American women to participate in the burgeoning consumer culture of the early twentieth century. The previous article illuminated how consumer culture changed gender expectations and created new standards of femininity that gradually transformed the lives of women in diverse communities. Fascination with fashionable clothing among young working girls was accompanied, in many cases, with growing cosmetic use. This development reflected cultural as well as economic shifts. In earlier decades, the use of cosmetics like face powder, rouge, or lipstick had been the sole province of prostitutes, actresses, and other morally suspect women. In the early twentieth century, "respectable" women embraced the use of cosmetics as a way to enhance their feminine allure. The purchase of commercial hair products and visits to beauty shops also became increasingly popular in this period.

Young New Yorkers were not the only ones who longed to "put on style"; women from all walks of life began to share a desire for a carefully crafted appearance that was enhanced by mass-produced "stylish" clothing and commercial cosmetics. For many women, wage earning provided the gateway into the new beauty culture. No matter how low their wages, young women hoped to earn enough to buy some face powder, visit a beauty salon, or at least learn how to use curling or straightening irons to set their own hair in the latest fashion. For the many working daughters who lived at home, the kitchen might serve as their beauty parlor, with friends and family members learning from each other how to set hair or put on makeup. Those women in a neighborhood who proved most skilled in these tasks often gained a following and might earn a few dollars doing hair at home.

Although women from all backgrounds were attracted to changing styles, racial prejudice existed in this area as it did in others. The mainstream beauty industry never perceived African American women as customers to cultivate; commercial products promising beautiful skin and luxuriant hair were designed specifically for women of European descent. In this chapter, Tiffany Gill describes how a group of African American women took advantage of this cultural and commercial segregation to build a beauty industry that later served as a base for social and political change. These women entrepreneurs pioneered innovative systems of marketing, production, and distribution that made cosmetics easily accessible to a wide range of black women.

In the twentieth century, African American beauty culture became a big business, but it owed its initial growth to small entrepreneurs. Learning to "fix" hair required a modest outlay of cash. Many beauty culturists practiced their trade out of their kitchens or in small shops. Some mixed hair tonics and other preparations at home and sold them door-to-door. This black beauty industry thus attracted women across the generations, including young wives and mothers who combined domestic responsibilities with wage earning. If their business flourished, husbands, daughters, or other female relatives joined the venture, assisting beauty culturists in the preparation, marketing, and sale of hair tonics, skin creams, and other goods and services.

The demand for the services of professional beauty culturists was growing in the first decades of the twentieth century thanks to the expansion of the African American consumer market. Black women increasingly linked respectability to neatly coiffed hair. In many towns the African American business community was dominated by beauty workers, who made up the largest number of black business owners.

The beauty industry offered African American women another important benefit: the chance to create spaces that were free from white economic, social, and political control. Beauty industry entrepreneurs combined business acumen with social awareness, marketing their products in ways that nurtured racial pride. Surrounded by black co-workers and clients, beauty culturists could afford to be more defiant than their sisters who hoed cotton, cleaned houses, or taught in the public schools. Many beauticians also prized the way their profession allowed them to avoid unwanted sexual advances from white employers. Since beauticians were dependent on other African Americans for their income, they did not have to answer to white employers, politicians, or business associates hostile to African American militancy. Beauty shops thus became institutional bases for political mobilization and networking. Hidden from white eyes, black women went to beauty shops to share stories, discuss events, and evangelize for racial justice. These spaces nurtured a passion for racial justice among women, who became central activists in the twentieth-century freedom struggle.

"I Had My Own Business . . . So I Didn't Have to Worry": Beauty Salons, Beauty Culturists and Black Community Life

Tiffany Melissa Gill

In 1939, after interviewing various beauty operators and clients in Harlem for the Works Progress Administration (WPA), Vivian Morris boldly proclaimed at the end of her analysis: "INTERESTING PLACES—THESE BEAUTY SHOPS." Unfortunately, sixty years later, very little scholarship has merged business history with the ever-expanding field of African-American women's history. In either literature, the existence of these uniquely autonomous black female worlds of beauty shops within black communities goes practically unnoticed. To that end, this essay seeks to fill a historiographic void by exploring the formation and evolution of a thriving industry based on black female beauty, specifically hair care, created primarily by black women and controlled by black female entrepreneurs for most of the twentieth century. By examining the work of beauty culturists in what has been called the "golden age of black business" (1900 to 1930) as well as the more politically based entrepreneurship of those I call "beauty activists" (1930 to 1960), this essay will demonstrate the role the hair care industry played in the development and redefinition of beauty culture, entrepreneurship, and social action in the lives of African-American women.

Beauty Culturists in the "Golden Age of Black Business"

The creation of the National Negro Business League (NNBL) by Booker T. Washington in many ways marked the genesis of the "golden age of black business." During his travels throughout the country in the late nineteenth century, Washington explained that he was "continually coming in contact" with a great number of "successful business men and women of the Negro race." This observation led him to "believe that the time had come for bringing together the leading and most successful colored men and women in the country who were engaged in business." These men and women, who met in Boston, Massachusetts, in August 1900, represented one of the earliest gatherings of black business people and ushered in changes that impacted not only this small yet burgeoning business community, but black America in general.

Prior to the Civil War, both enslaved and free black men and women owned a few small business ventures. Juliet E. K. Walker explains that African-American slaves operated as both "intrepreneurs," those who had some authority in managing their owner's business affairs, and entrepreneurs, those who hired out their services and

First National Convention –1917– Philadelphia, Pa.

The African American beauty industry provided an institutional base for women who sought to mobilize against intensified political and economic repression. Industry leaders like Madam C. J. Walker melded their business mission with politics, supporting civil rights organizations and providing agents with economic autonomy that emboldened them to challenge white racism and violence. This photo documents the first convention of Madam Walker Hair Culturists Union in Philadelphia in 1917. The assembled women sent a telegram to President Woodrow Wilson protesting recent white violence against African Americans during the East St. Louis riots.

established enterprises that they owned outright. She further argues that free blacks formed what should be considered capitalist enterprises in a multitude of venues. Based on the mutual aid and benevolent associations of free blacks in the seventeenth and eighteenth centuries, nineteenth-century antebellum free blacks entered business as jewelers, merchants, steamboat owners, restaurateurs, grocers, real estate speculators, barbers, and hairdressers.

From the onset of freedom until the turn of the century, most blacks engaged in entrepreneurship that was an extension of the activities of blacks in slavery—ventures based on performing tasks that whites did not wish to do. According to St. Clair Drake and Horace Cayton in their seminal study of Chicago, these "colored businessmen did not serve an exclusively Negro market [but] served a white clientele." However, as the nineteenth century drew to a close with the early stages of what would eventually become the Great Migration to northern and urban areas, the number of black businesses increased, coupled with a simultaneous decline in the number of whites as clients and customers. Booker T. Washington's NNBL was born in this moment of transition.

Washington was not the only black leader who desired to unite and organize the black business community. W. E. B. DuBois, often depicted as Washington's rival in all matters pertaining to black leadership and civil rights, called for black men to engage in business. As director of the Fourth Atlanta Conference in 1899, entitled "The Negro in Business," DuBois proclaimed the need for blacks to create an economic infrastructure, and called for an "organization in every town and hamlet where colored people dwell, of Negro Business Men's Leagues" and the eventual creation of "state and national organizations." Ironically, just two years later, it was Washington who brought this dream to fruition when he formed the NNBL.

Despite the fact that leaders like Du Bois and Washington generally described business as an honorable pursuit for the men of the race, black women in general, and beauty culturists in particular, were at the forefront not only of the NNBL, but of the black business community at large. According to the minutes of the NNBL's first meeting, the business success of the race was made synonymous with restoring the manhood of the race. Gilbert C. Harris delivered a speech entitled "Work in Hair," and admitted that he had "to do some business to be a man and be recognized among men," even if that meant entering into a profession that would eventually become female-dominated. Equating manhood and business pervaded the first meeting; only one woman was even allowed to address the convention. While most of the male orators spoke directly about the business enterprises they were involved in, the only female speaker, Mrs. Alberta Moore-Smith, theorized concerning "Women's Development in Business" in a monologue very much in line with the views of the men in attendance:

> To the minds of many there is a new woman but in actuality she does not exist. Theories have been put forth to show that she is new, but the only satisfactory evidence or conclusion agreed upon is that she is simply progressing; her natural tendencies having not changed one iota . . . on the contrary, with all the knowledge gained from free and unconventional education she takes her place in society as a faithful friend, in the business world as a judicious counselor, and in the home as a loving wife and queen.

Mrs. Moore-Smith's comments did little to challenge the placement of men at the center of the black business community. While she made no direct reference to restoring black manhood through involvement in business, she clearly did not see the black woman as upsetting black male leadership in business but as "taking her place" in a supportive role.

Just one year later at the Chicago convention, Alberta Moore-Smith gave a more demanding, albeit strangely titled speech, "Negro Women's Business Clubs: A Factor in the Solution of the Vexed Problem," where she tempered a pride in women's accomplishments with a sense of racial duty and declared:

> Negro women's business clubs do not desire to be known only by their names, but by their good works and the influence they exert in encouraging our women in opening establishments of their own, no matter how small the start may be. This is one of their main objectives, and no power on earth is strong enough to deter them from their purpose, for they are well on the high-road to success. They will also inevitably enlarge the education of women and assist them in the formation of opinions concerning the mooted questions of the day in which men are deeply interested.

Perhaps Moore-Smith was more assertive on behalf of her gender at this convention because she was no longer the lone female voice. She was joined by Mrs. E. Lewis of Chicago, who spoke on "Hair Dressing," and Mrs. Dora A. Miller of Brooklyn, who discussed the organizing activities and accomplishments of "Some Eastern Business Women." In fact, Miller's comments on the role of black women in business went even further than Moore-Smith's. "In the East as in other sections of the country, Negro women," Miller proclaimed, "are taking a firm grasp of business principles and in the struggle for capital are proving themselves the equal of men." Further demonstrating her point, Miller gave a list of successful businesswomen in New York City who were instrumental in organizing the Colored Women's Business Club of New York in 1900.

Still, women's roles in the early years of the convention, for the most part, were limited to speeches where women attempted to justify their place in a male-dominated business community—that is, until 1912. At this particular convention, held in Chicago, Madam C. J. Walker demanded time to speak on the lack of respect given to beauty culturists in particular and independent black female entrepreneurs in general, and in the process changed the NNBL's opinion of black female entrepreneurs. By 1912, Madam Walker (formerly Sara Breedlove) had already amassed a small fortune manufacturing beauty products and teaching her hair-care system. While Walker did not invent the straightening comb, as legend would suggest, she was by 1912 prominent in the black beauty industry, with her incorporated company grossing over $100,000 a year. The first member of her family born free, Walker worked her way out of the Louisiana cotton fields, migrated north, and toiled as a washerwoman as late as 1905. With $1.50, a young child, and a divine revelation, Walker began her hair-care empire. After two unsuccessful marriages—one that failed in part because of her former husband's desire to control her business—Madam C. J. eventually emerged in total control of the Walker Company.

Correspondence between Booker T. Washington and Madam Walker demonstrates that they clashed often—usually over whether or not Walker's beauty methods should be placed in the Tuskeegee Institute's curriculum and whether she could sell her hair products on the school's grounds. Washington usually objected on the grounds that beauty culture was not a worthwhile profession for his female students to pursue. However, their most public clash occurred at the 1912 NNBL convention, when Walker was snubbed by Washington and not given an opportunity to speak. This was even more of an affront since a male beauty manufacturer, Anthony Overton, founder of the Overton Hygenic Manufacturing Company of Chicago—a company that sold, among other goods, cosmetics (Overton's High Brown Face Powder) and hair-care products (High Brown Shampoo Soap and Pressing Oil)—received the utmost respect.

When George Knox, publisher of the Indianapolis newspaper *The Freeman*, asked the "convention for a few minutes of its time to hear a remarkable woman. She is Madam Walker, the manufacturer of hair goods and preparations," Washington ignored Knox, and instead recognized a male Texas banker as speaker. After the banker's long lecture and Washington's favorable response, Walker rose to her feet and began an impromptu passionate speech that described her rise from a washerwoman to an established businesswoman. She also questioned the lack of respect given to those in the beauty business—particularly the female entrepreneurs. "I have made it possible," Walker proudly announced when she finally reached the podium, "for many colored women to abandon the washtub for a more pleasant and profitable occupation." She went on to add: "the girls and women of our race must not be afraid to take hold of business endeavors and . . . wring success out of a number of business opportunities that lie at their very doors."

So many of the conference participants were moved by Walker's speech—including Washington himself—that at the convention one year later, Washington took pleasure in introducing Walker as "one of the most progressive and successful businesswomen of our race." Walker then gave another inspirational speech on the personal entrepreneurial progress and that of the race, after which Washington added, "You [Walker] talk about what the men are doing in a business way. Why, if we don't watch out, the women will excel us!" In fact, by 1915, Walker's female-dominated profession was so respected that the NNBL chose the "Beauty Parlor Business" as a major theme of its Sixteenth Annual Convention. Madam C. J. Walker's involvement demonstrates that black female entrepreneurs were at the forefront of the creation and evolution of the NNBL and that they understood that economic issues were important to the uplift of the race.

Studying black female beauty entrepreneurs in the golden age of black business not only compels a revision of black women's roles in the early formation of the black business community, but also a reconsideration of the very nature of black female organizing. Specifically, it demonstrates that ignoring the economic components of racial uplift greatly obscures much of what black women thought was important in the late nineteenth and early twentieth centuries. While a plethora of books and articles have focused on the black female club movement and the racial uplift programs they were involved in, few scholars have attempted to understand their economic- or business-driven activism. In fact, many beauty culturists were clubwomen actively involved in social reform. Tullia Brown Hamilton's dissertation provides biographical profiles of 108 women who were leaders in the National Association of Colored Women (NACW) from 1896 to 1920. Of the women profiled, 73 percent worked outside the home. Of these who worked outside the home, five women, Ezella Mathis Carter, Patricia Garland, Annie Turnbo Malone Pope, Maude Reynolds, and Madam C. J. Walker—were involved in the hair-care industry at some point in their lives. Examining the life of one of these women who was both an active clubwoman and a beautician will illustrate how her occupation as a beauty culturist and her activism complemented and even reinforced one another.

Ezella Mathis Carter was both the consummate clubwoman and an entrepreneur. Her life provides insight into how these seemingly incongruous worlds of business and social reform intersected one another. Her 1935 biography, written by Kathryn Johnson (who actually accompanied her on her journeys), sheds light on this historically obscure yet accomplished woman. While Johnson was more concerned with illuminating Carter's heroics than with providing the details that historians crave, the reader does manage to learn some aspects of Madam Carter's life. For example, Ezella Mathis was born in Girard, Alabama, and her family moved to Atlanta when she was one month old. Later in life, Carter earned money by teaching and eventually attended Spelman Seminary, where she specialized in

"Teachers' Professional and Missionary Training Courses." She graduated from Spelman in 1907 and subsequently went on to teach at Kowaliga Academic Institute, a school several miles from Booker T. Washinton's Tuskegee Institute.

Mathis's marriage in September 1909 to Mr. Carter (Johnson does not give any more information concerning her husband) "naturally changed her career." Shortly thereafter, she migrated to Chicago and studied to become a beauty culturist at the Enterprise Institute. Upon graduating, Carter received a certificate conferring the title of Madam, and opened up her own beauty shop where she taught the "art of hairdressing." Like the famous Madam C. J. Walker, Carter "experimented with various oils for the hair, and was finally successful in compounding her own hair preparations," which her biographer mentions were still in demand at the time the book was published in 1935.

Madam Carter merged the entrepreneurial with the philanthropic, a custom that beauty operators would adhere to throughout the twentieth century. Carter engaged in a door-to-door sales approach, entering black women's homes and teaching them how to care for their hair. She consciously sought out not only well-to-do women with disposable incomes, but poor ones as well:

> With her hair preparations, Mme. Carter began traveling and introducing them to the public and placing them on the market. She went back to her native Southland and into the far reaches of the rural sections, where she introduced her oils and taught the native backwoods woman, as well as the city woman, how to cultivate her hair, keep the scalp clean and healthful, and make the hair, which had been made harsh and brittle by exposure to the hot scorching, southern sun, soft and straight enough to be handled with ease.

Hair care and straightening were not linked to attaining whiteness but to cultivating healthy hair that had been damaged by the sun—an approach that would have resonated with women who spent a great deal of time outdoors doing harsh agricultural work. Madam Carter did more than sell products; she understood what she was doing as racial uplift work. Biographer Kathryn Johnson explains:

> She would go into the cabins, which probably had no more than two or three rooms; there she would heat water on the open fireplace, and with what conveniences she could find, shampoo the hair; then with infinite patience, apply the pressing oil; the straightening comb and the presser, and at the end of an hour and half or perhaps, two hours, she would be talking to the woman, giving her a lesson on how to improve her condition and her neighborhood.

Madam Carter seized the opportunity offered by entering black women's homes under the nonthreatening guise of selling beauty products, and used it to do race work. However, this aspect of racial uplift has not been addressed in the many books on the black woman's club movement.

The strategy used by Madam Carter, namely, meeting the needs of and administering to the poor within their homes, was a staple strategy of clubwomen in the early decades of the twentieth century. As a part of what they termed the "good" homes project, clubwomen targeted poor black women in their homes. Mary Church Terrell, the first president of the NACW, explained in a 1902 essay that it was only through the home: "that a people can become really good and great. More homes, better homes, purer homes is the text upon which sermons have and will be preached." Other clubwomen echoed the importance of the black household. "The Negro home," Josephine Bruce said, "is rapidly assuming the position designated for it. It is distinctly becoming the center of social and intellectual life; it is building up strength and righteousness in its sons and daughters, and equipping them for the inevitable battles of life which grow out of the struggle for existence." Paula Giddings accurately sums up what the home represented to black female reformers: "for these black women, the home was not so much a refuge from the outside world as a bulwark to secure one's passage through it."

Madam Carter clearly understood that the home was not only the site in which she could advance herself entrepreneurially but a place where she could act as a social reformer and establish herself as a true race woman. The NACW took notice of her abilities and named her the chair of the organization's Business Section. In addition, she also sponsored clubs on the local level. After training other women in the beauty trade and in their role as racial uplifters, Madam Carter gathered her sales agents into "Life Boat clubs," appropriately named since the clubs "were designed to save the people in the sections where [the agent] traveled." These clubs were educational, industrial, and benevolent in nature. They collected dues, distributed money to those who were ill, and in the event of death, provided funeral expenses. These Life Boat clubs were eventually incorporated under the laws of the State of Illinois and even became affiliated as an associate member of the National Council of Negro Women (NCNW). In 1927, the club expanded its mission and established a center for rural girls.

Carter's death in 1934 did not go unnoticed, as she was fondly remembered by Florence Read, President of Spelman College, and R. R. Moton, President of Tuskeegee Institute, and eulogized by Gwendolyn Brooks in a poem entitled "A Chicago High School Girl." Still, despite all of Madam Carter's accomplishments she has fallen into historical obscurity, and when she is remembered at all, it is for her work as a clubwoman and not for her entrepreneurial savvy. Carter is such a historical enigma, perhaps, because she did not fit neatly into categories. She was at once the consummate twentieth-century clubwoman, claiming moral and intellectual superiority over the women she wished to help, a role that an elite black woman was expected to fulfill. Yet she was also an astute businesswoman who studied Business Management at the LaSalle Extension University and traveled extensively teaching sales agents her system. More important, she exploited an underserved consumer—the rural black woman. These two ventures, beauty work and race work, while intelligently synergized by Carter, had a very complicated relationship in the early twentieth century. Although many clubwomen supported black women as entrepreneurs, some found the beauty business problematic and harmful to black women. In other words, beauty culturists not only had to establish themselves within a male-dominated black business community that was often less than welcoming, but also had to try and gain acceptance from many black elite clubwomen who felt threatened by their success.

Nannie Helen Burroughs, a clubwoman who founded the National Training School for Girls and Women to prepare and professionalize domestic workers, boldly and repeatedly expressed her disdain for the beauty industry as a whole, and asked: "What does this wholesale bleaching of the face and straightening of hair indicate? From our viewpoint, it simply means that the women who practice it wish that they had white faces and straight hair." However, most of the successful and established black female beauty manufacturers, such as Madam C. J. Walker and Annie Turnbo Malone, refused to sell skin-bleaching products and insisted that their hair systems were more about hair care, good grooming, and enhancing the beauty of black women, rather than hair-straightening and emulating white women. In fact, Noliwe Rooks explains that: "Walker did not argue that there was nothing wrong with African American women straightening their hair; she flat out denied that hair straightening was what she had to offer." In an examination of the advertisements of black-owned beauty manufacturers, Rooks finds that hairdressing was linked to racial uplift and an improvement in status. Black female beauty entrepreneurs, through their advertisements, emphasized cultivating, as opposed to creating, the beauty of black women that had been hidden due to poor health and historical and social denigration. For example, Rooks argues that white manufacturers of beauty products in the antebellum period were "driven primarily by popular ideas about race" that presented black women as "'suffering' from an African heritage and searching for the 'cure' that whiteness can offer." On the other hand, in the advertisements of African-American entrepreneurs, women were urged to strive for healthy hair. One advertisement declared that a particular treatment would: "cultivate, beautify and grow a person's hair, so long as there is no physical ailment which will prevent it." These black female manufacturers understood beauty work to be as much race work as the social programs of Nannie Helen Burroughs, Mary Church Terrell, and the other women of the NACW—even if it was not always regarded that way.

Although many beauty culturists joined the NACW, they understood that the manner in which they approached racial uplift set them apart from many clubwomen. To that end, beauty culturists organized on their behalf. Among the most influential organizations were those formed by Madam Walker, namely the Madam C. J. Walker Hair Culturists Union of America, founded in Philadelphia in 1917, and the National Negro Cosmetic Manufacturers Association, also founded in 1917. Darlene Clark Hine says of Walker's Hair Culturists Union:

> The national conventions honored and granted cash prizes to the clubs and individuals that had the largest number of agents, the greatest sales volume, and the most outstanding record of benevolent work. The conventions cemented a sense of community, promoted professionalism, and enabled black women to engage in political discussions even though they could not yet vote. The politicization of black beauty culturists was quickly manifested.

These organizations also had very practical functions pertaining specifically to the beauty industry. The charter of the National Negro Cosmetic Manufacturers Association stated that its founder members had formed the association in order to better protect themselves against the "dishonest and illegitimate" manufacturers of hair goods and to "promote the spirit of business reciprocity among ourselves, to encourage the development of Race enterprises and acquaint the public with the superior claims of high class goods. . . ." Similarly, in 1919 a group of beauticians formed the National Beauty Culturists League (NBCL), which soon was the first predominately female organization to become a part of the NNBL in 1921 and the largest organization in the black beauty industry. The organizers saw a need for beauticians to "encourage constant improvements as good citizens by participating in civic and community work, [to] seek legislation beneficial to the beauty profession" and "to promote the general welfare and raise the public image of those engaged in the beauty culture field."

For the NBCL, raising the public image of beauty culturists was paramount. Even though most beauty culturists did not become as wealthy as Madam Walker, professionally they considered their status to be among the best women of the race. In many ways, the beauty industry compromised the position of elite blacks whose uplift ideology and belief in the rule of the Talented Tenth became increasingly irrelevant to the lives of many blacks as the century progressed. By the late 1920s, black female organizations like the NACW faced a decline in popularity and in power. However, the female presence in the beauty industry and the organizational power they created lasted much longer and had a much wider appeal than any of the "woman's era" clubs. Indeed, as elite blacks began losing their prominence in the black community and were unable to hold rank based on color, education, and the financial security that such advantages afforded them, the hair-care industry and, to a large extent, beauty parlors became sites where tensions over class, color, and status were exacerbated. Although Madam C. J. Walker died in 1919, the fact that a dark-skinned, uneducated former laundress could not only make a fortune in this industry but in the process empower thousands of other women to believe that they could be considered the best women of the race posed a threat to elite black women.

Alice Dunbar-Nelson, poet and clubwoman, publicly and privately voiced her discomfort with the opportunities and attitudes of black beauty culturists. Kevin Gaines's examination of Dunbar-Nelson's life, as well as her posthumously published diary and writings, further illuminates the contradictory life of a woman who was quite conscious of issues of color, status, and class. In a 1928 *Washington Eagle* article, Dunbar-Nelson complained that: "women [working] in beauty parlors drag their social ambitions into their commercial life. A woman or girl from a class which they feel is superior socially to their own gets short shrift, poor service, and insulting discrimination."

Gaines notes that women were more vulnerable to distinctions made over issues of class and color, and makes a fascinating assessment of Dunbar-Nelson's encounter in the beauty salons, arguing that "the beauty parlor . . . is revealed here as a site of class conflict among black women." The perceived disrespect by beauty operators was such a problem for Alice Dunbar-Nelson that three years later, this self-proclaimed race woman stopped patronizing black-owned salons altogether. She recounted in her diary:

> I had made engagement to have waved at a beauty parlor at Ninth and King [Wilmington, Delaware]. Didn't know whether I'd "get by" [not be challenged because of race], but evidentially did. Nice wave. Nice place. Nice girls. Beauty problem solved.

In other words, the beauty salon provided a space where black women of different classes and hues congregated and often conflicted. Relationships between and among customers, as well as those between beautician and client, could foster a sense of community or exacerbate existing tensions.

Harlem in the first three decades of the century was at the center of the most volatile issues confronting the black community—namely, class and gender conflict and ideas about politics and leadership. This stretch of blocks in New York City also housed many black beauty salons, and "among the persons of wealth and social influence in Harlem were the community's great beauticians." In 1911, a black woman named Madam J. L. Crawford, originally from Virginia and educated at the New York School of Chiropody and Dermatology, opened one of Harlem's first beauty shops. Despite her training in the medical field, Crawford decided that the business world offered her the greatest possibilities. Starting in 1901, Crawford worked as an "itinerant hairdresser" in the Mt. Vernon section of New York for a white and black clientele. There, she also began manufacturing cosmetics, hair pomades, wigs, and toupees. By 1908, Madam Crawford owned and operated a beauty shop at 341 West 59th Street in Midtown Manhattan that exclusively served black customers. According to a report on "Negro Beauty Parlors in New York" compiled by the WPA in 1936, Crawford's combination dry goods store and beauty parlor "was the first Negro establishment of its kind in New York City."

Few in those early years would have predicted the success achieved by Crawford and the other black female beauticians who would follow in her footsteps. Harlem, in fact, became such a thriving place for the black beauty industry that Madam C. J. Walker decided to settle there in 1914. Already a woman of considerable wealth by this time, Walker, along with her daughter A'Leila, who would become one of the leading figures in the social life of blacks during the Harlem Renaissance, established not only a beauty parlor in Harlem, but also Leila College, the Walker Company's beauty school.

One of the first graduates of Leila College was Lucille Green. Described as a light woman of medium height and build with a head of short cropped hair, Green was born Lucille Campbell in Christianburg, Virginia in 1883. She attended Howard University, where she studied to become a schoolteacher and met and married Joseph Green, who died shortly after the couple moved to New York City. Lucille Green gave up schoolteaching upon the death of her husband and enrolled in Leila Beauty College. After graduating, Green "not only started her own salon on 135th Street, but also became a close friend of Madam Walker and a member of the 'society' that grew up around her in Harlem." It was during her trips back and forth to her hair salon on 135th Street and Lenox Avenue (which just happened to be down the corridor from Ernest Welcome, who in 1914 was the head of the Brotherhood of Labor), that Ms. Green caught the attention of twenty-five-year-old Asa Philip Randolph. Randolph's biographer Jervis Anderson describes their subsequent courtship as "brief and unspectacular," stating that Philip took Lucille to stage shows, movies, and of course political lectures. Anderson also explains that Mr. Randolph was not very fond of parties or dances, and that when Lucille invited him to Madam Walker's soirees, he declined and said that he did not have time to waste on "fly-by-night people."

However, even if A. Philip Randolph did not claim to be impressed with Madam Walker's parties and her cohort of "successful speculators of recent vintage, community clubwomen, new urban professionals, and other parvenu varieties," he certainly learned to respect the lucrativeness of the hair-care industry. In fact, it was the marriage of the "socialist and the socialite" in 1914 that made A. Philip Randolph's career and political activism possible. The new Mrs. Randolph joined the socialist party shortly after the marriage, and as a couple they committed themselves to political activism.

"I had a good wife. She carried us," A. Philip Randolph says of Lucille's financial backing of his socialist newspaper *The Messenger*. Lucille Randolph distributed the paper from her salon and periodically used her earnings to pay its debts. In 1919, the Justice Department described *The Messenger* as "by long odds the most dangerous of all the Negro publications," and when eulogizing Mrs. Randolph, a columnist for the *New York Post* later wrote:

> Lucille Greene Randolph seems entitled to the honor of being called the one time second most dangerous Negro in America. The title would certainly have once been official if the agents of the U.S. Justice Department had had the initiative and wit to intercept her postal money orders which helped support A. Philip Randolph's subversive activities.

When A. Philip Randolph was asked to organize the Brotherhood of Sleeping Car Porters (BSCP) in 1925, he discussed the job with Lucille, who enthusiastically supported his decision to assist the then-fledgling union. Her financial support became even more crucial while her husband held this post, since Philip did not receive a regular salary from the organization until 1936. She also persuaded her friend and colleague, A'Leila Walker (heir to the hair-care empire), to donate money to the BSCP, as well as organized other Walker salon operators to contribute money and prizes for the beauty contests that the Brotherhood held.

Mrs. Randolph's support of her husband was not only financial but social as well. Through her contacts, he met wealthy African Americans and prominent left-wing whites who added prestige to his political pursuits. She was also the one to introduce Philip to Chandler Owen—the person with whom he partnered at the Brotherhood. Clearly Lucille's relationship to her husband is an important area to study, but her accomplishment as a hairdresser and salon owner in Harlem should be explored in its own right. Jervis Anderson explains:

> Lucille became one of the more accomplished and sought after of the Walker students. Her customers ranged from the black elite in Harlem to well-to-do crinkly haired whites from "downtown." And one day a week she traveled out to the fashionable Marlborough Blenheim Hotel in Atlantic City, to serve a similar white clientele. Her prices seem to have been high, and brought her a considerable income.

However, Anderson argues that as Philip's reputation as a "wild-eyed radical" spread, Lucille's business declined, and by the 1930s she was no longer successful. On the other hand, in her dissertation on beauty culture, Gwendolyn Keita Robinson argues that: "nationalism, radicalism, and high classed life styles were often fused in those days. . . . Lucille, though a socialite, ran for the New York City Board of Alderman on the Socialist Party ticket in the 1930s, while at the same time, maintaining her beauty salon, without suffering any apparent pangs of contradiction."

In fact, Lucille Randolph's business problems in the 1930s probably derived less from her husband's reputation and more from the fact that the beauty industry, like most businesses, suffered during the Great Depression; in other words, the Depression brought the golden age of black business to an end. Labor historian Jacqueline Jones argues that during the Depression a personal beauty regimen had become too expensive for many black working women and that beauty operators were forced to lower their prices and even barter their services for food and clothing. A study of employment conditions of black- and white-owned beauty shops in four cities published by the U.S. Department of Labor in 1935 determined that:

> Wage reductions and lessened work opportunities in the last few years, resulting in curtailed purchasing power of the Negro Worker, have had a marked effect in reducing the number and activities of Negro shops. Hair pressing, previously indulged by many Negroes, especially by domestic workers, had by 1934 become a luxury to large numbers, even though prices in many shops had been materially reduced.

In 1938, the periodical *Opportunity* published a piece by Le Roy Jeffries, entitled "The Decay of the Beauty Parlor Industry in Harlem," where he described a dismal picture for black female beauticians. Jeffries explained that from February to June 1936 he made an "intensive survey of the conditions of beauty parlors in the Harlem area." Based on these findings, he felt qualified to declare that: "the road to fortune which was once open to beauty culture workers in the Harlem area has definitely curved into a dead end." He further noted that the New York State Department of Labor recently became interested in the plight of the black female beautician, and demonstrated that not only were most of the beauty operators in Harlem unlicensed but they also were not benefiting from the legislative enactments that came as a result of the New Deal:

> They are without workman's compensation, therefore may not be compensated for accidents incurred during the course of their employment; they are without the protective covering of unemployment insurance designed to offer some income for periods of unemployment; they will not be included among those who are guaranteed a minimum wage.

Despite the reality Jeffries described, there remained a great deal of optimism surrounding the black beauty industry, primarily because beauty operators fared better financially than their sisters employed as agricultural workers and domestics, whose already dubious financial stability the Depression worsened. For example, Sara Spencer Washington, founder of the Apex Beauty System, urged black women to enroll in her beauty school and "plan for [their] future by learning a depression-proof business." Similarly, the inability of black women to pay for hair-care services did not mean that beauty parlors lost their presence as a gathering place for black women. Elizabeth Cardozo Barker, the founder of the extremely successful Cardozo Sisters Beauty Shop in Washington, D.C., recalled that during the Great Depression, in the establishment where she first learned hair work, customers would come and sit in the beauty parlor "for hours, sometimes. They'd play cards; sometimes they'd gossip . . . they just came expecting to sit." In addition, the beauty industry, with its practice of door-to-door sales, hairstyling in one's home, and even styling in a salon became an integral part of black women's development of a leisure culture that was in many ways dependent upon traditional modes of black female gathering.

Historian Kathy Peiss describes these shifts in the black beauty industry and adds that during the Depression there was also a noticeable change in the marketing strategies of beauty manufacturers, as well as in the political nature of their beauty work. Before the 1930s in the periodicals produced by black hair-care companies: "beauty columns ran alongside stories on politics and notable African Americans; by the mid-thirties, these had disappeared, replaced by articles on romance, marriage, and the psychological effects of beautifying." Advertisements also began centering black women's identity on achieving beauty to attract men as opposed to enhancing beauty for self-worth.

In other words, Peiss argues that the "commercial images" portrayed by the beauty business during this period were much more depoliticized than previously, even though she acknowledges that beauty salons as sites involved themselves in civic matters and "endured as vibrant sources of economic, social and even political strength in black communities." Her elucidation of this shift is compelling; however, in addition to illuminating the way the manufacturing and commercial components of the beauty industry moved away from politics, I posit that it is important to examine the significance of beauty parlors as "political outposts" and hair-care workers as beauty activists. In the post-Depression era, black beauticians were once again at the forefront of expanding the very nature of business and the role of an entrepreneur. The beauty activists who came of age in this era inherited the political and philanthropic traditions of Madams Walker and Carter but modified them to meet the changing needs of their communities. In fact, for beauticians such as Rose Morgan, Ella Mae Martin, and Bernice Robinson, the hair-care industry in the post-Depression era represented endless possibilities, both entrepreneurial and political.

The Emergence of the Beauty Activist

The issue of state licensing, unimportant in the earlier decades, was one that was foremost in the minds of beauty culturists across the country in the 1930s and 1940s. Despite the fact that the New Deal era signaled the entrance of social legislation designed to protect workers from the perils of unfair labor practices, black women's work in the beauty industry, like their work in domestic labor and agriculture, remained unprotected for many years. Still, beauticians, both salon owners and employees, understood that their industry should benefit from government protection and representation on labor boards as well. Once beauty culturists realized that the government was not immediately willing to assist them in their profession, they relied upon a strategy that had served them well in the past—they organized on their own behalf. The National Beauty Culturists' League (NBCL) by the 1940s began pushing for better state regulation of beauty culture and "spearheaded the fight to eliminate segregation because of race on boards of beauty control, state beauty inspectors, and examiners."

New York, with its precedent of poor conditions in beauty salons, waited until the late 1940s to address the inequities in the beauty industry. In 1947, the New York

State Department of Labor convened the Beauty Service Minimum Wage Board to make recommendations to the Industrial Commissioner. Not only was this board groundbreaking in its attempt to examine the beauty industry thoroughly, but it also included "the first Negro beauty shop owner to hold membership on a New York State Wage Board." This board member was Rose Morgan, who in 1947 was one of the three employer members of the Wage Board. According to the report, Morgan's nomination: "for a place on the Wage Board, whose recommendations will affect the interests of some 12,500 workers in the industry throughout the state, was sponsored by the Manhattan Beauty Shop Owners Association of which she is a member." Rose Morgan's life, both personal and professional, offers insights into the role of beauty culturists from the 1930s to the 1960s.

Rose Morgan was an entrepreneur and philanthropist who likely would have been forgotten had the Schomburg Center for Research in Black Culture not decided to conduct a videotaped interview of her in 1988. James Briggs Murray interviewed an elderly but elegant Morgan at the Rose Morgan House of Beauty, 251 Adam Clayton Powell Boulevard in Harlem. Ironically, the perfectly coifed, sophisticated, elderly woman with the conservative mauve suit on the videotape was once incorrectly referred to by a magazine as a "plain Jane from Shelby, Mississippi." Morgan admitted that she had come a long way and was not embarrassed by her humble beginnings. Morgan was born in Edwards, Mississippi in 1912, moved to Shelby with her family when she was two years old, and remained there until she was six. In the interview, Morgan spoke fondly of her early years in Mississippi, where her father rented land on a cotton plantation and where the family—including her eight siblings—worked as sharecroppers. When Morgan was six years old, her family migrated north to Chicago, where her father embarked on a career in the hotel business.

Morgan admired her father's business initiative and says that he inspired her to begin her first informal business; she made and sold cut paper flowers door-to-door at the age of ten. At the age of twelve Morgan began experimenting with the profession that would ultimately bring her success—hairdressing—and began pressing hair informally for small wages. During this taped interview over fifty years later, Morgan admitted that she "never wanted to do anything but hair." Still, like most black women in that era, she was forced to drop out of school at sixteen to enter the workforce, and took a job shaking sheets in a laundry. The work was difficult, and young Rose knew immediately that this was not the path she wanted her life to take. She then decided to do hair full-time and began working in a salon as an apprentice while also styling hair out of her home.

In 1930, Morgan enrolled in Marcy's Beauty Academy to learn the scientific aspects of hair care in order to take the Illinois state board exams. She began meeting "theater people" and eventually ended up doing actress and singer Ethel Walter's hair at the Capitol Theater. A friend and fellow manicurist then suggested that Morgan come to New York City and pursue her cosmetology career there.

Harlem's "Sugar Hill" community of black elites proved to be the source of Morgan's success, and she remained there for over four decades. By 1946, after a failed partnership with Emmeta Hurley, sister of the owners of the Cardozo Sisters House of Beauty in Washington, D.C., and a performer in the Ziegfeld Follies,

Morgan became co-owner of the Rose-Meta House of Beauty, Inc. with Olivia Clarke. The salon boasted a clientele of luminaries such as dancer Katherine Dunham and Eslanda Robeson, the wife of Paul Robeson. Billed by *Ebony* magazine as the "biggest Negro beauty parlor in the world," the salon was located in a five-story brownstone at 148th Street and St. Nicholas Avenue, complete with twenty hair operators, three licensed masseurs, a registered nurse, and a full-service cafeteria. In 1955, Morgan withdrew from managing this salon and built a $225,000 enterprise with a surprisingly interracial staff of 80 beauty operators, complete with a children's department, a hat and clothes designer, a charm school, and a cosmetic and accessory counter. A young customer summed it up best when she said, "this place is the end. Under one roof it has everything a woman needs to get re-styled, upholstered and reconditioned."

When asked if communication and information was shared in her salons, Rose Morgan explained that her "girls" were not allowed to talk to customers beyond hair issues. She did not want her salon to be a "gossipy place." Still, while Morgan did not want the public sphere to enter her salon, she engaged in many public and philanthropic activities. She had a strong presence on the NYS Labor Board, was instrumental in raising the minimum wage for beauticians from $16 to $25 per week, and continued to lobby on the state level thereafter. In addition, Morgan worked on behalf of Nelson Rockefeller, Robert Kennedy, and Congressman Charles Rangel, and received an honorary degree from Shaw University for her many years of service to the black community.

Other contemporaries of Morgan—especially those in the South—were much more controversial in using their positions as beauticians within their communities as well as the use of their salons as public spaces. On an organizational level, they made a bold entrance into the public sphere as well. In 1952, the activities of the NBCL even captured the attention of the National Association for the Advancement of Colored People's (NAACP) executive secretary Walter White, who joined the organization for a pilgrimage to the grave of Madam C. J. Walker. Five years later, in 1957, the guest of honor at their annual convention was Dr. Martin Luther King. The leadership of the NBCL also initiated a voting campaign that year, commanding the members to make use of their right to vote:

> We have a distinguished right, as American citizens. Make use of our right to vote. Don't be denied of these rights. . . . You have seen Southern Senators in their last ditch fight to defeat President Eisenhower's Civil Rights Legislation. They have attacked bitterly every bill that would tend to free people of color in our shops and schools and we should interest ourselves enough to see to it that every customer, every student that goes in and out of our doors, are taking an active part in their city, state, and national government.

The then-president of the NBCL was Katie Whickham, who, as civil rights activist Ella Baker announced in a 1959 newsletter of the Southern Christian Leadership Conference (SCLC), was elected as the first female staff officer of SCLC:

> We believe that Mrs. Whickham will bring new strength to our efforts. The National Beauty Culturists's League, Inc., of which she is president, has strong local and state units throughout the South and voter registration is a major emphasis to its program.

In other words, while the activism of beauticians, both through their powerful national organization and through their strong presence on the local level, might be lost on historians of the modern Civil Rights movement, it was plainly evident to their contemporaries, who were aware of the strategic power of beauticians as "bridge leaders" in their communities.

Many beauty culturists heeded the call of the NBCL and continued this activism in their local communities. Those living in the South were especially active even though they must have been aware that the appeal broadcast by the NBCL was directed more at Northern beauticians who at least had the opportunity to vote. Instead, beauticians in the Jim Crow South had to deal with more immediate concerns surrounding the right to vote. Ella Martin, president of the Georgia State Beauty Culturists' League from 1946–1968, explains the situation in Atlanta:

> We would encourage the people. Some beauty shops we would use for the people to register to vote, to get them interested in voting and get them registered, and after getting them registered, to try our best to get them to go the polls, educate them to go to the polls to vote.

Martin's words show the extent to which beauticians were involved in political activism and thereby transformed their salons into the sole entrepreneurial and institutional spaces in the black community that were within the control and under the leadership of black women.

The life of Bernice Robinson demonstrates that beauty work was not only a key economic skill but a politically valuable one as well. Born in Charleston, South Carolina, in February 1914, the child of a bricklayer and a homemaker/seamstress, Robinson was raised to be self-reliant and specifically taught to avoid dependence on the white community. After completing high school (where she studied cooking, sewing, laundering, and piano), she, like many Southern blacks in the first three decades of the twentieth century, migrated north to New York City. There she lived with her sister and worked in the garment industry. However, according to Robinson, she found it necessary to return periodically to South Carolina and work as a domestic, for employment in the garment industry was not steady.

In her estimation, Robinson finally followed the advice of her parents to become economically self-sufficient by entering beauty school and becoming a beautician in the service of black women. With a friend in 1937, she opened a beauty shop in Harlem on 145th Street between Convent and Amsterdam Avenues. Robinson originally worked there part-time on the weekends but had so many customers after just three weeks that she then became a full-time beautician, often working eighteen hours a day. Still, once World War II began and government jobs slowly began opening up to black women, Bernice followed her sister to Philadelphia, passed the civil service exam, and secured a job with the Philadelphia Signal Corps. However, she later returned to New York, where she again passed a civil service exam and worked for the Internal Revenue Service and the Veterans Administration. In 1947, Robinson moved back to Charleston, planning to stay for only a few days to care for her ailing parents but actually remaining there until the 1990s.

Harsh segregation, voter discrimination, and poor employment prospects caused Robinson to become disappointed with Charleston and fueled her subsequent political involvement. After being repeatedly rejected for government jobs despite passing the civil service exam yet again in South Carolina and having extensive experience in New York and Philadelphia, she turned to the profession that had previously served her well, beauty work.

By 1952, Robinson had become involved with the NAACP while engaged in beauty work out of her home. Robinson admits: "It got to the point where we were working so hard getting people to register to vote that I would leave people under the dryer to take others down to the registration office to get them registered." In addition, Robinson was also instrumental in the growth of the NAACP's Charleston chapter. She encouraged her customers to join the organization, recognizing that her position as a beautician gave her freedom to engage in political activities that many other blacks did not have. Robinson explained:

> I didn't have to worry about losing my job or anything because I wasn't a schoolteacher or a caseworker with the Department of Social Services or connected with anything I might be fired from. I had my own business, supplied by black supply houses, so I didn't have to worry.

Her Charleston beauty shop became a "center for all sorts of subversive activity where many of her customers had their membership and any mail from the NAACP sent."

Robinson had firsthand knowledge of the peril of joining the NAACP when one was dependent upon whites for one's employment. In 1955, her first cousin Septima Clark lost her job as a public schoolteacher simply because she refused to renounce her membership in the NAACP. After her dismissal, Myles Horton, the founder of the Highlander Folk School based in Tennessee, approached Clark to direct a workshop to enlighten middle-class blacks about the work being done at Highlander. Myles Horton had opened the Highlander School in 1932 with the intention of educating "rural and industrial leaders for a new social order." After two decades working primarily in the labor movement, in 1953 the Highlander staff launched a series of workshops that focused on community desegregation. In 1957, with the assistance of Septima Clark, a Citizenship School project developed on the South Carolina Sea Islands. The primary goal was to teach black adults to read and write to prepare them to register to vote. Clark immediately thought of her cousin Bernice to run the first school that was established on Johns Island.

When asked to become the first teacher for Highlander's citizenship education program in the South Carolina Sea Islands, Robinson was surprised, for she had neither experience as a teacher nor a college education. This did not present a problem for Highlander's leadership—their main concern was that the islanders would have a teacher they could trust and who would respect them. Myles Horton articulated the strategic importance of beauticians to the success of his program and explained in his autobiography why he chose Robinson:

> Bernice was a black beautician. Compared to white beauticians, black beauticians had status in their own community. They had a higher-than-average education and, because they owned their own business, didn't depend upon whites for their incomes.

This advertisement from Madam C. J. Walker's company touts the benefits of her patented hair "grower" and the advantages of a career as a beauty culturist. Through ads like these, Walker recruited a national corps of agents who sold her products door-to-door to African American women who desired modern cosmetics and hair care products. This business model made her wealthy while also allowing thousands of local women to become entrepreneurs without a large capital investment.

We needed to build around black people who could stand up against white opposition, so black beauticians were very important.

On January 7, 1957, Robinson stood before her first class on Johns Island and quickly developed teaching methods that were so successful that by February of the next year, all of the voting-age adults with at least five months of classes were able to read the required paragraph in the state constitution and sign their names in order to receive their voter registration certificates. Horton acknowledged that more than anyone, Robinson "developed the methods used by the Citizenship Schools."

Robinson was not the only beautician involved in the Highlander Citizenship schools. Witnessing the success of the Johns Island school, hairdresser Marylee Davis of North Charleston asked for help in starting a school on Wadmalaw Island and offered her beauty parlor as a meeting place for adult literacy classes. Horton began to realize that many of the people most involved with Highlander were beauticians, and began running workshops specifically to enhance their leadership skills. While most people thought he was gathering them for vocational purposes, Horton explained:

> They thought that I was bringing these beauticians together to talk about straightening hair or whatever the hell they do, [but] I was just using them because they were community leaders and they were independent. . . . We used beauticians' shops all over the South to distribute Highlander literature on integration.

In many ways, Myles Horton's statement illuminates the key issues surrounding the unique ways beauty culturists throughout the twentieth century merged business with racial uplift and politics. He understood that members of their communities perceived them as community leaders and that their complicated status and class position placed them in an ideal situation for cultivating leadership. Beauty culturists, for the most part, were highly regarded in their communities and strove to be among the best women of the race. However, because of segregation and their indebtedness to the black community for a client base, beauty culturists were never removed from their respective communities. However, that is not to say that beauty parlors were homogenous utopias. Alice Dunbar-Nelson's experience is a reminder of the ways beauty salons policed race, class, color, and respectability.

Secondly, Horton's observations also point to the independence that black female beauticians had relative to other blacks—especially black women—whose occupations were usually under the watchful eyes of whites. Throughout the years this study treats, black women primarily worked as domestics, doing work that was often isolating and constantly supervised, clearly not offering a site to organize collective resistance. Even black professional women such as schoolteachers within segregated school systems faced constraints due to their dependence upon white-run school boards and city councils. Beauticians worked within black female-owned establishments, supplied by black manufacturers, patronized by black female clients, within segregated communities.

While Horton appreciated the work of beauticians in providing leadership, he was perhaps most thankful that these women had access to "free spaces." In fact, he utilized beauty salons as black-owned institutional spaces, similar to the black church. However, what is even more compelling about these spaces is that they were often hidden and even subversive. Even beauty culturists like Ezella Mathis Carter and the many Walker sales agents who used door-to-door sales created a hidden space within the home where they could engage in racial uplift work.

In many ways, like Myles Horton, this essay confirms that the hair-care industry in general and the black beauty parlor in particular should be examined as an important, albeit unique, institution in the black community, a space that was at once public and private, where the matrix of beauty, business, and politics allowed black women actively to confront the issues of their day. This journey through the first six decades of the twentieth century, with beauty culturists as our guides, provides a telling example of the need for historians to examine hidden spaces in order to unearth the ways black women created a political voice for themselves and their communities. Willie Coleman wrote in a 1983 poem that "beauty shops could have been a hell-of-a-place to ferment a . . . . revolution." As the beauty culturists in this essay demonstrate, they were.

Questions for Study and Review

1. Compare the work experiences and social networks in garment factories and beauty shops.

2. How did work in beauty culture differ from the jobs held by most African American women?

3. Why was beauty culture work so closely tied to political activism among African American women?

4. How might African American women who testified following the Memphis Riot of 1866 have viewed the black beauty culture industry that arose in the early twentieth century?

Suggested Readings and Web Sites

A'Lelia Perry Bundles, *On Her Own Ground: The Life and Times of Madam C. J. Walker* (2001)
Kathy Peiss, *Hope in a Jar: The Making of America's Beauty Culture* (1998)
Noliwe M. Rooks, *Hair Raising: Beauty, Culture and African American Women* (1996)
Stephanie Shaw, *What a Woman Ought to Be and to Do* (1996)
Julie Willett, *Permanent Waves: The Making of the American Beauty Shop* (2000)
Madame C. J. Walker's Career
    http://www.madamecjwalker.com/
Harlem 1900–1940: An African-American Community
    http://www.si.umich.edu/CHICO/Harlem/

Chapter 6

With the passage of the Nineteenth Amendment in 1920, the seventy-two-year campaign for women's suffrage came to an end. The ratification of this constitutional amendment guaranteeing full political citizenship for American women was a heady moment for female activists, who predicted a wave of female-driven legislation that would remake society. More pessimistic were African American women, who knew that Jim Crow laws would prevent most of them from exercising their political rights in the South. But all American women would soon discover that this much-anticipated measure did not open a new era of equality for women. Instead, female enfranchisement ushered in a period of diminishing political influence for women and a renewed emphasis on their domestic and maternal responsibilities.

The previous thirty years had been something of a "golden age" for women's activism, a period of female political influence still unmatched in American history. As Sklar, Orleck, and Gill have shown in Chapters Two, Three and Five, women from diverse backgrounds organized in these years to improve their own lives and those of their families and communities. Women from all backgrounds created institutions devoted to social reform, training cadres of women who became skilled political operatives and built female political subcultures. These efforts helped women gain public authority, especially on issues pertaining to women and children. Justifying much of this activism through their roles as "civic housekeepers," female activists broadened the definition of politics and initiated social, legal, and political changes on street corners and factory floors as well as in beauty shops and settlement houses. Though most of these women were far removed from voting booths or legislative chambers, they changed the way Americans thought about government, social responsibility, and economics.

Yet once women were armed with the vote, their influence actually ebbed. Women activists spent their first decade of enfranchisement battling one another, divided by concerns about the connections between activism, reform, and revolution. Hundreds of thousands of women joined conservative and far-right organizations in the 1920s. These groups were energized by concerns about immigration and radicalism, especially after the 1917 Russian Revolution sparked fears that the U.S. Communist Party might instigate a similar uprising in the United States. Political anxieties were reinforced by the changes occurring in urban dance halls, black beauty parlors, and other havens of cultural ferment. In response, some conservative women who had been active earlier in the anti-suffrage campaign, the crusade for Prohibition, women's clubs, and other voluntary organizations now joined groups driven by anti-communism, xenophobia, and old-fashioned sexual morality. Though these women, too, launched public political campaigns, they did so in the name of returning women to their "traditional" roles in the home and family.

The largest of these organizations was the Ku Klux Klan, which re-emerged in the 1920s and attracted six million men, women, and children. Already notorious for its violence against African Americans, the group now dedicated itself to a broad spectrum of racial and religious bigotry, targeting Catholics, Jews, and labor radicals as well as blacks. The first Ku Klux Klan launched a reign of racial terror that gripped the southern United States during and following Reconstruction. In the 1920s, however, the KKK was hardly confined to the South; the women Kathleen Blee examines in this chapter lived in Indiana. There, 250,000 women, 32 percent of the state's white native-born female population, joined the Women's Ku Klux Klan.

The KKK of the 1920s distinguished itself from its predecessors by heavily recruiting women, recognizing that they had the power to bring their entire family into the organization's fold. The organization cultivated women's loyalty through anti-vice campaigns, the enforcement of Prohibition, and the punishment of abusive or adulterous husbands. The WKKK suffused every aspect of life for these white, Protestant, native-born women who created Klan rituals to mark birth, marriage, and death. While the beauty operators described by Gill in Chapter Five saw the WKKK as a vicious race hate group, its members saw it as a way to enhance their friendship and solidarity among like-minded women, in much the same way that Orleck's labor activists viewed union militancy.

Blee shows that WKKK members combined race hatred with a desire for enhanced rights for white women in their families and communities. At the same time, these women understood their activism as a direct outgrowth of the suffrage campaign, which in many parts of the nation had played on nativist themes to win converts. These white supremacists illuminate the complex meanings of female enfranchisement, which they understood as a mandate for political activism in the service of race hatred rather than as a tool to achieve social justice.

Women and the Ku Klux Klan: Klan Women in Indiana in the 1920s

KATHLEEN BLEE

In 1920, women won the right to vote, culminating a seventy-two-year struggle for greater access to the political sphere. Yet, women's politics changed in another way in the 1920s. When women gained the franchise, the issue that had united women with different backgrounds and politics disappeared. Women's political goals and ideologies had grown more diverse even before the ratification of the Nineteenth

Kathleen M. Blee, "Women in the 1920s' Ku Klux Klan Movement" was originially published in *Feminist Studies*, Volume 17, Number 1 (1991): 57–77. Reprinted by permission of the publisher, *Feminist Studies, Inc.*

White women used the rituals and regalia of the Ku Klux Klan to deepen community solidarity in Indiana in the 1920s. Legendary for its violent support of white supremacy, the Klan is remembered as a terrorist organization that targeted immigrants, Catholics, Jews, and African Americans. Smiling women like these presented a different face for the organization. Women members were more likely to see the group as a way to bring like-minded neighbors together in an effort to enforce community moral standards.

Amendment as the separate gender spheres of the nineteenth century dissolved. The extent of this diversity became even more clear without the unifying cause of suffrage. Cleavages of class, race, ethnicity, and region, constant features of women's politics in the United States, now increasingly eroded gender unity in political goals.

The ways in which women became involved in postsuffrage politics were etched in the struggle for the franchise. Ideas born in the battle for the Nineteenth Amendment affected not only the activists but also their descendants and women who had refrained from politics. One outcome—the one most familiar in the popular imagery of the postsuffrage period—was the participation of women in progressive reform movements. Women whose belief in equality was nourished in the drive for the franchise found a logical extension of their suffrage politics in movements for social and urban reform. Women's votes supported candidates who favored maternity and infancy protection and opposed lynching and child labor. Female reformers of the 1920s led the fight for better schools, cleaner cities, more equitable labor relations, and honest politics. Another outcome of the franchise, however, was the involvement of postsuffrage women in reactionary and right-wing political movements. If most women worked for, or were influenced by, the fight for women's suffrage because of its emphasis on political equity, a significant minority found in the quest for votes for women an opportunity to solidify the political power of whites and native-born citizens. These women envisioned political equity between women and men as an issue relevant only within dominant racial and ethnic groups, as seen, for example, in campaigns to extend the franchise to white women. Such racist and anti-immigrant tendencies within the movement for women's suffrage shared aspects of the political vision of nationalistic, militaristic, and racial supremacist movements in the 1910s and 1920s. Women who interpreted the struggle for women's votes through the prism of racial, ethnic, and class privilege thus experienced an apparently easy transition from women's suffrage to the plethora of white supremacist, nativist, and racist political movements of the early twentieth century.

One of the largest and most influential right-wing women's organizations of the immediate postsuffrage period was the Women of the Ku Klux Klan (WKKK). From 1923 to 1930, women poured into the Klan movement to oppose immigration, racial equality, Jewish-owned businesses, parochial schools, and "moral decay." The mobilization of women into the 1920s' Klan was the product of a racist, nationalistic zeal, which also motivated men to join the Ku Klux Klan, combined with a specific, gendered notion of the preservation of family life and women's rights. The women's Klan copied the regalia, militarism, hierarchy, and political stances of the male Ku Klux Klan but insisted that they were no mere appendage of the KKK, claiming autonomy and a special mission for Klanswomen. They used the KKK's call for supremacy of white, native-born Protestants and interpreted it in a gender-specific way, as a vehicle to protect women and children, to preserve home and family life, and to demonstrate newly won women rights. A 1923 advertisement recruited women for the WKKK, using "American" rights and "pure womanhood" as code words for racial and national privilege:

> To the American Women of Washington: Are you interested in the welfare of our Nation? As an enfranchised woman are you interested in Better Government? Do you not wish for the protection of Pure Womanhood? Shall we uphold the sanctity of the American Home? Should we not interest ourselves in Better Education for our children? Do we not want American teachers in our American schools? IT IS POSSIBLE FOR ORGANIZED PATRIOTIC WOMEN TO AID IN STAMPING OUT THE CRIME AND VICE THAT ARE UNDERMINING THE MORALS OF OUR YOUTH. The duty of the American Mother is greater than ever before.

The appeal of the Klan to large numbers of women in the 1920s raises more general questions about how and why women become involved in movements of political protest. A particularly intriguing aspect of the 1920s' WKKK was its complex political ideology. Klanswomen carried into their struggle against Blacks, Jews, Catholics, labor radicals, socialists, Mormons, and immigrants a belief in gender equality among white Protestants in politics, work, and wages. Such an ideology cannot be understood within theoretical frameworks that assume a bifurcation between progressive and proequality movements, on the one hand, and conservative, antifeminist and "profamily" movements, on the other. The study of 1920s' Klanswomen is intended to contribute to an understanding of the varying, often contradictory, ideologies that underlie women's commitment to political movements, especially those of the political Right.

Feminist scholarship on women in contemporary and historical right-wing movements suggests two additional issues that can be explored through an analysis of the 1920s' women's Klan movement. One issue is that of motivation. Did women enter the Klan for the same economic, ideological, and political reasons that brought men into the Klan? Or did women and men differ in the motivations, or the political agendas, that led to Klan membership? Research on other movements suggests different possibilities for women's mobilization into the Klan. Scholars of U.S. antifeminist movements, for example, argue that women's participation in politics, ranging from Victorian-era social purity to modern anti-abortion and anti-ERA movements, has been motivated by a complex mixture of defending and resenting male privilege and female vulnerability in the economic and social spheres. Men's participation in these movements, however, reflects a simpler assessment of collective male self-interest. However, the little research that exists on women in right-wing movements other than those with antifeminist agendas suggests that these women may not differ significantly in ideology or political motivation from their male counterparts on the Right. The 1920s' WKKK, which supported both traditional right-wing politics and a certain degree of gender equality, provides an opportunity to examine gender differences in political motivation in a large and significant movement of the Right.

A second issue concerns political activity. What was the nature of women's involvement in the 1920s' Klan movement? Did women participate, as did men, in terroristic and violent activities, or were women's activities more peaceful, reformist, or "legitimate" than men's Klan activities? There is virtually no research on violent right-wing women's political activity in the United States with which to compare the WKKK. Is this, as traditional accounts imply, because women associated with the major reactionary and terroristic movements of the Right in U.S. history have played insignificant roles in these movements? Historians of the various Klan movements, for example, typically dismiss women's Klan activities as incidental, auxiliary, or merely cultural screens behind which men carried out the real politics of the Klan. Or, as feminist theory suggests, are women's political activities on the far Right undocumented precisely because, as women's activities, they have been invisible or seen as trivial by most historians? Traditional accounts of the Klan movement draw vivid images of episodic, deadly violence perpetrated by gangs of masked and hooded men. By defining the Klan movement through this image of male marauders, women disappear, becoming little more than peripheral onlookers to the crimes and violence of Klansmen. Such a picture distorts both women's role in the Klan and the reality of the Klan itself. If we take women's politics seriously, we find that in the 1920s, the activities of Klanswomen, commonly dismissed as inconsequential and apolitical, were responsible for some of the Klan's most destructive, vicious effects.

I explore these issues through analysis of the 1920s' Klan movement, using primary archival documents from the WKKK, the KKK, and from participants, observers, and critics of the Klan movement. I use documents from the national organizations of the WKKK and KKK to analyze the appeal of the Klan to women and the motivations that drew women into the Klan movement. The extensive propaganda machine of the 1920s' Klan left a considerable body of public documentation in the form of newspapers, pamphlets, and books, while surviving internal Klan letters, speeches, and memorandums preserve a sense of the ideology and goals of the organization.

To understand the specific processes of recruitment and activities of the WKKK, I also examine the large and powerful WKKK chapter in Indiana. With a membership estimated at 250,000 (half of Indiana's Klan membership of half a million), the Indiana WKKK was probably the largest state organization of Klanswomen. The Indiana WKKK was large but not unique; WKKK chapters existed in every state, with particularly strong chapters in Ohio, Pennsylvania, and Arkansas, in addition to

Indiana. To assess why women joined the Klan in Indiana it is important to understand what kinds of women became Klanswomen. Unfortunately, as a secret organization, the Klan closely guarded, and later destroyed, its membership roster. No comprehensive or even partial listing of Indiana Klanswomen survives. My analysis of the composition of the women's Klan, therefore, is based on more indirect methods. Women are considered Klan members if they used their names publicly as leaders or spokeswomen for the Indiana WKKK, if their Klan membership was reported in the influential anti-Klan papers, *Tolerance* (Chicago) or the *Post-Democrat* (Muncie, Indiana), or if their membership was publicized at their deaths by public funeral ceremonies performed by fellow Klanswomen. I then traced the personal histories of these Klanswomen through local newspapers, genealogies, obituaries, county histories, and other biographical sources. In addition, I examined propaganda materials written and distributed by the Indiana WKKK; archival data from the women's and men's Klan in Indiana; non-Klan and anti-Klan accounts of Klan activity; and personal recollections of participants, observers, and opponents of the Klan in Indiana.

Background to the 1920s' Klan

The Klan movement of the 1920s was the second historical occurrence of the Ku Klux Klan. The first Klan was organized in the rural South after the Civil War to assert claims of white, Southern supremacy during Reconstruction; it collapsed in the 1870s. The Klan lay dormant until the early twentieth century when it was reborn as a movement of white "100 percent American" Protestants, drawing strength from small towns and rural areas in the North, Midwest and West as well as in the South. This second wave of the Klan grew dramatically in the early 1920s, only to collapse precipitously in the late 1920s. In over a little more than a decade, the Klan managed to enroll an estimated three to six million persons in a crusade for a white, native-born Protestant America. A number of factors influenced the dramatic reemergence of the Klan movement in the 1920s. These included a public explosion of anti-Black racism and white supremacist sentiments that followed upon the postwar migration of Blacks from the South to the North, the nationalist hatred of immigrants and political "radicals" fueled in World War I propaganda, and the increase in bigotry and intolerance that accompanied the rise of religious and political fundamentalism.

Unlike its predecessor, the 1920s' Klan kept its organization in full public view, even as individual identities were safeguarded. The Klan movement built upon the network of lodges, Protestant churches, and clubs that structured daily life for many small-town and urban Protestant families. It recruited members in schools, clubs, and churches and used ministers and prominent local leaders as recruitment agents. In turn, the Klan built its own network of social ties. Numerous Klan newspapers and magazines were distributed across the United States. Klan lectures, rallies, and gatherings provided a focus for Protestant social life, and the Klan held out the promise of a Klan college to teach the children of loyal Klan parents. In a period of rapid change and great geographical mobility, the Klan positioned itself as the guarantor of the old virtues and the entrée into a cohesive social and cultural network.

Some of the Klan's rapid growth can be attributed to the local specificity of its campaigns. Klan chapters had substantial autonomy to address community issues and fashion appropriate scapegoats—from Mormons in Utah to Catholics in the

Midwest, Jews in the Northeast and Blacks in the South. While a national ideology of anti-Catholicism, anti-Semitism, and anti-Black racism and conservative moralism always underlay Klan actions, recruits varied widely in their commitments to these. Local chapters, too, varied in their activities, which ranged from electoral politics, lobbying, and cultural activities, to terrorism, vigilantism, and violence.

Women in the Klan Movement

Women's participation in the Klan movement began in the early 1920s, when male membership in the KKK was increasing rapidly. Various male Klan leaders throughout the country organized female auxiliaries, competing for membership and official chartering. The most successful of these affiliates was the WKKK, under the sponsorship of the powerful Klan leader, Hiram Evans. The WKKK was open to white, native-born, Protestant women over sixteen years old. Although there were personal and organizational ties between the women's and men's Klan, the WKKK worked to maintain some degree of autonomy from the male KKK.

Women entered the Klan in various ways and for different reasons. Initially, the women's Klan built upon, then absorbed, many of the women's patriotic societies and Protestant women clubs that began after World War I. Other women joined the Klan as the sisters, daughters, and wives of Klansmen, to assist the Klan cause and promote family togetherness. The WKKK also recruited women directly into a women's crusade for a white, Protestant America. The WKKK hired lecturers, organizers, and recruiters to establish new local chapters, usually in states where recruiters for the KKK had been successful. In this endeavor, the WKKK played upon notions of women's new status, as shaped in movements of female suffrage and gender equality. A recruitment ad for the Women's Klan in Indiana proclaimed: "Men no longer aspire to exclusive domination in any field of endeavor that is his authorship, and whether she wears the cool, sequestered veil of life in the home, or whether she is in the busy walks of business or fashion, woman is now called to put her splendid efforts and abilities behind a movement for 100 per cent American women."

The devotion of the WKKK to an elaborate hierarchy and ritual proved attractive to women, as it had to men in the KKK. An Imperial Commander governed the WKKK on a national level. Under her, a complex series of state, regional, and local officers, with titles of Klaliff (vice-president), Klokard (lecturer), Kligraff (secretary), Klabee (treasurer), and Klarogo/Klexter (inner/outer guard), enforced the code of Klan conduct, collected membership dues, initiated new members, and organized events. Like their male counterpart, the WKKK had an array of social, cultural, and economic units, including drill teams, bands, choirs, a social service agency, kindergartens, and a robe-making factory.

Recruitment of Women

What sort of women joined the women's Klan? The common dismissal of the WKKK as a dependent auxiliary of the male KKK does not accurately capture the process through which women became involved in the Klan. Many—but certainly not all—women in the WKKK were related to male Klan members. Of the sixty-two nonleadership Indiana Klanswomen who are named in the *Tolerance* and *Post-Democrat* or in the Indianapolis Klan paper, *Fiery Cross*, twelve were widows or unmarried women and, we can assume, made their own decisions to participate in the Klan. Furthermore, married women in the Klan were not necessarily led into the movement by Klan husbands; in fact, it was their wives who sometimes convinced men to join the Klan.

Further, most Indiana Klanswomen brought with them a history of extrafamilial involvement. Typically, they belonged to at least one voluntary organization, in addition to a Protestant church and the Klan, and a significant minority worked for wages, in occupations that ranged from positions such as physician, postmistress, real estate agent, and owner of a boarding house to skilled and semiskilled occupations that included dressmaker, office worker, courthouse employee, and nursing student.

Indiana Klanswomen in leadership positions, for whom more biographical information is available, clarify a pattern of Klan membership as an aspect of broad civic and social involvement. Daisy Douglas Barr, the fiery leader of the WKKK for Indiana and seven other states, was married to a bank examiner and raised a son but pursued an independent course. An ordained Quaker preacher, renowned for her oratory skills, Barr began preaching at sixteen; was ordained at eighteen; and served as pastor of churches in Muncie, Fairmount, and New Castle, Indiana. She was an active, powerful member of the Women's Christian Temperance Union (WCTU) and a famous crusader for the cause of the "drys" in Muncie. Barr also was a leader in the Indiana Republican party, serving as the first woman vice-chair of the Republican state committee and as a member of the Indiana Women's Republican Club. She was an active member of the American War Mothers (from which she was forced to resign when her Klan activities became known) and a member of the Women's Department Club. Daisy Douglas Barr, like many leaders of the women's Klan, was also an advocate of women's rights and public participation. In 1916, she wrote:

> One can hardly imagine, under our present day progress, that most of the religious denominations in our own country still refuse the rite of ordination to women applicants. Women have entered the professions of law, medicine, teaching, art, music and even are wrestling with the sciences. . . . And yet the relic of our barbarism and heathenism dogmas, when the belief was still current that women had no souls, is still evident in the fact that other doors are open while the holy ministry still bars her free entrance.

Mary Benadum, prominent leader of the WKKK in Muncie, Indiana, and a rival of Daisy Barr, had a similar background prior to joining the Klan. Married to a prosecuting attorney, she worked for twelve years as a schoolteacher in Muncie and was involved in a variety of state and local civic associations. She was president of the Delaware County (Muncie) Republican Woman's Club and was active in the Business and Professional Women of Indiana and the Methodist church. She also was a vocal and open leader of the women's Klan in Indiana. Benadum embroiled the WKKK in several lawsuits, charging Daisy Barr first with stealing WKKK funds and later with slander, when Barr claimed that Benadum was the true culprit. Her social prominence notwithstanding, Benadum did not fit the traditional conception of high-society womanhood. In 1924, she was arrested in Alliance, Ohio, in a battle with a rival faction of the WKKK in which one woman was injured seriously, and she and Daisy Barr competed intensively and viciously for leadership of the Muncie WKKK.

Lillian Sedwick, named as president of the Marion County, Indiana (Indianapolis), WKKK, was a highly influential and active leader in Indianapolis.

Married and the mother of three children, she served on the Indianapolis school board, through which she attempted to bring a Klan philosophy to questions of school policy and racial integration of the schools. She also was active in Eastern Star, the Rebekah Lodge, the WCTU (in which she served as state superintendent), the Methodist Episcopal church, and the International Order of Odd Fellows.

Klanswomen in Indiana not only were likely to be women with a personal history of social and political involvement, but many also violated accepted notions of gender and wifely duty to participate in the Klan. Stories of women who joined the WKKK against the wishes of their husbands and families are common. The 16 May 1924 Muncie *Post-Democrat* noted that "in many Protestant homes the klan has done it's [sic] work breaking the ties that would never have been severed. . . . Some husbands have parted from their wives who joined the Kamelias [Women's Klan] and wives have deserted husbands who enlisted in the army of Satan."

The Lynds' famous study of Muncie, Indiana, too, quotes a husband who attributed his divorce to his wife's participation in the Klan: "She and I split up over the G-d D— Klan. I couldn't stand them around any longer." Divorce proceedings, given prominent play in the anti-Klan press, claimed that women neglected children and household in favor of Klan activities. The press emphasized the Klan's negative effect on marriage and family life in order to convince women to return to their "rightful" role as wife and mother. "Edna Walling . . . led to believe that her sphere was politics and Klan activities, instead of the home life she deserved . . . was arrested."

Anti-Klan papers insisted that the Klan did not respect marriage and family life. Claims that the divorce rate was higher in the Klan stronghold of Muncie than in Nevada, that the Klan sponsored frivolous public weddings of fifty couples at a time, and that the Klan "placed Klangraft [Klan corruption] above the holy ordinance of marriage" were frequent. The existence of the WKKK was singled out as proof that the Klan was ignoring traditional morals and the rightful place of women and men. George Dale, the crusading anti-Klan editor of the Muncie *Post-Democrat* who was convicted of contempt of court by a local Klan judge, described Klanswomen spectators at his trial as "sister Amazons of Hate . . . bob-haired Amazons [who] demanded my death." The WKKK itself was accused of being nothing more than a front for women's adulterous trysts and of fomenting the murderous tendencies of women unleashed from male direction.

On the whole, this evidence offers a profile of Klanswomen that is remarkably congruent with decades of female activism in voluntary religious and reform associations. But why did they join the Klan? Recruitment literature from the WKKK played on the same racist and nativist themes as the male KKK, promising to safeguard the American family from "corrupting" influences; to guard against isolation and loneliness; to provide excitement; to preserve nationalistic pride; and to maintain racial, religious, and ethnic superiority. Other sources, however, indicate that women also joined the Klan to assert and increase their newfound political legitimacy. In a rare surviving document, an early women's Klan, the "Ladies of the Invisible Empire," of Shreveport, Louisiana, sought to simultaneously redirect American society and to assimilate women into the public, political life of the country. The group presented its objectives as the bringing together of the Protestant women of America . . . to cleanse and purify the civil, political and ecclesiastical atmosphere of our country; to provide a common meeting ground for American Protestant women who are willing to co-operate in bringing about better conditions in the home, church and social circles; to assist all Protestant women in the study of practical politics; to encourage a study by Protestant wives, mothers and daughters of questions concerning the happiness of the home and the welfare of the state.

Klanswomen bemoaned immorality, racial integration, and religious pluralism, as did Klansmen, but it was in terms of the effect of these on women, children, and the family. Men needed protection from the economic competition of foreigners, the WKKK insisted, for the sake of those who were dependent upon men's livelihoods: "Foreigners can live and make money where a white man would starve because they treat their women like cattle and their swarms of children like vermin, living without fear of God or regard for men. . . . You should by voice and vote encourage for your husband's sake the restriction of immigration. Let us have fewer citizens and better ones. Women of America, wake up."

The mobilization of women into the 1920s' Klan linked the racist, nationalistic zeal, which also motivated men to join the KKK, to a specific gendered notion of the preservation of family life and women's rights. Both Klansmen and Klanswomen promoted the idea of a white, Protestant America, but women, more so than men, were likely to fuse this political agenda with a vision of a perfected private family life. Advocates of a women's Klan organization, for example, linked antiforeign sentiments to a defense of the home and female morality. They charged that foreign influences were undermining morality by "public presentation of sex where the wife is always shown as inferior and the mistress as a heroine."

Similarly, the sermons of Quaker preacher and WKKK leader Daisy Douglas Barr adapted the rhetoric of the nineteenth-century temperance movement. Barr stressed the need for a "revival in our home [as] many of our family altars have been broken down," arguing that men's indulgence in the "serpent of alcohol . . . stings his family, degrades his wife, marks his children." She did not, however, consign women to the private sphere. Rather, she defended women's place in professional and civic life as necessary to the purification of the home.

Indeed, through active involvement in the Klan, white, Protestant women claimed to find a new weapon against male immorality. The Klan promoted its ability to protect women from sexual harassment on the job and from abuse by husbands. Both the KKK and the WKKK issued warnings to men who cheated on their wives, owed child support, or neglected their families.

As the WKKK recruited women on the basis of a conservative, racist ideology that stressed the interconnection between the public sphere of politics and the private sphere of the home, it expressed a political ideology that had been shaped in earlier women's political movements for temperance and moral reform. Like the WCTU, an organization to which many Klanswomen belonged and most Klanswomen probably were sympathetic, the WKKK expressed elements of a women's rights politics in which the interests of women were primary. The ideology of the women's Klan, however, was not identical to that of the temperance movement of the nineteenth century. Changes in women's roles in the early twentieth century were reflected in the politics of the 1920s' women's Klan. The restrictions of domesticity that gave rise to anger, antagonism, and resentment toward men's privileges and that motivated the women's rights politics of the WCTU no longer completely defined and circumscribed the lives of many white, Protestant, native-born women by the 1920s. Rather, the entrance of women into the world of politics and business made divisions of race, social class, and religion more salient for, and among, women. Klanswomen still used a rhetoric of women's subordinate status and collective interests similar to that which brought women into the temperance movement; but it was now mixed with appeals for racial, ethnic, and national unity, appeals which depended upon the unity and commonality of purpose of white, native-born, Protestant women *and* men. With this political ideology, the WKKK was able to mobilize women from a great variety of employment and family backgrounds.

Activities of Klanswomen

For the most part, the activities of Indiana Klanswomen did not differ significantly from those of Klansmen, except that Klanswomen were rarely involved in violence or vigilantism. Klansmen tended to be involved in either fraternal/social or terroristic activities. Klanswomen worked to solidify the Klan movement itself, led political assaults on non-Klan businesses, and organized to strengthen the Klan's political base, actions essential to the Klan's political and social impact.

On a national and state level, a central aspect of Klanswomen's work was organization building, antivice activities, and anti-Catholic propaganda and actions. The WKKK orchestrated rallies, festivals, and recreational events, some closed to all nonmembers, some for Klanswomen only, and others involving entire Klan families. The WKKK, like the KKK, specialized in ritual and spectacle, with day-long carnivals of sport and song followed by a twilight parade through town, a cross-burning, and an evening series of lectures and speeches in a field outside town. Klanswomen organized entertainment meant to build internal solidarity and heighten recruitment, including orchestras, quartets, and parades. A typical event, held in Sullivan, Indiana, involved 3,000 Klanswomen who paraded through downtown, then marched to a park. There,

> by the light of a burning cross, the speaking and demonstration were held. Floats, decorated autos, lady horseback riders, marching hosts, all the persons wearing the white robe and marks of the Ku Klux Klan with the exception of one young lady riding upon a specially decorated float. Mothers with sleeping babies in their arms marched with the others and the American flag was given a prominent place. At the park a speaker explained the aim and purpose of the women's organization and a male quartet sang.

Klanswomen were also prominent in the creation of a political culture of "Klannishness"—the use of family, leisure, social ties, and ritual to solidify the Klan movement internally and to mark the boundaries between insiders (Klan members) and outsiders ("aliens"). Although often regarded as politically insignificant, the political culture shaped by Klanswomen in the 1920s was critical to the Klan's success in convincing white, native-born, Protestants to enlist in the Klan's crusade and in shaping the solidarity of Klansmembers. Especially important in this culture were Klan rites of passage, including Klan wedding services, christening ceremonies, and funeral services to herald departed Klan sisters. These served both to create a sense of the totality of the Klan world and to present a politically palatable alternative to the culture, practices, and rituals of Catholicism, Judaism, Mormonism, and socialism that Klansmembers swore to oppose. Further, the WKKK had a public relations-oriented charity dimension. With great fanfare, they distributed food baskets to needy families and milk to public school children and raised money to build Protestant hospitals. They were also active in the effort to recruit churches into the Klan movement by descending on a church service in full regalia, striding to the front of the church and presenting an envelope of cash to the minister—sometimes a surprised potential recruit, but often a covert Klan propagandist. They crusaded against "immorality," drove liquor agents out of town, and worked to establish a "clean" motion picture company (the Cavalier Motion Picture Company).

A second activity of Klanswomen was the attempt to "reform" the public schools. Klanswomen frequently visited public schools to distribute Bibles or copies of the Ten Commandments, attempted to have Catholic teachers fired from public school positions, pushed for racial segregation of schools, worked against school closings and the teaching of German in public schools, sought to remove Catholic encyclopedias from the public schools, and raised money in their communities to support public schools to undermine parochial education. Klanswomen also ran for school board seats in order to implement the Klan's program to "Americanize" and make Protestant the public school system.

Third, Klanswomen worked to influence electoral politics, especially in Indiana. They were active in the drive to bring out the Klan vote by lobbying voters, distributing scandal sheets on non-Klan candidates, and caring for the children of women who pledged to vote the Klan ticket. More insidiously, Klanswomen were involved as "poison squads," organizing whispering campaigns to destroy the reputation of anti-Klan candidates by insinuating that they were Catholic or Jewish. Vivian Wheatcraft, a reputed Klanswoman and highly controversial vice-chair of the Indiana Republican State Committee, was accused of running an "organization of which she is pleased to call a 'poison squad of whispering women'"—five Klanswomen in each county in Indiana who could be counted upon to spread gossip and rumors for the Klan.

Similar tactics were used by Klanswomen who organized boycotts of Jewish-owned and Catholic-owned businesses and newspapers opposed to the Klan. These boycotts often were very effective, especially in smaller cities. They were a part of the overall Klan boycott program, in which women's role as household consumer was essential. Boycotts were implemented via a series of codes that encouraged trade only with fellow Klan members. Ads proclaimed "100 percent" dry cleaners, grocers, or photo studios or contained the code "TWK" (Trade with a Klansman).

Klanswomen took the message and vision of the Klan and acted upon it in a variety of ways, some of which were quite different from the actions of Klansmen. Although Klansmen tended toward more open displays of physical violence and intimidation, Klanswomen were the legitimators of the Klan, the covert manipulators of electoral plots, the cultural organizers of a Klan world, and the force behind the attempt to "Protestantize" the public schools of the 1920s. Certainly, Klanswomen demonstrated no more inclination toward progressive or peaceable politics than did men. On the contrary, the behind-the-scenes actions of

Klanswomen had the same goals, and perhaps a greater effect, than the openly violent actions of Klansmen. To a great extent, the destructive fury of the 1920s' Klan lay in its use of rumors, boycotts, and electoral strength—tactics that ruined countless lives across the nation. In these tactics, Klanswomen were key actors.

Conclusion

In many respects, the involvement of women in the 1920s' WKKK was motivated by factors similar to those that brought millions of men into the Klan. Both women and men, reacting to a fear of social, cultural, racial, and religious difference, joined a movement to preserve and elevate traditional white Protestant dominance. Women, no less than men, perceived heterogeneity as threatening; it was Indiana, one of the most homogeneous of states, that produced the nation's largest chapters of female and male Klans in the 1920s. From the limited data available, it also appears that female and male Klan members had similar backgrounds. Both women and men spanned a wide range of ages and occupational/class positions, with those in leadership positions more likely to be older and wealthier.

Women and men in the Klan movement, however, differed in one significant way. The political agenda of the women's Klan wove together appeals to racism, nationalism, traditional morality, and religious intolerance with other appeals to white women's vulnerability and to the possibility for increased equity between white women and men. Klanswomen described their reasons for participating in the Klan as related to the precarious or subordinate positions that they—as women—held in the family and in society. Women argued that the Klan was the best vehicle for protecting women and children, asserting the rights of women relative to men, and incorporating women's political savvy into the political arena.

It is clear that women's participation in the 1920s' Klan movement was not trivial or insignificant in its consequences. Although Klanswomen were not involved in the violent terroristic and vigilante actions of Klansmen, women did participate in a full range of racist, antipacifist, and right-wing activities. Klanswomen organized racially targeted boycotts, electoral strategies, and character assassinations, in addition to the cultural and social forums that bound the Klan movement together. Their actions contributed significantly to the persecution of racial and religious minorities and to the poisoning of American public life that was the legacy of the 1920s' Klan.

The history of women's participation in the 1920s' Klan movement should caution against a simplistic equation of progressive and proequality politics. Klanswomen, as fully as Klansmen, promoted a right-wing agenda of racism and bigotry. But they linked the preservation of their families to the rights of women (white, native-born, Protestant women) in the public sphere. They promoted white women's entrance into professions, white women's right to vote, and the need of white women to shape the nation's political agenda. Just as progressive political movements have not always promoted gender equality, so, too, reactionary political movements have at times included women's rights agendas.

The second Klan of the 1920s collapsed rapidly at the end of the decade, a victim of economic depression, internal battles, and financial scandals. In the Klan's next significant appearance in the 1950s, women and men no longer belonged to separate organizations. In the violent, extremist right-wing politics of today's Klan, women have become background figures, integrated with men in Klan organizations that no longer advocate gender equality. The fusion of women's rights with a reactionary and racist politics, at least in the Klan movement, did not stand the test of time.

What was it that permitted the inclusion of women's rights sentiments into the racist, reactionary political agenda of Klanswomen in the 1920s, but not thereafter? The answer rests on the specific historical conditions under which women joined the second Klan movement. The male Klan movement, desperate for female members to bolster the claims of competing Klan factions, recruited women who supported nativist and racist viewpoints but also supported women's rights politics. Further, antiimmigrant and racist sentiments within the women's suffrage, moral reform, and temperance movements created the historical possibility for a postsuffrage women's Klan that espoused women's rights while denying the rights of non-whites, non-Protestants, and the foreign-born.

Feminist scholarship has uncovered a rich legacy of women's involvement in progressive and proequality political movements. It is now possible to turn more attention to the disturbing, but important, question of women's involvement in racist, reactionary, and fascist movements. The study of women in extremist rightwing movements may provide us with a richer understanding of the complexities of women's activities in political movements, as well as better strategies by which to challenge racist, reactionary movements in contemporary society.

Questions for Study and Review

1. Who joined the Women's Ku Klux Klan, and what was the appeal of the organization to them?

2. Analyze the ways that women of the Klan combined advocacy for women's rights with race hatred and the meanings of such connections.

3. How was the activism of the WKKK different from that of the female trade unionists described by Orleck or the racial justice campaigns spearheaded by Gill's African American beauty operators?

4. Members of the Indiana WKKK professed hostility to immigrants. But many young women from small towns and farms in the Midwest found urban youth culture irresistible. How might women Klan members have reacted to New York working girls who were "putting on style" or the behavior of New York's "rowdy girls"?

Suggested Readings and Web Sites

Kathleen Blee, ed., *No Middle Ground: Women and Radical Protest* (1998)

Ruth Bordin, *Woman and Temperance: the Quest for Power and Liberty, 1873–1900* (1981)

Karen Cox, *Dixie's Daughters: The United Daughters of the Confederacy and the Preservation of Confederate Culture* (2003)

Nancy MacLean, "White Women and Klan Violence in the 1920s: Agency, Complicity, and the Politics of Women's History," *Gender & History* (1991): 285–303.

Kim E. Nielsen, *Un-American Womanhood: Antiradicalism, Antifeminism, and the First Red Scare* (2001)

Women and Social Movements in the United States, 1600–2000
    http://www.binghamton.edu/womhist/projectmap.htm

PART III

Decades of Turmoil

Photographer Dorothea Lange illuminated the repercussions of economic and environmental disaster for ordinary people like migrant farm worker Florence Owens, who in 1936 was reduced to huddling in a lean-to tent with her children.

F rom the 1880s through the 1920s, movement and change had been the watchwords of American development. Then, in 1929, a series of devastating economic upheavals plunged the nation, and the world, into the greatest depression of modern times. For more than a decade, women and men struggled to survive as banks and businesses collapsed, stores and factories closed their doors, families lost their livelihoods and their homes, and private charities and government leaders sought to stem the tide, or at least stave off the worst effects, of the Great Depression.

Women were among the foremost chroniclers of the Great Depression. Hired by the Works Progress Administration (WPA) and other government agencies to collect folktales, compile city guides, index local archives, and interview and photograph ordinary women and men, they documented the meaning of economic crisis for families and communities across the country. Dorothea Lange's *Migrant Mother* may be the most widely recognized of these Depression portraits, but it is only one of thousands that captured the pain and fortitude of common folk with many burdens and few resources.

Those whose lives were chronicled—whatever their region, race, ethnicity, or sex—shared some common problems. Unemployment, crowded quarters, family stress, personal anxiety, and limited options were the daily concerns of millions of Americans throughout the 1930s. Women who were bombarded during the 1920s with messages extolling the virtues of sexual attractiveness and a happy home faced the Depression from a slightly different stance than men, who perceived their role as that of family provider and household head. These differences were intensified by the alternatives offered each sex for coping with the collapse of their family's financial security.

As more individuals lost their jobs and fewer found new jobs, employers, politicians, and private citizens suggested a range of causes and offered a variety of cures for the crisis. One common theme was that women should not work if men lacked jobs. As Earl Leiby of Akron, Ohio, wrote to Franklin Roosevelt in 1933:

> You and we all know that the place for a wife and mother is at home, her palace. The excuse is often brought up that the husband cannot find employment. It is the writers' [sic] belief that if the women were expelled from places of business, . . . these very men would find employment.

Though most Americans seemed to accept the necessity of women working if they were the sole support of a family, legislators followed Leiby's logic in forbidding married women to work in certain occupations, such as teaching, or in government jobs where husbands were already employed.

Whatever the popular sentiment, however, women did work during the Depression, and in large numbers. At the level of national leadership more women than ever held high government posts. Many, like Secretary of Labor Frances Perkins, traced their political roots to the Progressive Era. Nearly all found in First Lady Eleanor Roosevelt a model and an advocate for women's expanded political influence. At the local level, women's work was less glamorous but just as important. Ironically, as a result of the sex-typing of jobs, "total female labor force participation rose in the period from 1930 to 1940 more than in any previous decade in the twentieth century." Not only did the number of jobs in such female-dominated occupations as nursing, domestic service, and typing decline less than jobs in those areas typically reserved for males but most men refused to take "women's work" even if no other employment was available.

The effects of these employment patterns on everyday life were often both dramatic and traumatic. Families in which men lost their breadwinning role to women suffered considerable economic and emotional stress. Women generally continued to perform the bulk of domestic work, perhaps to ease men's fear of a complete role reversal. With more children living at home, keeping up with housework and maintaining family harmony placed unusually heavy burdens on adult females. Families adjusted to these difficulties in different ways. In some cases, children and husbands took on added household chores, men accepted their new roles, and family members actually formed tighter bonds in response to crisis. In other cases, conflict, violence, and abandonment resulted from family tensions too deep to resolve.

The patterns of women's work varied as always by region, race, ethnicity, and age. Most notably, black women as well as younger and older women regardless of race were pushed out of the workforce as native-born white women aged twenty to forty-five sought jobs they once considered undesirable. African American women, who had long contributed to family well-being through paid employment, found themselves forced out of work alongside male kin. In addition, black and other minority families were discriminated against in the distribution of public assistance meant to alleviate their hardships. Some of these women joined the intensified union struggles of the period, participated in unemployment councils, or joined popular political movements that offered wide-ranging solutions to the crisis. Others appealed for help on an individual basis, many directly to President Franklin and First Lady Eleanor Roosevelt, whom they viewed as especially sympathetic to their plight. Pinkie Pelcher of Greenwood, Mississippi, pursued this latter path:

> "We are wondering," she wrote, "what is going to become of this large number of widow women with and without children. These white women at the head of the PWA [WPA] is still [telling us] colored women when we go to the office to be certified for work to go hunt washings. . . . The white people dont pay anything for their washing. [We] cant do enough washing to feed [our] family."

Entering the labor force, doing double duty at work and home, carrying both economic and emotional responsibilities for the family, joining unions and other protest movements, and appealing for a fair share of public assistance, women pursued a variety of strategies to combat poverty. In Chapter Seven Julia Kirk Blackwelder examines these strategies and women's part in them among Anglos, blacks, and Hispanics in San Antonio, Texas. She chronicles both the common roles played by women as women in crisis-ridden families and the distinct opportunities and barriers confronting them as members of different class, racial, and ethnic communities.

In San Antonio, as elsewhere, preparation for war ended the Depression. Beginning in the late 1930s, employment opportunities increased, this time more quickly for men than for women as heavy industry received the first infusion of federal money. Though World War II eventually brought minority, married, and older women into the workforce, and into industry, the process began slowly. Only the attack on Pearl Harbor, the mass mobilization of men that followed, the promise of government subsidies to industries hiring women, and a nationwide recruitment campaign finally brought the symbol of "Rosie the Riveter" to life.

From 1942 to the end of the war, millions of women entered the workforce. Most had worked before or would have sought paid work in the period with or without a military crisis. Only a small percentage, moreover, lived out the Rosie the Riveter image of "making history working for victory" by "working overtime on the riveting machine." Far more women were employed in traditional female jobs that also expanded during the war, such as food preparation, laundry, sewing, and nursing. And whatever the type of work performed, sex segregation and sex stereotyping continued.

Despite these limits on women's wartime opportunities, significant changes did occur. Black and Hispanic women found not only more but much better chances for employment. Married women over thirty-five with children entered the workforce in record numbers. Automation installed in munitions and aircraft factories to facilitate female employment transformed heavy industry forever. Female workers joined unions in unprecedented numbers; some headed women's locals; a few became unionwide leaders.

In addition, stores stayed open later to accommodate working mothers; short hair, which was safer and less time-consuming to fix, became fashionable; rationing of items such as sugar and stockings altered habits of cooking and dress; and, perhaps most important, a range of family issues such as publicly funded childcare became matters of national concern.

The wartime experiences of two groups of American women differed significantly from that of the majority of their sex. Panic generated by the Japanese attack on Pearl Harbor in December 1941, combined with long-held prejudice against Asian immigrants, led to the internment of more than 110,000 people of Japanese descent in remote camps throughout the western United States. At the same time, the demands of wartime mobilization drew more women into the U.S. armed forces than ever before. For women of Japanese descent and women in the military, World War II offered unique problems and opportunities.

Among those interred by the federal government during the war, some two-thirds were Japanese-Americans born in the United States. Sent to distant camps, families lived in barren lean-tos or barrack-like dormitories with outdoor pumps for water, shared latrines and showers, and mess tents for meals. Camps were surrounded with barbed wire, and they offered few activities to occupy children or adults. Mothers and wives tried to sustain family bonds and create a bit of domestic comfort despite extremely limited resources. Yet some younger women discovered new opportunities in the camps. They gained a modicum of financial independence by working as clerks or teachers in the camps, and they escaped the full weight of patriarchal authority, which eroded under conditions of internment.

Initially, administrators were reluctant to hire women of Japanese descent for jobs in the internment camps, but the demands of maintaining camp life over many years forced their hand. Similarly, despite the demands of wartime, most political and military leaders were opposed to women entering the armed forces. Although women had served in various capacities in every U.S. war from the American Revolution on, the idea of incorporating women into formal positions in the U.S. Army, Navy, and other services was widely opposed. Yet eventually the mass mobilization demanded by World War II opened some positions to women.

Most of the more than 300,000 women who joined the U.S. military during World War II were recruited into special women's divisions. These included the Women's Army Corps, or WACs, and Women Accepted for Volunteer Emergency Service, or WAVES. Many women served the military in stereotypically feminine jobs, such as clerical workers or nurses, but others entered positions normally reserved for men. The U.S. government sought to reassure female recruits as well as their families and communities back home that women in the armed forces would retain their respectability and femininity. Despite constant surveillance, some women in the WAC, WAVES, and other units managed to skirt surveillance and experiment with new gender and sexual relations. Still, most women who served during World War II focused their energies on training for their new positions and carrying out their military responsibilities with care and expertise.

Evelyn M. Monahan and Rosemary Neidel-Greenlee focus in Chapter Eight on the women who served as frontline Army nurses during the war. By following individual women like Claudine Glidewell from her home in Wichita through her training at Fort Riley, Kansas, her marriage to Lieutenant Frank Doyle, and her assignment to the 95th Evacuation Hospital, which was sent to North Africa in spring 1943, the authors trace the process by which military women formed new families and communities in the midst of war. Glidewell, like many women who joined the military, married a soldier. Yet husbands and wives in the military were separated for most of the war, and women like Glidewell thus relied on the bonds forged among the nurses in their units to provide the emotional and physical support so critical on the battlefront.

World War II affected American women's lives in dramatic ways. Some of these changes lasted only for the duration of the war; others affected women for generations to come. For many African American women, the war offered the possibility finally of leaving behind the narrow confines of domestic service and agricultural labor that had long served as their main occupational choices. Fanny Christina Hill, a black woman born in Texas who labored in domestic service until the age of twenty-four, landed a job at North American Aircraft during the war. She was one of a small percentage of female wage earners to return to work there in peacetime. Commenting on the effects of the war on black women, she concluded:

> It made me live better. It really did. We always say that Lincoln took the bale off the Negroes. . . . Well, my sister always said, . . . "Hitler was the one that got us out of the white folks' kitchens."

Still, when victory was declared in 1945, no one was quite sure how women and men would manage the return to peacetime. Demobilization generally meant that women who had been working in heavy industry lost their jobs or were relegated to traditionally female occupations. Though many women left high-paying jobs reluctantly, others saw peacetime as providing the opportunity to start families long postponed. Nonetheless, during the baby boom years (1946–64), the proportion of women in the workforce increased along with the nation's birthrate. The rising employment rate for women was due in part to the expansion of jobs sex-typed as female in the service sector, particularly clerical, sales, and health-care positions. In addition, more families began to rely on two incomes in order to take advantage of the availability of consumer goods—like televisions and washing machines—that had become central to a middle-class lifestyle.

In Chapter Nine, Stephanie Coontz explores postwar changes in representations as well as the shifting realities of American family life. She uses popular television shows like *Leave It to Beaver* and *Ozzie and Harriet,* which depicted happy families in their suburban homes with a working dad and a stay-at-home mom, as a starting point for illuminating the mythology of postwar gender and generational relations. While many of these shows highlighted traditional attitudes and values, Coontz argues that the family of the 1950s was a thoroughly modern institution that was often defined by unrealistic expectations. The suburban family, moreover, had only limited ties to wider family and community networks that in earlier generations had helped to meet the economic and emotional burdens of parents and children.

Both wartime experiences and the far-reaching economic changes that followed ensured that prewar sexual, class, and racial patterns would never be completely reinstated. Government intervention in the economy—and in many other areas of life—that seemed so necessary during the Depression and war continued to expand after 1945, reshaping relations among individuals, families, employers, unions, communities, and the state. At the same time, in everyday life the effects of two decades of upheaval could not be erased. Ordinary women and men had coped with economic, familial, communal, and military crises. They had taken on new roles, changed their expectations, traveled to different areas of the country and the world, formed new relationships and networks, and experienced previously unknown risks, responsibilities, and accomplishments.

Suggested Readings and Web Sites

Karen Anderson, *Wartime Women: Sex Roles, Family Relations, and the Status of Women during World War II* (1981)

Wini Breines, *Young, White, and Miserable: Growing Up Female in the Fifties* (1992)

Daniel Horowitz, *Betty Friedan and the Making of the Feminine Mystique* (1998)

Jeanne Houston and James D. Houston, *Farewell to Manzanar: A True Story of Japanese American Experience During and After World War II Internment* (1973)

Jacqueline Jones, *Labor of Love, Labor of Sorrow: Black Women, Work, and the Family, from Slavery to the Present* (1985)

Susan Ware, *Beyond Suffrage: Women in the New Deal* (1981)

Japanese American Relocation Digital Archives
http://jarda.cdlib.org

U.S. Government Response to the Great Depression
http://newdeal.feri.org/

Oral History Archives of World War II
http://fas-history-rutgers.edu/oralhistory/orlhom.htm

1950s Educational Films
http://www.archive.org/details/prelinger

Chapter 7

If the flapper, the Klan, and labor activists competed for women's attention in the 1910s and 1920s, economic crisis and family survival refocused women's vision in the 1930s. Daughters and sons who had eagerly left home in the earlier era often returned—with spouses and children in tow—in the Depression decade. Family strain took other forms as well: Husbands and fathers fought the economic and psychological burdens of unemployment and lower income, extended families sought to share small houses, and more women were pushed into positions as breadwinners.

Not all women and men experienced the Great Depression in the same ways. Some of the affluent escaped relatively unscathed. Middle-class families, who had the high expectations that came with prosperity, suffered emotionally as well as financially. Working-class families, who had fewer resources at the beginning of the crash, were pushed to the margins more quickly. Farmers of all races and ethnic backgrounds and African Americans, Hispanics, and other minorities regardless of occupation were perhaps the hardest hit. Within each of these class, racial, ethnic, and occupational groups, women and men often were affected differently as traditional expectations, the sexual division of labor, and federal relief programs shaped the hopes and opportunities for each sex.

By focusing on San Antonio, Texas, Julia Kirk Blackwelder reveals the ethnic and racial variations in the ways that Anglo, black, and Hispanic communities survived the Depression decade. At the same time, she notes similarities in the roles played by women in all three groups. In the absence of the massive and militant union relief drives staged by the Congress of Industrial Organizations in some cities, San Antonio residents were forced to rely on family resources, community charity, and federal relief. The first of these differed according to the long-term economic and social status of each group; the last two differed according to federal legislative and local bureaucratic assumptions about ethnicity, race, and gender.

By following the female life cycle before and during the Depression and comparing the private and public labors of Anglo, black, and Hispanic wives and daughters, Blackwelder shows how women in different racial and ethnic communities faced problems, both distinct and common, and how they reshaped their own roles in the family to address the economic crisis. Overall, economic necessity seems to have pushed women into more unconventional roles in the family and the workforce at the same time that the existing sexual division of labor and federal relief programs reinforced traditional expectations. The legacy of the Great Depression for women and the family was ambiguous and cannot be isolated from the effects of the war that finally revitalized the economy. What is clear is that women were simultaneously asked to take on new responsibilities and to remain within acceptable parameters of behavior for their sex, race, class, and ethnicity.

Women of the Depression: Anglo, Black, and Hispanic Families in San Antonio
JULIA KIRK BLACKWELDER

As San Antonio women articulated their concerns during the Depression and as they remembered the past, their thoughts ran first and last to family. Social worker Adela Navarro remembered her mother's watchful supervision of her children's education and her insistence on respectful behavior. Homemaker Ruby Cude recalled how hard her husband worked, sometimes holding down two jobs at one time, to make a comfortable life for his family. Store clerk Beatrice Clay reminisced about neighborhood sharing and backyard picnics that helped and cheered each of the families in her community. Family commanded deepest personal loyalties and constituted the primary economic unit in which a woman participated.

Marriage and the arrival of children were events that the average young girl expected in her life as well as the circumstances that most narrowly defined the roles she played in adulthood. Most girls coming of age in San Antonio in the 1920s married before or after a period of paid employment, stayed at home to rear the children, and did not enter the paid work force after marriage. The well-being of wives and of daughters living at home usually depended on the labor of male wage earners. For women who did not enter the work force, the vagaries of the labor market and the wage cuts of the 1930s were experienced second-hand in the form of sharply reduced household budgets, the sometimes awkward presence of husbands and fathers at home during their usual working hours, and male depression. The first responses of wives and daughters to financial setbacks were to adapt to a lifestyle of leftovers and hand-me-downs and to show support for male family members who felt shame for economic problems not of their making. As Navarro remembered of her father and her brothers, "I could see what had happened in my own family, that they just couldn't bear it."

Regardless of their family status, women's experiences during the Depression were not individual or solitary experiences. Their dependence on male wage earners profoundly influenced most women's perceptions and roles during the Depression. Women saw the Depression through the filter of emotional concerns and attachments that affect wives, mothers, and daughters in prosperous times as well. A woman did not achieve independence by remaining single and entering the work force; life was more comfortable if economic resources were pooled, and regard for parents or siblings was paramount if the woman had neither spouse nor child. The composition of the family and family changes over time defined the responsibilities of women as they moved through the Depression decade, but for most women family concerns of one kind or another were ever present. Women who wished or needed to work weighed their household responsibilities and attitudes of family members in the balance with the benefits of market labor and the difficulty of finding work.

In 1930 and in 1940 the vast majority of adult women were married. Marriage patterns were not the same for all population groupings, however, and marriage did not bring the same responsibilities to all women. Among San Antonio women blacks married earliest, 22 percent of all black women between the ages of fifteen and nineteen being married, widowed or divorced in 1930. Mexican-American and native born Anglo women married slightly later than blacks. As women reached their early twenties, life-cycle patterns manifested their greatest differences by ethnicity, though only among foreign-born Anglos was the majority single. After age twenty-five, differences in the percentages of the population who were married began to even out, but Anglo immigrant women remained the least likely to have married.

The age of marriage increased slightly between 1930 and 1940 with women in all age brackets somewhat more likely to be single at the end of the decade. Black women, a small percentage of the total female population, recorded a decline in both the number and the percentage of women reporting themselves as divorced, but the chances of other women experiencing divorce increased. Both the number and the percentage of women in the total population who were widows [also] increased over the course of the Depression.

The Depression exacerbated emotional as well as economic stress on the family, and either kind of stress might lead to the dissolution of the family unit or temporary separation of its members. Admissions of men and women to the state mental hospital in San Antonio increased dramatically during the early 1930s. Suicide increased, though it remained rare among women. The tensions created by poverty and overcrowded living conditions proved overwhelming to Janie Brown Katlan, who lived with her husband, two sisters, and four nieces in a two-room apartment. In 1938, after nine months of marriage, the twenty-year-old woman shot herself through the heart. Another San Antonio woman, Kate Clark, poisoned herself. She left a note in which she explained that she knew it was wrong to take her life but that she could not find work and suicide was "the only way out."

Abandonment was more likely to break up families than was mental illness or suicide. Unemployed fathers deserted their wives and children, who often had nowhere to turn for support. There were also instances of mothers abandoning their children. In May, 1936, an unemployed single mother left her three-month-old infant on the steps of the Salvation Army headquarters. The baby wore a note in which the mother said that she had gone to Austin in hope of finding a job. She promised, "I will send money every week if I have it."

In 1930 the state of Texas tried to minimize the effects of desertion by a spouse or parent in a law that facilitated support suits. As the law took effect in Bexar County, local officials reported encouraging signs that the legislation was slowing desertion. The county tried to counsel husbands, who were the primary targets, to keep families together. County-court records reveal, however, that mediation failed in many cases as wives took to the courts in hopes of forcing payments from their spouses or former spouses.

The reactions of Hispanic women to the new law reveal the limitations of cultural values in the depths of economic crisis. Despite cultural proscriptions that forbade wives from publicly shaming their husbands or even admitting that they had left home, Hispanic women were prominent among nonsupport plaintiffs. While they were unlikely to violate their husbands' authority as long as they remained at home, wives exercised considerable autonomy if their spouses deserted them.

Female family heads in all ethnic groups faced frightening circumstances during the Depression. When unemployment threatened the survival of their families, many women beseeched members of the Roosevelt administration to help them in some way. One mother wrote to Eleanor Roosevelt:

Aug 23—1939
San Antonio, Tex

Dear Mrs. Roosevelt:

I am trying hard to get on W.P.A. I'm a typist and just can't seem to find work. I have four little children depending on me. And I have no home and no money to buy food or pay rent. The relief has rejected me for W.P.A. work, because I have a three months old baby girl. The oldest boy is 6 and will go to school this year, but I don't know how I can send him if I dont get work.

My little baby needs milk and I can't buy it. Am living in one room in a basement which is warm and damp. . . .

Mrs. Roosevelt I'm begging you with all my heart to *please* help me if you can. I love my babies dearly and won't submit to them being put in a home away from me. I would simply die apart from them.

Mrs. Renee Lohrback

Despite the pressures of the Depression, most San Antonio families remained intact. In all ethnic groups most parents of young children stayed together during the Depression, but there were significant differences in family composition among Anglo, black, and Hispanic families. Overall, Anglo girls had greater chances than other San Antonio females of growing to adulthood in a family composed of two parents and their children and of imitating this pattern in their adult lives. Throughout the Depression the Anglo family was more stable than the minority family. The black family was the most likely of all San Antonio families to be broken by separation or abandonment, and the Mexican-American family was the most likely to be broken by death of a parent or child.

Mexican-American families were both larger and younger than other families, black families being the smallest. In 1930, Mexican Americans accounted for less than one-third of San Antonio families, but constituted three-fourths of families with three or more children under ten years of age and nearly two-thirds of families with four or more children under age twenty-one.

The San Antonio Health Department reported a decline in the birthrate during the Depression, especially during the early 1930s. The postponement of marriage and the practice of birth control were obvious factors in the declining birthrate, but abortion also persisted throughout the Depression as a means of family limitation.

When undertaken without proper medical assistance, abortion was dangerous. Each year a few San Antonio women died at the hands of untrained abortionists. The story of Mrs. Antonia Mena illustrates both the desperation of poor wives and the crude conditions under which abortionists operated. When she discovered that she was pregnant, Mrs. Mena, aged twenty-eight, sought the aid of an abortionist. With her sister she went to the home of Mrs. Leota Mowers, who told them that she had performed many abortions and that her clients had suffered no ill effects. Mrs. Mena paid Mrs. Mowers her last ten dollars and gave her a radio as security for the additional twenty-five dollars that Mrs. Mowers required. After the abortion had been performed, police were called to Mrs. Mowers's home, where Mrs. Mena was found dead on the living-room floor.

The declining birthrate that characterized the Depression, especially its early years, did not necessarily mean that household size decreased as well. The Depression discouraged persons in their late teens and early twenties from leaving home to begin their own households either as newlyweds or as single persons. Carmen Perry's brothers postponed marriage and remained in the parental home longer than they wished. A young single women named Schild lost her clerical job early in the Depression and returned to her parents' home after a period of independence. Married children might also share quarters with their parents. Ruby Cude and her husband and children moved in with her parents after a period of being on their own. As the Depression neared its end, large numbers of young adults found themselves in the same situation as Miss Schild and the Perrys.

One of the most common concerns of women who wrote letters to Eleanor Roosevelt and New Deal administrators asking for help was the reality that poverty could interfere with the education of their children. Few families considered allowing children to drop out of school to seek employment because almost no jobs were available for teenagers as the Depression deepened. Many mothers, however, confronted the prospect or the reality of children leaving school because they could not pay for books and supplies or because they did not have enough clothes to leave the house. One mother laid off from WPA employment wrote to Eleanor Roosevelt that "in September when school starts it will be impossible for mine to attend, they will have no shoes & there clothing is no better than rags."

In 1930 one in every ten San Antonio families included lodgers, who might be live-in servants, guests, boarders, or rent-paying family members. Beatrice Clay described the economic circumstances under which homeowners took in family members as boarders:

> I think there were some people who had a very very tough time because I had an uncle who lived almost on the same block that I lived. [He] was buying his home and he had not had a job for almost six months. And we were renting and he was buying so he came to me and asked me if I would move in with him. And he had his mother which is my grandmother and another nephew whose parents were both dead. And he said that they could make room and we could move in and what money we were paying for rent could pay the interest on his note to keep him from losing his house, which we did.

Black households like Clay's were the most likely to include boarders, and Mexican-American families were the least likely. While black San Antonians suffered residential segregation, they never experienced the intense overcrowding and slum conditions of the Mexican West Side. As Mexican immigrants flooded into the city in the 1920s, houses in the Mexican community were subdivided, and new one-room shacks were thrown up to accommodate the newcomers. Such close quarters discouraged adding outsiders to the household.

Regardless of the reasons, black households included more lodgers than did Mexican-American households. Since both the income from boarders and the responsibilites of caring for them may have discouraged married women from seeking work outside the home, it is surprising that black married women were both most likely to be in the labor force and most likely to keep lodgers. Conversely, married Hispanic women were least likely to seek work and least likely to have lodgers in their homes. Lodging arrangements are but one facet of the interaction between culture and economic conditions in San Antonio. The economic situation of the black family encouraged married women to bring money into the home in either wages or rent. Cultural values supported these economic motivations in black families. Female protectiveness in Hispanic families discouraged similar responses to need.

As mothers, both Anglo and black women worked with different goals from those of Mexican-American wives. Whereas a Hispanic mother taught her child obedience and devotion to family, an Anglo or black mother educated her child to "be somebody." In their adult lives Anglo women had a broader range of social contacts than either black or Hispanic women had and less emotional reliance on the extended family. Unlike Mexican-American wives, black wives frequently had close relationships with a few nonrelated women that involved some mutual dependence. Beatrice Clay, a black employee of Washer Brothers Department Store, maintained a mutually supportive friendship with a coworker that allowed both women to maintain steady incomes during the early years of the Depression. Anglo women, who were less likely to be employed, formed their extrafamilial friendships through churches, neighbors, social clubs, and their husbands. Even in the Depression years entertainment among Anglo women focused more around peer groups than around family. An evening's entertainment with other couples was an expected social activity of most wives, though the Depression may have reduced outings to a covered-dish supper at a friend's home. As an unmarried office clerk, May Eckles participated in similar activities with other unmarried friends or with a group of friends and relatives. Such get-togethers and group outings were not unknown to black and Mexican-American women, but they were less likely to center in relationships outside the family.

Women's understanding of their roles and responsibilities as daughters, wives, and mothers and as Anglos, blacks, or Hispanics predisposed them to cope with the realities of the Depression in different ways. A Hispanic mother ideally stayed at home to protect her family and her reputation, but there was no social disgrace for either her or her daughters if they sought pay for sewing or other tasks that they could undertake in their own homes. Black wives, accustomed to some autonomy in decision making, found employment outside the home easier to accept. Native-born

Anglo wives generally felt the least economic pressure to enter the work force, and most had not expected to work after marriage. Nevertheless, work outside the home did not carry the same stigma for the Anglo wife as for a Mexican-American wife. Regardless of marital status or cultural role definitions, women weighed a number of familial considerations in reaching their decisions about seeking employment. In such deliberations the pull of the labor market increasingly won out over the pull of the home, but the transition involved changes in the work lives of all family members, not just wives or daughters and not just the members of one racial or ethnic group.

[Family strategies for survival moved beyond purely private decisions as government programs began to offer new economic opportunities to women and men by the mid-1930s. Yet even these alternatives varied according to one's gender, ethnicity, and race.] The WPA educational programs in San Antonio offered hope and economic assistance, but the programs reflected local racial and ethnic prejudices as well. The vast majority of students and teachers were Anglo, but Mexican-American residents enrolled in some courses alongside Anglos and in other courses for Spanish-speakers. Adult classes in English, citizenship, and trade skills were offered through the "Americanization" program at the Sidney Lanier School, a Hispanic secondary school. Anglo and Hispanic women in San Antonio's education projects studied business and clerical subjects with the goal of gaining white-collar jobs. They also enrolled in such classes as furniture making that were created primarily to teach housewives to "make do" with home furnishings that could be constructed from scrap materials. Graduates of the home-improvement courses were expected to pass on their newly learned skills to female friends and neighbors. Under the WPA Anglo and Hispanic women were also employed in domestic work in the Housekeeping Aid Projects, programs to assist in home and child care when parents were ill or otherwise incapable of managing by themselves. The Housekeeping Aid Projects were totally separate from the Household Workers Project, the only educational program for black women, which taught them to be "capable domestics."

The first large public relief project for San Antonio women was a federally funded canning plant, which employed 900 women in the summer of 1934. Project administrators expected to double the plant payroll by the end of the year, but in January, 1935, only 450 women were employed. The second large project was a WPA sewing room. The first sewing room opened with 278 employees in October, 1935, and within a year sewing projects had expanded to employ 2,300 persons. The sewing rooms were the largest WPA projects for women, though various other programs employed lesser numbers of blue- and white-collar female workers. Women with clerical or administrative skills worked on all programs sponsored by the Federal Emergency Relief Administration and the WPA within and outside the Division of Women's Work, but more than half of all female WPA administrators in San Antonio worked with the sewing projects as supervisors or in some other administrative capacity.

While public works programs generally discriminated against women in a variety of ways, WPA projects offered a few women an unprecedented opportunity to develop and apply executive skills as project and agency administrators. In Texas as elsewhere women headed the offices and nearly all the projects of the Division of

Racial discrimination and ethnic bias were evident in the various educational, employment, and financial aid programs in San Antonio. The Housekeeping Aid Project, for example, trained Anglo and Hispanic women in home management and child care and placed them in temporary positions as live-in helpers to assist mothers who were ill or otherwise unable to manage by themselves. The Household Workers project was a separate program for black women designed to teach them skills related to their "appropriate" role as domestic servants.

Women's Work. A second category of white-collar jobs for women under emergency work programs was recordkeeping, both as administrative functionaries of public agencies and in special projects such as the Historical Records Survey and local projects to organize city ordinances and criminal records. Women in San Antonio served in various publicly funded positions as clinical aides, hospital workers, school cafeteria workers, and nursery-school workers. Librarians, editors, writers, artists, and musicians found work in the WPA professional programs. Women appeared regularly in WPA musical and theatrical performances in San Antonio and participated in arts programs under both the WPA and the National Youth Administration. Early in 1936 the San Antonio WPA office reported that 1,280 women and 2,739 men were employed in local professional projects.

In a city like San Antonio, where the Depression reached so broadly and deeply, the FERA and the WPA provided the margin of survival for many women and their families, though there was always more demand for work than either agency could begin to meet. Public works projects were late in coming to San Antonio, and women had an especially long wait for their meager share of emergency employment. Before the arrival of federal public assistance the legions of hungry and unemployed residents had few places to turn for help. Since neither San Antonio nor Bexar County dispensed local public relief funds, the unemployed could turn only to private charities during the early years of the Depression. The Salvation Army, the Junior League, the International Institute, Catholic and Protestant churches and convents, settlement houses, and other organizations helped feed and clothe destitute local residents and transients. The Bexar County Red Cross provided food, clothing, and shelter, and their relief expenditures increased 300 percent from 1928 through 1931. As San Antonian Veda Butler recalled, the relief commodities dispensed by the Salvation Army to the East Side black community were insufficient and barely edible, but people waited in line for hours for these handouts because of their desperate need.

There were virtually no Anglo-financed private social services other than the Salvation Army to which blacks could turn in times of need. However, a history of steady employment and the strong economic base of black churches provided the black community with some weapons to fight the ravages of the Depression. The Mexican-American community lacked the overall economic strength to see its members through hard times. A few private charities dispensed food and clothing on the West Side, but they could do little to mitigate the widespread starvation and disease. The concentration of poverty in San Antonio and its consequences are revealed in health statistics of the Depression years. In 1937, after public relief had alleviated some of the city's health problems, Mexican Americans suffered a death rate from tuberculosis of 310 per 100,000, blacks 138 per 100,000, and Anglos 56 per 100,000, giving San Antonio the worst record of any major American city. The infant death rate was 144 per 1,000 live births among Hispanics, 105 among blacks, and 51 among Anglos. For Mexican Americans housing conditions were as severe a threat as starvation. The high incidence of infant diarrhea and enteritis among Hispanic children testified to environmental dangers. Hundreds of mothers watched helplessly each year as their young children sickened and died.

Throughout the Depression local politicians and relief administrators discriminated against blacks and Hispanics. Racism was at the heart of the resistance to locally funded public relief, but early in the Depression, San Antonio leaders moved to improve the dispersal of private relief assistance. At the end of 1931, Mayor C. M. Chambers announced the formation of the Central Unemployment Relief Committee (CURC), which was authorized to collect private funds for relief efforts and to certify workers for the few public jobs funded by a recent bond issue. Encouraging charity was as far as either the city or the county would go in ameliorating local problems. The CURC exemplified Anglo antagonism to Hispanics in announcing that no aliens would be hired for jobs funded through contributions to the committee. The committee began providing make-work the following January, but the funds and foodstuffs the CURC could distribute made little impact, and by March the funds had been exhausted. During its three months of operation CURC distributed about $55,000 in money and food among the unemployed. The committee reported that "about 5,000 heads of families have registered with the committee and it is estimated that an additional 1,000 white families, who having been placed in such circumstances for the first time in their experience, due to a sense of humiliation and pride, have not registered."

Throughout 1932 stories of tragedy and suffering abounded. The *San Antonio Express* reported "five motherless children, living with a sick father in an old store-building, had no bed clothes and practically nothing to eat. Such instances of dire need are encountered frequently enough in normal times, but unemployment conditions have multiplied them." Private charities were unable to meet the demand for assistance during the same months that CURC offered relief. The Milk and Ice Fund, which had been established to provide a supply of sanitary milk to needy San Antonio children, assumed broader relief responsibilities early in the Depression. At the beginning of 1932 the fund warned that it could not continue its efforts through the remainder of the year without additional contributions, and in 1935 all fund activities terminated. The failure of public agencies to allocate general relief funds handicapped the city and county utilization of outside assistance. The Federal Farm Board's donation of 300,000 pounds of wheat flour nearly went unused because many families had no stoves and no funds were available to bake bread from the flour. The San Antonio Federation of Women's Clubs raised funds to bake 10,000 loaves of bread, and the rest of the flour was distributed to the needy.

Despite the obvious inadequacy of private funds to meet the local emergency, some civic leaders continued to oppose public relief. Commenting on President Hoover's plea in 1932 that relief administrators "make sure that no American this winter will go hungry or cold," the *San Antonio Express* argued that "Responsibility for that achievement rests, first of all, upon the individual citizen, who cannot evade his 'God-imposed obligation to look after his neighbor.' When that debt shall have been discharged, it will be time to appeal for government assistance, through the Reconstruction Finance Corporation." In fact, some RFC funds had already flowed into Bexar County, and in the fall of 1932 the city sought a $300,000 loan from the new corporation. The chamber of commerce estimated that twice that amount would be needed to sustain the unemployed through the winter.

Both the city and the county [also] benefited from expenditures of the NRA, the CWA, and the WPA. The CURC became a countywide committee under the guidance of the Texas State Relief Commission. In early August the committee, now federally funded, began making cash disbursements to relief clients. On August 5 more than one thousand persons lined up outside the Bexar County Courthouse to receive their payments of $4.50 per household head in exchange for two days' labor on relief projects.

Relief administrators heavily criticized cash payments as encouraging workers to refuse the jobs that were available. A. W. Greene, manager of the U.S. Employment Service office in San Antonio, asserted that he had been unable to meet requests for cotton pickers because of the cash payments. Greene insisted that hundreds of pickers, who had left San Antonio for the fields, turned back to the city when they learned that relief cash would be dispersed. A few days after Greene's statement to the press, police were called in to disperse a crowd that had besieged the farm-employment office on the West Side. The *San Antonio Light* reported that the crowd was composed of job applicants who had rushed to find picking jobs after hearing that all local work projects and cash relief payments would be suspended.

In September the relief committee, now known as the Bexar County Board of Welfare and Unemployment, replaced one central office with nine neighborhood relief offices. While bringing services closer to the clients, the decentralization also effectively segregated Anglo, black, and Mexican-American clients from each other. State and federal evidence of mismanagement of relief funds in Bexar County forced a second reorganization of the relief board in the late fall of 1933. Local work funds were cut back in February, 1934, when the CWA closed down. Relief rolls again rose to more than 17,000 families. The termination of work relief prompted disorder at the Mexican-American welfare office on the West Side.

The WPA and the NYA provided the major sources of help for the unemployed from 1935 through 1939. Federally funded relief provided the margin of survival for thousands of San Antonians, but there were never sufficient resources to meet the needs of all who qualified for assistance, and per capita relief expenditures in the city were low. In New Orleans, a city also hard-hit, monthly emergency relief expenditures under the FERA averaged $29.68 for a family of four, while in San Antonio the average was $15.74. Women workers in San Antonio, whether family heads or supplementary workers, faced special obstacles in obtaining emergency jobs.

Despite the establishment of women's divisions and the prominence of women in some New Deal agencies, women were second-class citizens under most work relief programs. Under the operating procedures of the WPA and other agencies, job preference was given to male family heads. Separated or widowed female family heads received first-priority ratings only if there were no adult male children in the household. A married woman whose husband was present in the home achieved first-priority certification only if her husband was disabled. An applicant of second-priority status stood no reasonable chance of employment in public works. Although the NYA created jobs for the youthful female workers who had been denied employment in the CCC, boys received preference over girls in NYA placement.

Overall, men dominated the better-paying emergency jobs. Among women the superior status of Anglos is revealed in statistics showing that a disproportionate number of women's jobs went to whites rather than blacks and no black or Hispanic women were prominent in the administration of federal programs for women in San Antonio. The general pattern of discrimination against women in the allocation of public or private relief jobs throughout the Depression also emerges in direct relief statistics. While needy men were given jobs, needy women were frequently extended only commodities. While men received most of the relief jobs in San Antonio, women comprised most of the direct relief clients.

As scholarly studies of the New Deal alphabet agencies have documented, the federal government accepted and reinforced southern laws and traditions of segregation in the administration of relief and public works programs. In San Antonio separate relief projects were maintained for blacks and whites. Mexican Americans and Anglos were not administratively segregated from each other in the work programs of the FERA or the WPA, but Anglo and Mexican-American clients rarely crossed paths in applying for relief commodities or emergency jobs. A relief office on the West Side served most of the Mexican-American clients, channeling Mexican-American men and women into unskilled work and reserving the few white-collar positions for Anglos. Similarly, federal and local relief agencies respected the tradition of occupational segregation by gender. The establishment of the women's division under both the FERA and the WPA generated segregation by sex in federal emergency job programs throughout the nation.

Particularly in San Antonio relief administrators regarded women as temporary workers whose primary role was in the home. Relief programs were structured to equip female clients with domestic skills that they could utilize after the Depression had passed. Relief programs developed around the assumption that additional women had been propelled into the labor market by declining male employment and that these women would retire to the home when the work of fathers and husbands returned to normal. Administrators recognized that some women would always be in the work force, and these workers were rigorously segregated into "appropriate" occupations. As the Texas relief director reported in 1935, "We believe our projects for women, in addition to keeping them from the despair of idleness, provide the more lasting benefit of permanently equipping these women to meet responsibilities in the home and to accept industrial opportunities as they develop."

Federal New Deal administrators demanded local support before they approved individual works projects. The refusal of San Antonio and Bexar County to appropriate relief funds presented a special problem in obtaining federal relief. Local support had to be obtained through private donations, usually of building use and supplies, or the allocation to federal projects of employees already on city or county payrolls and the use of space in city or county properties. Even after these initial barriers were overcome, lack of equipment and supplies frequently delayed or interrupted approved projects. The relief canning plant was forced to shut down for a period in 1935 because beef shipments failed to arrive. Shortages of machines and material in the sewing rooms caused especially severe problems because the sewing projects employed the most women.

Although sewing projects were created primarily as an appropriate alternative to direct relief for female family heads, Texas officials recognized the value of the workers' efforts in providing relief commodities. In 1935 the director of the WPA women's work division in San Antonio wrote the Washington office seeking continued support for sewing rooms:

> There is a most widespread and pressing need for garments for indigents, both for the unemployable of the Texas Relief Commission and also for those who are really employable but who have yet not been put to work. We feel that in operating these sewing rooms we can not only occupy our women profitably but can also do something of great value, particularly in clothing the school children of relief families, many of whom cannot attend school until such clothing is provided.

Texas officials frowned on any works project that employed women at tasks that they perceived as nontraditional. Although Texas women had worked as migrant agricultural laborers for generations, the state WPA head vetoed projects that required heavy outdoor labor. The WPA employed women on grounds improvements in several southern cities, but the Texas office refused to approve a similar project in the state, and the WPA in Texas also objected to federal funding of laundry work for women, though women were already extensively employed in commercial laundries throughout the state. Women's projects of the CWA, the FERA, and the WPA in Texas were largely confined to sewing, food processing, and domestic service or health care.

Programs for black women functioned on the assumption that the destiny of the black woman was domestic work. In an economic environment in which opportunities for the employment of domestic workers in homes were declining, the FERA and the WPA reinforced occupational segregation and participated in a discriminatory educational system that denied black women the skills to compete for the few areas of female employment that expanded during the Depression. In 1937, Mary Katherine Dickson, a local administrator, pointed out that a black church in San Antonio had been conducting a training program for black domestic workers and argued the need for such a program through the WPA adult-education program. Dickson reasoned that domestic training was the most suitable education for black women because "between 75% and 85% of persons employed in household service are black." In elaborating on her justification, Dickson revealed her personal perspective that the best interests of blacks and whites would be served by educating black women to function in an inferior place:

> In fact, the majority of housewives in San Antonio have a very real servant problem on their hands and, at present, no means of solving it satisfactorily. The public school system here, as elsewhere, has provided, in the past, essentially the same curriculum for the negroes as for the whites, in spite of the fact that their environments, their economic expectations, and their places in the social scale are mostly different.

The proposal went forward to federal officials in Washington with a supporting letter from Maury Maverick, the new congressman from San Antonio, whose election campaign had been marked by racist undercurrents. Maverick worked for household-worker projects through the following year. After an initial period of funding in 1938, Maverick cited the regional significance of the WPA Household Workers Training Project, noting that it was "the first attempt by the government to actually train these people for the jobs they are now performing. In the South . . . the field of labor for Negroes is restricted." Black women had a more difficult time than others in securing certification for WPA jobs. WPA supervisors and employees of the county employment office told black women that they should seek employment in private homes. As Lula Gordon complained to Eleanor Roosevelt, black women were forced into accepting domestic jobs, though such work often proved of short duration. Their employment in this manner might remove them from immediate consideration for any WPA jobs opening up, but if they refused the work, they would be taken off the WPA rolls altogether.

Justifiably, relief administrators in San Antonio were concerned about the possibility of charges of racial or ethnic discrimination, especially in the black community, which was better organized politically than the Hispanic West Side. Mary Taylor, the local WPA woman's work supervisor, sought to head off such charges in the face of budget cuts by publicizing programs for San Antonio blacks that had continued to function. In 1936 she wrote to her regional supervisor:

> As you know I had given considerable thought to developing good Negro projects—for obvious reasons! As soon as quota reduction was announced I asked Mr. Drought if he

would approve my having a series of articles on such projects prepared and sent to the big Negro newspaper in Pennsylvania. I thought it might forestall criticism as to racial discrimination.

WPA officials in San Antonio faced charges of racism not only because they did discriminate against blacks but also because San Antonio blacks had articulate spokesmen and organizations working on their behalf. Blacks in San Antonio suffered discrimination under the WPA that was unequaled in other parts of the state. Although Anglo and Hispanic garment workers were almost entirely segregated from each other in the private sector, no administrative decisions by the FERA or the WPA mandated separate public sewing rooms for the two groups. Nevertheless, officials assigned black women exclusively to separate projects. J. E. Thompson, a black San Antonio clergyman, supervised one project for black women in the city. In 1939, Thompson, who had conducted a private domestic-worker training program at the church he pastored, was fired as coordinator of the Household Workers Training Project. The National Association for the Advancement of Colored People and other groups unsuccessfully protested the dismissal. WPA administrators in San Antonio argued that blacks would not respect the authority of a member of their own race, though black supervisors had been successfully employed elsewhere.

WPA officials took a broader view of the occupational possibilities of Mexican-American women than of black women. The adult-education program of Sidney Lanier School, which enrolled more than three hundred Hispanic men and women, had Americanization as a unifying goal but presented various training and educational programs. Women were offered training in nutrition and home and child care. Clerical skills were another area of study, and some graduates of the school obtained employment as stenographers and bookkeepers. However, the majority of Hispanic WPA clients found jobs in sewing rooms and did not enter WPA classes.

Discrimination on the basis of marital status added to the liabilities of gender and ethnic origin that many women bore as they sought employment in Depression San Antonio. As Lois Scharf has documented with regard to the nation as a whole, the work rate among married women increased dramatically, but the increase occurred despite the disapproval of husbands, societal pressure, and some legal measures taken to deprive wives of employment. The Depression elicited unprecedented public pressure to drive women, particularly married women, from the work force. It did not matter that men were unlikely to prepare for or accept jobs as teachers, nurses, or secretaries; society demanded that married females withdraw from the work force. In 1931 the American Federation of Labor adopted a position endorsing discrimination in hiring against women whose husbands earned a decent wage.

Nationally the unfounded fears that women competed with men for a limited number of employment openings and that they displaced employed male workers was translated into a law prohibiting a husband and wife from simultaneous employment by the federal government. Section 213 of the Economy Act of 1932 did not specify which partner in a marriage would be hired or continued on the federal payroll, but since wives almost universally had less earning power than husbands, it was women who gave up federal jobs. Only a few states adopted similar legislation during the 1930s. Most states left the matter of working wives to local governments. At the local level female public employees were most visible in the schools, and married women teachers were the most common targets of discrimination.

Depression San Antonio was a city without a strong voice for women's rights. Although women in Atlanta, Georgia, and some other cities successfully fought policies preventing the employment of married female teachers, the dismissal of married women from the San Antonio schools met little opposition. In August, 1931, the San Antonio school board announced that married women would receive low priority in the hiring of new teachers. In June, 1932, all previously hired married women whose husbands earned a minimum of two thousand dollars a year were terminated. In 1931 offices in the Bexar County Courthouse began dismissing married women, a practice apparently opposed only by the victims. May Eckles noted in her diary:"There has been a mess stirred up in Jack Burke's office over cutting out the married women and Mrs. Achs is sure on the warpath, she says she is going to give Mr. Burke a piece of her mind at four o'clock this afternoon." Eckles registered her lack of sympathy with her coworkers when she noted, "Well all the married women are missing this morning and I aint sorry, for I certainly am not in favor of married women working unless they have to, there are too many unmarried ones without jobs." It did not trouble Eckles that there were three adult workers in her household while other households were being reduced to one or possibly no workers.

San Antonio's union voice was unsympathetic to the plight of the married female workers. William B. Arnold, editor of the pro-labor *San Antonio Weekly Dispatch,* accepted the fallacious argument that the firing of married women would create jobs for men, and he also argued that home and family suffered when wives went out to work. In 1939 he wrote:

> The wife is inescapably the builder of the home and the guardian of its children. These duties are necessarily neglected by working wives. We want no dictators telling women what to do; but the country cannot ignore the deterioration of the home, due to the pressure of married women in industry.

In drafting emergency employment programs for women, Texas relief officials were wary of drawing in married women. Texas officials balked at setting up household-worker projects in the state if second-priority female workers—women living with employed or employable fathers, husbands, or sons—were to be recruited. A Texas administrator reported that several organizations in San Antonio would donate space for conducting WPA training programs as long as no woman with an outside source of income was certified for entrance, because "the general feeling in this part of the country is that her husband and father should earn the livelihood for the family."

Although married women were discriminated against by the school board and had difficulty obtaining emergency jobs, personal influence in local administrative offices could break down the barriers that had been erected against their hiring. Anglo women, of course, were much more likely to have pull in city and county offices than black or Hispanic women. In 1933 an investigation by the Texas Senate of the Bexar County Board of Welfare and Employment involved accusations that wives of city and county employees were receiving emergency work wages while other San Antonians went hungry. The secretary of the welfare board presented evidence substantiating the complaints to the senate. Subsequent reorganization of the board eliminated the advantages that some wives had had, but complaints that privileged women received jobs to the detriment of the needy continued throughout the remainder of the Depression.

Women workers understood that their only competitors for emergency work were other women. The most likely critics of working women were unemployed women. Late in the Depression a widow with two dependents wrote Eleanor Roosevelt that her WPA salary had been cut while wives with no real need had experienced no reduction:

> I have been on the W.P.A at a salarie of $57.60 per month for the past few years. Recently I was cut to a $40.00 a month salarie. Instead of cutting the women who had other income and husbands to support them, they have cut the widow women with children and no other income. If the W.P.A had made this cut after an investigation to prove that people did not need their jobs, it would have been different, but they are taking the jobs away from the little people, while they have increased their own salaries. Why? Because the little fellow had no pull. It is not efficiency or education or refinement or need that counts in San Antonio, it is pull.

Thoughout the New Deal era women in supervisory positions were special targets of accusation that they did not need jobs or that they had obtained their positions through personal connections. Both the men and the women most likely to have influence were persons with white-collar skills. When supervisory positions on women's projects were filled, different criteria of selection were applied from those used in selecting women to perform the sewing, canning, cleaning, or inventorying that the projects involved. Mary Taylor wrote to Ellen Woodward that in the matter of supervisory personnel her office had not "made it a point to employ only needy people" but that when there were two equally qualified candidates the candidate with greater need was given preference.

In San Antonio as elsewhere in the nation, the administration of both public and private relief entailed endless bureaucratic red tape. Caseworkers were viewed with suspicion; almost all of them were Anglos and few were bilingual, though Mexican Americans comprised more than half the relief population. When Ruth Kolling was appointed to oversee local relief operations, she was characterized by the Bexar County Protective League as well seasoned in "the kind of charity where a poor woman is asked a bunch of impertinent questions and given a bunch of carrots and a bunch of beets and told not to eat it all at once."

Adela Navarro was the first Hispanic appointed as a caseworker in San Antonio, and it was more than a year before the second was hired. Often frustrated by official procedures or policies, she found ways to circumvent the rules when it seemed necessary. She refused to report to her superior that among her cases was a couple living together out of wedlock because she knew that they would be stricken from relief rolls if the information was divulged. However, said Navarro, someone was "so damn mean" that the information reached the relief office despite her silence on the issue. When her supervisor asked whether she knew that a particular couple were not married, she answered that she did not consider it her place to sit in moral judgment and that what she did know was that the people were hungry, and she could get them food. Satisfied with her response, the supervisor no longer interfered with her case reports.

Although public and private relief work was inconsistently administered and always inadequate to meet women's needs, clear patterns of preference and discrimination characterized the programs. Women were regarded merely as temporary and secondary workers who needed help getting by in hard times. The content of training programs generally militated against occupational advancement for women and was frequently unsuited to the local economy. Although black women were perceived as permanent workers, they received the fewest opportunities for training. Mexican-American women fared better than blacks in the variety of public works that employed them, but many Hispanics were turned away from relief and employment offices because of their alien status.

Questions for Study and Review

1. What was the impact of the Great Depression on the social, sexual, and technological developments of the preceding two decades?

2. How did women help their families cope with the Great Depression? How did Depression-era politics affect women's family and community roles in the long term?

3. Compare the family and community roles of San Antonio's Anglo, African American, and Hispanic women with those of black beauty culturists, female Klan members, and labor activists in New York City.

4. Economic crises often call into question the relation between women's paid labor and their domestic responsibilities. Compare responses to these concerns in Depression-era San Antonio; the Reconstruction-era South; and in early twentieth-century cities as they underwent another wave of industrialization.

Suggested Readings and Web Sites

Elna Green, *Looking for the New Deal: Florida Women's Letters during the Great Depression* (2007)
Ann Marie Low, *Dustbowl Diary* (1984)
Valerie Matsumoto, "Redefining Expectations: Nisei Women in the 1930s," *California History* (1994)
Susan Ware, *Holding Their Own: American Women in the 1930s* (1982)
The Library of Congress American Memory Site
    http://memory.loc.gov/ammem/index.html
The New Deal Network Site
    http://www.newdeal.feri.org
The 1930s Project
    http://xroads.virginia.edu
The Franklin D. Roosevelt Library and Digital Archives
    www.fdrlibrary.marist.edu

T he demands of "total war" set the entire country in motion during World War II. Huge waves of internal migration—around fifteen million Americans moved during the war—transformed many aspects of family and community life for women. Japanese-Americans were interned; husbands and fathers were drafted into the military. Military wives followed their husbands or decided to move in with their parents or in-laws while their men were in the service. Other women left rural towns for the nation's cities in search of well-paid defense industry jobs. The conflict also created a tremendous demand for nurses. Monahan and Neidel-Greenlee recount here how the Army enlisted close to sixty thousand of these female professionals to serve as combat nurses. Many traveled to dangerous situations overseas, situations they could have never imagined before the war.

This recruitment drive grew out of the War Department's determination to avoid asking men to perform the traditionally female job of nursing. Women responded with enthusiasm to the call for volunteers. The experience of these female recruits, however, illuminates the ironies of a rigid sexual division of labor. In the 1940s, the U.S. Army did not want women in combat, traditionally the exclusive province of men. But it needed nurses on the front lines to provide modern combat medical treatment. Thus, it either had to train men for a "woman's" job or send women into the masculine world of combat.

The Army resolved this dilemma by classifying nurses as noncombatants requiring minimal military training and half the pay of male servicemen. This decision did nothing to shield women from enemy fire or the physical hardships of combat. Nurses dodged bullets and bombs, ate C-rations, and washed in their helmets alongside male soldiers. Their determination to comfort maimed and dying men thrust them into nightmarish scenes that never faded from memory. Yet few Americans are aware—even today—that women served in World War II combat. Monahan and Neidel-Greenlee recorded the experiences of these female veterans in the hopes of contributing to current debates over women, citizenship, and military service.

Nurses were notable for their frontline service. But they were joined in the military by thousands of other women during these years. The War Department recruited women only with great reluctance. To allay public anxieties about women soldiers, the military worked to demonstrate how women could retain their feminine charms in the most masculine of environments. Recruiting posters featured women sporting military uniforms that accentuated their femininity and sexual allure; these women looked more like movie stars than rugged fighters. The uniforms may have been impractical for battlefield conditions, but these reassuring images had an important effect on the war effort. They asserted that traditional gender roles and images could be maintained even in the thick of "total war," and thus increased the acceptance, at least temporarily, of women in the military

Still, fashionable uniforms were probably less important than patriotic zeal in carrying women to the recruiting office. Ultimately, 140,000 women served in the Women's Army Corps (the WACs); 100,000 volunteered for the WAVES (the Navy's volunteer corps); 23,000 for the Marine Corps Women's Reserve; and 13,000 for the Coast Guard's Women's Reserve. Women also entered military service as Navy nurses. Yet these volunteers did little to dissipate the deep suspicion Americans harbored for women in uniform. The specter of unrestrained sexuality was most troubling for many observers, who predicted that enlistment would lead women into both lesbianism and heterosexual promiscuity. While most of these recruits ultimately returned to civilian life, the American military was permanently altered. Yet even as today's military depends on women to meet its enlistment quota, the War Department retains its World War II–era assumption that women will serve in limited "noncombat" roles.

The image of "Rosie the Riveter" has come to provide a visual reminder of women's contributions on the industrial home front during World War II. Monahan and Neidel-Greenlee hope that combat nurses will become equally iconic symbols of feminine strength and patriotism from this period. Their vivid account emphasizes how wartime exigencies brewed a complicated mix of exhilaration and anxiety for young women.

Women under Fire: Frontline U.S. Army Nurses in World War II

Evelyn M. Monahan and Rosemary Neidel-Greenlee

I ask for my boys what every mother has a right to ask—that they be given full and adequate nursing care should the time come when they need it. Only you nurses who have not yet volunteered can give it. . . . You must not forget that you have it in your power to bring back some who otherwise surely will not return.

—Eleanor Roosevelt, editorial,
American Journal of Nursing, August 1942

The federal government launched a sophisticated propaganda campaign when it made the decision to recruit women into military service for the first time during World War II. Posters like this packaged female military service for public consumption. The backdrop of ships and skyscrapers appealed to young women yearning for adventure. Yet the traditionally feminine appearance of these WAVES spoke to public anxieties about women in the military. The uniforms in this poster accentuated the recruits' femininity and sexual allure. These images reassured anxious Americans that gender roles could be maintained in the thick of "total war."

On 9 November 1942—one day after Lieutenants Helen Molony, Theresa Archard, Ruth Haskell, and the other nurses of the 48th Surgical Hospital landed with combat forces in North Africa—twenty-four-year-old Claudine Glidewell raised her right hand before a notary public in Wichita, Kansas, and was sworn into the U.S. Army Nurse Corps. The ceremony followed three days and nights of farewell parties where childhood friends, nursing school buddies, and longtime neighbors wished the pretty blue-eyed blonde well, and sent her off to war with their blessings and best wishes.

Claudine was now one of thousands of young women nurses who had been joining the armed forces in the months following America's entrance into the war in December 1941. In early 1942, the U.S. Army had announced that it would need at least fifty thousand military nurses to care for the wounded and sick of the battles to come, and set out to recruit women to fill this need. And in 1942, it was women—and only women—who were being recruited to fill the posts of army nurses.

There were male nurses in America. In the late 1930s and early 1940s, men were a very small minority in an occupation traditionally dominated by women. Despite the urgent need during wartime for military nurses, male nurses were barred from practicing their profession in the armed forces. During World War I, when seven male registered nurses petitioned Congress for the right to practice nursing within the Army Nurse Corps, the men were advised that ". . . all legislation strictly restricted membership in the Army Nurse Corps to women." The prevailing military opinion of the day was that the duties which naturally comprised a nurse's daily routine, such as bathing patients, emptying bedpans and urinals, and seeing that patients received nutritious meals or special diets, were too menial and degrading to be performed by men who had military status as officers. Some of the registered male nurses who had volunteered or were drafted into the military during World War II were placed in enlisted billets (jobs or positions) as medical technicians. Although the American Nurses Association ascribed to a philosophy that accepted and encouraged the employment of male nurses in both civilian and military life, military tradition and opinion was still firmly against male officers practicing nursing in the armed forces. It would be thirteen years before Second Lieutenant Edward Lyon, a nurse anesthetist from Kings Park, New York, would enter the Army Nurse Corps on 10 October 1955 as the first male nurse on active duty.

Since there was no legal compulsion—no draft—to conscript women into the military nurse corps, the 1901 law that had established the U.S. Army Nurse Corps directed the U.S. Surgeon General to establish and maintain a list of nurses who were qualified to serve during a national emergency. By 1933, the American National Red Cross, though not technically a government agency, was recruiting nurses into a "reserve" from which the government could call the women into service during national emergencies, including war. This official reservoir of nurses from which the U.S. Army and Navy could supplement their nurse corps was referred to as the First Reserve of the American National Red Cross Nursing Service.

With the threat of war in 1940, the American National Red Cross began to recruit nurses for the First Reserve. Although the American National Red Cross is a voluntary agency, it acted as a quasi-governmental agency since it officially held the responsibility for recruiting nurses for the First Reserve, processing their applications, and reviewing their nursing credentials, thus relieving the Army and Navy Nurse Corps of these responsibilities at that time.

On 30 June 1940, the U.S. Army had 942 regular army nurses on active duty. The First Reserve had a list of 15,770 qualified registered nurses who had volunteered to serve in times of emergency or disaster. On 27 May 1941, with global war looming and a declaration of a national emergency by the U.S. government, the American National Red Cross activated these First Reserve nurses. They were called up to serve a one-year tour of active duty with either the U.S. Army or U.S. Navy Nurse Corps. When Japan, Germany, and Italy declared war against the United States in December 1941, the American National Red Cross launched a nationwide search for fifty thousand more nurses. A national appeal went out by radio, posters, pamphlets, magazines, nursing journals, and newspapers for registered nurses to volunteer for wartime duty in the Army and Navy Nurse Corps.

A 1942 Red Cross pamphlet entitled *Uncle Sam Needs Nurses* appealed to the consciences of registered nurses: "You nurses of the country have an inescapable burden to bear. The moral obligation imposed upon you by your years of preparation gives you no choice of road to follow. No one else can do your job. It takes years to prepare a nurse and the Army and Navy need you now. The only decision you have to make is where you are needed the most . . . not where you will be safest or your work easiest or your career most promising."

On 12 April, the Sunday *New York Times* ran the following ad: "Needed: 50,000 nurses. Nursing is now a big-time career." The August 1942 *American Journal of Nursing* announced: "Nurses to the colors! Every nurse must serve—with the armed forces or at home. Which is your category? Priorities in nursing to meet the war emergency are here defined by the National Nursing Council for War Service."

In reply, thousands of young and not-so-young female registered nurses joined both the U.S. Army and U.S. Navy Nurse Corps. By 30 June 1943, approximately forty thousand women had been recruited for active duty, and the pressure to serve continued to be applied to civilian nurses. The American Nurses Association ran articles and editorials encouraging nurses to join the military. These volunteers could join either the "Regulars" or the "Reserves": The Regulars took women between the ages of twenty-two and thirty, while the Reserves took women up to the age of forty. For both, the women had to be unmarried, widowed, or divorced; to have graduated from an approved school of nursing as well as from high school; to hold U.S. citizenship or be a citizen of a friendly country; to hold state registration; and to be physically fit and "of good character and general suitability." A recruitment goal of two thousand nurses a month had been set; in some parts of the country local recruitment committees ferreted out civilian nurses who met the criteria and urged them to step forward and serve their country in either the army or the navy since ten thousand more nurses were needed. Thousands of civilian registered nurses did volunteer, passed the qualifications, and entered the military.

Thousands of these volunteers would volunteer again or raise no objection when assigned to serve in frontline hospitals in combat zones all over the world. In the opening months of the war, the young women, with little or no military training, were assigned to field and evacuation hospitals and shipped overseas to live and work in combat zones as few as three miles from the front lines. These women volunteered to serve despite the fact that . . . under the 1920 Army Reorganization Act, the army offered only "relative rank" to military nurses—that is, the army paid women only 50 percent of the salaries paid to male officers of the same rank. Added to the inequity in pay was the fact that U.S. Army nurses, although given the relative rank of officers, did not rate a salute. Despite these inequities, the number of military nurses on active duty steadily increased from the June 1940 level of 942, to 12,475 by June 1942, and 36,607 by June 1943.

If Claudine Glidewell had had her way, she would have signed up for the Army Nurse Corps almost a year earlier, immediately after America entered the war. But obligations at home stood in her way. Claudine's mother, Mrs. Hazel Glidewell, had been a widow for many years; moreover, Mrs. Glidewell had been seriously ill for two months before the Japanese launched their attack on Pearl Harbor. As the oldest of two children and the only daughter, Claudine assumed much of the responsibility for her younger brother, Stuart. Since Pearl Harbor, Stuart had been anxious to enlist in the army but, like his sister, had waited, hoping their mother's health would improve. For the first six months of 1942, Mrs. Glidewell's health was touch and go, and son and daughter considered it their responsibility to remain at home to support their mom.

Claudine was working as one of three nurses for Dr. Everett L. Cooper, Wichita's busiest obstetrician, and business was becoming more hectic with every passing month. Babies were arriving in record numbers from mid-September 1942 onward. The boom in births was beginning, understandably, nine months after the men of America had begun to take leave of their wives for the war. Claudine spent most of her time in the delivery room or on call. Despite the fact that three nurses were in Dr. Cooper's employ, Claudine's easygoing disposition and natural friendliness led to her being requested by name by expectant mothers when they went into labor. After a month of assisting at the births of scores of babies conceived on the eve of their fathers' departures for the war, Claudine decided to sign up for the Army Nurse Corps. Her mother was getting better every day, had resumed most of her household tasks, and with the monthly allotment from her daughter's military pay, and Stuart's help, would be able to get along well financially.

During the last week of October 1942, a letter arrived from the War Department ordering Claudine to report to Fort Riley, Kansas, in two weeks. When she broke the news to her family, Stuart had his own surprise. The twenty-two-year-old had enlisted in the army the previous day, and would leave for basic training before Claudine left for the Army Nurse Corps. Through tears, Mrs. Glidewell assured her children that, with allotments from both of them, she would be able to manage well financially, and otherwise. She told them she would miss them terribly, but was extremely proud that they wanted to serve their country. The evening was filled with reminiscences and laughter until the phone rang and Claudine was called out to assist Dr. Cooper with another delivery.

On Wednesday, 11 November, Claudine, her mother, and several of Stuart's friends from high school said good-bye to Stuart; they hugged and kissed the boy and shook his hand as he boarded a crowded train that carried him off to basic training with the U.S. Army Signal Corps. The next day, Mrs. Glidewell's heart would ache again as she and a half dozen friends accompanied Claudine to the Greyhound bus station. She held her daughter close and whispered through her tears, "I've already told God that I've only loaned my children to the army. He has to bring you back or listen to my complaints for a very long time."

"Honestly, Mom, I'll be fine," Claudine said. "Fort Riley is only one hundred miles away."

As the young woman stepped onto the bus, a familiar voice called out to her, "We'll be praying for you, Claudine." She knew without turning around that the voice belonged to her friend and Sunday school teacher, "Mom" Appleby. She took a window seat and waved to her mother and friends.

Mom Appleby had taught Claudine a lot over the years. As the driver closed the door and eased the bus toward the main road, Claudine could almost hear Mom Appleby advising her: "Always remember to trust in God; to have the courage to let Him watch over you; and for Heaven's sake, don't become a raving maniac when you're afraid."

If anyone had told the twenty-eight-year-old, brown-eyed brunette Evelyn "Andy" Anderson on 7 December 1941 that she would have to fight her way into the U.S. Army Nurse Corps, she would have laughed at such an absurd remark. The army had made it clear that they would need at least fifty thousand registered nurses to volunteer for the Army Nurse Corps. Yet when Evelyn Anderson raised her right hand and took the oath for admission, it was after two days of arguments with recruiters and examining physicians as to why being four pounds underweight should not keep her from serving her country as an army nurse. Finally, after many assurances that at five feet three and 107 pounds, she was "not underweight for her family," and that she "had always been thin but healthy," the army issued a waiver for her weight and allowed her to become an army nurse.

On 16 March 1942 the army ordered Anderson to report to Fort George C. Meade in Maryland. Andy worked there as a surgical nurse for three weeks before being directed to report to Camp Shanks, New York, to join the 93rd Evacuation Hospital, which was to sail for an overseas theater of war. A waiver for insufficient body weight not only got a short, thin nurse into the Army Nurse Corps, it got her a ticket to the combat zone and a reservation for frontline military nursing.

After a nearly one-hundred-mile trip, the bus from south-central Kansas carrying Claudine Glidewell and another new army nurse, June Gordon, Claudine's best friend, arrived at Fort Riley, in northeastern Kansas. As the bus made its way along the broad, tree-lined streets of the large military post, Claudine, from her window seat, could see neat red-brick houses standing behind the winter-bare branches of beautiful old oaks, hickories, and maples.

Fort Riley, a 100,000-acre military post, had been established in 1853. It was home to thousands of soldiers, including the First Infantry Division. The post included the U.S. Army correctional facility, an airfield, Irwin Army Community Hospital, and a smaller hospital facility called Camp Whitside. In addition to barracks, the post had multiple housing units for families, bachelor officers' quarters, and visiting officers' quarters.

The two station hospitals—Irwin Army and Camp Whitside—served thousands of troops at Fort Riley. Camp Whitside consisted of wards in multiple two-story wooden army buildings that were connected by outside wooden ramps to the nurses' quarters, a mess hall, and other buildings.

Lieutenant Glidewell was assigned to a medical ward where most of her patients were suffering from winter colds and seasonal flu, and the standard treatment was Brown's Cough Mixture and nosedrops administered every four hours. After several weeks at Camp Whitside, as other nurses who had been there longer were sent overseas, Glidewell's responsibilities increased until she was placed in charge of her ward—a long, open room with a center aisle lined by twelve beds on each long wall. The beds were white and each had a white nightstand at the head on the left side.

One morning, the chief nurse, First Lieutenant Gertrude Ryan, called Glidewell to her office and asked her to "special" a young African-American soldier who was ill with a serious case of pneumonia. In 1942, before penicillin was available, pneumonia was far more likely to prove fatal than it is today. Claudine spent her eight-hour shifts in the young man's private room, changing his position, getting him to cough at regular intervals, administering medication and oxygen, helping him with his meals, and talking to the soldier about his family and getting well. After ten days, the private first class seemed to be out of danger. On what would very likely be one of her last eight-hour shifts specialing this soldier, Claudine was shocked to find that the young man appeared to have had a relapse: His temperature had suddenly soared to 104°Fahrenheit. But on closer inspection, Claudine noted that he did not look feverish and his skin did not feel hot. After twenty minutes of conversation, the patient admitted that he liked talking to Lieutenant Glidewell and did not want to lose her as a private duty nurse. He confessed to holding the thermometer against a hot tube of his bedside radio and promised not to do it again. Glidewell took his temperature and recorded the 98.6°F on his chart. She said good-bye to him that afternoon, convinced that when she returned to duty the next day, he would have been moved to an open ward.

After her shift ended, she met two friends and went to the Post Exchange (PX) to shop, and to the Officers' Club for dinner. When she returned to her quarters that evening, she opened the door to a wonderful and unexpected fragrance, the heady bouquet of dozens of red roses. Two very excited nurses met Claudine at the door, bursting with the news that four dozen red roses had been delivered that day. A card beside one of the vases read: "Thank you for taking such good care of one of our men." It was signed: "Sincerely, Sgt. Joe Lewis." Joe E. Lewis was the reigning heavyweight boxing champion of the world at the time, and a sergeant stationed at Fort Riley. He was also an African-American—or "Negro" or "Colored," as African-Americans were called then. Lewis's extravagant thanks to Claudine, a white nurse, for having crossed the line to give special care to an African-American soldier, underscored the segregation enforced at that time between "Coloreds" and whites in the military.

When America entered the war in 1941, there were an estimated 8,000 female African-American registered nurses in the United States. Yet the U.S. Army set a recruitment quota of only 56 "Colored" nurses, who would be assigned to care only for Negro troops. During World War I, 18 African-American army nurses had served both black and white troops at Camp Sherman, Ohio, and Camp Grant, Illinois, during the influenza epidemic in late 1918. But the army would insist in 1941 that "Colored" troops be administered to by "Colored" nurses only and white troops be cared for by white nurses. In March 1941, the National Association of Colored Graduate Nurses (the American Nurses Association did not accept black nurses into its membership in 1941) initiated a campaign to convince the U.S. Army to increase the quota, but it was not until 1943 that the army raised its quota of African-American nurses to 160. At that time, African-American nurses were stationed at "Colored posts," such as Fort Huachuca, Arizona, and Tuskegee, Alabama. Not until mid-1944 did the army relax its segregation of "Colored" and white caregivers. By July 1945, approximately 500 African-American nurses were serving on active duty. Until segregation restrictions were lifted, white nurses and doctors treated injured and sick black troops stationed at segregated white posts like Fort Riley.

Life at Fort Riley was not all work. The approximately one hundred army nurses were surrounded by thousands of men and the women never wanted for a date or male companionship. One night, Claudine Glidewell agreed to a double-blind date with Artemese Kessler, a former classmate from civilian nursing school. When the two nurses went to the dayroom to greet their escorts, a tall, blond, blue-eyed twenty-six-year-old lieutenant stepped up to Claudine and said, "Hi, I'm Frank Doyle. You're going with me." The four went to the Officers' Club, where Claudine and Lieutenant Doyle danced and talked for hours. Near the end of the evening as they sat together, Frank announced, "I'm going to marry you." Claudine laughed in amusement and disbelief.

By Christmas, the couple had been on a half-dozen dates and Frank was increasingly more a part of Claudine's thoughts. When she developed a severe case of sinusitis two days after Christmas and was hospitalized at Fort Riley's main hospital, Claudine was surprised to learn that Frank had been admitted the night before with an upper respiratory infection. Since Frank was ambulatory and on the Officers' Ward, he was a frequent visitor. During his third visit, while Lieutenant Glidewell was floating in a haze brought on by an injection of morphine for a severe headache due to the sinusitis, Frank asked Claudine to marry him. She accepted without hesitation.

Toward the second week of January 1943, with both back on duty, Claudine received a phone call from Frank. In 1943, no one at Fort Riley, neither soldier nor nurse, had private phones in their rooms. One phone was stationed on each floor in the soldiers' or nurses' quarters and it was connected to the Fort Riley switchboard. When the phone rang, whoever was nearby answered and then tried to find the person being called. When Claudine came to the phone, she learned from Frank that he was leaving Fort Riley and being shipped to Paris, Texas. He asked to see her that night. They met and Frank presented his bride-to-be with an engagement ring that had been a gift from his grandparents. "I hope it's all right," he told Claudine. "It's the only ring I have, and it can be cut down to fit you." They said good-bye that night with the knowledge that Frank was to leave for Texas in a matter of hours, but they had made plans to marry in the spring.

The next morning, Lieutenant Glidewell was called to the phone on her ward. It was Frank. His train was not leaving until that night and he wanted to see Claudine again before he left. As it turned out, she had a half-day off, so the two met in the middle of a snowstorm and took the bus to Manhattan, Kansas, for the day. During the twenty-mile trip, Frank convinced Claudine to marry him that afternoon and they trudged through thick falling snow to the courthouse for a license. At the time, Kansas did not require a blood test or a waiting period, so their next job was to find a man of the cloth to perform the ceremony. There were five ministers in Manhattan, and the Methodist clergyman would be available in midafternoon. That gave the pair enough time to stop by a jewelry store to purchase a wedding ring. They agreed on a gold band encircled by engraved orange blooms.

It was not unusual for women to marry men in the armed forces just before the soldiers left for overseas duty. In a world where the future of couples in love could end with a bullet or a bomb, young people took whatever happiness they could be sure of at the moment. Many of the brides who saw their men off to war either went to live with their parents or the groom's parents until the end of the war. Other civilian wives bonded together and shared apartments or rented houses until their husbands returned. There would be many a young wife who received a telegram from the War Department informing her that her husband had been killed or was missing in action. Many counted themselves lucky if they were pregnant with or had already given birth to their husband's child before he left for the front.

The reverse scenario—that of a young husband receiving news of his wife's death at the front—was a rarity in the 1940s, given that women were not soldiers.

Nonetheless, it was a real possibility in the case of military nurses: The families of several army nurses who would later ship out for combat zones with Claudine Glidewell would receive a War Department telegram informing them that the women had been killed by enemy action in a combat area. Yet death was the last thing that concerned Claudine and Frank as they made their way through a Kansas snowstorm to the altar.

Three weeks later, in mid-February, Frank managed a fifteen-day leave and headed to Fort Riley to see his new wife. It was time for Claudine to tell the principal chief nurse of both hospitals at Fort Riley, First Lieutenant Pearl T. Ellis, that she was married. The chief nurse wished Claudine well, but told her that her maiden name could not be changed to her married name on the records. Claudine would remain "Lieutenant Glidewell" for the duration. However, Chief Nurse Ellis did give the new Mrs. Doyle permission to allow Lieutenant Doyle to stay in her room at night. The day after the first night Claudine and Frank spent together as husband and wife, Claudine and three other nurses received orders transferring them to Schick General Hospital in Clinton, Iowa. In the few days the women had left to them before leaving Fort Riley, Claudine managed to take Frank on a weekend trip to Wichita to meet her mother and friends. After returning, Frank spent the next leg of his honeymoon with his wife and three other army nurses in a crowded day coach headed for Clinton.

Given the nature of army barracks life, Claudine and Frank had not been able to spend much time alone together in the first month of their marriage. But once they reached Clinton, they were given a few hours alone. Since Schick General Hospital was brand new and had yet to receive its first patient, the principal chief nurse, First Lieutenant Jessie Locke, gave Lieutenant Glidewell permission to spend her off-duty hours at a hotel in Clinton. The newlyweds walked to the hotel hand-in-hand, looking forward to the novelty of privacy and time alone together, only to find Frank's mother sitting in the lobby waiting to meet her new daughter-in-law. The elder Mrs. Doyle had spent several days on the train from New York with the intent of surprising her son and his new wife. After three days spent with his bride and his mother, Frank boarded the train for Paris, Texas, while Lieutenant Glidewell reported to duty on the isolation ward of Schick General Hospital.

Glidewell was busy creating a nursing care plan for each type of communicable disease patient when the phone rang and she was asked to report to the chief nurse. She hurriedly reported to Lieutenant Locke, fearing she was about to receive bad news about Frank's train to Paris, Texas. Instead, Claudine was shocked to discover that she was being relieved of duty at Schick General and assigned to the 95th Evacuation Hospital, which was preparing to leave for a combat area. Someone had realized at the last minute that no nurses were assigned to the 95th Evac, so orders went out to twelve different army hospitals mobilizing one to six of their nurses for service overseas. The forty-four army nurses named were to join the officers and men of the 95th Evac at Camp Breckenridge, Kentucky.

Within twenty-four hours, Claudine left Clinton, Iowa, for Camp Breckenridge, Kentucky, on 5 March 1943. As was the case with all movements of troops and hospitals, exactly where Claudine and the 95th were headed and when were kept top secret from all, including the men and women of the 95th themselves. Claudine feared she would be shipped overseas before Frank had any knowledge that she had even left Schick General Hospital. At Breckenridge, on breaks between learning to pitch a pup tent and going on several long hikes, Claudine repeatedly placed long-distance calls to Paris, Texas, leaving messages with the switchboard operator for Frank to return her call. The process of placing long-distance phone calls in 1942, in the days before direct dialing and answering machines, was complicated: Claudine would call the switchboard and ask to be connected. Sometimes the call did not connect, or no one picked up, or Frank was unavailable to take the call. If he was unavailable, a message would be left with the switchboard at his camp. For days, Claudine had called and left messages; Frank called back several times only to find Claudine unavailable to take his call. On two or three occasions, Claudine missed Frank's return call by just five or ten minutes. After four days of near-heartbreaking misses, the chief nurse of the 95th Evac, First Lieutenant Blanche F. Sigman, allowed Claudine to leave a class on map reading to run to the orderly room and take her call.

Claudine and Frank talked for almost twenty minutes. It was ironic that Claudine was leaving for the front before Frank, and both remarked on how strange it seemed for a husband to be saying good-bye to his wife, who was being shipped to a combat zone. When each had told the other "I love you" for the third or fourth time, they said good-bye and Claudine clicked for the long-distance operator. In those days, the person who placed the long-distance call had to speak to a long-distance operator after the call was completed to get the charges and pay for the call. The military post where the long-distance call was placed billed the person placing the call. The operator's friendly voice told Claudine that the gentleman had paid for the call and Claudine went back to her map reading class. Three days later, she received a letter from Frank containing four one-dollar bills "to cover the charges"; obviously, Frank had understood that Claudine had arranged to pay for the call. As it turned out, neither had paid: The call had been placed so many times from each direction that the operators forgot who placed it originally and therefore failed to bill either party. Frank and Claudine's phone call was paid through the courtesy and confusion of Bell Telephone.

At Camp Breckenridge, the nurses spent a good amount of time learning how to pack a bedroll. "We were supposed to be able to roll the thing fast so we could clear out quickly in case of a retreat in the war zone," Claudine remembered. "In fact, that's how I got my nickname. I was rolling my bedroll for the third time when two nurses from Sioux City, Iowa, asked if I wanted to go to nearby Evansville, Indiana, to do some last-minute shopping. I shouted back that I'd be with them in a second, and that my middle name used to be 'Speed.' From there on everyone called me 'Speedy.' They even stenciled it on my equipment, duffel bag, bedroll, foot locker— everything had 'Speed' and the last three numbers of my service number stenciled on them."

Nicknames did not stop with Claudine "Speedy" Glidewell. Her closest friends, the two nurses from Sioux City, Iowa, Bernice Walden and Isabelle Wheeler, were affectionately christened and stenciled, respectively, "Hut Sut" after a popular song of the day, and "Bee Wee."

In late March, Chief Nurse Lieutenant Sigman gave Claudine permission to go to Louisville on an overnight pass to visit a friend who had just had a child. Once the L&N train pulled into the railroad station, Claudine caught the bus to

St. Matthews and the home of her new godchild. Marge, the child's mother, was waiting with a telegram in her hand when Claudine stepped off the bus. The telegram was short and to the point: "Return at once Stop Blanche Sigman."

Claudine was not the only off-duty member of the 95th to be summarily called back to camp. Military police had gone into Evansville, Indiana, and other nearby towns to gather up all off-duty members of the 95th Evacuation Hospital who were away from camp. The 95th was being mobilized for the front.

Three days later, on 2 April 1943, at 2000, the personnel of the 95th Evac, dressed with full field packs—bedrolls, map cases, musette bags (large military shoulder bags used by both men and women), canteens, and helmets strapped to their pistol belts—boarded a train and left for Camp Shanks, New York. The unit traveled on a private train and the nurses had a Pullman car all to themselves. "Between the excitement of each new experience was the realization that we were off to a combat zone where real bullets, shells, and bombs would bring wounds and death every day," Claudine recalled. "It added flashes of solemnity to the party atmosphere we were living in."

Their train arrived at Camp Shanks on 4 April, and they were the first troops to stay on the post. Like hundreds of other military camps in 1943, Camp Shanks had been thrown up virtually overnight to accommodate the training and movement of troops. Hence, everything was new, muddy, and untried. "The streets in the camp were rivers of mud and the wooden barracks had new army cots complete with new pillows," Claudine remembered. "I'll never forget those pillows. The feathers in them must have come straight from the chickens with no cleaning in between. They stunk to high heaven."

The next day, the nurses discovered that the PX had almost nothing a woman might need or want. In fact, the manager asked them to make a list of things they should stock for the next women who would come through camp. Claudine, Hut, and Bee Wee spent a lot of time trying to find items on a list that the army had given each to fill. One of the most difficult items to find were a dozen Curity cloth diapers. Feminine products such as sanitary pads were not stocked at most post exchanges and it was up to each individual army nurse to make certain she had a good stand-in—cloth Curity diapers. Where a nurse found and purchased the dozen diapers was totally the woman's responsibility. The washable cloth diapers would also double as turbans in the heat and dust of future hospital sites.

Most of the 95th's time at Camp Shanks was taken up with immunizations and the issuing of additional equipment. Every member of the hospital received a full issue of chemically impregnated clothing that was to be used in case of a poisonous gas attack by the Germans. The military planners in World War II were quite concerned that the Germans might employ some of the chemical agents they had used in World War I. The chemically impregnated clothing was intended to protect military personnel from the effects of chemical agents that could enter the body through exposed skin. One such agent was mustard gas, which when sprayed or exploded in shells would fall on exposed skin or untreated clothing and cause large balloonlike blisters, nausea, and vomiting. At the least, mustard gas was painful and disfiguring; at worst; it could be lethal. "They also made us carry two 'impregnated' mattress covers in our luggage," Claudine said. "We learned later that they were coverings for dead bodies in the combat zone. We never could figure out why they had to be treated for a gas attack." These impregnated clothes and mattress coverings were treated with a secret formula of chemicals and were to be used for the transport of corpses. Enlisted men referred to such clothes and mattress covers as "pregnant"; all members of the 95th were to turn these materials in to their quartermaster when they reached their frontline destination. "We kidded a lot," said Claudine, "about having to carry our own body bags overseas with us."

After several days at Camp Shanks, the nurses received a thirty-six-hour pass to go into New York City. Bee Wee had not been feeling too well, and when they were getting ready to leave the post, Hut and Claudine noticed that she was covered with pink-red spots. "You've got measles!" Claudine said. "You'll have to stay here and stay in bed. If anyone comes into the room, cover your head up, or they won't let you go overseas with the rest of us."

"How are we going to get her on the ship?" Hut said. "You can see those spots a block away."

"Frank just sent me *Their Hearts Were Young and Gay*," Claudine said, referring to a novel by Cornelia Otis Skinner that was popular that year. "Lucky for us, I read it. Cornelia Otis Skinner and Emily Kimbrough [a well-known actress who was in the stage production] had to cover up a case of measles in the book. We'll do the same thing. Just stay in bed until we get back tomorrow."

On 14 April, Claudine, Hut, and June Gordon met Frank's family at a fancy restaurant in New York City, had dinner, and promised to return the next evening, so Frank's sisters could give Claudine a bridal shower.

The next evening, while Frank's family waited for Claudine and her friends to appear for her bridal shower, Uncle Sam was throwing Claudine a going-away party. The 95th Evacuation Hospital, with full field packs and equipment, were boarding a train that would take them to a ferry, which would take them to a ship that would carry them to war.

At their destination, the Brooklyn Navy Yard, the nurses, doctors, and hospital personnel lined up in alphabetical order on the docks to board the USS *Mariposa*, a former luxury liner that had been refitted as a troopship. They were so heavily laden with field packs, bedrolls, "A" bags (suitcases), and "B" bags (duffel bags) that they were unable to sit down. "If we had sat down," Claudine said, "I'm not sure we could have gotten up again." Whatever extra energy Claudine and Hut had was directed to keeping an eye on Bee Wee and her cosmetically covered-up measles. They were not about to lose a buddy just when they were getting ready to sail.

In addition to the 95th Evac, also boarding the troopship were the 93rd and the 56th Evacuation Hospitals; the 54th Medical Battalion; Army Air Forces officers and enlisted men; tank crews and officers; and the African-American men of the fighter squadron later to be dubbed "The Tuskegee Airmen," led by Lieutenant Colonel Benjamin O. Davis. As a naval officer called the 95th's roll by last name, each person answered with their first name, middle initial, and service number. If the information matched that on the officer's clipboard, the nurse or soldier was allowed to lumber up the gangplank and onto the ship. There were five decks on board, designated "A" through "E." The nurses were assigned quarters in C Deck, midway down into the hold of the ship.

On 15 April, the *Mariposa* sailed out of the Brooklyn Navy Yard alone, without the protection of a convoy, and began zigzagging her way toward what "latrine rumors" said would be North Africa. The nurses believed the comments of male naval officers who said the *Maripsoa* was fast enough to outrun any German submarine and did not need to sail in a convoy. They did not add the sailors' next remarks that the nurses were placed on C Deck "because it's the safest from bombs and torpedoes."

Male officers and nurses were treated like first-class passengers. They were served two meals a day at tables covered with white linen and set with china and heavy silverware. Menus were printed and given out as souvenirs of the voyage. The same group met each day for meals. Claudine shared a table with Hut; Bee Wee; another nurse, Lieutenant Adeline Simonson, nicknamed "Si"; Lt. Neil Hansen, the hospital's adjutant and Bee Wee's steady beau since Camp Breckenridge; and two other officers of the 95th Evac.

The enlisted men were not so fortunate. They were billeted on lower decks, and bivouacked in the empty swimming pool and any other available corners. "Colored" soldiers were completely segregated from white soldiers; not only did the African-Americans have separate quarters, they were only allowed on the upper deck and in the mess hall for meals at different times from the whites.

Three days out to sea, on 19 April, all ships' passengers received a copy of a government-issue booklet, *How to Behave in North Africa,* and were told that they were headed for Casablanca in French Morocco. On 24 April, Lieutenant Claudine "Speedy" Glidewell and the rest of the 95th and 93rd Evacuation Hospitals landed there. The nurses got a quick look at some of the city as they climbed aboard 2.5-ton trucks and rode to what would be the new home for most of the nurses arriving at the port—the Internationale Première on the rue de la Gare. Before the war, the large building had been a boarding school for young French girls. Male officers and enlisted men had to march seven miles to Camp Don Passage, a staging area for American and Allied troops in the area.

Nurses of each hospital shared a large room that was divided into cubicles containing a bed, a chair, and a bureaulike storage cabinet. As soon as Bee Wee, Hut, and Claudine got their bearings and stowed their baggage, they got permission to look around the city.

In the following weeks in Casablanca, U.S. Army nurses met several groups of military nurses from Allied countries. "A group of nurses from the Belgian Congo were very sad about one of their nurses dying from amoebic dysentery and having to be left behind in a cemetery outside of Casablanca," Claudine remembered. The story came back to the nurses of the 95th Evac in earnest when they lined up at the quartermaster's to drop off the chemically impregnated clothing they had been issued in New York. They were told to keep and carry the two mattress-cover body bags.

While in Casablanca, Claudine developed a cough that concerned Chief Nurse Blanche Sigman enough to take her to the 8th Evacuation Hospital, which was operating in the area. The doctors told Sigman that there were some changes in Claudine's chest X-ray, and that if they had shown up in the States, she would never have been sent overseas. Since there were no antibiotics at this time, they followed the standard treatment of the day, issuing Claudine a bottle of Brown's Cough Mixture, and the cough got better.

Six teams of the 2nd Auxiliary Surgical Group that were assigned to the 48th Surgical Hospital had landed in North Africa on D-Day, 8 November 1942; months later, in March 1943, the rest of the 2nd Auxiliary Surgical Group with its hand-picked surgical specialists, experienced surgical nurses, and their enlisted men arrived in Rabat, French Morocco. For the first four days, the nurses were housed at a small hotel, L'Ecole de Jeanne, in the heart of the city. During this stay, Second Lieutenants Laura Ruth Hindman (known as "Ruthie") and Frances A. Miernicke ("Frenchie") learned that the rumors circulating among the natives were that the large group of American women at the hotel were concubines for the U.S. and Allied armies. "We took the rumors in good humor," Ruthie Hindman remembered. "The French Army did travel with concubines, and I guess the natives figured that all armies traveled with those amenities."

Ruthie had earned her RN at the University of Pennsylvania and had joined the U.S. Army Nurse Corps in June 1941 with the idea of serving a year and then returning to civilian nursing. She was on a train heading for her first leave at home in Johnstown, Pennsylvania, on 7 December 1941, when she and the other passengers heard the news break on the train's radio that the Japanese had attacked American forces at Pearl Harbor. When she returned to her hospital at Camp Claiborne, Louisiana, Lieutenant Hindman was told that she was in the Army Nurse Corps not only for the full year she had signed up for, but the duration of the war plus an additional six months. She could not leave in June 1942 when her year was up. Although it had not been her choice to remain in the army, she volunteered for the 2nd Auxiliary Surgical Group, knowing full well that they would be assigned close to the front lines. "People came through Camp Claiborne on the way overseas," Ruthie said. "It didn't take me long to get the itch to go overseas, too. I wanted to be where the action was and I could be of the most help." The chief nurse suggested that, with Ruthie's operating-room experience, she would be a natural for the 2nd Auxiliary Surgical Group.

The 2nd Aux was to be made up of 93 of the best surgeons in the country, 66 experienced army nurses, and 139 enlisted men to assist the doctors and nurses at surgery on the front lines. Second Auxiliary Surgical Group teams were to supplement the surgical staffs of various forward hospitals. The surgical teams would most often be stationed at those hospitals located three to fifteen miles behind the front lines, and would sometimes find themselves in enemy territory if American and Allied troops pulled back on short notice. Ruthie Hindman and Frances Miernicke had volunteered for an assignment that would guarantee them all the action they could stand.

On 22 March 1943, the entire 2nd Aux was transferred to Rabat, where they set up and operated a tent hospital on the Sultan's Racetrack. Each morning the Sultan's Guard, dressed in colorful, flowing materials and mounted on beautiful Arabian stallions, paraded past the racetrack to the accompaniment of trumpets and large drums.

This hospital would prove an interesting and challenging location for doctors and nurses alike. Most surgery performed at the location was to correct the results of training accidents and parachute-jump mishaps. The patient load was low, since the hospital was located approximately nine hundred miles from the front lines. Casualties from the fighting in Tunisia, the battles of El Guettar and Gabés, were taken to hospitals assigned to frontline areas.

Auxiliary surgical groups were composed of individual specialty teams: orthopedic, thoracic, neurological, maxillofacial, ophthalmic, general surgery, and shock. Each specialty team was usually made up of a surgeon—the officer in charge—an assistant surgeon, an anesthetist, an operating-room nurse, and two OR technicians. One physician, one nurse, and two technicians usually comprised a "a shock team": a medical team whose specialty was to stabilize a trauma victim in order to prepare him for surgery. The kind and number of specialty teams was based on the number of casualties expected with various types of wounds. Since broken bones from a bullet, shell, land mine, or booby trap were most common, several orthopedic surgical teams had to be assigned to more hospitals in more areas. Head and spinal injuries were relatively fewer than orthopedic injuries; therefore, fewer neurosurgical teams were needed, and these were positioned to serve larger areas in sites where they could receive wounded with spinal and head injuries from several frontline areas.

Rabat was one of the few places where all teams of the 2nd Aux were stationed together for any length of time. Friendships developed among the doctors and nurses who spent their off-duty hours playing gin rummy and sharing bull sessions. Assignments to the front would break the 2nd Aux into its individual teams. These assignments took the teams to specific combat zones or frontline hospitals and could last for days, weeks, or months, depending on the need. During such assignments, team members who traveled, worked, and played together were family in every sense but blood. Frequently, at the end of a particular campaign and before staging for the next assignment, teams were brought back together at 2nd Aux Headquarters—wherever it might be—to share the knowledge they had gained, and to be instructed on any new techniques or procedures that had been developed since their last time together as a surgical group. Such information gathering and sharing was due to the foresight and planning of the commanding officer, Colonel James H. Forsee, MC.

Forsee had determined before leaving the States, during the organization of the 2nd Auxiliary Surgical Group at Lawson General Hospital in Atlanta, that ongoing clinical education and detailed record keeping were critical to the progress of military medicine. Forsee set up periodic returns of the various surgical teams from the front lines to headquarters to ensure that all teams would share the new medical techniques they were rapidly developing ad hoc on the battlefields to treat the war wounded. These periodic returns by the surgical teams were times when members of various teams got to renew friendships and enjoy the closeness of an extended family. After a few days or a week, the teams were reassigned again and would look forward to their next "gathering."

On 9 April, after a few hours of leave in Rabat, Ruthie Hindman returned to her tent to find her belongings packed and orders waiting for her surgical team to leave immediately. Ruthie's team, Orthopedic Team 4, consisted of Major John Adams, a surgeon and graduate of the University of Virginia; Lieutenant Anna Bess Berret, a surgical nurse from Natchez, Mississippi; and Tech Sergeant 5 Theron G. McComb, an enlisted man. Ruthie and Orthopedic Team 4 rushed to catch a flight for Algiers and the British 95th General Hospital.

On 26 April, the 2nd Aux Headquarters was transferred to a dusty, rock-strewn hill southeast of Oran known as "Goat Hill." Battles were still going on in Tunisia, where American and Allied forces were still trying to drive the Germans out of Tunis and Bizerte. The 22nd marked the beginning of the final phase of the Tunisian campaign as the Allied forces battled their way into the northeast corner of Tunisia to capture Mateur and finally Bizerte in the weeks that followed. The 2nd Aux personnel were ordered to put up pup tents for living quarters and lived on C-rations until Colonel Forsee found them a villa in Ain-el-Turk, twenty odd miles southwest of Oran. More teams were sent to frontline hospitals, but the majority of personnel were still waiting for their assignments.

On 10 May 1943, the forty-three nurses of the 16th Evacuation Hospital arrived in Mers-el-Kebir harbor aboard the USAT *Fobn Erickson*. Rather than disembark immediately, the 16th was ordered to wait on board. Fourteen hours later, at 1600, the public address system crackled to life and the ship's captain announced the surrender of all German and Italian troops in North Africa.

Nurses, doctors, and enlisted men of the 16th were assigned to temporary duty at various operating hospitals in the area until 26 May, when Prisoner of War Camp 129 opened at Saint-Barbe-du-Tlelat, Algeria, fourteen miles outside Oran. The 16th Evacuation Hospital was assigned to the POW camp hospital and moved into tents in the barbed-wire-enclosed compound. The camp hospital housed three thousand wounded and ill German and Italian prisoners in need of surgery or suffering from dysentery, malaria, and jaundice.

Running and working in a POW camp hospital brought its own special problems. Since few people in the 16th Evac spoke fluent German or Italian, interpreters were employed on every ward and service. Even medical records that arrived with the POWs had to be translated in order that medical personnel could review their patients's medical histories.

Added to the language problems were problems born of cultural biases: German and Italian soldiers had a strong animosity toward each other. Thus, to avoid outbreaks of hostility between German and Italian POWs, it was necessary to keep the two nationalities separated. Further segregation was necessary among the German soldiers themselves, since men in the *Schutzstaffel* (the notorious elite "Special Services," or SS) and men in the Wehrmacht (regular foot soldiers of the German army) had distinctly different attitudes toward their captors. The SS men were stern and obeyed orders grudgingly, often refusing to cooperate fully with surgeons, nurses, and other medical staff. The SS used their rank and training to order regular German soldiers to be insolent toward and uncooperative with the Americans as well. Separating these different factions was one way to decrease friction and, hopefully, prevent the minor, petty revolts that threatened to disrupt the operation of the camp.

Hot, stagnant summer weather added mightily to the camp's problems. During the 16th Evac's stay in the compound, hot and humid sirocco winds blew steadily for more than two months without rain. The heat was oppressive and unrelenting, with temperatures during the day reaching as high as 132°F, and, of course, there was no air-conditioning in the hospital.

On 15 May, a few days after the Allied defeat of the Germans in North Africa, the nurses of the 95th Evacuation Hospital were issued three days of C-rations, loaded onto trucks, and taken to Camp Don Passage, where they met the enlisted men of the 95th Evac for the first time and ate lunch with them in the crowded mess tent. The next day, the entire hospital loaded onto 2.5-ton trucks and started a two-day journey to their new hospital site, over three hundred miles away in Oujda, French Morocco.

On the first night of their trip, the 95th Evacuation Hospital bivouacked in a deserted field and GIs dug the nurses' latrine about thirty yards from their tents. Lunch and dinner had been C-rations, and by 2030, diarrhea had hit in earnest. Pedestrian traffic to and from all latrines grew heavier as the night wore on. About midnight, Claudine Glidewell ran as fast as she could toward the nurses' latrine. The moon was full and as she neared the canvas surrounding the slit trenches, she saw a GI stagger out the front opening. He pulled himself to attention and shouted, "Halt! Who goes there?"

"We had been given a password to tell the guards, but all I could think of was getting into the latrine," Glidewell remembered. "I never slowed down. I shouted, 'Me!,' and ran into and past the guard, knocking him and his rifle to one side. He didn't try to stop me. I guess he figured there wouldn't be too many German soldiers dressed in red polka-dot pajamas running for the nurses' latrine with a full moon lighting their way."

On 24 May, the 95th Evacuation Hospital opened for business in a large wheat field that backed up to an olive grove. The nurses were quartered five to a pyramidal tent and each group marked their quarters with a small sign out front. Claudine, Bee Wee, Hut, Edna G. Ray, and Anita M. "Foo" Foss shared one tent and named it "Hut Two." Next to them was the "Fall Inn," shared by Si Simonson, Lillie H. "Pete" Peterson, Othelia "Oats" L. Rosten, Dora E. Witte, and Jennette "Jan" Smit.

The Rangers of the 509th Parachute Infantry Regiment were assigned to the 95th Evac for all necessary medical care. After a week, a call went out for nurses to volunteer for training as anesthetists, and Claudine and Si stepped forward. The next unit assigned to the 95th Evac for care was the Eighty-second Airborne Divison. The division was taking part in a parachute exhibition for visiting "top brass" when a freak accident landed scores of them in surgery.

"The guys had jumped and were about three hundred feet from the ground when the wind shifted and collapsed about fifty chutes," Claudine remembered. "One by one the troopers hit the ground, breaking ankles, feet, legs, and arms. And one by one Si and I put them to sleep to have their injuries repaired. We'd ask them to count as we gave them Pentothal and most of them never got beyond four."

During off-duty hours, Claudine, Si, and the other two nurse anesthetists prepared sterile packs for surgery and occasionally worked as scrub nurses in the OR. One hot 130° afternoon, General Eisenhower visited the 95th Evacuation Hospital. Lieutenants Glidewell, Simonson, and several other nurses and corpsmen

This poster was part of the War Department's campaign to recruit at least 50,000 women into the military nursing corps during World War II. This image of a carefully coiffed woman ministering to a handsome veteran was calculated to support the claim that military service would actually enhance women's femininity and prepare young women for family life after the war. The romantic scene depicted here had little relation to the brutal combat conditions experienced by tens of thousands of battlefield nurses.

were cleaning up after surgery when Eisenhower paid an unannounced visit to the operating-room tent. "We were all surprised to see him," Glidewell remembered. "He chatted with us for about fifteen minutes in that hot tent. We were all sweating and mopping our faces with handkerchiefs or the sleeves on our OR gowns as we talked. Tents seem to catch and focus the desert heat and everyone was suffering from its effects."

Like Claudine Glidewell, Eisenhower was a Kansan and no stranger to hot weather. The heat of the OR tent, however, would have been extreme even for a Kansas prairie dog. About an hour after the general left, a big truck loaded with narrow-diameter pipe pulled up and parked by the OR tent. As three GIs got out and began unloading the pipe, Glidewell and Simonson went to the door to investigate. "What's all the pipe for?" Glidewell remembered her question, and a GI's response: "General Eisenhower sent you people a present. Once we get it up and running, you'll love it." "Not unless it's a shower." Gildewell went back to work inside the OR tent. About an hour later, the soldiers had finished their job and a long line of narrow-diameter pipe ran along the top of the OR tent and hooked up to a water supply nearby. One of the GIs opened a valve and water shot through the pipe and out the many holes along its length. It flowed along the canvas roof and down the canvas walls of the large tent, providing the U.S. Army's 1943 version of air-conditioning to a hot and sweating OR crew. "It was wonderful," Glidewell remembered. "It was one of the nicest presents a commanding general could have given to an evacuation hospital set up in a desert."

The 95th Evac's staff had another way to beat the heat. On several sweltering afternoons, nurses, doctors, and enlisted men traveled forty miles by GI trucks to swim at Fort Said. As the French-style bathing suits were more revealing than the nurses were used to, several of them created their own bathing suits out of white Turkish towels and blue bloomers they had purchased at the PX. The bathing suits worked fine and traveled with the nurses to other beaches in the months and years that followed.

Since troops and equipment were now assembled in North Africa, it was decided that a joint invasion of Sicily would be the Allies' next blow against Axis forces. "Operation Husky"—the invasion of Sicily—was secretly set for July 1943.

On 21 May 1943, Lieutenant Evelyn Anderson, along with the 41 other nurses, 38 officers, and 246 enlisted men of the 400-bed 93rd Evacuation Hospital, left Staging Area #2, nicknamed "Agony Hill," for Oran, Algeria. All boarded trucks that carried the staff over mountainous roads to a campsite near Mascara, about fifty miles southeast of Oran. They arrived at 1530 and immediately began setting up the hospital in a wheat field. But just a few weeks after setting up, the 93rd received word to mobilize for the next planned invasion, which, as yet, was a secret. "We evacuated our patients," Anderson recalled, "and began preparing for our move to care for new frontline casualties."

The 93rd Evac began sorting and packing its equipment into "twenty 'cut-down cab-height' vehicles including two ambulances and two 750-gallon water trucks." With this combat loading, the trucks would be able to drive off LSTs (landing ship tanks) onto the beaches of the new invasion site, which rumor said would be Sicily.

To make setting up faster, the supply officer divided all ward equipment into twenty-two parts. Each individual part contained all the equipment needed for one particular ward. Each part was then subdivided into four large chests to facilitate the reconstruction of the ward: chest 1 contained plasma, saline solution, and medicines; chest 2 was packed with mess equipment and patient pajamas; chest 3 held soap, towels, and mosquito bars to support netting around patient beds; and chest 4 carried mosquito bar spreaders to hold the nets in place. Several supplemental chests were packed with specific ward equipment and clearly marked so everything could be found and accessed quickly. Surgery, X-ray, and laboratory subdivided their equipment in the same way so that hospital staff could accept and treat the wounded as quickly and efficiently as possible.

Careful planning by the supply staff even included the placement of the trucks aboard so that no two similarly loaded trucks were on the same ship. Troops in the Sicilian invasion would benefit from lessons learned in supply problems that had occurred during Operation Torch. As a final precaution, hospital personnel were divided so that no one ship carried all the surgeons, all the corpsmen, or all the X-ray or laboratory technicians.

During the first days of July 1943, the staff of the 93rd Evac began loading and boarding ships in preparation for their participation in the invasion of Sicily.

Questions for Study and Review

1. How did World War II disrupt established communities and family relations? What did military mobilization mean for different groups of women?

2. "Rosie the Riveter" is the iconic symbol of feminine patriotism from World War II. How accurately does she reflect the role of American women in the war?

3. How did race shape the opportunities for and experience of women nurses during World War II?

4. Do you think that wartime labor shortages changed the lives of union activists in New York City? Women in San Antonio, Texas? African American beauty culturists?

Suggested Readings and Web Sites

Susan M. Hartmann, *The Homefront and Beyond: American Women in the 1940s* (1982)

Melissa A. Herbert, "Amazons or Butterflies: The Recruitment of Women into the Military during World War II," *Minerva* 9 (1991)

Darlene Clark Hine, *Black Women in White: Racial Conflict and Cooperation in the Nursing Profession, 1890–1950* (1989)

Maureen Honey, ed., *Bitter Fruit: African American Women in World War II* (1999)

Leisa D. Meyer, *Creating GI Jane: Sexuality and Power in the Women's Army Corps during World War II* (1996)

Female Aviators during World War II:
   http://www.pbs.org/wgbh/amex/flygirls/

Women in the U.S. Navy
   http://www.history.navy.mil/photos/prs-tpic/females/wave-ww2.htm

Women Marines
   http://www.nps.gov/archive/wapa/indepth/extContent/usmc/pcn-190–003129–00/sec1.htm

The WASPs Oral History Project
   http://www.twu.edu/wasp/oral.htm

World War II Posters
   http://digital.lib.umn.edu/warposters/warpost.html

Chapter 9

Before enlisting as an Army combat nurse in 1942, Claudine "Speedy" Glidewell worked as a nurse for Wichita's leading obstetrician. She witnessed first-hand how the war pushed young people into marriage and parenthood. Highly paid defense jobs and allowances for the dependents of enlisted men provided financial support for young families. At the same time, the prospect of their own mortality made many young men and women eager to cement relationships through matrimony and parenthood. They rushed to marry and conceive babies before the war took them away from one another. Only months after entering the Army, Glidewell married Frank Doyle after a whirlwind courtship at Fort Riley, vowing fidelity to her new husband only days before shipping overseas.

Domesticity for the Doyles had to wait until the fighting ended. Peacetime reunited Claudine and Frank and they settled in New England, where they began raising a family. Family life was the sanctuary of choice for young couples like the Doyles who had been buffeted by economic hardships and war. In the ten years after World War II, new family values combined with unprecedented prosperity to reshape American life. This new domestic ideology became deeply embedded within the white American middle class. The enthusiastic embrace of suburbanization, consumer culture, and large, child-centered families even began to affect working-class aspirations. Communities such as Levittown promised a suburban lifestyle to every hard-working family. Many Americans may have enjoyed the comforts of new homes, the convenience of the car culture, and the chance to get away from overcrowded urban neighborhoods. Yet life in these new suburbs was not carefree.

The ruling culture of conformity was not kind to women, who were constantly being measured by their ability to perform time-consuming domestic duties as standards for cleanliness and sociability escalated. Magazines, movies, advertising, and, perhaps most powerfully, television produced images of femininity for millions of postwar mothers to emulate. No woman could match the domestic harmony achieved by television housewives like June Cleaver and Harriet Nelson. Cheerful and prosperous, these women devoted themselves with zeal to tending their suburban houses, raising their children, and baking cookies. At the end of each day, they greeted their breadwinner husbands with a kiss and home-cooked dinner prepared in a gleaming, modern kitchen.

These televised images provided the standards against which most American women were judged. Those who fell short or failed to find joy in the operation of their household appliances were labeled neurotic. Women were also held responsible for any problems that surfaced. Divorce was blamed on bad cooking and female frigidity; children's problems were attributed to mothers who showered too much or too little love on their children. Many women chafed under rigid gender roles that demanded their unquestioning subservience to male family members.

Few of her neighbors would have recognized Claudine as a combat veteran or skilled professional. Her earlier accomplishments were eclipsed by the post-war preoccupation with domesticity that cast her exclusively as a wife, mother, and homemaker. Proud of her wartime service, Claudine was still happy to trade combat duty for peacetime childraising. But many American women were loath to give up the independence and autonomy that had accompanied a good paycheck during the war.

After the war, many women wanted to continue in challenging jobs that brought the rewards of personal fulfillment and decent pay. But demobilization closed these types of jobs to women, whose deteriorating opportunities did not diminish their need for money. A rising number of women were shoulder-ing the double shift of wage work and housework. Even in middle-class com-munities, more mothers than ever were going out to work. Women sought even the paltry paychecks they could earn in more traditional female occupa-tions to allow their families to participate fully in the postwar consumer society.

African American women, radical women, and labor activists probably never had any illusions about their ability to emulate June Cleaver. These women made the decade much less placid than it appeared on television. Behind a façade of affluence and conformity, the country seethed with anxiety. Discontent boiled over into postwar labor unrest and renewed racial violence. Fears about Communism erupted into McCarthyism while rising inflation sparked new economic worries. In turn, critics denounced the era's consumerism, anti-Communism, and racial oppression. In tandem with nonconformist "Beat" writers and musicians, they brought a generation's unease to light. Another iconic woman of the period—Rosa Parks—illuminated the nation's racial hypocrisy.

Stephanie Coontz analyzes the myths about American families in the 1950s, unraveling the connection between ideology and reality. She demonstrates that the ideal family of the 1950s was an entirely modern construction that grew out of suburbanization, consumer culture, attenuated ties to extended family, and an intensified emphasis on parenting and marital sexual satisfaction. While many Americans may have been happy during the 1950s, Coontz illuminates why the period was hardly a "golden age" for women, families, and American communities.

Leave It to Beaver and *Ozzie and Harriet*: American Families in the 1950s
STEPHANIE COONTZ

Our most powerful visions of traditional families derive from images that are still delivered to our homes in countless reruns of 1950s television sit-coms. When liberals and conservatives debate family policy, for example, the issue is often framed in terms of how many "Ozzie and Harriet" families are left in America. Liberals compute the percentage of total households that contain a breadwinner father, a full-time homemaker mother, and dependent children, proclaiming that fewer than 10 percent of American families meet the "Ozzie and Harriet" or "Leave It to Beaver" model. Conservatives counter that more than half of all mothers with preschool children either are not employed or are employed only part-time. They cite polls showing that most working mothers would like to spend more time with their children and periodically announce that the Nelsons are "making a comeback," in popular opinion if not in real numbers.

Since everyone admits that nontraditional families are now a majority, why this obsessive concern to establish a higher or a lower figure? Liberals seem to think that unless they can prove the "Leave It to Beaver" family is on an irreversible slide toward extinction, they cannot justify introducing new family definitions and social policies. Conservatives believe that if they can demonstrate the traditional family is alive and well, although endangered by policies that reward two-earner families and single parents, they can pass measures to revive the seeming placidity and prosperity of the 1950s, associated in many people's minds with the relative stability of marriage, gender roles, and family life in that decade. If the 1950s family existed today,

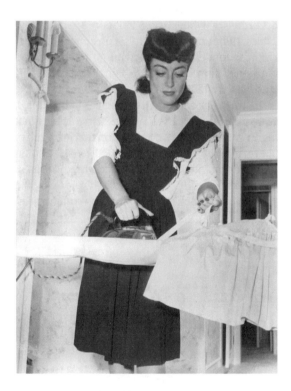

As the nation demobilized after World War II, women faced an onslaught of images encouraging them to embrace a new version of traditional femininity. Even movie stars like Joan Crawford—pictured here ironing—felt the pressure to embrace these new feminine norms. This publicity photo sought to enhance Crawford's mass appeal by portraying her as a woman who relishes routine household duties. Although Crawford does not deliver a convincing performance as a happy housewife, images like these reinforced the message that feminine fulfillment could only be found in traditional domesticity.

both sides seem to assume, we would not have the contemporary social dilemmas that cause such debate.

At first glance, the figures seem to justify this assumption. The 1950s was a pro-family period if there ever was one. Rates of divorce and illegitimacy were half what they are today; marriage was almost universally praised; the family was everywhere hailed as the most basic institution in society; and a massive baby boom, among all classes and ethnic groups, made America a "child-centered" society. Births rose from a low of 18.4 per 1,000 women during the Depression to a high of 25.3 per 1,000 in 1957. "The birth rate for third children doubled between 1940 and 1960, and that for fourth children tripled."

In retrospect, the 1950s also seem a time of innocence and consensus: Gang warfare among youths did not lead to drive-by shootings; the crack epidemic had not yet hit; discipline problems in the schools were minor; no "secular humanist" movement opposed the 1954 addition of the words *under God* to the Pledge of Allegiance; and 90 percent of all school levies were approved by voters. Introduction of the polio vaccine in 1954 was the most dramatic of many medical advances that improved the quality of life for children.

The profamily features of this decade were bolstered by impressive economic improvements for vast numbers of Americans. Between 1945 and 1960, the gross national product grew by almost 250 percent and per capita income by 35 percent. Housing starts exploded after the war, peaking at 1.65 million in 1955 and remaining above 1.5 million a year for the rest of the decade; the increase in single-family homeownership between 1946 and 1956 outstripped the increase during the entire preceding century and a half. By 1960, 62 percent of American families owned their own homes, in contrast to 43 percent in 1940. Eighty-five percent of the new homes were built in the suburbs, where the nuclear family found new possibilities for privacy and togetherness. While middle-class Americans were the prime beneficiaries of the building boom, substantial numbers of white working-class Americans moved out of the cities into affordable developments, such as Levittown.

Many working-class families also moved into the middle class. The number of salaried workers increased by 61 percent between 1947 and 1957. By the mid-1950s, nearly 60 percent of the population had what was labeled a middle-class income level (between $3,000 and $10,000 in constant dollars), compared to only 31 percent in the "prosperous twenties," before the Great Depression. By 1960, thirty-one million of the nation's forty-four million families owned their own home, 87 percent had a television, and 75 percent possessed a car. The number of people with discretionary income doubled during the 1950s.

For most Americans, the most salient symbol and immediate beneficiary of their newfound prosperity was the nuclear family. The biggest boom in consumer spending, for example, was in household goods. Food spending rose by only 33 percent in the five years following the Second World War, and clothing expenditures rose by 20 percent, but purchases of household furnishings and appliances climbed 240 percent. "Nearly the entire increase in the gross national product in the mid-1950s was due to increased spending on consumer durables and residential construction," most of it oriented toward the nuclear family.

Putting their mouths where their money was, Americans consistently told pollsters that home and family were the wellsprings of their happiness and self-esteem. Cultural historian David Marc argues that prewar fantasies of sophisticated urban "elegance," epitomized by the high-rise penthouse apartment, gave way in the 1950s to a more modest vision of utopia: a single-family house and a car. The emotional dimensions of utopia, however, were unbounded. When respondents to a 1955 marriage study "were asked what they thought they had sacrificed by marrying and raising a family, an overwhelming majority of them replied, 'Nothing.'" Less than 10 percent of Americans believed that an unmarried person could be happy. As one popular advice book intoned: "The family is the center of your living. If it isn't, you've gone far astray."

The Novelty of the 1950s Family

In fact, the "traditional" family of the 1950s was a qualitatively new phenomenon. At the end of the 1940s, all the trends characterizing the rest of the twentieth century suddenly reversed themselves: For the first time in more than one hundred years, the age for marriage and motherhood fell, fertility increased, divorce rates declined, and women's degree of educational parity with men dropped sharply. In a period of less than ten years, the proportion of never-married persons declined by as much as it had during the entire previous half century.

At the time, most people understood the 1950s family to be a new invention. The Great Depression and the Second World War had reinforced extended family ties, but in ways that were experienced by most people as stultifying and oppressive. As one child of the Depression later put it, "The Waltons" television series of the 1970s did not show what family life in the 1930s was really like: "It wasn't a big family sitting around a table radio and everybody saying goodnight while Bing Crosby crooned 'Pennies from Heaven.'" On top of Depression-era family tensions had come the painful family separations and housing shortages of the war years: By 1947, six million American families were sharing housing, and postwar family counselors warned of a widespread marital crisis caused by conflicts between the generations. A 1948 *March of Time* film, "Marriage and Divorce," declared: "No home is big enough to house two families, particularly two of different generations, with opposite theories on child training."

During the 1950s, films and television plays, such as "Marty," showed people working through conflicts between marital loyalties and older kin, peer group, or community ties; regretfully but decisively, these conflicts were almost invariably "resolved in favor of the heterosexual couple rather than the claims of extended kinship networks. . . . homosociability and friendship." Talcott Parsons and other sociologists argued that modern industrial society required the family to jettison traditional productive functions and wider kin ties in order to specialize in emotional nurturance, childrearing, and production of a modern personality. Social workers "endorsed nuclear family separateness and looked suspiciously on active extended-family networks."

Popular commentators urged young families to adopt a "modern" stance and strike out on their own, and with the return of prosperity, most did. By the early 1950s, newlyweds not only were establishing single-family homes at an earlier age and a more rapid rate than ever before but also were increasingly moving to the suburbs, away from the close scrutiny of the elder generation.

For the first time in American history, moreover, such average trends did not disguise sharp variations by class, race, and ethnic group. People married at a younger age, bore their children earlier and closer together, completed their families by the time they were in their late twenties, and experienced a longer period living together as a couple after their children left home. The traditional range of acceptable family behaviors—even the range in the acceptable number and timing of children—narrowed substantially.

The values of 1950s families also were new. The emphasis on producing a whole world of satisfaction, amusement, and inventiveness within the nuclear family had no precedents. Historian Elaine Tyler May comments: "The legendary family of the 1950s . . . was not, as common wisdom tells us, the last gasp of 'traditional' family life with deep roots in the past. Rather, it was the first wholehearted effort to create a home that would fulfill virtually all its members' personal needs through an energized and expressive personal life."

Beneath a superficial revival of Victorian domesticity and gender distinctions, a novel rearrangement of family ideals and male-female relations was accomplished. For women, this involved a reduction in the moral aspect of domesticity and an expansion of its orientation toward personal service. Nineteenth-century middle-class women had cheerfully left housework to servants, yet 1950s women of all classes created makework in their homes and felt guilty when they did not do everything for themselves. The amount of time women spent doing housework actually *increased* during the 1950s, despite the advent of convenience foods and new, labor-saving appliances; child care absorbed more than twice as much time as it had in the 1920s. By the mid-1950s, advertisers' surveys reported on a growing tendency among women to find "housework a medium of expression for . . . [their] femininity and individuality."

For the first time, men as well as women were encouraged to root their identity and self-image in familial and parental roles. The novelty of these family and gender values can be seen in the dramatic postwar transformation of movie themes. Historian Peter Biskind writes that almost every major male star who had played tough loners in the 1930s and 1940s "took the roles with which he was synonymous and transformed them, in the fifties, into neurotics or psychotics." In these films, "men belonged at home, not on the streets or out on the prairie, . . . not alone or hanging out with other men." The women who got men to settle down had to promise enough sex to compete with "bad" women, but ultimately they provided it only in the marital bedroom and only in return for some help fixing up the house.

Public images of Hollywood stars were consciously reworked to show their commitment to marriage and stability. After 1947, for example, the Actors' Guild organized "a series of unprecedented speeches . . . to be given to civic groups around the country, emphasizing that the stars now embodied the rejuvenated family life unfolding in the suburbs." Ronald Reagan's defense of actors' family values was especially "stirring," noted one reporter, but female stars, unlike Reagan and other male stars, were obliged to *live* the new values as well as propagandize them. Joan Crawford, for example, one of the brash, tough, independent leading ladies of the prewar era, was now pictured as a devoted mother whose sex appeal and glamour did not prevent her from doing her own housework. She posed for pictures mopping floors and gave interviews about her childrearing philosophy.

The "good life" in the 1950s, historian Clifford Clark points out, made the family "the focus of fun and recreation." The ranch house, architectural embodiment of this new ideal, discarded the older privacy of the kitchen, den, and sewing room (representative of separate spheres for men and women) but introduced new privacy and luxury into the master bedroom. There was an unprecedented "glorification of self-indulgence" in family life. Formality was discarded in favor of "livability," "comfort," and "convenience." A contradiction in terms in earlier periods, "the sexually charged, child-centered family took its place at the center of the postwar American dream."

On television, David Marc comments, all the "normal" families moved to the suburbs during the 1950s. Popular culture turned such suburban families into capitalism's answer to the Communist threat. In his famous "kitchen debate" with Nikita Khrushchev in 1959, Richard Nixon asserted that the superiority of capitalism over communism was embodied not in ideology or military might but in the comforts of the suburban home, "designed to make things easier for our women."

Acceptance of domesticity was the mark of middle-class status and upward mobility. In sit-com families, a middle-class man's work was totally irrelevant to his identity; by the same token, the problems of working-class families did not lie in their economic situation but in their failure to create harmonious gender roles. Working-class and ethnic men on television had one defining characteristic: They were unable to control their wives. The families of middle-class men, by contrast, were generally well behaved.

Not only was the 1950s family a new invention, it was also a historical fluke, based on a unique and temporary conjuncture of economic, social, and political factors. During the war, Americans had saved at a rate more than three times higher than that in the decades before or since. Their buying power was further enhanced by America's extraordinary competitive advantage at the end of the war, when every other industrial power was devastated by the experience. This privileged economic position sustained both a tremendous expansion of middle-class management occupations and a new honeymoon between management and organized labor: During the 1950s, real wages increased by more than they had in the entire previous half century.

The impact of such prosperity on family formation and stability was magnified by the role of government, which could afford to be generous with education benefits, housing loans, highway and sewer construction, and job training. All this allowed most middle-class Americans, and a large number of working-class ones, to adopt family values and strategies that assumed the availability of cheap energy, low-interest home loans, expanding educational and occupational opportunities, and steady employment. These expectations encouraged early marriage, early childbearing, expansion of consumer debt, and residential patterns that required long commutes to work—all patterns that would become highly problematic by the 1970s.

A Complex Reality: 1950s Poverty, Diversity, and Social Change

Even aside from the exceptional and ephemeral nature of the conditions that supported them, 1950s family strategies and values offer no solution to the discontents that underlie contemporary romanticization of the "good old days." The reality of these families was far more painful and complex than the situation-comedy reruns or the expurgated memories of the nostalgic would suggest. Contrary to popular opinion, "Leave It to Beaver" was not a documentary.

In the first place, not all American families shared in the consumer expansion that provided Hotpoint appliances for June Cleaver's kitchen and a vacuum cleaner for Donna Stone. A full 25 percent of Americans, forty to fifty million people, were poor in the mid-1950s, and in the absence of food stamps and housing programs, this poverty was searing. Even at the end of the 1950s, a third of American children were poor. Sixty percent of Americans over sixty-five had incomes below $1,000 in 1958, considerably below the $3,000 to $10,000 level considered to represent middle-class status. A majority of elders also lacked medical insurance. Only half the population had savings in 1959; one-quarter of the population had no liquid assets at all. Even when we consider only native-born, white families, one-third could not get by on the income of the household head.

In the second place, real life was not so white as it was on television. Television, comments historian Ella Taylor, increasingly ignored cultural diversity, adopting "the motto 'least objectionable programming,' which gave rise to those least objectionable families, the Cleavers, the Nelsons and the Andersons." Such families were so completely white and Anglo-Saxon that even the Hispanic gardener in "Father Knows Best" went by the name of Frank Smith. But contrary to the all-white lineup on the television networks and the streets of suburbia, the 1950s saw a major transformation in the ethnic composition of America. More Mexican immigrants entered the United States in the two decades after the Second World War than in the entire previous one hundred years. Prior to the war, most blacks and Mexican-Americans lived in rural areas, and three-fourths of blacks lived in the South. By 1960, a majority of blacks resided in the North, and 80 percent of both blacks and Mexican-Americans lived in cities. Postwar Puerto Rican immigration was so massive that by 1960 more Puerto Ricans lived in New York than in San Juan.

These minorities were almost entirely excluded from the gains and privileges accorded white middle-class families. The June Cleaver or Donna Stone homemaker role was not available to the more than 40 percent of black women with small children who worked outside the home. Twenty-five percent of these women headed their own households, but even minorities who conformed to the dominant family form faced conditions quite unlike those portrayed on television. The poverty rate of two-parent black families was more than 50 percent, approximately the same as that of one-parent black ones. Migrant workers suffered "near medieval" deprivations, while termination and relocation policies were employed against Native Americans to get them to give up treaty rights.

African Americans in the South faced systematic, legally sanctioned segregation and pervasive brutality, and those in the North were excluded by restrictive covenants and redlining from many benefits of the economic expansion that their labor helped sustain. Whites resisted, with harassment and violence, the attempts of blacks to participate in the American family dream. When Harvey Clark tried to move into Cicero, Illinois, in 1951, a mob of 4,000 whites spent four days tearing his apartment apart while police stood by and joked with them. In 1953, the first black family moved into Chicago's Trumbull Park public housing project; neighbors "hurled stones and tomatoes" and trashed stores that sold groceries to the new residents. In Detroit, *Life* magazine reported in 1957, "10,000 Negroes work at the Ford plant in nearby Dearborn, [but] not one Negro can live in Dearborn itself."

More Complexities: Repression, Anxiety, Unhappiness, and Conflict

The happy, homogeneous families that we "remember" from the 1950s were thus partly a result of the media's denial of diversity. But even among sectors of the population where the "least objectionable" families did prevail, their values and behaviors were not entirely a spontaneous, joyful reaction to prosperity. If suburban ranch houses and family barbecues were the carrots offered to white middle-class families that adopted the new norms, there was also a stick.

Women's retreat to housewifery, for example, was in many cases not freely chosen. During the war, thousands of women had entered new jobs, gained new skills, joined unions, and fought against job discrimination. Although 95 percent of the new women employees had expected when they were first hired to quit work at the end of the war, by 1945 almost an equally overwhelming majority did not want to give up their independence, responsibility, and income, and expressed the desire to continue working.

After the war, however, writes one recent student of postwar reconstruction, "management went to extraordinary lengths to purge women workers from the auto plants," as well as from other high-paying and nontraditional jobs. As it turned out, in most cases women were not permanently expelled from the labor force but were merely downgraded to lower-paid, "female" jobs. Even at the end of the purge, there were more women working than before the war, and by 1952 there were two million more wives at work than at the peak of wartime production. The jobs available to these women, however, lacked the pay and the challenges that had made wartime work so satisfying, encouraging women to define themselves in terms of home and family even when they were working.

Vehement attacks were launched against women who did not accept such self-definitions. In the 1947 bestseller, *The Modern Woman: The Lost Sex,* Marynia Farnham and Ferdinand Lundberg described feminism as a "deep illness," called the notion of an independent woman a "contradiction in terms," and accused women who sought educational or employment equality of engaging in symbolic "castration" of men. As sociologist David Riesman noted, a woman's failure to bear children went from being "a social disadvantage and sometimes a personal tragedy" in the nineteenth century to being a "quasi-perversion" in the 1950s. The conflicting messages aimed at women seemed almost calculated to demoralize: At the same time as they labeled women "unnatural" if they did not seek fulfillment in motherhood, psychologists and popular writers insisted that most modern social ills could be traced to domineering mothers who invested too much energy and emotion in their children. Women were told that "no other experience in life . . . will provide the same sense of fulfillment, of happiness, of complete pervading contentment" as motherhood. But soon after delivery they were asked, "Which are you first of all, Wife or Mother?" and warned against the tendency to be "too much mother, too little wife."

Women who could not walk the fine line between nurturing motherhood and castrating "momism," or who had trouble adjusting to "creative homemaking," were labeled neurotic, perverted, or schizophrenic. A recent study of hospitalized "schizophrenic" women in the San Francisco Bay Area during the 1950s concludes that institutionalization and sometimes electric shock treatments were used to force women to accept their domestic roles and their husbands' dictates. Shock treatments also were recommended for women who sought abortions, on the assumption that failure to want a baby signified dangerous emotional disturbance.

All women, even seemingly docile ones, were deeply mistrusted. They were frequently denied the right to serve on juries, convey property, make contracts, take out credit cards in their own name, or establish residence. A 1954 article in *Esquire* called working wives a "menace"; a *Life* author termed married women's employment a "disease." Women were excluded from several professions, and some states even gave husbands total control over family finances. There were not many permissible alternatives to baking brownies, experimenting with new canned soups, and getting rid of stains around the collar.

Men were also pressured into acceptable family roles, since lack of a suitable wife could mean the loss of a job or promotion for a middle-class man. Bachelors were categorized as "immature," "infantile," "narcissistic," "deviant" or even "pathological." Family advice expert Paul Landis argued: "Except for the sick, the badly crippled, the deformed, the emotionally warped and the mentally defective, almost everyone has an opportunity [and, by clear implication, a duty] to marry."

Families in the 1950s were products of even more direct repression. Cold war anxieties merged with concerns about the expanded sexuality of family life and the commercial world to create what one authority calls the domestic version of George F. Kennan's containment policy toward the Soviet Union: A "normal" family and vigilant mother became the "front line" of defense against treason; anticommunists linked deviant family or sexual behavior to sedition. The FBI and other government agencies instituted unprecedented state intrusion into private life under the guise of investigating subversives. Gay baiting was almost as widespread and every bit as vicious as red baiting.

The Civil Service Commission fired 2,611 persons as "security risks" and reported that 4,315 others resigned under the pressure of investigations that asked leading questions of their neighbors and inquired into the books they read or the music to which they listened. In this atmosphere, movie producer Joel Schumacher recalls, "No one told the truth. . . . People pretended they weren't unfaithful. They pretended that they weren't homosexual. They pretended that they weren't horrible."

Even for people not directly coerced into conformity by racial, political, or personal repression, the turn toward families was in many cases more a defensive move than a purely affirmative act. Some men and women entered loveless marriages in order to forestall attacks about real or suspected homosexuality or lesbianism. Growing numbers of people saw the family, in the words of one husband, as the one "group that in spite of many disagreements internally always will face its external enemies together." Conservative families warned children to beware of communists who might masquerade as friendly neighbors; liberal children learned to confine their opinions to the family for fear that their father's job or reputation might be threatened.

Americans were far more ambivalent about the 1950s than later retrospectives, such as "Happy Days," suggest. Plays by Tennessee Williams, Eugene O'Neill, and Arthur Miller explored the underside of family life. Movies such as *Rebel Without a Cause* (1955) expressed fears about youths whose parents had failed them. There was an almost obsessive concern with the idea that the mass media had broken down parental control, thus provoking an outburst of "delinquency and youthful viciousness." In 1954, psychiatrist Fredric Wertham's *Seduction of the Innocents* warned: "The atmosphere of crime comic books is unparalleled in the history of children's literature of any time or any nation." In 1955, Congress discussed nearly 200 bills relating to delinquency. If some of these anxieties seem almost charmingly naïve to our more hardened age, they were no less real for all that.

Many families, of course, managed to hold such fears at bay—and it must be admitted that the suburbs and small towns of America were exceptionally good places for doing so. Shielded from the multiplying problems and growing diversity of the rest of society, residents of these areas could afford to be neighborly. Church attendance and membership in voluntary associations tended to be higher in the suburbs than in the cities, although contact with extended kin was less frequent. Children played in the neighborhoods and cul-de-sacs with only cursory warnings about strangers.

In her autobiographical account of a 1950s adolescence, Susan Allen Toth remembers growing up "gradually" and "quietly" in a small town of the period: "We were not seared by fierce poverty, racial tensions, drug abuse, street crimes." Perhaps this innocence was "constricting," she admitted, but it also gave a child "shelter and space to grow." For Toth, insulation from external problems meant that growing up was a process of being "cossetted, gently warmed, transmuted by slow degress."

For many other children, however, growing up in 1950s families was not so much a matter of being protected from the harsh realities of the outside world as preventing the outside world from learning the harsh realities of family life. Few would have guessed that radiant Marilyn Van Derbur, crowned Miss America in 1958, had been sexually violated by her wealthy, respectable father from the time she was five until she was eighteen, when she moved away to college. While not all family secrets were quite so shocking, author Benita Eisler recalls a common middle-class experience:

> As college classmates became close friends, I heard sagas of life at home that were Gothic horror stories. Behind the hedges and driveways of upper-middle-class suburbia were tragedies of madness, suicide, and—most prevalent of all—chronic and severe alcoholism. . . .
>
> The real revelation for me was the role played by children in . . . keeping up appearances. Many of my new friends had been pressed into service early as happy smiling fronts, emissaries of family normalcy, cheerful proof that "nothing was really wrong" at the Joneses.

Beneath the polished facades of many "ideal" families, suburban as well as urban, was violence, terror, or simply grinding misery that only occasionally came to light. Although Colorado researchers found 302 battered-child cases, including 33 deaths, in their state during one year alone, the major journal of American family sociology did not carry a single article on family violence between 1939 and 1969. Wife battering was not even considered a "real" crime by most people. Psychiatrists in the 1950s, following Helene Deutsch, "regarded the battered woman as a masochist who provoked her husband into beating her."

Historian Elizabeth Pleck describes how one Family Service Association translated this psychological approach into patient counseling during the 1950s. Mrs. K came to the Association because her husband was an alcoholic who repeatedly abused her, both physically and sexually. The agency felt, however, that it was simplistic to blame the couple's problems on his drinking. When counselors learned that Mrs. K refused her husband's demands for sex after he came home from working the night shift, they decided that they had found a deeper difficulty: Mrs. K needed therapy to "bring out some of her anxiety about sex activities."

We will probably never know how prevalent incest and sexual abuse were in the 1950s, but we do know that when girls or women reported incidents of such abuse to therapists, they were frequently told that they were "fantasizing" their unconscious oedipal desires. Although incest cases were common throughout the records of caseworkers from 1880 to 1960, according to historian Linda Gordon's study of these documents, the problem was increasingly redefined as one of female "sex delinquency." By 1960, despite overwhelming evidence to the contrary, experts described incest as a "one-in-a-million occurrence." Not until the 1970s, heartened by a supportive women's movement, were many women able to speak out about the sexual abuse they had suffered in silent agony during the 1950s; others, such as Marilyn Van Derbur, are only now coming forward.

Less dramatic but more widespread was the existence of significant marital unhappiness. Between one-quarter and one-third of the marriages contracted in the 1950s eventually ended in divorce; during that decade two million legally married people lived apart from each other. Many more couples simply toughed it out. Sociologist Mirra Komarovsky concluded that of the working-class couples she interviewed in the 1950s, "slightly less than one-third [were] happily or very happily married."

National polls found that 20 percent of all couples considered their marriages unhappy, and another 20 percent reported only "medium happiness." In the middle-class sample studied by Elaine Tyler May, two-thirds of the husbands and wives rated their marriages "decidedly happier than average," but an outside observer might well have scaled this back to a percentage much like Komarovsky's, for even the happiest couples reported many dissatisfactions and communication problems. "The idea of a 'working marriage' was one that often included constant day-to-day misery for one or both partners."

A successful 1950s family, moreover, was often achieved at enormous cost to the wife, who was expected to subordinate her own needs and aspirations to those of both her husband and her children. In consequence, no sooner was the ideal of the postwar family accepted than observers began to comment perplexedly on how discontented women seemed in the very roles they supposedly desired most. In 1949, *Life* magazine reported that "suddenly and for no plain reason" American women were "seized with an eerie restlessness." Under a "mask of placidity" and an outwardly feminine appearance, one physician wrote in 1953, there was often "an inwardly tense and emotionally unstable individual seething with hidden aggressiveness and resentment."

Some women took this resentment out on their families. Surely some of the bizarre behaviors that Joan Crawford exhibited toward her children, according to her daughter's bitter remembrance, *Mommie Dearest*, flowed from the frustration of being forced into a domestic role about which she was intensely ambivalent. Other women tried to dull the pain with alcohol or drugs. Tranquilizers were developed in the 1950s in response to a need that physicians explicitly saw as female: Virtually nonexistent in 1955, tranquilizer consumption reached 462,000 pounds in 1958 and soared to 1.15 million pounds merely a year later. Commentators noted a sharp increase in women's drinking during the decade, even though many middle-class housewives kept their liquor stash hidden and thought no one knew that they needed a couple of drinks to face an evening of family "togetherness."

But not even "the four *b's*," as the mother of a colleague of mine used to label her life in the 1950s—"booze, bowling, bridge, and boredom"—could entirely conceal the discontents. In 1956, the *Ladies' Home Journal* devoted an issue to "The Plight of the Young Mother." When *McCall's* ran an article entitled."The Mother Who Ran Away" in the same year, the magazine set a new record for readership. A former editor commented: "We suddenly realized that all those women at home with their three and a half children were miserably unhappy." By 1960, almost every major news journal was using the word *trapped* to describe the feelings of the American housewife. When *Redbook's* editors asked readers to provide them with examples of "Why Young Mothers Feel Trapped," they received 24,000 replies.

Although Betty Friedan's bestseller *The Feminine Mystique* did not appear until 1963, it was a product of the 1950s, originating in the discontented responses Friedan received in 1957 when she surveyed fellow college classmates from the class of 1942. The heartfelt identification of other 1950s women with "the problem that has no name" is preserved in the letters Friedan received after her book was published, letters now at the Schlesinger Library at Radcliffe.

Men tended to be more satisfied with marriage than were women, especially over time, but they, too, had their discontents. Even the most successful strivers after the American dream sometimes muttered about "mindless conformity." The titles of books such as *The Organization Man*, by William Whyte (1956), and *The Lonely Crowd*, by David Riesman (1958), summarized a widespread critique of 1950s culture. Male resentments against women were expressed in the only partly humorous diatribes of *Playboy* magazine (founded in 1953) against "money-hungry" gold diggers or lazy "parasites" trying to trap men into commitment.

Contradictions of the 1950s Family Boom

Happy memories of 1950s family life are not all illusion, of course—there were good times for many families. But even the most positive aspects had another side. One reason that the 1950s family model was so fleeting was that it contained the seeds of its own destruction. It was during the 1950s, not the 1960s, that the youth market was first produced, then institutionalized into the youth culture. It was through such innocuous shows as "Howdy Doody" and "The Disney Hour" that advertisers first discovered the riches to be gained by bypassing parents and appealing directly to youth. It was also during this period that advertising and consumerism became saturated with sex.

In the 1950s, family life was financed by economic practices that were to have unanticipated consequences in the 1970s. Wives and mothers first started to work in great numbers during the 1950s in order to supplement their families' purchasing power; expansion of household comforts came "at the cost of an astronomical increase of indebtedness." The labor-management accord of the 1950s helped erode the union movement's ability to oppose the takebacks and runaway shops that destroyed the "family wage system" during the 1970s and 1980s.

Family and gender strategies also contained some time bombs. Women who "played dumb" to catch a man, as 40 percent of Barnard College women admitted to doing, sometimes despised their husbands for not living up to the fiction of male superiority they had worked so hard to promote. Commitment to improving the quality of family life by manipulating the timing and spacing of childbearing led to the social acceptability of family planning and the spread of birth-control techniques. Concentration of childbearing in early marriage meant that growing numbers of women had years to spare for paid work after the bulk of their child-care duties were finished. Finally, 1950s families fostered intense feelings and values that produced young people with a sharp eye for hypocrisy; many of the so-called rebels of the 1960s were simply acting on values that they had internalized in the bosom of their families.

Teen Pregnancy and the 1950s Family

Whatever its other unexpected features, the 1950s family does appear, at least when compared to families in the last two decades, to be a bastion of "traditional" sexual morality. Many modern observers, accordingly, look back to the sexual values of this decade as a possible solution to what they see as the peculiarly modern "epidemic" of teen pregnancy. On closer examination, however, the issue of teen pregnancy is a classic example of both the novelty and the contradictions of the 1950s family.

Those who advocate that today's youth should be taught abstinence or deferred gratification rather than sex education will find no 1950s model for such restraint. "Heavy petting" became a norm of dating in this period, while the proportion of white brides who were pregnant at marriage more than doubled. Teen birth rates soared, reaching highs that have not been equaled since. In 1957, 97 out of every 1,000 girls aged fifteen to nineteen gave birth, compared to only 52 of every 1,000 in 1983. A surprising number of these births were illegitimate, although 1950s census codes made it impossible to identify an unmarried mother if she lived at home with her parents. The incidence of illegitimacy was also disguised by the new emphasis on "rehabilitating" the white mother (though not the black) by putting her baby up for adoption and encouraging her to "start over"; there was an 80 percent increase in the number of out-of-wedlock babies placed for adoption between 1944 and 1955.

The main reason that teenage sexual behavior did not result in many more illegitimate births during this period was that the age of marriage dropped sharply. Young people were not taught how to "say no"—they were simply handed wedding rings. In fact, the growing willingness of parents to subsidize young married couples and the new prevalence of government educational stipends and home ownership loans for veterans undermined the former assumption that a man should be able to support a family before embarking on marriage. Among the middle class, it became common for young wives to work while their husbands finished school. Prior to the 1950s, as David Riesman wrote of his Depression-era classmates, it would not "have occurred to us to have our wives support us through graduate school."

Contemporary teenage motherhood in some ways represents a *continuation* of 1950s values in a new economic situation that makes early marriage less viable. Of course, modern teen pregnancy also reflects the rejection of some of those earlier values. The values that have broken down, however, have little to do with sexual restraint. What we now think of as 1950s sexual morality depended not so much on stricter sexual control as on intensification of the sexual double standard. Elaine Tyler May argues that sexual "repression" gave way to sexual "containment." The new practice of going steady "widened the boundaries of permissible sexual activity," creating a "sexual brinksmanship" in which women bore the burden of "drawing the line," but that line was constantly changing. Popular opinion admitted, as the *Ladies' Home Journal* put it in 1956, that "sex suggestiveness" was here to stay, but insisted that it was up to women to "put the brakes on."

This double standard led to a Byzantine code of sexual conduct: "Petting" was sanctioned so long as one didn't go "too far" (though this was an elastic and ambiguous prohibition); a woman could be touched on various parts of her body (how low depended on how serious the relationship was) but "nice girls" refused to fondle the comparable male parts in return; mutual stimulation to orgasm was compatible with maintaining a "good" reputation so long as penetration did not occur.

The success of sexual containment depended on sexual inequality. Men no longer bore the responsibility of "saving themselves for marriage"; this was now exclusively a woman's job. In sharp contrast to the nineteenth century, when "oversexed" or demanding men were considered to have serious problems, it was now considered "normal" or "natural" for men to be sexually aggressive. The "average man," advice writers for women commented indulgently, "will go as far as you let him go." When women succeeded in "holding out" (a phrase charged with moral ambiguity), they sometimes experienced problems "letting go," even after marriage; when they failed, they were often reproached later by their husbands for having "given in." The contradictions of this double standard could not long withstand the period's pressures for companionate romance: By 1959, a more liberal single standard had already gained ground among older teenagers across America.

The Problem of Women in Traditional Families

People who romanticize the 1950s, or any model of the traditional family, are usually put in an uncomfortable position when they attempt to gain popular support. The legitimacy of women's rights is so widely accepted today that only a tiny minority of Americans seriously propose that women should go back to being full-time housewives or should be denied educational and job opportunities because of their family responsibility. Yet when commentators lament the collapse of traditional family commitments and values, they almost invariably mean the uniquely female duties associated with the doctrine of separate spheres for men and women.

Karl Zinsmeister of the American Enterprise Institute, for example, bemoans the fact that "workaholism and family dereliction have become equal-opportunity diseases, striking mothers as much as fathers." David Blankenhorn of the Institute for American Values expresses sympathy for the needs of working women but warns that "employed women do not a family make. The goals of women (and of men, too) in the workplace are primarily individualistic: social recognition, wages, opportunities for advancement, and self-fulfillment. But the family is about collective goals . . . , building life's most important bonds of affection, nurturance, mutual support, and long-term commitment."

In both statements, a seemingly gender-neutral indictment of family irresponsibility ends up being directed most forcefully against women. For Blankenhorn, it is not surprising that *men's* goals should be individualistic; this is a parenthetical aside. For Zinsmeister, the problem with the disease of family dereliction is that it has spread to women. So long as it was confined to men, evidently, there was no urgency about finding a cure.

The crisis of commitment in America is usually seen as a problem associated with women's changing roles because women's family functions have historically mediated the worst effects of competition and individualism in the larger society. Most people who talk about balancing private advancement and individual rights with "nurturance, mutual support, and long-term commitment" do not envision any serious rethinking of the individualistic, antisocial tendencies in our society, nor any ways of broadening our sources of nurturance and mutual assistance. Instead, they seek ways—sometimes through repression, sometimes through reform—of rebuilding a family in which women can continue to compensate for, rather than challenge, the individualism in our larger economy and polity.

Questions for Study and Review

1. Describe the domestic ideal that reshaped the United States in the 1950s. When and why did these new family values take root, and how did they shape the aspirations of many Americans?

2. How did demobilization transform families and communities, and the expectations for women between 1945 and the 1950s?

3. How well do stereotypical images of 1950s domesticity describe the lives of women, families, and communities in this period? What do they leave out?

4. How do you think Claudine "Speedy" Glidewell and other World War II combat nurses reacted to these new ideals of domesticity and life in the suburbs?

Suggested Readings and Web Sites

Susan J. Douglass, *Where the Girls Are: Growing Up Female with the Mass Media* (1994)
Ruth Feldstein, *Motherhood in Black and White: Race and Sex in American Liberalism, 1930–1965* (2000)
Joanne Meyerowitz, ed., *Not June Cleaver: Women and Gender in Postwar America* (1994)
Katherine J. Parkin, *Food is Love: Advertising and Gender Roles in Modern America* (2006)
Jessica Weiss, *To Have and To Hold: Marriage, the Baby Boom, and Social Change* (2000)
The Prelinger Archive on Gender Roles
    http://www.archive.org/details/prelinger
American Experience Web Site for the Documentary *Tupperware*
    http://www.pbs.org/wgbh/amex/tupperware/
Levittown and Suburbanization
    http://server1.fandm.edu/levittown/default.html

PART IV

Mobilizing Communities

Fannie Lou Hamer led the Mississippi Freedom Democratic Party, a group determined to integrate the official all-white Mississippi delegation at the 1964 Democratic National Convention. Here, before television cameras at the convention, she declares, "If the Freedom Democratic Party is not seated now I question America."

While new concepts of family, domesticity, and motherhood flourished in the 1950s, so too did new claims for justice, dignity, and equality. In the case of the civil rights movement, demands for change were first voiced in the midst of postwar adjustments. *Brown v. Board of Education* (1954), the Montgomery Bus Boycott (1955), and the desegregation of Little Rock's Central High (1957) are among the most well-documented challenges to racism during the decade. In each of these episodes, women or girls—Linda Brown, Rosa Parks, Jo Ann Gibson Robinson, Carlotta Walls, Mabel Patillo, Minnijean Brown, Elizabeth Eckford, and Daisy Bates—were in the front lines and on the front pages of national periodicals. They were not alone. Thousands of African American women joined men in community-based movements and civil rights organizations, while girls and boys entered schoolhouse doors long closed to blacks.

Black women in the civil rights movement, carrying the double burden of race and gender, symbolized the despair, anger, and hope of African Americans of both sexes. In Chapter Ten, Danielle McGuire traces the specific ways that sexual violence against black women, and women's resistance to it, sparked civil rights efforts in Tallahassee, Florida. She argues that similar incidents of rape and sexual abuse inspired black political mobilization in communities across the South. Indeed, the courageous decision by individual African American women in the 1950s and 1960s to testify publicly against the white men who raped them ignited local, national, and even international movements for racial justice. Moreover, for the first time in the history of the southern United States, the testimony of these women and the movements that supported them led, at least in some cases, to the conviction and incarceration of white male rapists, who had for so long felt safe from prosecution for crimes against black women.

The struggle for black equality sparked a range of social movements in the 1960s and brought women and men from different races, ethnic groups, classes, and regions into the political arena. Many of these activists were inspired by demands for gender as well as racial equality, and growing numbers joined the movement against U.S. involvement in the Vietnam War. Civil rights activists were especially outspoken in criticizing the high percentage of black men drafted into military service and the high price of the war effort, which diminished funds for the fight against poverty and other social problems at home. Only men could be drafted into the U.S. Army in the 1960s, but large numbers of women were recruited into the antiwar movement. Older women argued that as mothers they were obligated to protect their sons from the unnecessary risks of an imperialist war, while younger women claimed a right equal to that of young men to protest national policies that affected not only the United States but also men, women, and families in Vietnam and other countries in Southeast Asia.

While movements for peace and social justice flourished in the 1960s, they did not go unchallenged. The Sixties, though often portrayed as a time of radical activism, gave birth to the New Right as well as the New Left. In Chapter Eleven, Michelle Nickerson traces the emergence of conservative campaigns in California, many created and nurtured by white women. These women and their families were convinced that radical activists threatened America's moral values and, in the context of the Cold War against Soviet Communism, put the nation at risk. Despite ideological differences, conservative women, like their counterparts in progressive social movements, organized first in their neighborhoods and local communities. Then they, too, gradually expanded their efforts, ultimately reshaping state and national politics by recasting the Republican Party as a bastion of social and political conservatism. Indeed, some scholars would later argue that activists on the right were just as radical as those on the left even if they were in the service of an opposing perspective.

Women had long been active in social movements, but the scope of their activism in the 1960s and 1970s and the sheer number of women who entered the public arena on behalf of one cause or another marked a dramatic change. Women were more often organizers and participants than leaders and spokespeople in these movements, but they did take on increasingly important roles in both conservative and progressive campaigns over time. Moreover, they gained a wide range of political and organizational skills as they labored for racial equality, against nuclear weapons and the burgeoning war in Vietnam, and on behalf of rights for workers, American Indians, and other marginalized groups as well as in movements that opposed each of these efforts.

For some women activists, sex discrimination and gender inequities—in society at large and in activist organizations—slowly emerged as critical issues on their agenda. Calling themselves feminists, a term that first came into use in the United States in the late nineteenth century, these women drew heavily on the ideas, tactics, and rhetoric of civil rights and black freedom struggles. Two white women—Casey Hayden and Mary King—embraced the message of racial liberation that was formulated in the 1964 Freedom Summer campaign organized in Mississippi by the Student Nonviolent Coordinating Committee (SNCC). They then modified it to encompass women's grievances and with like-minded co-workers carried these feminist insights into the antiwar movement. Participation in the civil rights and antiwar movements bolstered women's confidence in their ability to speak and act, and profoundly shaped their feminist activism. These women were especially taken with the ideals of participatory democracy that characterized the work of SNCC and of the Students for a Democratic Society (SDS). Yet some of the male leaders who so eloquently articulated such ideals nonetheless assumed that traditional sexual hierarchies and gender roles should prevail within their organizations. Raising demands for women's equality within New Left organizations often fueled tension and conflict. Nonetheless, women in these organizations had the opportunity to develop skills and to debate issues that served them well when they turned their attention to rights for women.

Both inspired and frustrated by their experiences in civil rights and antiwar movements, a generation of feminists—many young, single women or young mothers—formulated a critique of the social and sexual order and demanded women's liberation. Although many feminist groups were comprised entirely of white women from middle-class backgrounds, African American, Puerto Rican, Asian American, and American Indian women as well as working-class white women also organized on behalf of women's liberation. A Black Women's Liberation Committee was formed in SNCC in

1968, for instance, and Puerto Rican feminists within the Young Lords insisted that reproductive rights be included on the political agenda of that organization.

The enthusiasms of these women's liberationists converged and at times conflicted
with proposals offered by an older generation of women who combined frustration over
the "feminine mystique" with experience in labor unions, more moderate civil rights
organizations, and partisan politics. After gaining experience on President John F.
Kennedy's Commission on Women, or the state commissions modeled on it, more mainstream feminists forged an agenda and an association to implement it—the National
Organization for Women, or NOW. Although once again dominated by middle-class
white women, NOW also attracted support from African American, Chicana, and blue-
collar women. Many of these older feminists had participated in or supported the civil
rights movement, but they focused more on the benefits gained from legislative victories
than on community organizing and participatory democracy. One of the most important
victories for them was the inclusion of the word "sex" in the Civil Rights Act of 1964.
Although Congressman Howard W. Smith of Virginia inserted the word sex into the bill
as a way to ensure its failure, he miscalculated. When the bill was passed and signed into
law by President Lyndon Johnson, it thus banned gender as well as racial discrimination
in numerous areas, including employment.

Despite ideological differences between members of NOW and advocates of
women's liberation, feminists in many local communities attempted to work together
across political, generational, racial, and class differences. Issues such as equal pay,
domestic violence, rape, and access to birth control and abortion gained support from a
wide range of feminists as well as from large numbers of women and men who rejected
that label. In cities and towns across the country, rape crisis centers, spouse abuse shelters, day care centers, women's health clinics, and similar institutions blossomed and
attracted the attention and support of diverse groups of women.

In Chapter Twelve, Anne Enke examines one of the nation's first battered-women's
shelters—Women's Advocates in St. Paul, Minnesota, which opened in 1972. Through the
history of Women's Advocates, she explores the emergence of a community-based feminist movement that drew on women's experiences in antiwar and other social justice
campaigns. Yet in confronting domestic violence, these feminists were forced to reimag-
ine the relationship between private and public space, between safety and danger.
Moreover, once the shelter opened and women began using its resources, its founders
had to rethink questions of class, race, gender, and sexuality and to confront tensions
and conflicts among women themselves.

Feminists alone could not have placed women's issues at the center of public
debate. They were aided by dramatic social, economic, cultural, and political transformations in the decades following World War II. As the chapters in this section make
clear, many of the changes that fueled feminist activism also inspired conservative reactions. These changes include the massive expansion of service-sector occupations; a
huge influx of women, including married women, into the paid labor force; increased
numbers of college-educated and professionally trained women; a continued wage
gap between women and men and between white women and women of color; a
heightened awareness and perhaps incidence of rape, domestic violence, and incest;
the promise of control over reproduction through safe contraceptives and abortions;

declining rates of marriage and childbirth alongside rising rates of divorce; and increasing numbers of women and children living in poverty.

As women confronted these transformations in their individual lives, families, and communities, they often differed about how to define both the problems and the solutions. Nonetheless, in the 1960s and 1970s women across the political spectrum claimed new roles and forged new organizations and institutions. In the process, they brought issues and ideas long relegated to the private domain into public view and demanded political action and accountability.

Suggested Readings and Web Sites

Dorothy Sue Cobble, *The Other Women's Movement: Workplace Justice and Social Rights in Modern America* (2004)

Rachel Blau DuPlessis and Ann Snitow, eds., *The Feminist Memoir Project: Voices from Women's Liberation,* 2nd edition (2007)

Sara M. Evans, *Tidal Wave: How Women Changed America at Century's End* (2003)

Michelle Nickerson, *Mothers of Conservatism: Women and the Postwar Right* (2008)

Barbara Ransby, *Ella Baker and the Black Freedom Movement: A Radical, Democratic Vision* (2003)

Vicki Ruiz, *From Out of the Shadows: Mexican Women in Twentieth-Century America* (1998)

Susan K. Cahn, *Sexual Reckonings: Southern Girls in a Troubling Age* (2007)

Civil Rights in Mississippi Digital Archive
   http://www.lib.usm.edu/~spcol/crda/index.html

Agents of Social Change
   http://www.smith.edu/libraries/libs/ssc/agents/index.html

Chicago Women's Liberation Herstory Project
   http://www.cwluherstory.com/CWLUMemoir/memoir.html

The postwar ideology of domesticity exhorted women to devote themselves to suburban mothering and homemaking. Yet most American women did not live in the suburbs, did not belong to the white middle class, and did not see themselves solely as mothers and wives. In fact, substantial numbers of women in this period embraced activist roles in the public sphere. Still, maternity and domesticity frequently shaped women's activism in this period, whether the issue was world peace, the rights of workers, or other areas of social justice. Moreover, both activists who were mothers and those who were not won moral legitimacy for their work by framing it as an outgrowth of maternal concern. Some of the most courageous of these women were the driving force behind the civil rights movement, the most powerful campaign for freedom in twentieth-century American history.

The experiences of black soldiers in World War II and the claims that the United States would make the world safe for democracy had raised the hopes of African Americans that they could finally achieve full equality. During the late 1940s and throughout the 1950s, however, black Americans faced continued discrimination as well as physical violence as they tried to claim first-class citizenship. Efforts to desegregate public schools and public transportation, to regain voting rights, and to increase access to managerial and professional jobs led to confrontations with those who continued to advocate white supremacy. The movement accelerated during the 1950s, which was marked by a number of landmark events. The Supreme Court's 1954 decision in *Brown v. Board of Education*, the murder of Emmett Till, and the Montgomery Bus Boycott that brought Martin Luther King, Jr., into the national headlines are among the most well known of these events.

Although men like Reverend King often filled the formal leadership positions in these civil rights struggles, women, in the words of civil rights leader Ella Baker, were the "backbone" of the movement. "When demonstrations took place and when the community acted," she claimed, "usually it was some women who came to the fore." Baker was only one of the movement's heroines: Septima Clark, Rosa Parks, Jo Ann Gibson Robinson, Daisy Bates, and Mamie Till Bradley all joined her at the forefront of the struggle in the 1950s. They spoke to other African Americans and to the nation at large about the hardship and grief of being a black woman in a racist society. Some of these women were charismatic leaders while others were behind-the-scenes organizers; by example and design they nurtured the grassroots leadership of hundreds of other female community leaders. Together, these women instigated and sustained the massive protests of the civil rights movement into the 1960s. Female freedom fighters won renown for their efforts as community organizers, as facilitators within and across organizations and generations, and as frontline soldiers in the efforts to desegregate schools and lunch counters and to register and vote.

African American women fostered the social networks that kept churches, neighborhoods, and civic organizations operating in their communities. In their hands, beauty parlors and similar establishments blurred the lines between business and politics. As the civil rights movement gained momentum in the 1940s and 1950s, female community leaders mobilized their social connections to advance racial justice. In doing so, they put their own lives in danger. They were humiliated, threatened, arrested, beaten, and shot alongside their male counterparts. They were fired from jobs and forced out of their homes. In addition, they confronted the particular threats of sexual violence that had long plagued black women. Despite these women's courage, their work was largely overlooked for many years. Only recently have historians recognized that the black freedom movement would have collapsed without its female organizers.

Narratives of the civil rights movement look very different with women at their core. Gender and sexuality become central to understanding the genesis and development of the movement, and the focus shifts from federal court cases and legislation to local families and communities. The histories in this volume reflect this realization. In Chapter One, Hannah Rosen illuminates sexual assault as a critical tool of white supremacy. Danielle McGuire builds on these insights in this chapter, which describes how rape continued to shape the lives of women, families, and African American communities in the years after 1866. Yet McGuire focuses less on the brutal victimization of black women and more on their willingness to fight back in the face of sexual violence. Certainly, the oppressive character of white supremacy cannot be understood without an analysis of rape, but neither can massive female resistance be adequately explained without acknowledging the desire of black women to maintain control over their own bodies.

McGuire explores the choices made by African American women when they decided to speak publicly about their rapes by white men. Cognizant that they might be tarred by pernicious stereotypes about black female promiscuity, these women nonetheless recognized the political power of testifying publicly about sexual assault. Exposing white rapists struck at the core of white supremacy. White supremacists argued that the races needed to be separated in order to protect white womanhood from sexually voracious black men and white men from morally suspect black women. By establishing white men as sexual predators, African American women exposed these segregationist arguments as lies and thereby undermined one of the most powerful justifications for racial segregation.

Black women's testimony provided more than an intellectual challenge to white America. It also served as a catalyst for direct action. Public discussion of sexual assaults transformed the violation of one individual into a transgression against an entire community. The resulting trials fueled community outrage that activists were able to channel into political mobilization. McGuire uses one 1959 Florida case to illuminate the connection between a horrifying rape and the mobilization of a community. She argues that this was hardly an isolated incident; some of the era's most well-known civil rights protests began as reactions to a rape. In numerous cases, African American communities launched sit-ins, marches, boycotts, and other actions out of a determination to erase the racial hierarchies that allowed white men to rape black women without suffering any consequences. Although the testimony of African American women in the 1950s echoed that of their foremothers in the 1860s, the time was now ripe for a civil rights revolution, what historians have termed a Second Reconstruction.

"It Was Like All of Us Had Been Raped": Sexual Violence, Community Mobilization, and the African American Freedom Struggle

DANIELLE L. MCGUIRE

On Saturday, May 2, 1959, four white men in Tallahassee, Florida, made a pact, one of their friends testified in court later, to "go out and get a nigger girl" and have an "all night party." That evening, they armed themselves with shotguns and switchblades and crept up behind a car parked alongside a quiet road near Jake Gaither Park. At about 1:00 a.m. on May 3, Patrick Scarborough pressed a sixteen-gauge shotgun against the driver's nose and ordered Richard Brown and his companions out of the car. Dressed in formal gowns and tuxedoes, the four African Americans—all students at Florida A&M University who had spent the evening dancing at the Green and Orange Ball—reluctantly stepped out of the car. Scarborough forced the two black men to kneel, while his friend David Beagles held the two black women at knifepoint. When Betty Jean Owens began to cry, Beagles slapped her and told her to "shut up" or she "would never get back home." Waving his gun, Scarborough ordered Richard Brown and his friend Thomas Butterfield back in the car and told them to leave. As Brown and Butterfield began to move toward the car and then slowly drove away, Edna Richardson broke free and ran to the nearby park, leaving Betty Jean Owens alone with their attackers. Beagles pressed the switchblade to Owens's throat and growled, "We'll let you go if you do what we want," then forced her to her knees, slapped her as she sobbed, and pushed her into the backseat of their blue Chevrolet; the four men drove her to the edge of town, where they raped her seven times.

This newspaper photo from May 4, 1959, depicts the large crowd of students who rallied on behalf of Betty Jean Owens, a Florida A&M student who had been raped by a gang of white men two nights earlier. Owen's testimony about her assault mobilized both her fellow students and the town's African American community. The outrage generated by this and other well-publicized rape cases fueled the escalating civil rights movement.

Analyses of rape play little or no role in most histories of the civil rights movement, even as stories of violence against black and white men—from Emmett Till to Andrew Goodman, Michael Schwerner, and James Chaney—provide gripping examples of racist brutality. Despite a growing body of literature that focuses on the roles of black and white women and the operation of gender in the movement, sexualized violence—both as a tool of oppression and as a political spur for the movement—has yet to find its place in the story of the African American freedom struggle. Rape, like lynching and murder, served as a tool of psychological and physical intimidation that expressed white male domination and buttressed white supremacy. During the Jim Crow era, women's bodies served as signposts of the social order, and white men used rape and rumors of rape not only to justify violence against black men but to remind black women that their bodies were not their own.

African American women frequently retaliated by testifying about their brutal experiences. I argue that, from Harriet Jacobs to Ida B. Wells to the women of the present, the refusal of black women to remain silent about sexualized violence was part of a long-standing tradition. Black women described and denounced their sexual misuse, deploying their voices as weapons in the wars against white supremacy. Indeed, their public protests often galvanized local, national, and even international outrage and sparked campaigns for racial justice and human dignity. When Betty Jean Owens spoke out against her assailants, and when the local black community mobilized in defense of her womanhood in 1959, they joined in this tradition of testimony and protest.

The arrest, trial, and conviction of Owens's white rapists by an all-white jury marked a dramatic change in the relations between this tradition of testimony and a tradition of silence that Darlene Clark Hine has termed the "culture of dissemblance." The verdict not only broke with southern tradition but fractured the philosophical and political foundations of white supremacy by challenging the relationship between sexual domination and racial inequality. For perhaps the first time since Reconstruction, southern black communities could imagine state power being deployed in defense of their respectability as men and women. As a result, the 1959 Tallahassee rape case was a watershed event that remains as revealing now as it was important then.

The sexual exploitation of black women had its roots in slavery. Slave owners, overseers, and drivers took advantage of their positions of power and authority to rape slave women, sometimes in the presence of their husbands or families. White slave owners' stolen access to black women's bodies strengthened their political, social, and economic power, partly because colonial laws made the offspring of slave women the property of their masters. After the fall of slavery, when African Americans asserted their freedom during the interracial experiment in democracy that briefly characterized Reconstruction, former slaveholders and their sympathizers used violence and terror to reassert control over the social, political, and economic agency of freedpeople. At the heart of this violence, according to Gerda Lerner, rape became a "weapon of terror" to dominate the bodies and minds of African American men and women.

"Freedom," as Tera Hunter notes, "was meaningless without ownership and control over one's own body." During Reconstruction and Jim Crow, sexualized violence served as a "ritualistic reenactment of the daily pattern of social dominance," and interracial rape became the battleground upon which black men and women fought for ownership of their own bodies. Many African American women who were raped or assaulted by white men fought back by speaking out. Frances Thompson told a congressional committee investigating the 1866 Memphis race riot that seven armed white men broke into her house on a Tuesday afternoon, "drew their pistols and said they would shoot us and fire the house if we did not let them have their way with us." Four of the men raped Frances, while the other three choked and raped sixteen-year-old Lucy Smith and left her close to death. In 1871, Harriet Simril testified in front of a congressional committee investigating Ku Klux Klan terror during Reconstruction that she was beaten and "ravished" by eight men in South Carolina who broke into her house to force her husband to "join the democratic ticket." Essic Harris, appearing before the same committee, reported that "the rape of black women was so frequent" in the postbellum South that it had become "an old saying by now." Ferdie Walker, who grew up during the height of segregation in the 1930s and 1940s in Fort Worth, Texas, remembered being "scared to death" by a white police officer who often exposed himself to her while she waited at the bus stop when she was only eleven years old. The sexual abuse of black women, she recalled, was an everyday occurrence. "That was really bad and it was bad for *all black girls*," she recalled.

John H. McCray, editor of the South Carolina *Lighthouse and Informer*, reported that it was "a commonplace experience for many of our women in southern towns . . . to be propositioned openly by white men." He said, "You can pick up accounts of these at a dime a dozen in almost any community." African American women that I interviewed in Birmingham, Alabama, in March 2003 echoed Ferdie Walker's and McCray's comments. Nearly all of them testified about being sexually abused or intimidated by white men—particularly bus drivers, police officers, and employers.

The acclaimed freedom fighter Fannie Lou Hamer knew that rape and sexual violence was a common occurrence in the segregated South. *For Freedom's Sake*, Chana Kai Lee's biography of Hamer, is one of the few histories of the modern-day civil rights movement that openly deals with and documents the legacy of sexual assault. Hamer's grandmother, Liza Bramlett, spoke often of the "horrors of slavery," including stories about "how the white folks would do her." Bramlett's daughter remembered that "this man would keep her as long as he want to and then he would trade her off for a little heifer calf. Then the other man would get her and keep her as long as he want—she was steady having babies—and trade her off for a little sow pig." Twenty of the twenty-three children Bramlett gave birth to were products of rape.

Hamer grew up with the clear understanding that a "black woman's body was never hers alone." If she was at all unclear about this lesson, the forced hysterectomy she received in 1961 and the brutal beating she received in the Winona, Mississippi, jail in 1963 left little room for confusion. After being arrested with other Student Nonviolent Coordinating Committee (SNCC) activists for desegregating a restaurant, Hamer received a savage and sexually abusive beating by the Winona police. "You bitch," one officer yelled, "we going to make you wish you was dead." He ordered two black inmates to beat Hamer with "a long wide blackjack," while other patrolmen battered "her head and other parts of her body." As they assaulted her, Hamer felt them repeatedly "pull my dress over my head and try to feel under my clothes." She attempted to pull her dress down during the brutal attack in order to "preserve some respectability through the horror and disgrace." Hamer told this story on national television at the Democratic National Convention in 1964 and continued to tell it "until the day she died," offering her testimony of the sexual and racial injustice of segregation.

By speaking out, whether it was in the church, the courtroom, or a congressional hearing, black women used their own public voices to reject the stereotypes used by white supremacists to justify economic and sexual exploitation, and they reaffirmed their own humanity. Additionally, African American women's refusal to remain silent offered African American men an opportunity to assert themselves as *men* by rallying around the protection of black womanhood. Many other men, however, remained silent since speaking out was often dangerous, if not deadly. Most important, women's testimonies were a political act that exposed the bitter ironies of segregation and white supremacy, helped to reverse the shame and humiliation rape inflicts, and served as catalysts in mobilizing mass movements.

Only after local and national groups were organized, black women's testimony began to spark public campaigns for equal justice and protection of black womanhood. In this respect, World War II served as a watershed for African Americans—especially in the South. Black women's testimony and the willingness of black leaders to protect black womanhood must be viewed as part of these resistance movements. For example, in Montgomery, Alabama, the organizational infrastructure that made the Montgomery bus boycott possible in 1955 stemmed in part from decades of black women's activism and a history of gendered political appeals to protect black women from sexual assault. The majority of leaders active in the Montgomery Improvement Association in 1955 cut their political teeth demanding justice for black women who were raped in the 1940s and early 1950s.

In 1944, the kidnapping and gang rape of Mrs. Recy Taylor by six white men in Abbeville, Alabama, sparked what the *Chicago Defender* called "the strongest campaign for equal justice to Negroes to be seen in a decade." Taylor, a twenty-four-year-old African American woman, was walking home from the Rock Hill Holiness Church near Abbeville on September 3 when a carload of six white men pulled alongside her, pointed a gun at her head, and ordered her to get into the car. They drove her to a vacant patch of land where Herbert Lovett pointed his rifle at Taylor and demanded she get out of the car and "get them rags off or I will kill you and leave you down here in the woods." Lovett held her at gunpoint while each of the white men took turns "ravishing" her. After the men raped her, Lovett blindfolded her, pushed her into the car, and dropped her off in the middle of town. That night, Recy Taylor told her father, her husband, and Deputy Sheriff Lewey Corbitt the details of her harrowing assault.

Within a few weeks, the Committee for Equal Justice for Mrs. Recy Taylor formed and was led on a local level by Rosa Parks, E. D. Nixon, Rufus A. Lewis, and E. G. Jackson (editor of the *Alabama Tribune*), all of whom later became pivotal figures in the Montgomery bus boycott. By utilizing the political infrastructure designed to defend the Scottsboro boys a decade earlier and employing the rhetoric of democracy sparked by World War II, Parks, Nixon, and their allies secured the support of national labor unions, African American organizations, women's groups, and thousands of individuals who demanded that Gov. Chauncey Sparks order an immediate investigation and trial. "The raping of Mrs. Recy Taylor was a fascist-like, brutal violation of her personal rights as a woman and as a citizen of democracy," Eugene Gordon, a reporter for the *New York Daily Worker,* wrote in a pamphlet about the case; "Mrs. Taylor was not the first Negro woman to be outraged," he argued, "but it is our intention to make her the last. White-supremacy imitators of Hitler's storm troopers [will] shrink under the glare of the nation's spotlight." Gordon closed by universalizing the rape: "The attack on Mrs. Taylor was an attack on all women. Mrs. Taylor is a Negro . . . but no woman is safe or free until all women are free." Few African Americans were surprised when the Henry Country Grand Jury twice failed to indict the white men—despite the governor's belief that they were, in fact, guilty. Still, Recy Taylor's testimony launched a national and international campaign for equal justice that must not be ignored.

Five years later, African Americans in Montgomery, Alabama, rallied to the defense of a twenty-five-year-old black woman named Gertrude Perkins. On March 27, 1949, Perkins was walking home when she was arrested for public drunkenness and attacked by two white police officers in uniform. After forcing her into their squad car, they drove her to the edge of town and raped her repeatedly at gunpoint. Afterwards, they threw her out of their car and sped away. Somehow, she found the strength to stagger into town, where she went directly to Rev. Solomon Seay Sr.'s house. Awaking him, she told him the details of her brutal assault through sobs and tears. "We didn't go to bed that morning," remembered Seay; "I kept her at my house, carefully wrote down what she said, and later had it notarized." Seay sent Perkins's horror story to the syndicated columnist Drew Pearson, who let the whole country know what happened in his daily radio address before Montgomery's white leaders knew what hit them.

The leaders of the local Interdenominational Ministerial Alliance, the Negro Improvement League, and the National Association for the Advancement of Colored People (NAACP), led by E. D. Nixon and the Reverend Mr. Seay, joined together to form the Citizens Committee for Gertrude Perkins. Mary Fair Burks and her newly formed Women's Political Council may have been involved since one of their early goals was to "aid victims of rape." Although the community mobilized on behalf of Perkins, a grand jury failed to indict the assailants a few weeks later, despite running the full process of "the Anglo-Saxon system of justice." Still, Joe Azbell, editor of the *Montgomery Advertiser*, thought Gertrude Perkins, who bravely spoke out against the men who raped her, "had as much to do with the bus boycott and its creation as anyone on earth." The Perkins protest did not occur in isolation. In February 1951, Rufus A. Lewis, whose influence was crucial to the 1955 campaign, led a boycott of a grocery store owned by Sam E. Green, a white man, who was accused of raping his black teenage babysitter while driving her home. Lewis, a World War II veteran and football coach at Alabama State University, organized other veterans and members of the Citizens' Coordinating Committee in the successful campaign to close the store and bring Green to trial.

The 1955 Montgomery bus boycott itself can be viewed as the most obvious example of the African American community coming to the rescue of a black woman, Rosa Parks, though not because of rape. When Parks sat down in a bus's "no-man's land" and was arrested for refusing to give up her seat to a white man, Montgomery blacks found the *perfect* woman to rally around. "Humble enough to be claimed by the common folk," Taylor Branch notes, Rosa Parks was "dignified enough in manner, speech, and dress to command the respect of the leading classes." Rosa Parks fit the middle-class ideals of "chastity, Godliness, family responsibility, and proper womanly conduct and demeanor" and was the kind of woman around which all the African Americans in Montgomery could rally. It is clear that her symbolic role as icon of virtuous black womanhood was decisive in Montgomery. Rev. Martin Luther King Jr.'s first speech at Holt Street Baptist Church stressed this point. "And since it had to happen," the young preacher told the crowd, "I'm happy it happened to a person like Mrs. Parks. Nobody can doubt the height of her character; nobody can doubt the depth of her Christian commitment."

By selecting Rosa Parks as the symbol of segregation instead of other, less exemplary black women who had been arrested on buses earlier in 1955, black leaders in Montgomery embraced the "politics of respectability" and adhered to what Darlene Clark Hine calls the "culture of dissemblance" as a matter of political necessity amidst the burning white backlash that the 1954 Supreme Court decision in *Brown v. Board of Education* sparked. The White Citizens' Councils, a kind of uptown Ku Klux Klan, led the movement for massive resistance to school integration by relying heavily on sexual scare tactics and white fears of racial amalgamation. As a result, any gender or racial impropriety on the part of African Americans could be viewed as threatening the social order. For the supporters of segregation, "integration always meant miscegenation." Headlines in the *Citizens' Council* warned that "mixed marriage," "sex orgies," and accounts of black men raping white girls were "typical of stories filtering back from areas where racial integration is proceeding 'with all deliberate speed.'"

In this environment, respectability and dissemblance required that silence surround black sexuality, a "cult of secrecy" that helped counter negative stereotypes and kept the inner lives of African Americans hidden from white people. This self-imposed reticence, Hine argues, "implied that those [African American women] who spoke out provided grist for detractors' mills and, even more ominously, tore the protective cloaks from their inner selves." Silence as strategy did not emerge in the mid-twentieth century; it had been a staple of black clubwomen's politics since Reconstruction, when whites continued to use racist violence and sexual abuse to shore up white supremacy.

The culture of dissemblance does not mean there was an unbroken wall of silence. There are moments in history when the pain of violation or the opportunity for justice forced women to come forward to speak out against their abusers. Yet this code of secrecy, a political imperative during the Montgomery bus boycott, helped create a void in the historical record. As a result, violence toward black women has not been as "vividly and importantly retained in our collective memory," Elsa Barkley Brown claims, as the lynching of and violence against black men.

In many ways, this culture of dissemblance silenced more than the survivors of rape; it also trained historians of the black freedom struggle to ignore the subject of black women's dissemblance. Over the past two decades, historians have sharpened their focus on the gendered meanings of respectability, but they have lost sight of the role rape and the threat of sexual violence played in the daily lives of African American women as well as within the larger black freedom struggle. Yet throughout the Jim Crow South African American women such as Recy Taylor in 1944, Gertrude Perkins in 1949, and Betty Jean Owens in 1959 refused to shield their pain in secrecy, thereby challenging the pervasiveness of the politics of respectability. Following in the footsteps of their Reconstruction-era counterparts, they testified about their assaults, leaving behind critical evidence that historians must find the courage to analyze.

To be sure, black women's refusal to remain silent about sexual violence during and after slavery suggests that the culture of dissemblance functioned in tension and in tandem with a tradition of testimony. Even after respectability became the key to black women's symbolic place in the civil rights movement in the early 1950s, however, a number of African American women continued to speak out publicly about being raped, and African American community members rallied to their defense. Unfortunately, too many of these stories remain buried in the archives, yellowing newspapers, or the memories of the survivors, contributing to the historical amnesia about black women's experiences. And Montgomery, Alabama, was not the only place in which attacks on black womanhood fueled protests against white supremacy. Betty Jean Owens's experience in Florida is evidence that a significant story has been missed across the South.

When the four armed white men in Tallahassee forced Thomas Butterfield and Richard Brown to get into their car and drive away, leaving Betty Jean Owens and Edna Richardson at the mercy of their assailants, the two black men did not abandon them but drove around the corner and waited. As the blue Chevrolet disappeared down the street, Brown and Butterfield hurried back to the scene. Edna Richardson, the black woman who was able to get away, saw her friends from her hiding spot, called out to them, and then ran to the car. Hoping to save Owens, the Florida A&M students rushed to the local police station to report the crime.

Similar situations in other southern towns had typically left African Americans without police aid. The officer on duty that night in Tallahassee was Joe Cooke Jr., a nineteen-year-old intern from the all-white Florida State University. Much to the surprise of the three black students, he agreed to look for Owens and her assailants. After a lengthy search, one of the students finally spotted the blue Chevrolet and shouted, "That's it!" It was just after 4:00 a.m. Deputy Cooke turned on his flashers and drove alongside the car. Attempting to escape, the kidnappers led Cooke "twisting and turning through the dark streets of Tallahassee at speeds up to 100 miles per hour." One of the white men suggested "dumping the nigger," but William Collinsworth replied, "we can't now, he's on our tail." Finally, Collinsworth pulled the car to the curb, grabbed his shotgun, and got out of the car. Deputy Cooke drew his pistol and ordered all four to line up against the car or, he threatened, "I will shoot to kill."

As they waited for assistance from Cooke's supervisor, they heard muffled screams coming from the car. Richard Brown and Deputy Cooke peered through the rear window and saw Betty Jean Owens, bound and gagged, lying on the backseat floorboards. Brown tried to help her out of the car, but, as her feet touched the ground, she collapsed. Cooke drove Betty Jean Owens and her friends to the local colored hospital at Florida A&M while Deputy Sheriff W.W.Slappey arrested the four white men and drove them to the jailhouse.

Laughing and joking on the way to the police station, the four white men apparently did not take their arrest seriously, nor did they think they had done anything wrong. Collinsworth, for example, worried less about the charges against him than about the safety of his car. Deputy Sheriff Slappey revealed his disgust when he handed the men over to Sheriff Raymond Hamlin Jr. "They all admitted it," Slappey said; "they didn't say why they did it and that's all I'm going to say about this dirty business." William Collinsworth, David Beagles, Ollie Stoutamire, and Patrick Scarborough confessed in writing to abducting Betty Jean Owens at gunpoint and having "sexual relations" with her. When Sheriff Hamlin asked the men to look over their statements and make any necessary corrections, David Beagles, smiling, bent over the table and made one minor adjustment before he and his friends were hustled off to jail.

If the four white men did not take their arrests seriously, students at Florida A&M University flew into a rage. Many of them were veterans of the Tallahassee bus boycott in 1957, a Montgomery-inspired campaign that highlighted the trend in students' preference for direct action rather than the more respectable and slower litigation favored by the NAACP throughout the 1940s and 1950s. When the students heard news of the attack on Owens and the subsequent arrest of four white men, a small group planned an armed march to city hall to let city officials know that they were willing to protect black womanhood the same way whites "protected" white womanhood—with violence or at least a show of force. Mainstream student leaders persuaded them that an armed march was "the wrong thing to do" and patched together a "Unity" demonstration on Sunday, May 3, only twelve hours after Betty Jean Owens was admitted to the hospital and the four white men were taken to jail.

Fifteen hundred students filled Lee Auditorium, where Clifford Taylor, president of the Student Government Association, said he "would not sit idly by and see our sisters, wives, and mothers desecrated." Using language white men in power could understand, student leaders professed their "belief in the dignity, respect, and protection of womanhood" and announced that they would petition the governor and other authorities for a "speedy and impartial trial."

Early the next day, a thousand students gathered in the university's grassy quadrangle with signs, hymns, and prayers aimed at the national news media, which sent out stories of the attack across the country. The students planned to show Tallahassee and the rest of the nation that white men could no longer attack black women without consequence. Student protesters held signs calling for "Justice"; other posters declared, "It could have been YOUR sister, wife, or mother." Some students linked the attack in Tallahassee to larger issues related to the black freedom struggle: Two students held up a poster depicting scenes from Little Rock, Arkansas, which read, "My God How Much More of This Can We Take."

It was the deeply personal violation that rape inflicts, however, that gave the students their focus. Patricia Stephens Due remembered feeling helpless and unsafe. She recalled, "We all felt violated, male and female. It was like all of us had been raped." The student leader Buford Gibson, speaking to a crowd, universalized the attack when he said, "You must remember it wasn't just one Negro girl that was raped—it was all of Negro womanhood in the South." By using Betty Jean Owens as a black Everywoman, Gibson challenged male students to rise up in protest and then placed the protection of black womanhood in their hands. Gibson's exhortation inspired students at Florida A&M to maintain their nonviolent demonstration, unlike white men who historically used the protection of white womanhood to inspire mob violence against black men.

At about the same time, white men in Poplarville, Mississippi, used the protection of womanhood as justification for the lynching of Mack Charles Parker, a black man who was charged with the kidnapping and rape of a twenty-four-year-old white women who could barely identify him in a police lineup. On April 25, 1959, two days before his trial, a group of eight to ten white men obtained keys to Parker's unguarded jail cell, savagely beat him, and then dragged him down three flights of stairs and out of the building while he screamed "I'm innocent." Federal Bureau of Investigation (FBI) agents located Parker's bloated body floating in the Pearl River on May 4, 1959, just two days after four white men gang-raped Betty Jean Owens. The Parker lynching cast a shadow over Tallahassee, brutally reminding the black community that white women's bodies were off limits, while the bodies of black women were fair game.

Accelerating media coverage, student-led protests, and a threat to boycott classes at Florida A&M forced Judge W. May Walker to call members of the grand jury into special session in Tallahassee on May 6, 1959. Over two hundred black spectators, mostly students, squeezed into the segregated balcony at the Leon Country Courthouse to catch a glimpse of Betty Jean Owens and her attackers before they retreated into the secret hearing. Still undergoing hospital treatment for injuries inflicted during the attack and for "severe depression," Owens was accompanied to the courthouse by a nurse, the hospital administrator, and her mother.

Gasps and moans emanated from the balcony when, after two hours behind closed doors, William Collinsworth, David Beagles, Patrick Scarborough and Ollie Stoutamire emerged, calmly faced the judge, and pleaded innocent to the charge of rape, making a jury trial mandatory. African Americans in the balcony roared with disapproval. Dr. M. C. Williams, a local black leader, shouted, "four colored men would be dead if the situation had been reversed. It looks like an open and shut case." Defense attorneys for Collinsworth and Scarborough argued for a delay, insisting that public excitement threatened a fair trial, but Judge Walker ignored their objections. For the first time in Florida history, a judge sent the white defendants charged with raping an African American woman back to jail to await their trial. Echoing the sentiments of the people around him, a young boy traced "we want justice" in the dust on the railing of the segregated balcony.

Justice was the last thing the black community expected. In the thirty-four years since Florida began sending convicted rapists to the electric chair instead of the gallows, the state had electrocuted thirty-seven African Americans charged with raping white women. Before this, Florida led the country in per capita lynchings, even surpassing such notoriously violent states as Mississippi, Georgia, and Louisiana. From 1900 to 1930, white Floridians lynched 281 people, 256 of whom were African American. Throughout its history, Florida never executed or lynched a white man for raping a black woman. In this respect, Florida followed the entire region. Florida's violent history included the "little Scottsboro" case involving Samuel Shepard, Walter Irvin, and Charles Greenlee, black men accused of raping a white woman in Groveland, Florida, in 1949. After the U.S. Supreme Court overturned their guilty verdicts in 1951, Sheriff Willis McCall picked up Shepard and Irvin from Raiford State Prison to transfer them back to the county. On the way there, McCall pulled to the side of the road and asked the two handcuffed men to change the tire and then shot them both in the chest. He radioed his boss and muttered, "I got rid of them; killed the sons of bitches." Walter Irvin survived the shooting, but Samuel Shepard died that day.

In Tallahassee, memories of the "little Scottsboro" case hung over many members of the African American community in 1954 when the state electrocuted Abraham Beard, a seventeen-year-old black youth accused of raping a white woman. Apart from the races of the accuser and the accused, the Beard case featured a cast of characters almost identical to that of the Tallahassee case five years later: An all-white jury had tried and convicted Beard in the same courtroom where Betty Jean Owens faced her attackers. Judge W. May Walker presided, and William D. Hopkins served as the state prosecutor. Harry Michaels, Patrick Scarborought's attorney in 1959, served as Beard's court-appointed attorney in 1954. Both the "little Scottsboro" and the Beard cases revealed the extent to which the protection of white women served as the ultimate symbol of white male power and the foundation of white supremacy. When

African Americans in Tallahassee demanded equal justice for Betty Jean Owens, that foundation began to crumble.

News that four white men would actually face prosecution for raping a black woman plunged both whites and blacks into largely unfamiliar territory. It not only highlighted the bitter ironies of segregation and "social equality" but allowed African Americans to publicize them. According to the *Pittsburgh Courier,* the arraignment made the "arguments for white supremacy, racial discrimination, and segregation fall by the wayside" and the arguments against school desegregation seem "childishly futile." "Time and again," another newspaper editor argued, "Southern spokesmen have protested that they oppose integration in the schools only because it foreshadows a total 'mingling of the races.' The implication is that Negroes are hell-bent for intimacy, while whites shrink back in horror." "Perhaps," the writer argued, "as Lillian Smith and other maverick Southerners have suggested, it is not quite that simple."

While prominent members of the white community expressed their shock and horror at the rape, they continued to stumble into old narratives about race and sex. The indictment helped incite age-old fears of miscegenation and stereotypes of the so-called black beast rapist. William H. Chafe argues that "merely evoking the image of 'miscegenation' could often suffice to ring the alarm bells that would mobilize a solid phalanx of white resistance to change." For example, white women around Tallahassee began to speak openly about their "fear of retaliation," while young white couples avoided parking "in the country moonlight lest some Negroes should be out hunting in a retaliatory mood." Reflecting this fear as well as the larger concern with social equality, Florida legislators, like other lawmakers throughout the South, passed a series of racist bills designed to segregate children in schools by sex in order to circumvent the *Brown v. Board of Education* decision and "reduce the chances of interracial marriage." The extent to which the myth of the black beast rapist was a projection of white fears was never clearer than when the gang rape of a black woman conjured up terror of *black-on-white* rape. The fact that the black community rallied around Betty Jean Owens and her womanhood threatened white male power—making the myth of the black savage a timely political tool.

Black leaders from all over the country eagerly used the rape case for their own political purposes as well. Most focused on the lynching of black men in similar cases, placing the crime against Betty Jean Owens into a larger dialogue about the power struggle between black and white men. As A. D. Williams, a black businessman in Tallahassee, put it, "the white men are on the spot." Rev. Dennis H. Jamison felt that the indictment of four white men indicated a "better chance at Justice than any involving the races in the South," but, he added, "still no white men have ever been executed." Elijah Muhammad, leader of the Nation of Islam, expressed this viewpoint forcefully. Using almost the exact same language as white supremacists, he accused the "four devil rapists" of destroying the "virginity of our daughters." "Appeals for justice," he fumed, "will avail us nothing. We know there is no justice under the American flag." Nearly all the editorials in major black newspapers echoed his sentiments.

Ella Baker, director of the Southern Christian Leadership Conference (SCLC), felt that the evidence in the Tallahassee case was so strong that "not even an all white Florida jury could fail to convict." Reminding whites of their tendency to mete out unequal justice toward black men, she warned, "with memories of Negroes who have been lynched and executed on far less evidence, Negro leaders from all over the South will certainly examine every development in this case. . . . What will Florida's answer be?" The *New York Amsterdam News* called for equal justice, noting that the "law which calls for the death sentence does not say that Negro rapists should be punished by death and white rapists should be allowed to live." The *Pittsburgh Courier* bet on acquittal, despite the fact that the case "is as open and shut as a case can be."

Martin Luther King Jr., at the annual SCLC meeting in Tallahassee a few days after the indictment, praised the student protesters for giving "hope to all of us who struggle for human dignity and equal justice." But he tempered his optimism with political savvy, calling on the federal government to force the country to practice what it preached in its Cold War rivalry with the Soviet Union. "Violence in the South can not be deplored or ignored," King declared, directing his criticism at President Dwight D. Eisenhower; "without effective action, the situation will worsen." King exploited a political context in which America's racial problems were increasingly an international issue. The British Broadcasting Corporation (BBC) broadcast segments of the Florida A&M University student speeches condemning the rape and racial injustice, while newspapers throughout Europe closely watched the case unfold. "It is ironical that these un-American outrages occur as our representatives confer in Geneva to expand democratic principles . . . it might well be necessary and expedient," King threatened, "to appeal to the conscience of the world through the Commission on Human Rights of the United Nations." This international angle was a strategy shared by mainstream integrationists, leftist radicals, and black nationalists alike. Audley "Queen Mother" Moore, leader of the Universal Association of Ethiopian Women, Inc., petitioned the United Nations Human Rights Commission in person to end the "planned lynch terror and willful destruction of our people." She tied issues of race, gender, sex, and citizenship together by demanding Justice Department assistance for Betty Jean Owens's rape case, an FBI investigation of the Mack Charles Parker lynching, and basic voting rights.

Robert F. Williams, militant leader of the Monroe, North Carolina, chapter of the NAACP, suggested African Americans stand their ground and defend themselves. The Parker lynching, the Tallahassee rape case, and two Monroe, North Carolina, cases in which white men stood accused of attacking black women forced Williams to defend racial pride and black womanhood. On May 6, 1959, B. F. Shaw, a white railroad engineer, had been exonerated on charges of beating and kicking a black maid at the Hotel Monroe, even though he did not show up for court. That same day, white jurors giggled while Mrs. Mary Ruth Reed, a pregnant black woman, testified that Lewis Medlin, a white mechanic, beat and sexually assaulted her in front of her five children. Medlin's attorney argued that he was just having a little fun, that he was married to a "lovely white woman . . . the pure flower of life," whom he would not dare leave for "that." The jury deliberated for less than ten minutes before returning the not guilty verdict. It was the defilement of black womanhood and the humiliation of black manhood that inspired Williams to hurl his infamous vow to "meet violence with violence." His exhortation set off a national controversy, culminating at the 1959 NAACP convention where Executive Secretary Roy Wilkins suspended Williams for his remarks. Williams defended his position by citing the tragedy in Tallahassee. Had the "young black men who escorted the coed who was raped in Tallahassee" been able to defend her, Williams argued, they would have been justified "even though it meant that they themselves or the white rapists were killed."

Roy Wilkins shared Williams's gender and race politics but not his methods for achieving them. In a letter to Florida governor LeRoy Collins, Wilkins invoked the lynching of Mack Charles Parker and Emmett Till, noting that the victims' skin color alone kept them from receiving a fair trial and that their deaths threatened political embarrassment at home and abroad. "Full punishment has been certain and swift in cases involving a white victim and a Negro accused," he said, "but the penalty has neither been certain nor heavy in cases involving a Negro victim and a white accused . . . for these reasons," Wilkins warned, "all eyes will be upon the state of Florida."

On June 11, 1959, at least four hundred people witnessed Betty Jean Owens face her attackers and testify on her own behalf. Owens approached the witness box with her head bowed. She wore a white embroidered blouse and a black-and-salmon checked skirt with gold earrings. The African American press had cast her in the role of respectable womanhood by characterizing her as a God-fearing, middle-class college co-ed "raised in a hard-working Christian household" with parents devoted to the "simple verities of life that make up the backbone of our democracy." Unlike white women, who were often able to play the role of "fair maiden" before a lynch mob worked its will on their alleged attackers, Betty Jean Owens had to tell her story knowing that the four white men who raped her might go unpunished. Worse, Owens had to describe the attack in front of hundreds of white people in a segregated institution that inherently denied her humanity. Though it may seem unnecessary, even lurid, to bear witness to the details of her testimony today, it is crucial that we hear the same testimony that the jurors heard. Owens's willingness to identify those who attacked her and to testify against them in public broke the institutional silence surrounding the centuries-long history of white men's sexual violation of black women, made a white southern judge and jury recognize her womanhood and dignity, and countered efforts to shame or stereotype her as sexually unchaste. As a result, her testimony alone is a momentous event.

Owens remained strong as state prosecutor William Hopkins asked her to detail the attack from the moment she and her friends left the Florida A&M dance. This she did powerfully and emotionally. "We were only parked near Jake Gaither Park for fifteen minutes," she said, when "four white men pulled up in a 1959 blue Chevrolet." She identified Patrick Scarborough as the man who pressed the shotgun into her date's nose and yelled, "Get out and get out now." When Owens began to cry, David Beagles pressed a "wicked looking foot long knife" to her throat and forced her down to the ground. He then pulled her up, slapped her, and said, "You haven't anything to worry about." Owens testified that Beagles pushed her into the car and then "pushed my head down in his lap and yelled at me to be quiet or I would never get home." "I knew I couldn't get away," she stated; "I thought they would kill me if I didn't do what they wanted me to do."

She continued with the horrid details. As the car pulled off the highway and into the woods, "the one with the knife pulled me out of the car and laid me on the ground." Owens was still wearing the gold and white evening gown as they tugged at the dress and "pulled my panties off." She pleaded with them to let her go and not hurt her when Beagles slapped her again. She then told how each one raped her while she was "begging them to let me go . . . I was so scared, but there was nothing I could do with four men, knife, and a gun . . . I couldn't do anything but what they said." Owens testified that the men eagerly watched one another have intercourse with her the first time around but lost interest during the second round. "Two of them were working on taking the car's license plate off," she said, "while the oldest one" offered her some whiskey. "I never had a chance to get away," she said quietly; "I was on the ground for two or three hours before the one with the knife pushed me back into the car." After the men had collectively raped her seven times, Ollie Stoutamire and Beagles blindfolded her with a baby diaper and pushed her onto the floorboards of the car, and they all drove away. When she heard the police sirens and felt the car stop, she pulled the blindfold down and began yelling for help. After police ordered the men out of the car, Owens recalled, "I was so scared and weak and nervous that I just fell on the ground and that is the last thing I remember."

Betty Jean Owens then described the physical injuries she sustained from the attack. "One arm and one leg," she said, "were practically useless" to her for several days while she was at the hospital. A nurse had to accompany her to the grand jury hearing a few days after the attack, and she needed medication for severe depression. She also had a large bruise on her breast where the bodice stay from her dress dug into her skin as the four men pressed their bodies into hers. Asking her to identify some of the exhibits, Hopkins flipped open the switchblade used the night of the attack, startling some of the jurors. Immediately the four defense attorneys jumped up and vehemently called for a mistrial, arguing that "by flashing the knife Mr. Hopkins tried to inflame the jury and this prejudiced their clients' constitutional rights to a fair trial." Judge Walker denied their motion, signaling Hopkins to continue. When asked whether she consented, Owens clearly told Hopkins and the jury, "No sir, I did not."

Defense attorneys grilled Owens for more than an hour, trying to prove that she consented because she never struggled to get away and that she actually enjoyed the sexual encounter. "Didn't you derive any pleasure from that? Didn't you?" the attorney Howard Williams yelled repeatedly. He kept pressing her, "Why didn't you yell or scream out?" "I was afraid they would kill me," Owens said quietly. She showed signs of anger when Williams repeatedly asked if she was a virgin in an attempt to characterize her as a stereotypical black jezebel. Owens retained her composure, refused to answer questions about her chastity, and resisted efforts to shame her. The defense made a last-ditch effort to discredit Owens by arguing that, if the young men had actually raped her and threatened her life, she would have sustained more severe injuries.

Proceeding with the state's case, William Hopkins called the doctors, both black and white, who examined Owens after the attack. They told the jury that they found her in a terrible condition and that she "definitely had sexual relations" that caused the injuries that required a five-day hospital stay. Richard Brown, Thomas Butterfield, and Edna Richardson took the stand next. They all corroborated Owen's testimony, adding that after the attack Owens was "crying, hysterical, and jerking all over." Brown testified that Scarborough pointed the shotgun into his car window and ordered him and Butterfield to kneel in front of its headlights. Defense attorney John Rudd asked Brown on cross-examination, was it a "single or double barrel shotgun they pointed into your car?" Brown replied, "I only saw one barrel, sir." Laughter rolled down from the balcony, upsetting Rudd. "I can not work with this duress and disorder at my back, a boy's life is at stake here!" Judge Walker called for order and reprimanded the spectators. When the prosecution finally rested its case at 8:30 p.m. on June 11, defense attorneys moved for a directed verdict of acquittal, claiming the state failed to prove anything except sexual intercourse. Judge Walker vigorously denied the motion and insisted the defense return the next day to present their defense.

Amid a sea of people in the tiny courtroom, David Beagles, an eighteen-year-old high school student, sat rigidly on the stand, pushing a ring back and forth on his finger as he answered questions from his attorney. His mother buried her head in her arms as she listened to her son tell the jury his side of the story. Beagles testified that he had a knife and William Collinsworth had a shotgun. The four of them were out "looking around for Negroes who had been parking near Collinsworth's neighborhood and bothering them." When they came upon the Florida A&M students, Beagles admitted holding the switchblade but then said he put it away when he saw they were dressed in formal wear. He admitted that they ordered Brown and Butterfield to drive away but insisted that he "*asked* the girls to get into the car." He denied the rape, arguing that Owens consented and even asked them to take her "back to school to change her dress." Under cross-examination, Beagles admitted that he "pushed her, just once . . . not hard," into the car, that he said, "If you do what we want you to, we'll let you go," and that he blindfolded her with a diaper after the attack. Defense attorney Howard Williams then asked Judge Walker to remove the jury as Beagles detailed the confession he made the night of the crime. Williams argued that when police officers arrested the young men, they "were still groggy from a night of drinking," making their confessions inadmissible. Under Hopkins's cross-examination, however, Beagles admitted that he was not pressured to say anything, that his confession was voluntary, and that he actually looked over the written statement and made an adjustment.

Patrick Scarborough, who admitted that he was married to a woman in Texas, testified that he had intercourse with Owens twice but emphatically denied using force. When Hopkins questioned him, Scarborough admitted that Owens pleaded, "please don't hurt me," but he insisted that she offered "no resistance." He denied kissing her at first and then said he kissed her on the neck while he had sex with her.

Defense attorneys focused on discrediting Owens instead of defending their clients because the prosecution repeatedly drew self-incriminating information from them. State prosecutor Hopkins argued that "they simply have no defense." Defense attorneys tried to use each man's ignorance to prove his innocence, highlighting their low IQ's and poor educations. When that failed, they detailed the dysfunctional histories of each defendant, as though to diminish the viciousness of the crime by offering a rationale for the men's depravity. Character witnesses for William Collinsworth, for example, described his sordid home life and drinking problem. Nearly every member of Collinsworth's family took the stand, spilling sorrowful stories about their poverty and dysfunction. His sister, Maudine Reeves, broke down on the stand and had to be rushed to the hospital. His wife, Pearlie, told the jury through sobs and tears that he was "not himself when he was drunk," but when he was sober "you couldn't ask for a better husband." On the stand, she failed to mention what her letter to the judge had made explicit: that her husband regularly beat her. When that did not seem to work, defense arrorneys switched gears and attempted to portray their clients as reputable young men who were incapable of rape. Friends and family members all testified that these young men "were good boys," and that in particular Ollie Stoutamire, a cousin of Tallahassee police chief Frank Stoutamire, had "nothing but pure and moral intentions."

Finally, the defense appealed to the jury's prejudices. Collinsworth blamed his actions on the "Indian blood" pulsing through his veins; the Pensacola psychiatrist Dr. W. M. C. Wilhoit backed him up when he argued, "It is a known fact that individuals of the Indian race react violently and primitively when psychotic or intoxicated." When Collinsworth added alcohol to his "Indian blood," Wilhoit argued, "he was unable to discern the nature and quality of the crime in question." The attorney for Ollie Stoutamire, city judge John Rudd, blamed "outside agitators." The defendants are "being publicized and ridiculed to satisfy sadists and people in other places," Rudd yelled during closing arguments. "Look at that little skinny, long legged sixteen-year-old boy. Does he look like a mad rapist who should die . . . should we kill or incarcerate that little boy because he happened to be in the wrong place at the wrong time?"

In their summations to the jury, defense attorneys S. Gunter Toney and Harry Michaels followed Rudd's lead. Michaels insisted that "the crime here is insignificant . . . the pressure, clamor, and furor are completely out of proportion." Pointing to Scarborough, Michaels told the jury, "his motives, intentions, and designs that night were wholesome, innocent and decent." The fact that Owens could "have easily walked ten feet into the woods where nobody could find her," Michaels said, proved she consented. Waving her gold and white gown in front of the jury, he pointed out that it was "not soiled or torn," which he said proved no brutality was involved. Finally, he called for an acquittal, arguing that the jury could not possibly convict on the basis of "only one witness—the victim, and confessions that admitted only one fact—sexual intercourse." Sitting in the segregated balcony, Charles U. Smith, a sociologist at Florida A&M University, said he gasped when he heard Howard Williams yell, "Are you going to believe this nigger wench over these four boys?"

In his summation, prosecuting attorney William Hopkins jumped up, grabbed the shotgun and Betty Jean Owens's prom dress, and appealed to the jury for a conviction.

Suppose two colored boys and their moron friends attacked Mrs. Beagles' daughter . . . had taken her at gunpoint from a car and forced her into a secluded place and regardless of whether they secured her consent or not, had intercourse with her seven times, leaving her in such a condition that she collapsed and had to be hospitalized?

Betty Jean Owens, he said, "didn't have a chance in the world with four big boys, a loaded gun and a knife. She was within an inch of losing her life . . . she was gang-raped SEVEN times." "When you get to the question of mercy," he told the jury, "consider that they wouldn't even let that little girl whimper."

Restless spectators, squeezed into every corner of the segregated courthouse, piled back into their seats when jurors emerged after three hours of deliberation with a decision. An additional three hundred African Americans held a silent vigil outside. A. H. King, the jury foreman and a local plantation owner, slowly read aloud the jury's decision for all four defendants: "guilty with a recommendation for mercy." The recommendation for mercy saved the four men from the electric chair and, according to the *Baltimore Afro-American*, "made it inescapably clear that the death penalty for rape is only for colored men accused by white women." A. H. King defended the mercy ruling by arguing that "there was no brutality involved" and insisted, implausibly enough, that the decision would have been the same "if the defendants had been four Negroes." Judge Walker deferred sentencing for fifteen days, cleared the courtroom, and sent the four white men to Raiford prison.

African Americans who attended the trial quietly made their way home after the bittersweet verdict. Betty Jean Owens's mother told reporters that she was "just happy that the jury upheld my daughter's womanhood." Rev. A. J. Reddick, former head of the Florida NAACP, snapped, "If it had been Negroes, they would have gotten the death penalty." "Florida," he said, "has maintained an excellent record of not veering from its pattern of never executing a white man for the rape of a Negro," but he acknowledged that the conviction was "a step forward." Betty Jean Owens showed a similar ambivalence in an interview by the *New York Amsterdam News*. "It is something," she said; "I'm grateful that twelve white men believed the truth, but I still wonder what they would have done if one of our boys raped a white girl."

Florida A&M students, who had criticized Butterfield and Brown for failing to protect black womanhood a week earlier, were visibly upset after the trial. In fact, letters to the editors of many African American newspapers condemned the two men and all black men for failing to protect "their" women. Mrs. C. A. C. in New York City felt that all Negro men were "mice" and not worthy of respect because "they stand by and let the white men do anything they want to our women." She then warned all black men that they "would never have freedom until [they] learn to stand up and fight." In a letter to the *Baltimore Afro-American*, a black man accepted her challenge: "unless we decide to protect our own women," he argued, "none of them will be safe." Some African American women felt they should protect themselves. A white woman sent her black maid home one day after she came to work with a knife, "in case any white man came after her," reported the *Tallahassee Democrat*. Still, many felt that "someone should have burned."

Despite their anger at the unequal justice meted out, some African Americans in the community considered the guilty verdict a victory. The Reverend C. K. Steele Jr., head of the Tallahassee chapter of the SCLC, said it showed progress, reminding others that four white men "wouldn't have even been arrested twenty years ago." The Reverend Leon A. Lowery, state president of the Florida NAACP, saw a strategy in the mercy recommendation. He thought that it could help "Negroes more in the long run" by setting a precedent for equal justice in future rape cases. After Judge Walker handed down life sentences to the four white men, some African Americans in Tallahassee applauded what they felt was a significant step in the right direction; many others, however, exhibited outrage. Roy Wilkins openly praised the verdict as a move toward equal justice but acknowledged in a private letter the "glaring contrast that was furnished by the Tallahassee verdict." In light of the recent lynching of Mack Charles Parker, no one really had to wonder what would have happened had the attackers been black. Editors of the *Louisiana Weekly* called the trial a "figment and a farce" and insisted that anyone who praised the verdict "confesses that he sees nothing wrong with exacting one punishment for white offenders and another, more severe for others."

Any conviction was too much for some whites who felt that sending four white men to jail for raping a black woman upset the entire foundation of white supremacy. Many believed the guilty verdict was the result of a Communist-inspired NAACP conspiracy, which would ultimately lead to miscegenation. Letters to Judge Walker featured a host of common fears and racist stereotypes of black men and women. Fred G. Millette reminded the judge that a conviction "would play into the hands of the Warren Court, the NAACP, and all other radical enemies of the South . . . even though the nigger wench probably had been with a dozen men before." Mrs. Laura Cox wrote to Judge Walker that she feared this case would strengthen desegregation efforts, posing a direct threat to white children who might attend integrated schools. "If the South is integrated," she argued, "white children will be in danger because the Negroes carry knives, razors, ice picks, and guns practically all the time." Petitioning Judge Walker for leniency, Mrs. Bill Aren reminded him to remember that "Negro women like to be raped by the white men" and that "something like this will help the Supreme Court force this low bred race ahead, making whites live and eat with him and allow his children to associate with the little apes, grow up and marry them."

It is ironic that a rape case involving a black woman and four white men would conjure up images of the black brute chasing white women with the intent to mongrelize the white race. The Tallahassee case attests to the persistence of such images decades after Reconstruction, when the mythological "incubus" took flight, justifying mob violence and a reign of terror throughout the South. Anxieties about the black beast rapist and fears of miscegenation conveniently surfaced when white men feared losing their monopoly on power. As Frederick Douglass noted nearly a century earlier, the myth of the black man as a rapist was an "invention with a well defined motive." The rape of Betty Jean Owens reminds us that the maintenance of white supremacy relied on *both* the racial and sexual domination of black men *and* women.

While the verdict was likely the confluence of localized issues—a politically mobilized middle-class African American community, the lower-class status of the defendants (who were politically expendable), Florida's status as a "moderate" southern state dependent on northern tourism, and media pressure—it had far-reaching consequences. The Tallahassee case focused national attention on the sexual exploitation of black women at the hands of white men, leading to convictions elsewhere that summer. In Montgomery, Alabama, Grady F. Smith, a retired air force colonel, was sentenced to fourteen months of hard labor for raping a seventeen-year-old African American girl. In Raleigh, North Carolina, Ralph Lee Betts, a thirty-six-year-old white man, was sentenced to life imprisonment for kidnapping and molesting an eleven-year-old African American girl. And in Burton, South Carolina, an all-white jury sent a white marine named Fred Davis to the electric chair—a first in the history of the South—for raping a forty-seven-year-old African American woman. In each case, white supremacy faltered in the face of the courageous black women who testified on their own behalf.

Betty Jean Owens's grandmother recognized the historic and political significance of the verdicts. "I've lived to see the day," she said, "where white men would really be brought to trial for what they did." John McCray, editor of the South Carolina *Lighthouse and Informer,* wondered if the convictions in Tallahassee and elsewhere pointed to "defensive steps" taken by the South to "belatedly try to disprove that it discriminates against colored people." Still, he realized the importance of guilty verdicts. "This forced intimacy," he argued, "goes back to the days of slavery when our women were the chattel property of white men." For McCray, the life sentences indicated a new day: "Are we now witnessing the arrival of our women? Are they at long last gaining the emancipation they've needed?"

John McCray's connection between the conviction of white men for raping black women and black women's emancipation raises important questions that historians are just beginning to ponder. How did the daily struggle to gain self-respect and dignity, rooted in ideas of what it meant to be men and women, play out in the black freedom struggle? It is not just a coincidence that black college students, struggling for their own identity and independence, sparked the sit-in movement soon after Betty Jean Owens was brutally raped. In Tallahassee, Patricia Stephens Due, who felt that the rape symbolized an attack on the dignity and humanity of all African Americans, organized the city's first Congress of Racial Equality (CORE) chapter just six weeks after Owens's trial. Florida A&M CORE members launched an uneventful sit-in campaign that fall, but, like other black students throughout the South, successfully desegregated local lunch counters, theaters, and department stores in the spring of 1960. The students later led the "jail, no bail" tactic popularized by SCLC and SNCC. While the rape alone may not have been the galvanizing force that turned students into soldiers for freedom, the sexual and racial dynamics inherent in this case speak to larger themes in the African American freedom struggle.

The politics of respectability—Betty Jean Owens's middle-class background, her college education, and her chastity—may have enabled African Americans on the local and national level to break through the "culture of dissemblance" and speak out against her rape. But it was the convergence of the politics of respectability, Owens's testimony, and African Americans' growing political influence on the national and international stage in the late 1950s that made the legal victory possible. Still, the long tradition of black women's testimony, stretching back to slavery and Reconstruction, makes it clear that some elements of the Tallahassee case were not aberrations. The testimonies and trials of Betty Jean Owens, Gertrude Perkins, and Recy Taylor, to name just a few, bear witness to these issues, forcing historians to reconsider the individual threads that make up the fabric of African American politics. Black women not only dissembled where it was necessary but testified where it was possible. Not only silence but often protest surrounded the sexualized violence against African American women. If we are are fully to understand the role of gender and sexuality in larger struggles for freedom and equality, we must explore these battles over manhood and womanhood, frequently set in the context of sexualized violence, that remain at the volatile core of the modern civil rights movements.

Questions for Study and Review

1. Compare the 1866 statements of the five Memphis freedwomen to the 1959 courtroom testimony of Betty Jean Owens. Explain the similarities and differences in terms of the context and outcomes of these two episodes.

2. How did sexual violence against women shape the civil rights movement in the 1940s and 1950s?

3. How did race shape the politics of rape in the 1950s? Why didn't rape unite women across race and class lines?

4. In what ways does McGuire's description of African American women in the 1950s challenge Coontz's characterization of this period?

Suggested Readings and Web Sites

Christina Green, *Our Separate Ways: Women and the Black Freedom Movement in Durham, North Carolina* (2005)

Darlene Clark Hine, "Rape and the Inner Lives of Black Women in the Middle West: Preliminary Thoughts on a Culture of Dissemblance," *Signs: A Journal of Women in Culture and Society* (1989)

Steven F. Lawson, "Civil Rights and Black Liberation," in *A Companion to American Women's History* (2002)

Chana Kai Lee, *For Freedom's Sake: The Life of Fannie Lou Hamer* (1999)

Charles M. Payne, *I've Got the Light of Freedom* (1995)

Mississippi Oral History Project
    http://www.usm.edu/msoralhistory

Voices of Civil Rights Exhibit
    http://www.loc.gov/exhibits/civilrights/cr-exhibit.html

"The Sixties" has become shorthand for the social movements and social changes that rocked the country from the 1950s through the 1970s. During the decade of the 1960s, especially powerful images of social protest dominated the airwaves. Footage of civil rights marchers under attack by police dogs made some Americans sympathetic to protesters. Yet the defiance of flower children and student radicals who burned draft cards alienated many others, who feared nothing was sacred to those demanding the right to "question authority." Rejecting the notion that protesters were seeking to fulfill the promise of American democracy, these horrified citizens interpreted the protesters' actions as harbingers of political, economic, and moral decline.

Far from the television cameras, groups of concerned citizens resolved to halt what they viewed as the nation's deterioration. Seated around kitchen tables in new tract homes across the South and West, in a region called the Sunbelt, local activists planned a campaign designed to restore traditional American freedoms and celebrate the nation's heroic heritage. Drawing on neighborhood networks, these activists recruited like-minded people to sustain letter-writing campaigns, study groups, and "Freedom Forum" bookstores. Roiled by the threat of Communism, many of these affluent suburbanites had already acknowledged their Cold War fears by constructing bomb shelters in their backyards. But they were not content to stock up on canned goods and pray that they would not have to retreat to their family bunker. They channeled anxiety into activism, determined to unmask the pernicious influence of Communists in American society.

The movement created by conservative anti-Communists became one of the most powerful legacies of the 1960s. Its core ideology was fueled by a reactionary populism that dominated the last two decades of the twentieth century. The movement won widespread support among white middle-class Christians who were animated by the sense that their values were under siege. As Michelle Nickerson explains, women were at the heart of this conservative campaign. Like their counterparts in the civil rights movement, female conservatives mobilized at a local level to build a grassroots movement that ultimately reshaped national politics.

Within movements on the right and left, men were elevated to visible leadership positions, but women were the ones who organized their communities. For conservative causes, this meant that white middle-class mothers in the nation's new suburbs were doing more than baking cookies in their modern kitchens. They were also cooking up a highly politicized domesticity that cast political organizing as integral to their work as homemakers and mothers. In this sense, they echoed the arguments of women suffragists and settlement house workers in the early twentieth century, who justified their activism by arguing that they needed to protect their families from harm. This time, however, women activists rejected the progressive priorities of an earlier age to embrace a conservative agenda. These suburban women activists took advantage of their flexible schedules to canvass voters and mimeograph political pamphlets between diaper changes, car pools, and meal preparation.

Outraged by what they observed in their children's schools, female conservatives in California cut their political teeth in educational politics. They wrested control over institutions like Parent-Teacher Associations (PTAs) and school boards from more liberal leaders. Eventually, they remade the statewide educational bureaucracy according to conservative principles. But they soon extended their political reach beyond the realm of education. As they entered partisan politics, they took the Republican Party from a bastion of the eastern elite, many of whom held moderate views on a range of social issues, and recast it as a stronghold of a more conservative populism that motivated masses of women and men across the nation.

The unflagging efforts of these new political activists propelled candidates who embraced their uncompromising conservatism to national prominence. Elated by the 1980 election of Ronald Reagan, these militant conservatives charted a new course in American politics that transformed the way many citizens thought about government. At the same time, grassroots conservatives expanded women's roles in politics, although not by attacking traditional gender roles. Rather, they created a new breed of conservatism that emphasized family values and drew its legitimacy from the support of politicized mothers like themselves.

Moral Mothers and Goldwater Girls: Women and Grassroots Conservatism in the American Sunbelt
MICHELLE NICKERSON

In November 1961, a group of parents in Los Angeles' San Fernando Valley gathered at Gledhill Elementary School for their regular PTA meeting. School board member J. C. Chambers was their speaker that evening and his topic was "How the Communist Menace Influences the Minds and Thinking of Our Youth." Chambers warned his audience that communists at Harvard and Columbia were using textbooks to brainwash American schoolchildren. Some women stood up to point out that communists were closer to home than that: they taught at U.C.L.A.,

Women volunteers stand behind the display of conservative literature at the Main Street Americanism Center, a bookstore in Southern California that supplied conservative activists with books, magazines, and patriotic paraphenalia for most of the 1960s. This South Pasadena bookstore served as a model for other conservative bookstores in the Los Angeles metropolitan area. Institutions like these bookstores helped activists spread the gospel of a newly militant conservatism that reshaped national politics in the last decades of the twentieth century. Women provided the volunteer labor essential to these efforts.

U.C. Berkeley, and other California colleges. The discussion then turned to a recent development at Gledhill. The patriotic hymn "Columbia, Gem of the Ocean" no longer appeared in the second-grade songbook. Instead, folk tunes like the Ukraine's "Cut the Grain" took its place. When one woman spoke up to defend the decision, noting that "Columbia" was too difficult for second graders, the others booed her: They believed that "Cut the Grain's" peasant themes and place of origin should be taken seriously—that this was precisely the way communists slowly and insidiously opened vulnerable minds to radical thinking.

The tension and suspicion that underlay this gathering at Gledhill was characteristic of the high-pitched political battles happening around Los Angeles and all over America during the Cold War. Dominating the discussion was a formidable group of political agitators—homemakers and mothers. From Orange County to Pasadena, from Hollywood to the San Fernando Valley, women increasingly made it their business to stop communism from infiltrating their communities. After World War II, when California reached new heights of electoral importance as the most populous state in the nation, Los Angeles and its burgeoning suburbs became a hotbed of grassroots right-wing activism. The region's economic boom, fueled by the growing military-industrial complex, kindled a pro-defense, free-enterprise, limited-government program of conservatism. In the 1960s, the movement picked up energy and supporters in response to civil rights activism and Vietnam War protests; and in 1966 it propelled Ronald Reagan to the governorship. Just as the Free Speech Movement in Berkeley and Gay Liberation in San Francisco have made northern California a focal point of the standard 1960s narrative, southern California deserves equal recognition as a nucleus of conservative activism.

The conservative movement spread quickly and pervasively throughout Los Angeles because its organizers mobilized effectively at the grassroots. Women, mostly homemakers and mothers, executed much of the work behind these home-grown efforts. Women conservatives built important organizing networks from their living rooms and kitchens, balancing these tasks with child-rearing and house-keeping, embracing political work as an extension of their household duties. Few of these women participants in the conservative movement actually sought high polit-ical office for themselves or made any efforts to secure gains for women as a group. Sometimes they invoked their roles as housewives and mothers to get attention, but most often they spoke up on the basis of their own political expertise, cultivated through intense study and research with other women. They entered politics as informed, self-educated super citizens. Mostly white, middle and upper class, few of these women worked at paid full-time jobs. Instead, they took advantage of their time and flexible schedules to do political work. These activists shaped the conserv-ative movement in ways that reflected their concerns for children, family, and community. They politicized their PTAs and school boards, opened patriotic bookstores, formed anticommunist study groups and letter-writing networks, wrote politically conservative literature, and composed anticommunist music. With these activities, women drew the battle lines of the Cold War at the most fundamental levels of civic and cultural life and built a grassroots movement in the process. As one South Pasadena housewife active in the Republican Women's Club and John Birch Society remembered, women were "the core of the conservative movement."

Women's involvement in right-wing politics increased alongside an emerging conservative era in the California Republican Party. When conservative Senator William Knowland became the Republican front-runner for governor in 1958, his more militant anticommunist, anti-labor faction began to dominate the party. Although Knowland ultimately lost to Democrat Pat Brown, his candidacy signaled the decline of President Eisenhower's moderate "Modern Republicanism" in the California GOP. By the early 1960s, a vibrant, energetic conservative movement swept Los Angeles and its environs, helped Barry Goldwater win the 1964 Republican presidential nomination, and contributed to Ronald Reagan's victory in the 1966 gubernatorial race.

This conservative movement was jump-started by charismatic figures like Barry Goldwater, Robert Welch, and Fred Schwarz, who put forth a fresh, exciting, and intelligent vision of conservatism. Goldwater's *Conscience of a Conservative* (1960), for example, outlined a compelling "Conservative position," declared war on the nation's moral and spiritual decay, and summoned patriotic Americans to mount "Conservative demonstrations." Robert Welch, who founded the John Birch Society (JBS), named after a Baptist missionary slain for his anticommunist efforts in China, offered a "total program" for fighting communism in 1958. Men and women all over the country formed JBS chapters in their homes. Although the communist conspiracy theories propagated by the society struck most Americans as extremist, Welch's patriotic, antistatist message resonated even with conservatives who chose not to join. The society also educated and cultivated many of the most important leaders, both men and women, of the burgeoning movement in L.A. At roughly the same time, Australian Dr. Fred Schwarz, who based his operation in Long Beach, opened immensely popular "schools of Anti-Communism" and held youth rallies in several U.S. cities. Schwarz's Christian Anti-Communist Crusade introduced a highly appealing evangelical conservatism that electrified audiences from the Disneyland Hotel to Patriotic Hall, the Hollywood Palladium, and the L.A. Sports Arena. The breadth and popularity of this invigorated conservatism became apparent with the right-wing takeover of the Republican Party. The three major Republican volunteer organizations, the California Republican Assembly (CRA), the Young Republicans (LAYR), and the newly formed United Republicans of California (UROC), became a powerful conservative bulwark within the party. The members of these groups proved instrumental in the election of Birchers John Rousselot and Edgar Heistand, in Barry Goldwater's 1964 presidential nomination, and in Ronald Reagan's 1966 gubernatorial victory.

While white men played the most visible roles in this conservative movement, women dominated the activist grassroots. As historical subjects, conservative women of the 1950s and 1960s do not fit the mainstream women's history written about their era, which focuses on Cold War domesticity and feminism. By not calling attention to themselves as women and not working toward a set of goals specifically for women, these activists fit awkwardly in the history of the women's liberation movement. Politically aware and active, they defy Betty Friedan's *Feminine Mystique* model of the depressed, unfulfilled housebound American homemaker. As housewives and mothers, they mobilized behind conservatism while accepting and even leveraging their traditional feminine roles. Although the lives of activist wives and mothers mirror the revived domesticity often associated with the 1950s, they challenge the assertion that this ideology, as historian Elaine Tyler May argues, effected an "apolitical tone." On the contrary, southern California's women conservatives shored up traditional gender roles and laid the groundwork for the conservative movement. Within the John Birch Society, the CRA, the Young Republicans, and UROC, men and women worked together—but women worked during the daytime, weekday hours as well. Women generally expressed the reasons for their conservatism in the same terms as men. They thought government was getting too big, that domestic communism posed a serious threat, and that social disruptions like loosening sexual standards, student activism, and civil rights demonstrations made America vulnerable to communism. Gender might not have colored their core beliefs, but women experienced politics differently from men and chose to confront the threat of communism in their own ways. Believing that the educational system was the nation's Achilles heel—where children would become either patriotic Americans or disillusioned radicals—many women felt compelled to become political. They often viewed their work as a crusade. As the president of California's Federation of Republican Women challenged her 50,000 members in 1958, "No longer is it possible for [women] to stay home keeping aloof from all outside. . . . Are we through apathy and ignorance going to allow this great dynamic idea we call the U.S.A. to go down the drain of governmental controls and dominance under Socialism?"

Education battles presented women with the opportunity to extend the domestic realm into the larger world of politics. Though the not-so-cold war over education started well before the 1960s, the grassroots movement turned a corner with the election of Max Rafferty as state superintendent in 1962. His shocking victory represented a new show of strength for conservatives. Rafferty was a firebrand educator, writer, speaker, and school superintendent in the wealthy LaCañada school district. He championed a "back to basics" program for education: local control of schools, the use of wholesome *McGuffey* Readers, the emphasis on patriotic "heroes" in American history, and the "three R's." Dr. Rafferty excoriated the "red psychological warfare" being waged on school children and denounced the "unwashed, leather-jacketed slobs" and "greasers" who disrupted classrooms and terrorized other students. Though roundly criticized for the racial undertones of his rhetoric, Rafferty resonated with Angelenos who were anxious about rebellious youths and afraid of communism. He came to personify the educational agenda of the conservative movement in Los Angeles.

In 1961, a "Draft Rafferty" office opened in Orange County. A group of wealthy businessmen from the California Club—oil company executives, bankers, and real estate giants—made hefty contributions to Rafferty's campaign that played a major role in his election. Women, however, played the key role as the grassroots activists in his campaign. When draft Rafferty efforts got underway in Orange County, Newport Beach homemaker Patricia Gilbert, the wife of a traveling salesman, invited ten women to her house to strategize. "We sat around the table," she remembers, "just like we were planning a senior prom or something." The women merged their Christmas card lists into a mailing roster and organized a letter-writing campaign to draft Rafferty. When Rafferty finally decided to run, Gilbert formed Parents for Rafferty. Adopting the little red schoolhouse as their symbol, Parents for Rafferty set out to reach as many Californians as possible; theirs was a genuinely "homespun effort." The group distributed over three million pieces of literature, most of which were printed on a mimeograph machine in the Gilberts' garage. Parents for Rafferty built an 8,000-person mailing list and opened 260 chapters around the state. Telephone calls, canvassing, mass mailings—all activities that mixed well with their daily routines as mothers—became their modus operandi.

Patricia Gilbert's own political awakening originated from her interests as a mother. Busy at home with small children, she had paid little attention to politics before the Rafferty campaign. She had, however, grown concerned about communism enough earlier that year to attend Fred Schwarz's School of Anti-Communism. Schwarz left a strong impression on her political thinking, but it was her focus on children and education that catalyzed her activism:

> I always loved children and I always worked with them . . . teaching them numbers and colors. . . . And I had observed that often perfectly bright children went off to school and . . . then just had trouble learning. I could never understand why that was.

Acting on these concerns, she read more about education, attended talks, and sat in on school board meetings. She agreed with Rafferty that children were not acquiring the basic skills they needed to get excited about learning; they were also not exposed often enough to inspirational, patriotic heroes of history. Gilbert threw herself into the Rafferty campaign and became a savvy political organizer. She worked with other women out of a shared interest in education and common patterns of everyday life. "Our main basis and ground," she points out, "was the drafting of somebody to help out education." Thanks largely to the efforts of Parents for Rafferty and similar groups, Max Rafferty won a landslide victory in 1962. That same year California reelected liberal governor Pat Brown, but Rafferty organizers demonstrated the power of grassroots conservatives to turn out their voters.

Perhaps more important, Rafferty's campaign highlights some of the burning education issues that fomented conservatives and embroiled women in the movement. Many activists focused on school politics because they thought that American educators were too liberal, that their labor unions were too powerful, and that their progressive teaching methods were downright socialistic. Although most educators considered John Dewey's philosophy of progressive education passé by mid-century, conservatives warned that the liberal overtones and experimental spirit of progressive education still lingered in the public schools. Rafferty and others championed phonics and back-to-basics techniques over the latest "new math" and "look-say" reading methods. Also, many conservative parents were politicized by John Stormer's *None Dare Call It Treason*, published in 1964. Stormer cautioned them that American children were learning to think like communists through the presentation of U.S. history "as a class struggle." He charged that many widely used textbooks downgraded American heroes, the U.S. Constitution, and religion. For similar reasons, Robert Welch urged John Birch Society members to take over their PTAs. He warned that liberalism's twin by-products were social upheaval and centralized government and both eventually led to communism. Trends like premarital sex and experimentation with drugs, moreover, were threats to the social order that invited revolution. Max Rafferty, who shared these views, described the University of California at Berkeley as a "four year course in sex, drugs and treason." This rhetoric played no small role in his 1962 election and that of Governor Ronald Reagan in 1966.

The Gledhill Elementary episode illustrates how women took the lead on school board fights and in Parent Teachers Association debates. Some of these imbroglios brought female agitators into the local spotlight. In 1963, Emily Philips of Sepulveda, president of the local PTA, gained many supporters and notoriety because of the strong stance she took against communism, even though her protests eventually landed her in a Van Nuys courtroom. Philips was tried for, and cleared of, two counts: loitering and trespassing. The thirty-five-year-old mother interrupted a dance in the school gymnasium, charging that the Latin number's sexual overtones were inappropriate for youths. On another occasion she refused to release the hand of a five-year-old boy whom she encountered running away from school. She insisted on waiting for the boy's mother instead of turning him over to school administrators, believing the child might have good reasons for running away.

Philips had long been a thorn in the side of the San Fernando Valley school officials and Parent Teachers Association. For three years she had been speaking to groups, railing against the 31st district PTA, the Community Chest, the San Fernando State College Welfare Council, and other social agencies that she linked in a "mysterious advocacy of Socialism." Tired of her accusations, the Sepulveda school principal took advantage of Philips' trespasses and called the police. The prosecutors made no effort to conceal the principal's real purposes. "You can't hit her and you can't shoot her," said the Deputy City Attorney, "so we've done the only other thing we can do—bring her to trial." If San Fernando Valley educators thought Emily Philips was a crackpot, legions of concerned parents around Los Angeles believed she was dead right. A group called the Valley Association to Preserve Freedom sponsored a talk by Philips in the Woodland Hills American Legion Hall. Three hundred came to hear her lecture that evening about how public schools propagated the welfare state. Two months later she gave that talk twice at the Encino Community Center, both events sponsored by the same Valley Association group, and both drawing crowds of over four hundred. Jim Collins, one of the event organizers, urged parents to spread the word because "it would take Emily a hundred years to go to every house in Woodland Hills."

Gender shaped Emily Philips' particular concerns about communism and influenced how others responded to her claims against the school system. Philips identified herself as a housewife and mother above all, yet spoke with authority about education. Motherhood was a major component of her political cachet. For hours at a time, parents sat in community centers and churches to hear her talks. Women only rarely ran for high office in the early sixties, but they did run for PTA president and frequently won. Though Philips never made an issue of gender, the media did so with verve. Philips' Hollywood-style beauty and tailored suit outfits made her a wholesome-yet-titillating news story. Local newspapers called her "personable" and usually mentioned that she was a mother of five. Although a common enough description of women at that time, the mother-activist image evoked a set of connotations: selflessness, good intentions, and genuine concern, among them. Philips' homemaking credentials helped make her a martyr. The *Los Angeles Times* called her a "Crusader." "She had the cloak of a saint," reflected one of her lawyers. No doubt many Angelenos read "hysterical housewife" between the lines, but Philips won admirers, enough to become a local celebrity among conservatives. Just a few weeks after the trial, a Los Angeles Young Republicans unit passed a resolution commending her and her attorney "for their successful defense against harassing legal charges."

Marion Miller, often described as "mother of three children and a former FBI spy," was another recognizable anticommunist housewife who ran for a seat on the Los Angeles school board in 1963. "Most of you have heard her speak on her experiences as an undercover agent for the FBI," advertised the Beverly Hills Republican Club in their January meeting announcement. "Many of you have read her revealing book, *I Was a Spy*. Now she comes to us." Miller's work in espionage made her a popular lecturer even though she never was a paid agent. "While never an employee of the FBI," confirmed J. Edgar Hoover to the *Los Angeles Times* in 1965, "Mrs. Miller did furnish information in a confidential capacity regarding security matters." Miller lost the election, but the spy-mother-housewife image won her a following. She represented a blend of global and local knowledge. Miller's FBI resume gave her claim to expertise on the international communist threat and she offered community-based solutions to meet that threat. During her school board campaign, Miller echoed Max Rafferty, promising to return Los Angeles City Schools to the three R's and phonics and vowing to inculcate an "appreciation of our American Heritage."

Emily Philips and Marion Miller became notable community mobilizers in Los Angeles; their concerns as parents guided their activism. Volunteerism, though far less powerful than paid political office, was more valuable in grassroots politics. Neatly dressed, well-mannered women caught school officials off guard when they went to war against "communism" in public education.

As Parents for Rafferty, Marion Miller and Emily Philips entered the political scene in Los Angeles, while other southern California parents ignited similar battles over textbooks, teachers unions, and school prayer. The San Fernando Valley's Parents for Education (PBE) declared war on the California Teachers Association in 1962, charging that the union's "powerful hierarchy" undermined local control of schools. Two years later, Hollywood-based Project Prayer enlisted the celebrities Pat Boone, Susan Seaforth, Dale Evans, Ronald Reagan, and John Wayne in the campaign for a Constitutional amendment to legalize religious expression in schools. In 1965, Mrs. Virginia Zebold of Granada Hills took her textbook research on the road, appearing before a variety of L.A. clubs to demonstrate how the "irresponsible and rebellious" behavior among students at U.C. Berkeley derived from "indoctrination [through] schools, books, movies and television." The next year, *Land of the Free*, a history textbook adopted by L.A. schools, unleashed a torrent of protest. Parents in Protest of Sierra Madre and the Textbook Study League in San Gabriel complained that the book's author, John Caughey, not only refused to sign a loyalty oath in 1950, but portrayed anticommunists as witch-hunters, characterized slavery as a "shortcoming of the free enterprise system," and depicted the radicals Sacco and Vanzetti as victims.

This parental activism was a reflection of the "family-centered" culture often associated with the 1950s, but that continued for many Americans well past the end of "Ike's America." Although mothers and fathers shared concerns about education, women, as full-time parents, usually assumed leadership and extra responsibility in this realm. In many cases, as with Parents for Rafferty, women were more effective organizers; many groups even played up the social value accorded their gender. In 1964, the San Fernando Valley organization "Women for America, Inc." billed itself as "an organization dedicated to the defeat of totalitarianism using education as a weapon." They raised money for "patriotic" libraries and sponsored "Americanism" quizzes for college students in Los Angeles. Some clubs, like the Liberty Torchbearers, the Network of Patriotic Letter-Writers, Facts in Education, Inc., and the Encino Legislative Research group, were women's organizations not in name, but certainly in numbers and usually in leadership as well.

Many conservative ideologues saw great potential in the deep-rooted moral outrage that drove mothers and housewives to enlist in the fight against communism. One popular anticommunist speaker in Los Angeles, Paul Neipp, wrote a manual for conservative study groups in 1962 called *Let's Take the Offensive!* Neipp highlighted housewives as a special group of "common people" who often demonstrate uncommon resolve. "These are the very ones who could do a lot," he emphasized in the manual's "Call to Housewives" section. Neipp, a Lutheran minister, claimed responsibility for helping to start over five hundred study groups around the country and attributed part of his success to women's heightened sense of awareness to the communist threat. In another of his pieces, a leaflet called "For Women Only," he warned recalcitrant housewives that "if we are to survive, it must come through the women of our country . . . our men are too busy to be concerned. They are too selfishly occupied with making money." Presidential candidate Barry Goldwater was another conservative who recognized homemakers and mothers as an important grassroots force. Women were important vote-getters and their support affirmed his vows to reverse the nation's moral and spiritual decline. Citizens for Goldwater-Miller, the grassroots arm of his campaign, went so far as to form a separate organization, Mothers for Moral America, that appealed directly to women's maternal instincts and sense of moral righteousness. They launched the organization in Nashville, Tennessee, two months before the election, hoping for "a spontaneous, public movement—carefully coordinated with and through the Citizens committee." A Mothers unit formed in the San Fernando Valley in October and Orange County's Carol Arth Waters became the organization's national coordinator.

Gender was clearly an operative force in conservative politics—organizing the division of labor, influencing why men and women entered politics, and determining how they would assert themselves—but "women's" and "men's" issues never drove the debates. Women organized together out of political necessity; men were simply not as available most hours of the day. Whether they chose to acknowledge gender or not, though, a distinctive women's political culture emerged out of their concentrated spheres of activism. While cowboy conservatives Barry Goldwater and Ronald Reagan captured the national spotlight with their masculine, western populist personas, women concentrated their own feminine style of politics on the grass roots. In these ways, they expanded the reach of the conservative movement, as well as their own political domain, well beyond school boards and PTAs.

By the 1960s, women had long been mixing domesticity and politics, mainly through political clubs. In fact, many conservative women started their activist careers in the California Federation of Republican Women, California's first club formed in Los Angeles in 1920 as a wedge for GOP women into the male-dominated world of partisan politics. Over the next few decades, clubs proliferated in California and fashioned a distinctly feminine style of political organizing for themselves in the process. By 1954, there were 123 Republican women's clubs in southern California and 234 statewide. Their political luncheons and coffees, get-out-the-vote drives, and monthly newsletters eventually became the bread-and-butter practices of more conservative grassroots organizations in the postwar era. Republican women's clubs also popularized study groups which, as Paul Neipp was well aware, often inspired housewives to intensify their political involvement.

Over the 1950s, right-wing activist women increasingly adopted the study group model as a way to foster a more militant conservatism that went beyond Eisenhower's "Modern Republicanism." Women in these groups volunteered to research a particular issue and make themselves experts on current topics like the United Nations, mental health legislation, or school integration policies. Meeting at a regular time, often with a scheduled outside speaker, group members updated each other on political developments and often wrote letters to senators and representatives together. One of the most visible and active study clubs in Los Angeles, for example, was American Public Relations Forum. Headquartered in Van Nuys, the forum spun out of a Catholic women's church group and grew rapidly. They were "wives and mothers . . . vitally interested in what is happening in our country," declared president Stephanie Williams at the founding meeting in 1952. The forum received national notoriety in 1956 when they organized a letter-writing campaign that held up passage of the Alaska Mental Health Bill, a measure, they claimed, that would have empowered psychiatrists to institutionalize political dissidents gulag-style in Alaska.

A sizable force of citizen-housewives and political organizers emerged out of this decade of study, research, and correspondence and the conservative movement spread quickly through their extensive networks. The Tuesday Morning Study Club (TMSC) of Pasadena is a case in point. The club originally met as a group of friends, reading pending legislation and discussing politics in one member's home overlooking the Rose Bowl. However, several of the TMSC women eventually went in their own directions, applying their copious study to different grassroots projects. Jane Crosby, for example, formed an early Birch Society chapter in South Pasadena. She also helped establish the United Republicans of California (UROC) and partic-ipated in the conservative takeover of the Republican Party in the early 1960s. When Crosby's husband, Joseph, became chairman of UROC in the mid-1960s, she managed the UROC office on Wilshire Boulevard as a full-time volunteer. "My husband bought me this beautiful air-conditioned home," remembers Crosby, "and I was down in that hot headquarters. I used to think about that." Another outgrowth of TMSC was the Network of Patriotic Letter-Writers (NPLW). The purpose of NPLW, which formed in the late 1950s and lasted into the 1970s, was to "shape trends through letter writing." By 1959, the network was mailing its newslet-ters to subscribers all over the country, two-thirds of whom were women and one-half of whom were non-California residents. NPLW bulletins routinely praised FBI Director J. Edgar Hoover and the House Un-American Activities Committee, attacked the Kennedys, demanded the impeachment of Chief Justice Earl Warren, and called for U.S. withdrawal from the United Nations. The network also urged members to start their own groups. "We will be happy to help you get started," wrote chairman Gertrude Bale to subscriber Della Root, of nearby Alhambra. "This I think is the best way to get into the swing of a letter-writing group."

Conservative study groups reflected not only their women's club origins, but also the new reliance on expertise in postwar American society. Activists were not merely housewives, they were experts by virtue of their intense study. Technological experts built the military industrial complex; think tanks like the Rand corporation advised U.S. national security agencies; and health professionals like Dr. Benjamin Spock advised couples how to raise children. In the same vein, Marie Koenig of Pasadena, self-described "housewife, researcher, lecturer," spoke out against the textbook, *Land of the Free,* but not until she finished checking every footnote. Elaine Tyler May argues that "the era of the expert" diverted middle-class Americans away from political activism by advocating "adaptation" over "resistance," however many housewives cultivated their own expertise to make themselves politically adept. In her own study of Queens, New York, historian Sylvie Murray observes how postwar housewife activists on the other coast also relied less often on "prescribed maternal responsibilities" and more often on "facts and figures" to speak with political authority. Marion Miller and Emily Philips similarly emphasized their extensive experience with domestic communism in their lectures, one as a PTA president and the other as an ex-spy.

The study clubs of the 1950s were the means by which women politicized themselves through familiar rituals and institutions, but housewife activism came even further out into the open in the early 1960s. Around that time, women began opening patriotic bookstores and libraries in the greater Los Angeles area. "We have been lending books back and forth between ourselves so we can become informed," explained Jane Crosby when she founded the Main Street Americanism Center in South Pasadena, "now we want to come out from behind the bushes and get right out on the main street." The center's fifty-odd volunteers, all mothers, made the store a comfortable, handsome space where people would want to walk off the street and sit down to read. "It had a big round oak table," remembers Crosby, "it was cozy . . . so pretty, and so patriotic-looking." The Americanism Center title caught on; it implied a wholly American ideology, a counterpoint to communism. The Wilshire Americanism Center opened in 1964, promising to emphasize "the culturally important and noteworthy aspects of America's growth." Promoting "faith and allegiance" to the United States was the central mission of the Long Beach Americanism Center, which opened in 1965.

Poor Richard's Bookshop opened on Hollywood Boulevard as a patriotic bookstore and more. Frank and Florence Ranuzzi of Los Feliz created Poor Richard's, but Florence operated the shop because Frank was busy with the family's insurance agency. In addition to books like Goldwater's *Conscience of a Conservative* and Whittaker Chamber's *Witness,* Poor Richard's stocked copies of pending bills and legislative hearings, "survival literature" for bomb shelter construction and *McGuffey* children's readers. Florence also turned the shop into a political headquarters. She and Frank designed bumper stickers, printed leaflets, and organized protests. During the 1962 gubernatorial race between Pat Brown and Richard Nixon, Florence's popular "Brown Is Pink" bumper sticker raised quite a furor. Under Florence's guidance, Poor Richard's became a bookstore for the whole family, a conservative "salon" for the community. Men, women, and teenagers would drop in on Saturdays to sit around a big captain's table and hear Florence give talks about communism. "If somebody started an argument . . . she'd grab this book [and] that book," remembers her daughter, "[and] she'd say read it for yourself." The bookstore was a family operation. The Ranuzzis gave away political materials at their own expense. The store never turned a profit. As a result, Frank continued to work at the insurance agency to support the family's activism. Their daughter, then a teenager, cooked and cleaned their home because Florence worked at the store six days a week. Mary also became a "Goldwater Girl." Like a cheerleader, she waved pompoms and shook bottles of gold water (ginger ale) at political rallies.

The Americanism Centers and Poor Richard's provided conservatives in Los Angeles with a sense of community. Poor Richard's, for example, served as a local think tank for speakers and writers in the area. Corinne Griffith, former film star turned anti–income tax lecturer, shopped there for her speech material. So did John Wayne, spokesperson for Project Prayer. Similarly, the South Pasadena center became an information clearinghouse. People called the store volunteers for references on everything from local anti-pornography initiatives to Christian histories of the Constitution. The center also rented out audiovisual materials and sold copies of JBS's *American Opinion* magazine. Patriotic bookstores embodied the new image of conservatism in the early 1960s; they were wholesome, upbeat, and intellectually alive.

Women activists, including the bookstore volunteers, also took the rough edges off of militant conservatism with their feminine warmth and hospitality. Some exerted this same influence through books and music. For example, two southern California women, Patty Newman and Joyce Wenger, wrote a paperback parody of President Johnson's war on poverty in 1966 called *Pass the Poverty Please!* The back cover promised readers, "Two American mothers bring you this exciting story which will make you gnash your teeth at the facts while you laugh along with their adventures." Newman and Wenger's smiling head shots, along with the book's light and satiric tone, softened what was actually a heavy-handed indictment of civil rights and anti-poverty programs. The publisher identified the authors as wives and mothers to pitch *Pass the Poverty Please!* as a practical, down-home guide to politics, grounded in real life for all levels of readers.

Janet Greene, anticommunist folk singer, was another conservative spokesperson who made femininity and domesticity a part of her popular image without talking about gender outright. Greene performed at Fred Schwarz's anticommunism rallies, often with her two daughters. Billed as "a new and effective anti-Communist weapon," the June Cleaver–looking Greene offered a wholesome alternative to the bohemian left-wing folk icons of her time. Greene fit a central organizing strategy of the Christian Anti-Communist Crusade—to fight fire with fire, to turn leftist movement tactics back on itself. "The communists have been using folk-singing for years," they advertised, "now the tables have been turned." Janet Greene was the Joan Baez of the Right. The Crusade's Long Beach office sold Greene's songs, "Fascist Threat," "Commie Lies," "Poor Left-Winger," and "Comrade's Lament" as fund-raisers. "One billion conquered should reveal," she sang, "the danger that is very real. The greatest fascist threat, you see, is the Communist conspiracy."

Singing, writing, operating bookstores, mailing letters and giving lectures, politically active conservative women reveal another 1960s. For the legions who built effective and meaningful political lives for themselves in the conservative movement, their roles allowed them to be activists as well as mothers and wives. For them, the late 1960s did not give birth to a new and exciting era of movement politics and culture, as it did for American leftists. Like second wave feminists, these activists fought hard to expand women's role in politics, but not by attacking hierarchies of gender. They embraced an entirely different vision of women's political advancement, one that conformed to the traditional social order. The activism of middle- and upper-class Los Angeles women shows that their lives were highly conducive to grassroots political work well before the women's liberation movement. While their own movement underwent major changes in the 1960s, its emphasis on family issues, especially education, remained a powerful force in U.S. political culture. So did conservative women in California and around the United States.

Questions for Study and Review

1. Why did affluent suburban Californians believe that their values were under siege in 1961, and why did they feel threatened enough to organize politically?

2. The grassroots conservatives described by Nickerson did not organize as women, yet their activism was shaped by gender. On the one hand, how did gender roles and household duties determine the outlines of their activism? On the other, how does the story of political organizing by California housewives challenge traditional stereotypes about suburban family life in the postwar period?

3. How was conservative women's activism different from or similar to that of more progressive women such as civil rights activists and feminists?

4. Does the mobilization of female conservatives change your understanding of women and politics or of late twentieth-century conservatism?

Suggested Readings and Web Sites

Donald T. Critchlow, *Phyllis Schlafly and Grassroots Conservatism: A Woman's Crusade* (2005)
Elaine Tyler May, *Homeward Bound: American Families in the Cold War Era* (1988)
Lisa McGirr, *Suburban Warriors: The Origins of the New American Right* (2001)
Sylvie Murray, *The Progressive Housewife: Community Activism in Suburban Queens 1945–1965* (2003)
Catherine E. Rymph, *Republican Women: Feminism and Conservatism from Suffrage Through the Rise of the New Right* (2006)
1964 Presidential Election
   http://livingroomcandidate.movingimage.us/election/

Labor militants and anti-Communists, civil rights activists and WKKK supporters all viewed family as a refuge from injustice, violence, and economic uncertainty, a sanctuary linking them to a broader community that inspired and shaped their activism. Women from across the political spectrum also viewed their activism through the lens of family preservation. Taken as a whole, the articles in this volume reveal how "family values" were central to female mobilization even before a supercharged domestic ideology reshaped post–World War II American society.

The feminists described by Anne Enke in this chapter drew inspiration from these earlier social movements. Many of them had come of age politically in either the antiwar movement or the civil rights movement, which offered searing critiques of American democracy and awakened them to the importance of social change. But these militant women in St. Paul, Minnesota, diverged from other activists of the period over the question of the family. For these activists, the family was a highly problematic institution that often engendered violence against women and children. In their analysis, the protective family was a myth that obscured unequal power relations and sanctioned brutality against women. After observing that wives and mothers in crisis had no place to go, this group of feminists decided to create an institution to shelter women seeking safety from family members who abused them. In 1972 they banded together to build Women's Advocates, one of the most enduring battered-women's shelters in the United States.

Women's Advocates is part of the rich institutional legacy of the women's liberation movement of the 1960s and 1970s. Women's liberationists created an array of female-controlled institutions designed to ensure women's equality, dignity, and freedom: rape crisis hotlines, abortion services, health clinics, schools, birthing and day care centers, newspapers and magazines, bookstores and music festivals. These social action projects were just one element of women's liberation, and women's liberation formed just one branch of second-wave feminism. The larger feminist movement was devoted to women's equality and over the course of the late twentieth century transformed the way Americans perceived sex, gender, family, community, and power.

The feminist activism of the 1960s to 1990s had its roots in the nineteenth century, when women first articulated a feminist identity and agenda. These early feminists developed a radical and far-reaching vision for social change but are best known for one achievement: the passage of the Nineteenth Amendment that guaranteed female enfranchisement. Second-wave feminists sought to put the electoral and legal rights hard-won by the earlier movement to the service of new political and social visions.

Most second-wave feminists could agree on the pressing need for change in politics, laws, education, health care, reproductive rights, household structure, work, and conceptions of female sexuality. They could not, however, reach any consensus on priorities or tactics. Yet most feminists spent little time worrying about their lack of central organization or strategy. Women's liberationists in particular poured their energy into social action projects on the local level. Indeed, disagreements among women who shared a feminist identity seemed only to engender more activism. An amazing array of feminist ideologies inspired small groups of women all over the country to pursue the creation and transformation of all kinds of community institutions.

Feminists devised agendas and practices around a long list of political philosophies, including socialist feminism, liberal feminism, radical feminism, black feminism, lesbian feminism, and cultural feminism. One of the most important distinctions noted by scholars of this period has generally been between liberal and radical feminism. Liberal feminism was focused on equality. In the broadest terms, liberal feminists sought to advance women's position within existing institutions. Their major concerns included electing women to office, gaining equal access to universities and professional schools, receiving equal pay for equal work, and enhancing social services—such as day care and health care—that would allow women to balance family, educational, and occupational responsibilities. The most well-known liberal feminist organization is the National Organization for Women (NOW), founded in 1966.

Radical feminism, which in many communities was synonymous with women's liberation, had a completely different style. These activists were generally young, anti-authoritarian, and revolutionary. They did not seek access to established institutions like political parties. Instead, they wanted to abolish these institutions of formal power as well as structures like the family and the church that they believed had engineered male domination over women. Women's liberationists founded few national associations. Instead, they formed local organizations like Women's Advocates that responded to pressing needs. Many of these women embraced alternate family forms, from lesbianism to communal living, and refused to abide by dominant norms regarding feminine appearance and behavior.

One of the most innovative tactics employed by women's liberationists was consciousness-raising, which brought small groups of women together in communities all over the country to explore the meaning of sex and gender in American life. These democratically run groups employed wide-ranging questions to spur discussions about members' personal histories and current lives. Inspired by the slogan "the personal is political," these groups helped women connect their experiences to a larger political analysis. Women emerged from these sessions with a new understanding of their commonalities and new tools to analyze obstacles, abuses, and insecurities as the product of structural inequities rather than personal failings. While members provided support to one another, the ultimate purpose of these groups was political rather than therapeutic.

It was the revelations of a consciousness-raising group in St. Paul that led to the creation of Women's Advocates. As these activists labored to create a haven for abuse survivors that brought together women from diverse class and race backgrounds, they grappled with the challenge of making the personal "political." In this chapter, Enke describes this process, narrating the way activists examined every aspect of their daily lives in order to take over and transform domestic space.

Taking Over Domestic Space: Feminism and the Battered Women's Movement
ANNE ENKE

> When we finally went to the "dirty money" [corporate] sources to help fund shelter space, they told us we needed a director, governing board and this whole hierarchy to run it. Well we had *already* provided shelter for over 1,200 women, for two years, from *our* homes. . . . So . . . the first thing we did was to make the governing board identical to—*composed of*—the whole *membership*, and the membership consisted of everyone who *stayed* at or worked for Women's Advocates.
>
> —Sharon Rice Vaughan

Women's Advocates in St. Paul, Minnesota, is one of the most well-known and longest-lasting battered-women's shelters in the country. Though evidencing the lasting and far-reaching impact of women's movements of the 1970s, it is rarely included in the history of radical social movements. In 1972, the year of Women's Advocates' founding, an international movement against domestic violence against women was in its fledgling stage, lacking even a name for itself, but based in part on a perceived need for "a place" that offered temporary residence and resources for women trying to get away from violent partners. Critiquing the structural conditions that made women economically and socially vulnerable to male violence, the battered-women's movement shared roots, analyses, and strategies with women's movements that addressed rape, welfare, and homelessness, and similarly gained strength by building broad-based coalitions with other activist groups and public agencies. By the end of the 1970s, activists in the United States had created hundreds of housing facilities for battered women in both urban and rural locations, making "shelter" the signature stamp of the battered-women's movement. During the 1980s and 1990s, women of color especially elaborated movement networks and strategies to take advantage of the particular resources

Political buttons were central to feminist movement culture in the late 1960s and 1970s. Combining fashion and protest, feminist buttons broadcast irreverent slogans and powerful symbols. A cheap and easy way to communicate a message, buttons allowed the wearer to make a public statement and attract the attention of like-minded women. Buttons were created to highlight certain issues, commemorate people or events, or declare allegiance to particular groups.

available to specific Indian, Latina, African American, and Asian communities, and in the process have shown that "shelter" and "advocacy" for battered women can and must take on a vast array of forms.

In the historiography and memory of the 1960s and 1970s, militant, direct action—sit-ins, takeovers—and mass protests have been so valorized that it is difficult to recognize radicalism in other forms and contexts. The battered-women's movement and much of the feminist and gay and lesbian liberation movements have been represented as concerns about personal, private, or "lifestyle" issues. However, those movements not only are continuous with radical movements of the 1960s, but also have expanded radical critiques and strategies. Many of the founders of Women's Advocates first came together years earlier, through their involvement in the antiwar movement. There, they developed a critique of a violent society, a critique that meshed well with their budding feminist consciousness. Another thing that those white women brought with them from the antiwar movement was a feeling of constant emergency and the need to act *now*—taking risks, creating protests, and taking over spaces—to save people's lives. I argue here that one of the most important strategies of the battered-women's movement involved nothing less than a radical takeover, not of a government office for a few hours, but of *domestic space*, to create a place in which a woman could rightly demand public protection, privacy, and the inviolability of her own body at all times. Doing so required coalitional action and outreach to thousands of people beyond the existing feminist movement.

Feminists have argued that domestic space, far from being a woman's place, has taken shape firmly within male-dominated social structures. In the United States, ideals originating in the early nineteenth century suggest that the privacy of domestic space is a (white, middle- or upper-class, heterosexual) male right, based on the inviolability of his property, including his domicile, his wife, and his progeny; as owner, he protects his wife's social and sexual status and the purity of his bloodline. In the post–World War II years (largely in response to women's actual departure from the home), popular representations of domesticity as a private—yet nationalist—endeavor further painted a vision of the white, middle-class, nuclear-family "home" as the unassailable space essential to individual and national security. Deviations from dominant domestic ideals made those ideals no less potent in their ability to privatize and support men's violence against women "in their own homes." The women's movement, perhaps more than any other post-1960 social movement, not only condemned the lingering nineteenth-century liberal ideal of separate private and public realms, but also showed that personal and political realms were inseparable or even indistinguishable.

Women's Advocates' mission was not simply to add to or reform social services for women; instead, women in that grassroots organization launched a deep critique of society's division into public and private, and they organized to transform it by creating a domestic space that was intensely political. They argued that the notion of dichotomous public and private realms functioned to privilege white, middle- and upper-class, heterosexual men. The privatization of domestic space, in particular, isolated and confined women, reinforced men's "property rights" over them, and condoned violence as a private matter not subject to public intervention. Neither social services nor legal practices had challenged the privatization of battering; indeed, many argued, existing services even contributed to the isolation of women who experienced domestic battering. Normative conceptions of "home" as an apolitical space furthered women's invisibility. While women's liberation in general challenged this conception by asserting that "the personal is political," the battered-women's movement in particular went further, both critiquing domestic norms and creating an alternative homelike space that women embraced as a site of protection, politicization, and political resistance.

Women's Advocates battered-women's shelter entailed three important aspects of social change. First, it generated a politicized and politicizing "domestic" space. Second, Women's Advocates demanded that "public" institutions such as law enforcement agencies change to accommodate and support that new space. Third, Women's Advocates deepened their own social critique and vision by developing coalitions to address problems of race and class that emerged in the process of running a shelter. Far from cutting themselves off from people who did not share their feminist or leftist analyses, leaders in the battered-women's movement engaged state agencies and capitalist funding sources to create a lasting network of institutions that addressed domestic violence. Most importantly, as the Women's Advocates case reveals, the movement began with the ideas and needs of battered women themselves, and over the years a diversity of shelter residents and advocates innovated strategies to increase resources for women in violent relationships, decrease domestic violence, and sustain the movement.

Politicizing Domestic Space

The founders of Women's Advocates emerged from one of many eclectic consciousness-raising collectives in the Twin Cities. They were "ten or so" white women in their midtwenties to late thirties, of working- and middle-class backgrounds, and had in common prior work with the Honeywell Project, which sought to prevent Honeywell's production of cluster bombs used in Vietnam. Sharon Vaughan of St. Paul had gained local prominence through her activism in the Honeywell Project; she had also been active in the local Catholic Left, but, recently divorced and with three children, she chafed at "St. Paul's Catholic values," which denied women accurate legal information related to marriage and divorce. Minnesotans Monica Erler and Bernice Sisson each had years of traditional civic volunteer work behind them and a growing frustration with the lack of emergency services for women. Susan Ryan, a young VISTA volunteer originally from New York, was perhaps least tolerant of the establishment and demanded nothing less than community-based devotion to ending violence and hierarchies of gender, race, and class.

Upon learning that most female clients of the county legal assistance offices lacked basic legal rights information, especially regarding divorce and custody issues, the collective first created a divorce-rights booklet for women and worked to distribute information about custody, support, and name changes. Drawing on Ryan's VISTA program grants, they also established a telephone hotline, housed in an office donated by the legal assistance office. Countless women throughout Minnesota called the phone service, alerting workers to a shocking reality: So many women were battered in their homes, but most had no place to go and no financial resources. While there were thirty-seven emergency shelters for men in the Twin Cities, the only place that a woman with children could receive emergency shelter—for one night only—was in a motel booked through Emergency Social Services. Lack of safe shelter and legal recourse led this first group of activists to found Women's Advocates in March 1972, a nonprofit group of volunteers who provided legal advocacy for women in abusive relationships. As contact with women increased, advocates began to develop a vision of "a place" for "women who 'need to get away right now.'"

Women seeking Women's Advocates' services almost invariably came from situations of extreme isolation, the result of domineering partners and a society that did not acknowledge battering. While long-enduring peace and civil rights movements strengthened critiques of all kinds of violence, even they did not focus on violence in the home. Few battered women had been touched by the social upheavals of the 1960s. Activists offered clients shelter in their own homes and apartments. Women and children crowded onto floors and couches, an experience that was indeed politicizing for many, but it was a short-term solution that was politically weakened by its relatively privatized nature. Thus arose the idea of a formal shelter; it would be "like home" but collectively run, and not one person's property.

In part, it was the opposition Women's Advocates faced that prompted activists to envision wide-reaching, almost utopian, change. Their early efforts to help battered women—such as housing women in their own homes and later building a formal shelter—were policed with neighborhood suspicion, evictions, and threats of lawsuits by actors concerned with "men's rights." From the outset, therefore, advocates adopted a role as "protector" of women, usurping a prerogative traditionally belonging to fathers and husbands. But advocates also demanded a "response from the whole public community." They envisioned "a house on every block" in which the whole neighborhood would be involved, "like McGruff houses for kids, only they would be shelters for women." Such houses would not only act as discreet zones of safety for women, but would also signal neighborly intervention in battering, making visible a formerly privatized issue. Women's Advocates, then, offered a vision of a dramatically changed public landscape that would support an alternative domestic space.

In challenging normative notions of domesticity, and in nurturing the politicization of residents and staff, Women's Advocates' shelter itself represented a concerted challenge to the boundary between public and private. This was another kind of takeover, one which—in keeping with feminist ideologies—also challenged the boundaries between the movement and the mainstream. Like other social movements, it incorporated dramatic and at times militant acts aimed at radical social transformation. Unlike others, it aimed to take over the home, usurping it from a public order that supported male violence within it, and reappropriating it as a space safe for women.

Most accounts of the battered-women's movement narrate the movement's engagement with "the public" through a shift from grassroots funding to public and private funding sources. This exclusive focus on funding generates a familiar narrative of declining control over resources and discourses. A very different story can be told, however, by tracing the process through which Women's Advocates laid claim to a new kind of space and insisted that existing social entities change to support it. Initially, Women's Advocates activists seemed to believe that the protection of women depended on constructing impenetrable walls between the shelter and the public world. But Women's Advocates constantly renegotiated those boundaries, forging new relationships with local police departments, batterers, the neighborhood, and the larger metropolitan community.

For the energetic founders of Women's Advocates, sheltering women was a logical and necessary extension of social movements that protested institutionalized racism, class stratification, and U.S. colonization of other countries. By 1972, advocates with homes took on an increasing number of women needing shelter. While their homes functioned as a sort of underground shelter system, advocates and residents caught their first glimpse of alternative domesticity: "Women and children slept in spare beds and on our living room floors, sharing our food and belongings. Our children met a succession of new friends." Through opening their homes to a diversity of women and children, advocates, along with clients, further "realized the importance of women being together in one house, sharing their experiences and getting support from one another." This experience, along with a feminist belief in democracy, shared authority, and female empowerment, prompted Women's Advocates to insist on a governing structure in which all residents, as well as advocates, were members of the board of directors, and all members had voting rights. It was this moment—critical to the movement—during which formerly privatized individuals experienced, as a group, a shift from perceiving the world from within a nuclear-family framework to strategizing about the world as a community under one roof. This shift in perception also encouraged a coalitional approach—seeking involvement from a diversity of politicized groups—that would become an inherent and far-reaching aspect of the battered-women's movement.

Advocates saw their actions as radical challenges to society. Many advocates opened up their homes to women facing all manner of crises, convinced that such direct action "was part of working there and being an advocate." Their work as shelterers and advocates thus took place in the space of their own "private" lives, giving them their first taste of danger (e.g., men armed with knives or guns) intruding into their homes. As activists had for the civil rights and antiwar movements, many advocates believed that "taking risks and chances" was also "what you did for Women's Advocates." More importantly, doing so convinced advocates that U.S. domestic norms and the privatization of nuclear households allowed, rather than protected women from, domestic violence. As Bernice Sisson, Women's Advocates volunteer for twenty-six years, explained, battering depended on "private homes" since "most batterers do not batter in front of others." Equally important, this led to an intense focus on the boundary between outside and inside, as advocates tried to convert the exterior walls of their homes (and later the shelter) from barriers that hide violence within to barriers that keep violence out. Advocates at that time interpreted violence explicitly in gendered terms. They determined that the most important thing was that women be able to get to a space "free of violence," where they could "keep the man out" long enough for women to envision a further solution.

As if to confirm that Women's Advocates was challenging the public order and the hierarchies that supported it, backlash came from many fronts. After only a few months, one advocate got evicted from her apartment because neighbors complained that she was bringing too many women and children into what was supposed to be an adults-only property. Sharon Vaughan, Women's Advocates' first director, explained that it helped that early activists tended not to have male partners. "I had kids, but I don't think I could have done any of [Women's Advocates work] with [my former husband]. . . . I didn't have to check in with anybody, to see if it was okay to have somebody sleep in my house." But it was not long before advocates discovered that even their own private homes were under a tangible net of public surveillance. Vaughan eventually stopped housing women and children in the home she owned due to pressure from several sources: In her "homogenously white" neighborhood, neighbors noticed the many women and children of color coming and going at all times of the day and night, and they pressured local legislators to find out and put an end to "what is going on in there." At the same time, a men's rights group threatened to sue Vaughan for housing only women and children. She recalled: "I was really scared of them, because when all you have is a house, you know that's what you'll lose." It was the "public"—neighbors, civic groups, legislators, and so on—who seemed to secure (or deny) privacy in accordance with gendered and racist norms about the use of space. Housing only women and children, Vaughan broke neighborhood and social codes about the gender, as well as the number and ethnicity, of residents and thereby forfeited her "right" to the privacy of the home she owned.

The challenge of housing women in their own homes prompted Women's Advocates to transfer to a new location their ideals of communal living and their challenge to the links between domesticity and violence. By July 1974, Women's Advocates had raised enough funds through public agencies and private donors to purchase a large Victorian house on Grand Avenue, a short bus ride from downtown St. Paul. Vaughan explained that "one of the best things about [the neighborhood] was that it wasn't really a neighborhood. There was a big apartment building next to us, and a rooming house on the other side. . . . That makes it a great place for a shelter: because it's very visible and public, but it's not right in the middle of a residential neighborhood." As shelters opened in other areas over the years, neighborhood acceptance proved to be critical to a shelter's survival. The battered-women's movement narrates countless incidents of local shelters being pushed out of their neighborhoods by angry neighbors, primarily in white or upper-class neighborhoods in which residents espouse homogeneity and longevity of property owners and occupants. Women's Advocates chose its block so well that, within a decade, they owned and occupied three adjacent houses on the block and thereby gained an unchallenged presence in and influence over an area otherwise on its way to gentrification.

Central to the advocates' vision was the desire to make the shelter feel like home, albeit a temporary one, rather than like a treatment facility. In the 1970s, that meant "scrounging" for "castoff" furniture, "covering the tatters with brightly colored throws," and finding things "to help create a homey atmosphere." They sanded wood floors, stripped off old paint, installed louvered shades and drapes over all the windows, and filled the house with plants. While many commented on the beauty of the shelter, Pat Murphy's affectionate comment points even more to the meaning of the space: "We made do. It was *never* a *showplace*, it was a *home*. . . . It was ticky-tacky right from the start." The shelter implied that battered women could and should make a public claim on their right to a home. In the words of one former volunteer: "*Women* were not the ones who were crazy or needed to be institutionalized."

Staff often felt ambivalent about changes that seemed institutional, and such measures became points of conflict. For example, finding that residents often took house bedsheets with them when they left, Women's Advocates eventually built locks on the cupboards. Vaughan recalled that the locked sheets were "the thing that made me totally wild with anger. You know, putting sheets behind these cages, and it was like putting women in cages so they wouldn't take them. There would be that kind of feeling." To mitigate against this hierarchy, Women's Advocates instituted nightly meetings in which residents and staff would collectively develop house policy, forming and reforming rules usually through consensus and as need arose.

To keep women safe in this new, politicized domesticity, advocates attempted to create a shelter that was impervious to intrusion by emphasizing a commitment to house security. In the first year or two of the shelter's operation, there were a number of incidents in which violent men broke into the shelter, endangering the well-being of residents and staff. Other scares included telephone bomb threats and angry men pounding on doors and throwing rocks to break windows. The sense of ever-present threat led advocates to take two actions: One involved building an elaborate security system around the house; the other involved pressuring the local police department to change its policies. Both measures reveal some of the ways that the movement perceived and analyzed patterns of violence against women, as well as their strategies for taking over domestic space and introducing it to the realm of public protest.

The house security system signaled Women's Advocates' determination to keep women inside safe even without public support. The system received a great deal of attention in local papers. A 1976 *Minneapolis Tribune* article subtitled "Battered: Security Is Essential" began its description of the shelter, "Women's Advocates looks like most of the large old houses on Grand Avenue in St. Paul, except for the wire mesh over the door and the highly visible alarm system across every window." The reporter implied that security systems were not typical—indeed, they were newsworthy—on residential houses in that neighborhood. Attention to the security system disrupted the normative images of domestic space in which men protect women inside from threats outside; Women's Advocates painted a counterimage of violent men intruding into (an all-female) domestic space.

Advocates also attempted to control all the permeable elements of the house's boundary with the neighborhood outside. Not only did they cover windows with heavy-duty mesh wiring and alarm systems, but also they kept heavy drapes and shutters pulled across all windows at all times. The front door was kept closed and women constantly checked to see that locks were secured. Because of the electronic alarm system, residents were required to notify a staff person before opening any outside door or changing the position of any window. At the time, advocates saw no alternative to maintaining this system, which sealed off the shelter from any relationship to its neighbors, as well as from the rest of the outside world. The darkness of the house, the rules against touching windows, and the surveillance of passersby were all intended to create security. Unwelcome intrusions only reinforced advocates' sense of dependence on a barrier that even the sun could not penetrate.

Women's Advocates did not intend, however, to reproduce the centuries-old image of the cloister as an impermeable, safe, and even chaste space. Ultimately, rules and alarm systems smacked of institutions and were thus at odds with advocates's vision of the shelter as home and private residence. Security rules implied that staff held exclusive power to draw the defining boundaries between inside and outside the shelter. Staff mediation, further, implied that residents bore a problematic relationship between inside and outside the shelter—indeed, that residents were vulnerably situated somewhere near that boundary, poised either to fall off to the exterior, or to add threatening potential to the interior. This element of an institutional relationship between residents and staff could be dispensed with only when Women's Advocates figured out how to create a shelter that was not cut off from the world, but that was part of it.

In the summer of 1976, advocate Pat Murphy visited a working shelter in Toronto. Murphy returned to Women's Advocates with a new vision of how a shelter could feel more like a safe home, and she still vividly recalls how her trip to Toronto altered her perspective on security. The Toronto shelter, in Murphy's opinion, was staffed by women "just like the women at Women's Advocates—collective, smart, great politics, great women," and the "very big, old house" itself was "very like Women's Advocates' house." Residents similarly came from all walks of life and included children of all ages. But the "feeling" of the house, compared to Women's Advocates, was like day compared to night:

> There was such a sense of openness! The light! It was so light! . . . this place was wide open and the light was there and the doors were open and the windows were open. . . . There was clearly no sense of crisis going on. . . . And there was a foyer where men could come visit their girlfriends or visit with the kids . . . there were no rules like we had about "you can't tell him we're here" and all that kind of stuff. And the feeling in that house was so much better . . . the staff weren't fearful, the women in that house were not fearful. They and their kids went outside, played outside, came and went and were not fearful. It was just like a home.

Suddenly, to Murphy, the "feeling" at Women's Advocates stood in stark contrast: She saw Women's Advocates "all holed up against the fearful men out there . . . it was like a fortress, a fortress holding women in, imprisoning them here, we have them in this little prison, and we're going to get the walls high enough and nobody's going to hurt us or them."

Murphy's visit to the Toronto women's shelter prompted a reevaluation of the effects of Women's Advocates' security measures, as well as a decision to open the house by publishing the address, opening the drapes, and letting in the light. To Murphy, it was apparent that living in a "fortress" where the walls can never be quite high enough actually contributed to a feeling of fear. Murphy blamed advocates and staff for setting the fearful tone of the house: "*We* projected the need for that fear, with our rules: Don't tell him you're here, don't give out the phone number. . . . *We* projected that fear." Others agreed that the symbolism of an "open" house was crucial, and wanted to project a message that "women are not here to hide, and that women can be here and do not need to be afraid, that this is safe, this is a good place." Most residents, most of the time, did experience Women's Advocates as a safe and good, even life-saving, place. But to go from "hiding behind a fortress" to being "open" required renegotiating Women's Advocates' relationship with the public, and reconceptualizing the relationship between gender, space, and power. Women's Advocates transformed normative ideologies about "private" domestic space as they discovered that to create a private and impenetrable domesticity was, in practice, to create a fortress or even a prison. Residents and advocates alike had much to celebrate: "Letting in the light" was an act that irrefutably politicized a domestic space by opening it up to engagement with the public world.

Residents' representations of the shelter revolved around a slightly different set of spatial images than those of many advocates. Generally, residents represented the shelter neither as an institution nor as a home. They were not typically critical of house rules that governed women's manipulation of shelter boundaries; locked doors meant greater security, not entrapment. As one resident put it: "There's safety and emotional support here. Just having the door closed behind you and knowing you're safe is half of it." For residents, inside/outside and public/private did not define a stable dichotomy between essentially different spaces. Abusive partners took over even the privacy of women's own bodies and at the same time walled women in to a space of extreme isolation. Domestic violence proved the contingency and malleability of the relationship between women's security and *all* spaces. While they preferred a place that felt "open," residents struggled more with a critical set of concepts: "leaving," for them, could imply banishment, exile, failure, danger, being alone or the end of being alone, escape, resistance, and liberation.

"Reaching Out, Looking In"

While advocates tried to create a place that felt like home, their initial representation of violence as perpetrated by males outside and something that could be kept out crumbled in the face of their experience. At the shelter, women encountered violence among each other and in disciplining children. A simple gender analysis proved inadequate, as all women at the shelter were forced to grapple with complex and ubiquitous dynamics of violence and power. Residents, some of whom became advocates, helped Women's Advocates shape itself around the difference that race and class made in uses of space and in experimental solutions to domestic violence. Through practice, Women's Advocates gradually exposed and redressed the white, middle-class bias of the shelter's policies. As soon as advocates acknowledged the multiple ways that hierarchy shaped the interior, as well as exterior, of the house, they brought the meaning of violence and nonviolence under closer scrutiny.

Advocates, most of whom had cut their political teeth in the antiwar movement, created and posted a set of house rules named "House Policy" to "protect everyone's safety." Initially, rules on house security focused only on the risk of violence from outside. And yet advocates became aware of women's own violent potential early on, through a few incidents in which clients verbally or physically attacked staff members. To address this, advocates reiterated their ability to keep it out: As one advocate told the *Milwaukee Journal* in 1976, "violence in the house is simply not tolerated." Rules portrayed violence within the house as a very simple matter with a simple and workable solution, and rules granted staff the right to evict anyone acting in a "violent or threatening" way. Staff thereby implied that they had the power to keep the shelter free of violence.

"House Policy" did not initially elaborate what would constitute "violent or threatening" behavior among women, nor did advocates see any need to explain why there was a code against violence among women in the house. The definition of, and reason for prohibiting, violent behavior among adults was self-evident to advocates, at least in the early years of operation. Initially, advocates put forth their lengthiest interpretation and discussion of violence *within* the house not under the "House Security" section, but rather under the section called "House Policy Regarding Children":

> It is important that Women's Advocates be a safe and secure place for the children who stay here as well as the women. For this reason we have general rules concerning care and behavior of children.

Violence is frequently a learned behavior. Children who grow up with it as part of family life and discipline may well incorporate it into their adult lifestyle. This is one of the reasons there is no violent discipline of children allowed during the time they are here. This includes spanking and slapping hands. The staff, especially the child care staff, are willing to work with women to find workable alternatives.

Vaughan retrospectively explained the "Regarding Children" policy as an instance in which staff imposed white, middle-class values on residents.

We had a rule that you couldn't spank children because that was a form of violence. And there wasn't any question in our minds that this was just. I remember [intervening when] a woman was whopping her kid, a woman of color who came from a really tough situation in her neighborhood, and she turned around and looked at me, and in this calm voice said, "It's normal to spank." Just like that. I never forgot that, because I thought, "Well, what *is* normal?" So even the radical philosophy [about violence] was up for grabs. . . . She said, "I teach her to whip anybody who comes up to her, because otherwise she's going to get whipped." And I thought, . . . "I have a daughter too, and why would this not be the way I raise my kids?" I thought a lot about the social context of violence and nonviolence, and how . . . we did a lot of things that . . . came from our own context, not necessarily from the women we served.

It was the very definition of violence that was suddenly "up for grabs" for Vaughan. "Violence" and "nonviolence" proved not to be self-explanatory or essential categories; rather, the terms were culturally and spatially specific.

Initially, advocates put forth a philosophy about child rearing that explicitly equated spanking and hand slapping with violence, assumed that those practices would make Women's Advocates space unsafe for children, and implicitly held parents responsible for normalizing battering as a form of violent control over others. Advocates thus acknowledged—and attempted to reform—one kind of women's behavior that they interpreted as "violence." In keeping with much of the feminist movement of the time, they defined power and violence so that, stereotypically, men were physically, economically, and socially more powerful than women, and adults more powerful than children. As women in the shelter discovered that hierarchy, control, and violence were part of the internal dynamics shaping the shelter space, they revised their simple gender analysis and definition of violence to one that recognized hierarchies of class, ethnicity, race, and sexuality. The experience of living in the shelter thus launched this idealistic, if initially naïve, group of activists into the forefront of emerging feminist theory and critique of the multiple dimensions of social hierarchies.

Revising definitions of gender and violence opened up Women's Advocates by the late 1970s to the reality of violence in lesbian relationships. Until then, advocates presumed males to be the perpetrators of violence, and sheltered women to be in heterosexual relationships. As Women's Advocates wrestled against their preconceived notions, lesbian clients increasingly demanded that Women's Advocates develop awareness of the particular needs and resources of lesbians. During the 1980s, lesbians then built on the battered-women's movement to develop a movement that would specifically challenge the multiple social roots of lesbian battering.

In addition to definitions of violence, the first group of shelter workers discovered that their own assumptions about food and waste disposal actually created class distinctions between residents and staff. While many staff members came from working-class backgrounds and did not identify with the shelter's initial consumption plans, residents experienced the emphasis on whole grains, alfalfa and bean sprouts, and recycling as an imposition of values that they themselves had neither the leisure nor interest to pursue. Advocate Pat Murphy described this as a huge "culture clash" between women for whom "brown rice" was "real big" (many staff), and women who were "making it just living" or who were on public assistance or who simply preferred meat, sweet potato pie, chips, and pop (many residents). In distinction from social services that operated out of offices, Women's Advocates took the opportunity for transforming their own assumptions because, as Murphy put it, "you're not in an office seeing people for an hour. You're *living together.* So *all* of your cultural patterns and behaviors are there." Staff conceded that consumption practices were one of the most tangible markers of class and ethnic hierarchy at the shelter and accordingly reprioritized around residents' preferences.

Claiming public space for a shelter included more than creating a functional house; it also meant transforming the existing social landscape. All residents had experienced the ways that existing public institutions kept them in violent relationships. Vaughan recalled the "image" that prevailed in her mind as she staffed the shelter: "Women would come into Women's Advocates, and it would be this shelter, and our back door was a cliff, and we'd push'em out the back door and they'd fall off the edge." Under one roof, women developed a picture of systemic violence against women—a system supported by norms about gender, privacy, and domesticity. Beyond a roof, Women's Advocates addressed a long list of residents' needs: school arrangements for their children; visits to hospital emergency rooms; support from welfare, police, and courts; the search for affordable long-term housing; and retrieval of women's possessions from their former homes. Meeting those needs involved intervention in all manner of public agencies and institutions.

Advocates' struggle to gain police protection revealed the ways that law enforcement was organized to protect established hierarchies. From the moment Women's Advocates opened, activists demanded that the St. Paul Police Department change its practices in order to protect women against abusive men. Thirty to forty residents and advocates marched down the mile-long hill to the state Capitol to confront the mayor about Women's Advocates' relationship with the police. They also showed up as a group at the police department, demanding attention. Direct action had been an inherent part of Women's Advocates from the beginning; protests at the Capitol flowed naturally from their basic goal to change the public landscape into one that supported a violence-free domesticity.

The struggle between Women's Advocates and the police department shows the influence that the battered-women's movement had on common notions of acceptable and unacceptable violence. Women's Advocates records show that during Women's Advocates' first year of operation, police response to emergency calls was slow at best. Officers were generally dismissive of women's demands for protection and treated calls from Women's Advocates as routine "domestics"—the term police used in cases of violence between heterosexual couples. They were reluctant to intervene in what they defined to be private matters or, worse, arrived on the scene with statements such as, "My job is to protect marriage."

Women's Advocates insisted that women have a right to be protected even from private violence. But police department responses as late as September 1975 indicate that any such rights were yet to be won. Chief of Police R. H. Rowan recorded an incident in which an officer dispatched to Women's Advocates found a man aggressively demanding "visiting privileges" with his children at the shelter. The officer, rather than removing the man or intervening in the escalating tension, referred the couple to court arbitration and told the advocate on duty: "You're a women's advocate, I'm a man's advocate." Notably, Chief Rowan found no fault with the officer's behavior and concluded that "[Women's Advocates'] complaint can not be sustained." Advocates, familiar with this outcome, insisted that "public servants" such as police officers have "no right" to be "partial" in their protection of any citizens.

Women's Advocates began submitting formal complaints to the police department in May 1975. The department initially responded to complaints with arguments about "legal procedure." In instances of armed break-in to Women's Advocates, officers sometimes dismissed Women's Advocates' request for intervention, arguing that they could only arrest a man if his wife explicity demands his arrest at the time of his initial break-in, or if she demands his arrest in the event of future violent contact. In response, Women's Advocates emphasized that their own primary function was to shelter and protect women, and that the police department should similarly bear *public* responsibility for ensuring the safety of everyone at Women's Advocates.

Normative assumptions about (male) property ownership made police unwilling to recognize Women's Advocates as a private property against which men could be considered trespassers; police assumed that even when women owned a property, men retained a right of access to "their" women and children on that property. In mid-September 1975, Women's Advocates voiced their criticisms of the police department at a formal meeting with the department and Mayor Cohen of St. Paul. Their protests did change the department's practices to the increased satisfaction of Women's Advocates. But their success depended to a large extent on subsequent legal confirmation that Women's Advocates shelter was, in fact, private property. During the meeting itself, Chief Rowan was "very concerned about the legal rights of men who wished access to their wives and children." Only after a representative from the city attorney's office determined that men do *not* have a "right" to "self-help" in seeking access to women or children, and that a man may be considered "at the very least a trespasser on Women's Advocates' property," did the police department begin to take seriously their role in protecting the shelter. Before this legal clarification, common notions of private property were essentially gendered. Not only did privacy protect male property owners from social surveillance, but also it granted men the right to access "their" women on *any* property. Women, though they might become property owners, would gain privacy against social surveillance and protection against intruders and trespassers only through protracted struggle with public agencies.

By August 1976, the police department had adopted new policies to "relieve some of the difficulties," including "to give calls to your facility [Women's

Advocates] a high priority designation." Women's Advocates thereby successfully instituted an unprecedented relationship with the St. Paul Police Department, which included the presence and input of advocates at officer training sessions to educate officers on domestic violence and the options available and unavailable to women. Women's Advocates saw to it that officers would not treat the cases as "private" matters and therefore inappropriate for police intervention.

Living the Coalition, 1975–1980

Women's Advocates was a politicizing space for both advocates and residents. Many shelter residents did not consider themselves feminists, nor even about to become feminists. But Women's Advocates was "a place to go" where individuals suddenly became part of a broad-based movement. After isolation and demoralization, Women's Advocates was a space that was both radicalizing and empowering for battered women across race and class differences. In early 1976, while talking with other residents and staff after her first day at the shelter, Lois remarked: "This is the first time I've felt like a human being. I've kept quiet for so long." Being with other battered women at the shelter helped women begin to transform the meaning of leaving into a positive act that affirmed that they had the right to run their own lives. Most residents experienced life-changing moments of community and support, such as the celebration parties they held whenever a woman found an apartment after a long search. Among their liberating actions were en masse marches to the St. Paul Police Department or down the hill to the Capitol, where they interrupted legislative sessions to demand laws and programs that would meet women's needs for safe domestic space.

Women's Advocates was a specifically politicizing space that gave many women their first consciousness-raising experience not segregated according to race and class. One resident wrote of her arrival at Women's Advocates in fall 1975:

> I was given a bed the first chance I got I lay down to rest. . . . [Later] I went downstairs and found that a woman named Manuella had prepared a fried chicken and potato dinner. There were ten or so women sitting around the table eating. . . . I felt pleased and part of the pleasure came from the fact that here were women from several different racial groups all sitting together and sharing. . . . Often one hears, "Really, that sounds just like my husband/boyfriend." The revelation is quick in coming that the woman is not alone in her situation.

Consciousness-raising came in the context of crisis and the first successful mobilization for change in these women's lives. By 1978, residents had also helped increase public awareness of battering and of the movement created to stop battering. In that year, Minnesotan Ellen Pence, a leader in linking the battered-women's movement with other movements, reflected: "Most people think there's more wife-beating than before. I don't think that's true. They also think because of women's liberation, women are getting more uppity so they're getting beaten up more. But it's just the opposite. Most of the women in shelters are not feminists. . . . They've just never had a place to go before." Shelters like Women's Advocates became one place in which feminism extended beyond the lives of self-named activists to become a broader movement.

The shelter also created an unparalleled opportunity for experiencing, confronting, analyzing, and changing racist dynamics within its own walls and within feminist activism. Changes did not happen overnight; in the words of one advocate: "It wasn't like we just opened the doors and in came women of color and we figured it out. It was a long, three-year process." Women at the shelter functioned as an unnamed coalition, learning about the ways that race, class, and (later) homophobia shaped battered-women's experience. As former resident Eileen Hudon put it: "It was in shelters that I first started talking about racism. What does that have to do with battering? Or what does homophobia have to do with battering? Well, it all has to do with a woman's safety, that's all. If you can't say the word 'homophobia' or 'lesbian,' if you don't understand a woman's community, how're you going to help? If you don't know what resources or powers are there, or what particular kind of dangers or isolation she has to deal with, then you're not doing your job." This accomplishment of the movement, too often overlooked in histories of radicalism, was based on innovative responses to difference and power; not without struggle, Women's Advocates became one place that gave concrete meaning to the idea of coalition.

Early residents of the shelter—particularly women of color—felt they were largely on their own to deal with racism without the support and understanding of the (virtually all white) staff. Indeed, according to Hudon, they thought that the staff "had no idea of the racism going on" among residents or between residents and staff. At least initially, some residents actively hid from the staff their perception of conflict between white women and women of color at the shelter. They perceived racism at the shelter to function similarly to racism in the wider society, but with one crucial difference: Whereas most urban space was defined by racial segregation, the shelter brought otherwise segregated women together under the same roof. Hudon recalled an escalating argument between a black woman, a Chicana woman, and a white woman in the second year of the shelter's operation. Hudon believed that "[the advocate] was instrumental in creating a division between white women and women of color at the shelter." Ultimately, the argument came to physical threat: "You had two women, a white woman and a black woman, facing off in the kitchen with knives." Hudon (an Indian woman) and a Chicana woman were actively but not physically involved. Before an assault occurred, "an advocate comes walking in. Everybody immediately acted like nothing happened. She asked what was going on, and everyone was just, 'Oh, we're just talking about what we're going to have for dinner.' Which was an absolute lie. She fortunately walked in at the right time, otherwise somebody probably would have been injured. But they [staff] did not know about this fight; I don't know if anybody [staff] knows—ha ha ha!"

Being together under one roof allowed residents to share, for the first time, the trials of being battered women and simultaneously facing the racism and classism of social services, and therefore to foster a movement for radical change that incorporated race, class, gender, and sexuality. Through their activism, advocates learned about and responded to race and class conflict by devising tools to undermine the tendency toward hierarchies between staff and residents. From the moment advocates began sheltering women in their own homes, residents impressed upon them that "battered women are *all* women." Residents also revealed that every woman came for shelter with her own specific resources and challenges; for the shelter to be a safe space, advocates needed to understand the cultural contexts that shaped residents' needs. Some residents, like Beatrice during the shelter's second month of operation, quite vocally criticized staff for being "do-gooders," "liberals" who were separated from and "better than" residents. Women's Advocates began to keep a residents' notebook in which residents could anonymously evaluate staff as well as bring up conflicts they wanted addressed. Activists throughout the country—including former shelter residents—expanded this innovative strategy over the next decade by incorporating battered-women's needs assessments, service evaluations, and ideas for solutions to design increasingly effective shelter and advocacy programs.

Staff perceptions of racism led to two critical policy changes by 1978. Women's Advocates created a statement against racism and prominently posted that statement alone on the kitchen wall: "As a reminder to the staff, residents, and visitors: Racism is a form of violence which will not be tolerated at the shelter." Racism incurred the same consequences as violence toward others in the shelter, namely, eviction. The introduction of this policy reveals an acknowledgment of racist conflict at the shelter, due entirely to residents' increasing willingness to discuss or write about their perceptions of racist dynamics.

Even more significant, after several grueling house meetings and staff retreats, Women's Advocates made a decision to hire and maintain a staff that proportionally matched the ethnic and racial composition of the residents—at that time, 35 percent women of color. Women's Advocates' insistence on maintaining a staff that was ethnically representative of residents arose initially out of the understanding that many women of color did not receive enough support or "safety" at the shelter; the original white staff, by themselves, were not aware of the specific challenges that faced battered Indian, Latina, or black women or the resources available to them. The meetings that resulted in Women's Advocates' new hiring policy did not simplistically envision that a black woman would best be served by a black advocate, or an Indian by an Indian. Rather, the policy, hinting at the value of coalition, was instated to draw *more* resources to the shelter, and to hold everyone accountable for being aware of the specific "intersectional" issues facing women of color.

Conclusion

In the early 1970s, advocates focused on creating a shelter, a place for women to get away from their batterers long enough to make longer-term plans. This became the focus of the movement through the 1970s. As Pat Murphy told the *Minneapolis Tribune* in 1976: "The reason women who are battered continue to be battered is that they have no place to go. At least one or two or three or five or ten houses like this are needed in every town in the country." By 1978, having received unprecedented state and national recognition of battering, advocates were critical of all the bills and programs that provided only for more shelters and counseling. "The shelter thing is really a stop-gap remedy. We have to get to the point where women and children are safe in their homes and are not forced to leave," Marlene Travis, chair of the State Task Force on Battering, told the *Minneapolis Star.* Each of several shelters in the cities received four to seven times more requests for shelter than they could provide, turning away hundreds each month.

But, while shelters may be a stopgap, the process of creating one of the first shelters, as a resident or staff-member, was a radicalizing experience and generated far-reaching changes in the social landscape. As Lisbet Wolf, current director of Women's Advocates, recalled of her work with Women's Advocates in the 1970s: "It was absolutely the most transforming thing in my life, absolutely unique. We had nothing to model ourselves after. We did things right and we made devastating mistakes." Many residents' lives were transformed too, as they collectively experienced "the power of women in crisis trying to make changes." The act of creating and maintaining a space that is safe for women challenged normative gender-, class-, and race-laden conceptions of domesticity and privacy. Alone of all exclusively women's spaces in Minnesota during the 1970s, Women's Advocates was not just open to, but *did* serve, *all* women; to best advocate for and shelter—and ensure the safety of—a diversity of women, Women's Advocates became a space defined by coalition.

The battered-women's movement was similar to earlier social movements in that it arose through community organizing that originated in spaces not usually represented as political, in this case, women's private homes. The collective nature of southern civil rights organizing, for example, depended on spaces such as churches and kitchens not only because that was where black people *could* gather, but also because those spaces were normatively imagined and represented as apolitical spaces. During the 1950s and 1960s, ironically, dominant media representations of civil rights organizing both reinforced a norm of domestic security and masked the community-based nature of the movement by dwelling excessively on private, nuclear-family (i.e., specifically depoliticized) scenes in activists' homes, to the exclusion of formal and informal meetings in churches and the importance of extended kin and community networks. A decade and a half later, the battered-women's movement was uniquely constructive because collective political alliances were realized not only within, but also about, domestic space. Thus from its inception, the battered-women's movement necessarily *resisted* a definition of "home" as a privatized, nuclear-family space that masks both the politics of security (national or personal) and the power relations inherent in domestic norms. Instead, the act of turning a private house into a shelter created a home built of collective action, a place that directly intersected with the public and political world.

As Women's Advocates created specifically politicizing shelters, it generated a social movement that was successfully built through the involvement of a broad range of people—self-identified feminists, women who distanced themselves from feminism, Indian women, black women, Latina women, and white women across all classes. The movement, thanks largely to the involvement of formerly battered women, has proven itself to be highly flexible, adapting to (and surviving) the vicissitudes of federal and state funding, and also imaginatively tapping community resources to minimize violence against women in disparate contexts, from Indian reservations throughout the country (each with unique financial and political resources) to multiethnic or homogeneously white neighborhoods in urban and

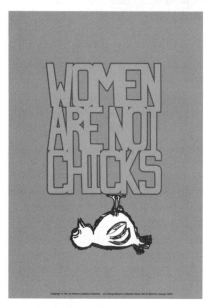

These posters illuminate the range of issues embraced by feminist activists. The dramatic images featured here were created by a group organized through the Chicago Women's Graphics Collective, which sought to create revolutionary art that advanced the agendas of women's liberation. Each piece was the product of collaboration, part of the artists' effort to create a feminist artistic process that undermined the patriarchal practices of the traditionally male-dominated art world.

suburban settings. While Women's Advocates' early vision of a neighbor-run "house on every block" has not been realized, the persistence and success of the battered-women's movement can in fact be measured by increased community involvement, networks, and coalitions at local, regional, national, and international levels. The movement thus achieved a goal fundamental to most progressive movements that arose in the 1960s, in that it radically challenged the relationship between the personal and the public, political world. While nineteenth-century ideals about the separation of domestic and political realms lingered well into the twentieth century, the women's movement proved that such separation was no longer viable. The battered-women's movement did not shelter itself from the rough and tumble real world. Rather, the movement learned to create shelters that served a diversity of women across political, ideological, and cultural differences and also engaged the larger social world in the interest of radical change.

Questions for Study and Review

1. How did the activists of Women's Advocates challenge conventional assumptions about family privacy, and why did they think it was so important to make "private" issues "public"?

2. The activists of Women's Advocates and conservative "Goldwater Girls" had very different perceptions of the family. Could they have found any common ground on the issue of domestic abuse?

3. How have the ideas and institutions developed by feminists reshaped American families and communities?

4. What developments in post–World War II American society fueled the emergence of the feminist movement, and how was it related to other social movements of the period?

Suggested Readings and Web Sites

Rosalyn Baxandall and Linda Gordon, eds. *Dear Sisters: Dispatches from the Women's Liberation Movement* (2000)

Estelle B. Freedman, *No Turning Back: The History of Feminism and the Future of Women* (2002)

Premilla Nadasen, *Welfare Warriors: The Welfare Rights Movement in the United States* (2005)

Becky Thompson, "Multiracial Feminism: Recasting the Chronology of Second Wave Feminism," *Feminist Studies*, Vol. 28 (Summer 2002)

Anne M. Valk, "Living a Feminist Lifestyle: The Furies Collective," *Feminist Studies* Vol. 28 (Summer 2002)

Women's Liberation
http://scriptorium.lib.duke.edu/wlm/

The Women of Color Web
http://www.hsph.harvard.edu/Organizations/healthnet/WoC/mission.html

Alexander Street Press's "The 'Second Wave' and Beyond"
http://scholar.alexanderstreet.com/display/WASM/Home+Page#

Black American Feminisms
http://www.library.ucsb.edu/subjects/blackfeminism/introduction.html

The Feminist Chronicles
http://www.feminist.org/research/chronicles/chronicl.html

Photographs by Jo Freeman
http://www.jofreeman.com/photos.htm

PART V

Families in Transition

Protesters staged work stoppages and rallies in 2006 to highlight the importance of immigrant workers to the nation's economy. Demonstrations like this one in Miami, Florida, were meant to draw attention to the difficulties faced by new migrants as they sought to establish families and communities in the United States.

Although many of the conflicts between the New Left and the New Right focused on political issues—the Vietnam War, civil rights, and equality for women—there was a deep cultural divide between the two sides as well. Members of the New Left often accused their conservative adversaries of being old-fashioned and authoritarian, harboring outmoded ideas about race relations, women's subordination, and unquestioned loyalty to U.S. policies. Activists on the right replied that black power advocates, feminists, and peace activists undermined the basic fabric of American society by challenging established authorities in the family, the church, and the government; practicing promiscuity; and belittling patriotism.

While supporters on each side caricatured their opponents, there was some truth to the contrasting images they presented. The New Left attracted large numbers of young, single, well-educated women and men who questioned mainstream religion, traditional race relations, government expertise, and corporate values. Many experimented with drugs, new sexual identities, nontraditional family forms, and alternative community structures. But the New Left agenda also spoke to poor and working-class families—black, white, and Hispanic—whose sons were most likely to be drafted and whose families depended on multiple wage earners or the federal welfare system to make ends meet. Ending the war abroad would provide more resources for social welfare programs at home, and racial and gender equality in education and the workplace would help lift poor Americans, whatever their race, out of poverty. The New Right's most outspoken adherents were mainly white, middle-aged women and men, many of them married, living in suburban communities or affluent towns, and employed in law, medicine, business, or government. Yet it also attracted support among blue-collar families who had embraced the American dream after World War II and were appalled by antiwar and feminist activists' seeming rejection of all they had worked so hard to gain. Whatever their class background, most conservative activists belonged to mainstream Protestant churches or embraced evangelical religion, viewed patriotism as central to their identity as Americans, eschewed sex outside of marriage, and rejected interracial and homosexual relations.

The battle over cultural values—later dubbed the "culture wars"—escalated in the 1970s and 1980s. Through debates over abortion, homosexuality, women's employment, prayer in school, immigration, and a host of other issues, conservative and progressive activists raised fundamental questions about the roles of women, the structure of the family, and the meaning of community. The fight over the Equal Rights Amendment (ERA) in the late 1970s and early 1980s illuminated many of the issues at stake. The ERA stated simply that "Men and women shall have equal rights throughout the United States and every place subject to its jurisdiction." Most feminists viewed passage of the Amendment as a logical step in the long march toward fulfilling the democratic promises of the Declaration of Independence and the U.S. Constitution. Following the civil rights acts of the 1960s, the ERA would finally ensure equal treatment of women of all races, classes, and regions. The opponents of the ERA, led by conservative activist

Phyllis Schlafly, claimed that the Amendment would necessitate the creation of unisex bathrooms in public places, ensure that divorced women were denied alimony from their husbands, and demand that the military draft be extended to women. They believed that the ERA would disrupt every aspect of American life by eliminating all legal distinctions between the sexes. In the early 1970s, feminists seemed to be on the road to victory. The ERA was approved by Congress in 1972 and within a year was approved by thirty of the thirty-six states required for ratification. But Schlafly and her STOP-ERA (Stop Taking Our Privileges) campaign lobbied vigorously in the state legislatures that had not yet ratified the ERA and gradually eroded support for the Amendment. By 1977, the ERA remained three states short of ratification, and efforts to gain final approval of the Amendment ultimately failed.

Although the New Right defeated the ERA, some of the changes that New Right members had most feared—such as women's entry into military service—occurred anyway. Indeed, significant transformations in women's roles and rights in the 1980s and 1990s resulted less from legislation than from changes in the economy and society. Perhaps most importantly, growing numbers of women gained high school and college degrees and entered the paid labor force. Although many women chose to work outside the home, others were forced to do so to meet the financial needs of their households. African American women and working-class women of all races had long faced the burden of combining wage work with domestic labor; but from the mid-1970s on, middle-class women increasingly confronted this double day as well. Some of these women entered business and the professions, especially law. But others moved into the expanding service sector, working in restaurants, hotels, hospitals, nursing homes, offices, schools, and shopping malls. At the same time, the percentage of men in full-time employment declined. Nonetheless, it was mainly women who juggled the double burden of full-time wage labor and primary responsibility for the household and family. They did so, moreover, just as the demand for elder care, that is, the care of elderly parents, increased in many families.

As more American women tried to balance wage labor and domestic labor, some working women began to demand that men play a greater role in childcare and housework. And men's participation in domestic chores did increase slightly in the late twentieth century. However, just as important to resolving these tensions was the increased availability of domestic laborers, due in large part to the passage in 1965 of the Immigration Reform Act. This act opened the door for a new wave of immigrants, including many women forced to seek low-paid jobs as housecleaners, nannies, cooks, and home health aides. The flow of immigrants into the United States was shaped not only by federal legislation, but also by the growth of multinational corporations; changes in the global labor market; the deforestation of vast territories in Asia, Africa, and Latin America; the collapse of agricultural economies in many parts of the world; and by civil wars and foreign invasions. These forces fueled decisions by families in other parts of the world to send husbands and wives, sons and daughters to the United States seeking work. Since 1965, women have outnumbered men among immigrants to the United States, and most have entered the country eager for work. Some have sought short-term employment to provide much-needed funds for family members back home; others have come to the United States hoping to gain permanent residency and to bring their families to live with them in the future.

The flow of women and families into the United States, especially from poor countries in the Caribbean, Latin America, the Philippines, Eastern Europe, and Africa, provided much-needed labor, but it also re-energized debates among U.S. citizens over the value and rights of immigrants. Once again, foreigners were represented alternately as valuable workers who contributed to the economy and cultural vitality of the nation and as alien parasites that took jobs away from "real" Americans, introduced drugs and other vices into American society, and sucked economic resources out of the nation. The benefits and dangers posed by legal versus illegal immigrants also emerged as a critical issue with a wide range of policies proposed by big business, including agribusiness, politicians of all ideological persuasions, immigrant rights' groups, and immigrants themselves. These debates were further complicated by the September 11, 2001, attacks on the World Trade Center and the Pentagon. Concern over immigrants has intensified since 9/11, with more attention focused on young men from Iraq, Iran, Afghanistan, and the Middle East and on Muslims regardless of their national background or their immigration status. Still, despite hostile attitudes toward "aliens" among many native-born U.S. citizens, the demand for cheap labor on farms and in factories and homes continues to fuel the flow of immigrants into the United States.

Since the 1970s, immigrant women have provided the bulk of household labor, childcare, and elder care for large numbers of native-born U.S. women who work for wages outside the home. In Chapter Thirteen, Pierrette Hondagneu-Sotelo examines the lives and work experiences of this latest cohort of domestic laborers through a case study of Los Angeles, California. She reveals the exploitative labor conditions and anti-immigrant prejudice such women face and notes the necessity of organizing these workers in response to both.

While changes in patterns of wage work, immigration, and household labor fueled one set of debates about family life, innovations in medical and especially reproductive technology inspired another. By the 1970s, improved prenatal testing, such as amniocentesis, allowed parents to determine whether children would be born with severe disabilities or with genetic abnormalities that could cause devastating and deadly illnesses. About the same time, in vitro fertilization, sperm banks, and other means that allowed women to be inseminated in a laboratory or doctor's office became available. These medical advances in planning and monitoring pregnancies appeared alongside the 1973 *Roe v. Wade* decision by the Supreme Court, which granted women the Constitutional right to terminate a pregnancy during the first trimester (roughly the first three months). In the 1970s and 1980s, then, the seemingly natural course of pregnancy was dramatically transformed, allowing individuals and couples to plan for children more self-consciously, to end a pregnancy that was considered problematic, or to intervene medically to save a fetus in distress.

The Supreme Court's affirmation of a woman's right to abortion has remained a highly contested issue since 1973, and medical advances in monitoring pregnancies and in sustaining the lives of babies born prematurely have only heightened questions about when life begins or when a fetus is viable. Yet these questions are matters not only of science, but also of faith. A large percentage of Catholics, evangelical Protestants, and members of orthodox branches of many religions oppose abortion at any time and for any reason. Of course, church law and personal practice are often at odds, and public opinion polls suggest that religion is only one factor that shapes attitudes toward abortion. Nonetheless, evangelical Protestants and Catholics have been among the most outspoken critics of *Roe v. Wade*. Abortion opponents have worked persistently to limit a woman's right to end a pregnancy by restricting abortion funding for poor women, eliminating monies for abortion information and referrals, using a variety of tactics to close down family planning clinics, advocating laws that require young women to notify their parents before getting an abortion, and pursuing court cases that will narrow or overturn the *Roe v. Wade* decision. Others have campaigned just as hard to support *Roe v. Wade* and to ensure access to abortion for women regardless of income, age, race, or region.

Abortion is not the only reproductive issue that has polarized Americans in recent decades. Some women who want to have children have also found themselves victims of harassment, hate mail, and legal regulation. In this case, it is women seeking to have children outside of traditional nuclear families who are the focus of attention. Some conservative groups have condemned single mothers, especially single mothers who are black, immigrant, or poor, arguing that their children will become economic burdens on the state. Others claim that these mothers are by definition morally deficient because their pregnancies resulted from sexual relations outside of marriage. Yet single motherhood is not always equated with "bad" mothering. Indeed, in vitro fertilization and sperm banks have allowed many affluent women, including Hollywood celebrities, to bear children outside of marriage, and their mothering skills are less likely to be condemned despite the absence of a husband.

More controversial in the past decade has been the desire for motherhood among lesbians. As gay men and women became freer to openly express their sexuality, the diversity among same-sex individuals and couples also became evident. Some couples settled into jobs, houses, and communities and then sought to adopt or, in the case of lesbians, to bear children. Some demanded the right to marry or, at the least, to gain legal recognition of their long-term partners through civil unions. Others focused less on legal concerns and more on the medical innovations that make pregnancy more widely accessible for single women, gay or straight. Interestingly, just as the desire for a conventional family life (a couple committed to a lifelong partnership with children) has increased among lesbians and gay men, such families are declining in the population as a whole. The rise over the past four decades in divorce, remarriage, blended families, and single mothers has meant that the once-dominant family form in the United States— a husband, a wife, and their birth children—now defines only a minority of households. Nonetheless, those who are the most ardent in their advocacy of this "traditional" family form are also the least supportive of same-sex couples who embrace that very ideal. In Chapter Fourteen, Maureen Sullivan uses interviews with lesbian couples in the San Francisco Bay area to illuminate why they chose to have children and how they navigated the terrain of medical options available to them. Through their voices, she provides a window into the formation of families that both mirror and challenge traditional notions of the American household.

In the twenty-first century, women, families, and communities will face new opportunities and new crises. Historians are not equipped to gaze into the future, but we can be fairly certain of two things: First, differences of race, class, nationality, sexual orientation, region, religion, age, and ideology will continue to shape the ways that women, families, and communities respond to changes in the economy, culture, society, and politics of the United States. Second, the place of the United States in the wider world will transform the lives of women, families, and communities around the globe, bringing millions from other parts of the world to the United States and sending millions more from the United States out into the world.

Suggested Readings and Web Sites

Dorothy Sue Cobble, ed., *The Sex of Class: Women Transforming American Labor* (2007)
Cynthia Enloe, *The Curious Feminist: Searching for Women in a New Age of Empire* (2004)
Rebecca E. Klatch, *Women of the New Right* (1987)
Dorothy Roberts, *Shattering Bonds: The Color of Child Welfare* (2003)
Judith Stacey, *In the Name of the Family: Rethinking Family Values in the Postmodern Age* (1996)
Arlene Stein, *The Stranger Next Door: The Story of a Small Community's Battle over Sex, Faith and Civil Rights* (2006)
The City/La Ciudad
  http://www.pbs.org/itvs/thecity/immigration4.html
Contemporary Families
  http://www.contemporaryfamilies.org/

Until the first decades of the twentieth century, the largest portion of U.S. women who worked outside their homes for wages performed domestic work. That is, they served as household workers for another family, cooking, cleaning, doing laundry, and caring for children. As soon as other occupational opportunities opened up, however, most women fled their posts at the laundry tub and the stove. Earlier articles in this volume describe how young Jewish women entered garment industry sweatshops at the turn of the century, and African American women became beauticians or sold beauty products in this same period. For these women, as well as for white native-born women who struggled to support themselves as shop girls and department store clerks in the nation's growing cities, a domestic job was the occupation of last resort. Factory work may have been difficult, dirty, and sometimes dangerous, but it offered the promise of better pay, limited working hours, greater autonomy, and camaraderie. Beauty culture, too, had its challenges; but compared to domestic service, it offered African American women safety, decent pay, and respectability. By the mid-twentieth century, the dwindling supply of willing workers—paired with the spread of labor-saving appliances—prompted observers to herald the end of domestic labor as an occupation.

Yet bucking these predictions, domestic labor became a growth occupation by the closing years of the twentieth century. Huge numbers of American families continue to employ individuals to mop their floors, scrub their toilets, prepare their meals, and care for their children. Defined more rigidly than ever by race and sex, these jobs are filled exclusively by women, mostly immigrants from Mexico, Central America, and the Caribbean. Moreover, the domestic labor of immigrant women in the United States has reshaped the landscape of domesticity among women, families, and communities around the globe.

These new domestic workers are part of an immigrant influx that is remaking the United States. The last great wave of immigration transformed the United States at the turn of the twentieth century, when native-born Americans decried the flood of southern and eastern Europeans as racially unassimilable. The country capitulated to these fears, instituting new immigration regulations in the 1920s that heavily favored applicants from northern and western Europe. By the 1930s, immigration to the United States had tapered off to a trickle. Then in 1965, racially discriminatory quotas were abolished by the Immigration Reform Act, which opened the door for the next great wave of newcomers to the United States.

Relatively few Europeans have come to the United States as immigrants in the last forty years; most hopeful new Americans have originated instead in Latin America and Asia. War and economic turmoil in these regions have sent women and men looking for a better life. Devastating economic fluctuations have been a by-product of the intensifying process of globalization, by which the world's capitalist markets have been increasingly integrated. This global integration has fueled the free movement of goods, capital, and workers across national borders. The profits generated by this process have been distributed very unequally, producing yawning chasms between rich and poor both within the United States and between nations. These inequities have pulled immigrants to the United States.

The stark disparity between the affluent and the poor within the United States has fueled the demand for domestic labor. Well-to-do Americans are working longer hours and raising children with both parents in the workforce. With more money than time, affluent Americans use the labor of new immigrant women to make their domestic lives manageable. This heightened demand for domestic labor has shaped the immigrant stream. By 1995, for the first time in American history, women comprised the majority of all legal immigrants to the United States. These women have pioneered new patterns of migration. Female immigrants of the early twentieth century were most likely to arrive in this country with their families and were less likely to work outside their homes for wages than native-born women. More recent immigrants come to the United States to work and frequently travel without their families or even their children, whom they leave in the care of another relative in their home country.

In this article, sociologist Hondagneu-Sotelo analyzes the social, economic, and political context of domestic work in Los Angeles. She approaches her research from a personal angle, writing as both the daughter of a domestic worker and the current employer of a housecleaner. Determined to expose American dependence on immigrant women, Hondagneu-Sotelo illuminates how these women operate outside the regulatory structure that governs the work of most Americans. Employers of domestic workers largely ignore the laws that stipulate minimum wages, maximum hours, and other conditions of work. As a result many immigrants endure extreme exploitation, afraid to seek help or unaware that they could seek redress from government or legal authorities. These fears have been heightened by anti-immigrant sentiment, which has taken legal form in measures barring immigrants from using public schools, hospitals, and social welfare programs. Some militant Latinas have turned to unionizing drives in an effort to claim their dignity. Hondagneu-Sotelo echoes the demands of these organizers, calling on the country to recognize and reward the work performed by these new Americans.

Domestica: Globalization and the Female Face of Recent Immigration in California
PIERRETTE HONDAGNEU-SOTELO

Contemplating a day in Los Angeles without the labor of Latino immigrants taxes the imagination, for an array of consumer products and services would disappear (poof!) or become prohibitively expensive. Think about it. When you arrive at

Women now make up the majority of legal immigrants to the United States, where they most commonly find jobs as nannies and housekeepers. Most American families—even those with young children—perceive the need for two paychecks to make ends meet. They rely on often poorly paid domestic workers to keep their households running when both parents work sometimes long hours. The women they employ often leave their own children behind in their home country in the care of other relatives.

many a Southern California hotel or restaurant, you are likely to be first greeted by a Latino car valet. The janitors, cooks, busboys, painters, carpet cleaners, and landscape workers who keep the office buildings, restaurants, and malls running are also likely to be Mexican or Central American immigrants, as are many of those who work behind the scenes in dry cleaners, convalescent homes, hospitals, resorts, and apartment complexes. Both figuratively and literally, the work performed by Latino and Latina immigrants gives Los Angeles much of its famed gloss. Along the boulevards, at car washes promising "100% hand wash" for prices as low as $4.99, teams of Latino workers furiously scrub, wipe, and polish automobiles. Supermarket shelves boast bags of "prewashed" mesclun or baby greens (sometimes labeled "Euro salad"), thanks to the efforts of the Latino immigrants who wash and package the greens. (In addition, nail parlors adorn almost every corner mini-mall, offering the promise of emphasized femininity for $10 or $12, thanks largely to the work of Korean immigrant women.) Only twenty years ago, these relatively inexpensive consumer services and products were not nearly as widely available as they are today. The Los Angeles economy, landscape, and lifestyle have been transformed in ways that rely on low-wage, Latino immigrant labor.

The proliferation of such labor-intensive services, coupled with inflated real estate values and booming mutual funds portfolios, has given many people the illusion of affluence and socioeconomic mobility. When Angelenos, accustomed to employing a full-time nanny/housekeeper for about $150 or $200 a week, move to Seattle or Durham, they are startled to discover how "the cost of living that way" quickly escalates. Only then do they realize the extent to which their affluent lifestyle and smoothly running household depended on one Latina immigrant woman.

This article focuses on the Mexican and Central American immigrant women who work as nanny/housekeepers and housecleaners in Los Angeles, as well as the women who employ them. Who could have foreseen that at the dawn of the twenty-first century, paid domestic work would be a growth occupation? Only a few decades ago, observers confidently predicted that this occupation would soon become obsolete, replaced by labor-saving household devices such as automatic dishwashers, disposable diapers, and microwave ovens, and by consumer goods and services purchased outside of the home, such as fast food and dry cleaning. Instead, paid domestic work has expanded. Why?

The Growth of Domestic Work

The increased employment of women, especially of married women with children, is usually what comes to mind when people explain the proliferation of private nannies, housekeepers, and housecleaners. As women have gone off to work, men have not picked up the slack at home. Grandmothers are also working, or no longer live nearby; and given the relative scarcity of child care centers in the United States, especially those that will accept infants and toddlers not yet toilet trained, working families of sufficient means often choose to pay someone to come in to take care of their homes and their children.

Even when conveniently located day care centers are available, many middle-class Americans are deeply prejudiced against them, perceiving them as offering cold, institutional, second-class child care. For various reasons, middle-class families headed by two working parents prefer the convenience, flexibility, and privilege of having someone care for their children in their home. With this arrangement, parents don't have to dread their harried early-morning preparations before rushing to day care, the children don't seem to catch as many illnesses, and parents aren't likely to be fined by the care provider when they work late or get stuck in traffic. As the educational sociologist Julia Wrigley has shown in research conducted in New York City and Los Angeles, with a private caregiver in the home, parents feel they gain control and flexibility, while their children receive more attention. Wrigley also makes clear that when they hire a Caribbean or Latina woman as their private employee in either a live-in or live-out arrangement, they typically gain something else: an employee who does two jobs for the price of one, both looking after the children as a nanny and undertaking daily housekeeping duties. I use the term "nanny/housekeeper" to refer to the individual performing this dual job.

Meanwhile, more people are working and they are working longer hours. Even individuals without young children feel overwhelmed by the much-bemoaned "time squeeze," which makes it more difficult to find time for both daily domestic duties and leisure. At workplaces around the nation, women and men alike are pressured by new technology, their own desires for consumer goods, national anxieties over global competition, and exhortations from employers and co-workers to work overtime. As free time shrinks, people who can afford it seek relief by paying a housecleaner to attend to domestic grit and grime once every week or two. Increasing numbers of Americans thus purchase from nanny/housekeepers and housecleaners the work once performed by wives and mothers.

Of course, not everyone brings equal resources to bear on these problems. In fact, growing income inequality has contributed significantly to the expansion of paid domestic work. The mid-twentieth-century trend in the United States toward less income inequality, as many researchers and commentators have remarked, was short-lived. In the years immediately after World War II, a strong economy (based on an increasing number of well-paying unionized jobs in factories), together with growing mass consumption and federal investment in education, housing, and public welfare, allowed many Americans to join an expanding middle class. This upward trend halted in the early 1970s, when deindustrialization, the oil crisis, national inflation, the end of the Vietnam War, and shifts in global trade began to restructure the U.S. economy. Gaps in the occupational structure widened. The college educated began to enjoy greater opportunities in the professions and in corporate and high-technology sectors, while poorly educated workers found their manufacturing jobs downgraded—if they found them at all, as many were shipped overseas. During the 1980s and 1990s, income polarization in the United States intensified, setting the stage for further expansion of paid domestic work.

Specific location is important to this analysis, for the income distribution in some cities is more inequitable than in others, and greater inequality, as an important study directed by UCLA sociologist Ruth Milkman has shown, tends to generate greater concentrations of paid domestic work. When the researchers compared cities around the nation, the Los Angeles–Long Beach metropolitan area emerged as the nation's leader in these jobs (measured by the proportion of all employed women in paid domestic work), followed by Miami-Hialeah, Houston, and New York City.

Los Angeles' dubious distinction is not hard to explain. All of the top-ranked cities in paid domestic work have large concentrations of Latina or Caribbean immigrant women, and Los Angeles remains the number-one destination for Mexicans, Salvadorans, and Guatemalans coming to the United States, most of whom join the ranks of the working poor. Moreover, Los Angeles is a city where capital concentrates. It is a dynamic economic center for Pacific Rim trade and finance—what Saskia Sassen, a leading theorist of globalization, immigration, and transnational capital mobility, refers to as a "global city." Global cities serve as regional "command posts" that aid in integrating the new expansive global economy. Though Los Angeles lacks the financial power of New York or London, it has a large, diversified economy, supported both by manufacturing and by the capital-intensive entertainment industry. The upshot? Los Angeles is home to many people with highly paid jobs. As Southern California businesses bounced back from the recession of the early 1990s, many already handsomely paid individuals suddenly found themselves flush with unanticipated dividends, bonuses, and stock options. And as Sassen reminds us, globalization's high-end jobs breed low-paying jobs.

Many people employed in business and finance, and in the high-tech and the entertainment sectors, are high-salaried lawyers, bankers, accountants, marketing specialists, consultants, agents, and entrepreneurs. The way they live their lives, requiring many services and consuming many products, generates other high-end occupations linked to gentrification (creating jobs for real estate agents, therapists, personal trainers, designers, celebrity chefs, etc.), all of which in turn rely on various kinds of daily servicing that low-wage workers provide. For the masses of affluent professionals and corporate managers in Los Angeles, relying on Latino immigrant workers has become almost a social obligation. After relocating from the Midwest to Southern California, a new neighbor, the homemaker wife of an engineer, expressed her embarrassment at not hiring a gardener. It's easy to see why she felt abashed. In New York, the quintessential service occupation is dog walking; in Los Angeles' suburban landscape, gardeners and domestic workers proliferate. And in fact, as Roger Waldinger's analysis of census data shows, twice as many gardeners and domestic workers were working in Los Angeles in 1990 as in 1980. Mexicans, Salvadorans, and Guatemalans perform these bottom-rung, low-wage jobs; and by 1990 those three groups, numbering about 2 million, made up more than half of the adults who had immigrated to Los Angeles since 1965. Hundreds of thousands of Mexican, Salvadoran, and Guatemalan women sought employment in Los Angeles during the 1970s, 1980s, and 1990s often without papers but in search of better futures for themselves and for their families. For many of them, the best job opportunity was in paid domestic work.

Mexican women have always lived in Los Angeles—indeed, Los Angeles *was* Mexico until 1848—but their rates of migration to the United States were momentarily dampened by the Bracero Program, a government-operated temporary contract labor program that recruited Mexican men to work in western agriculture between 1942 and 1964. During the Bracero Program, nearly 5 million contracts were authorized. Beginning in the 1970s, family reunification legislation allowed many former bracero workers to legally bring their wives and families from Mexico. Immigration accelerated, and by 1990 there were 7 million Mexican immigrants in the United States, concentrated most highly in Southern California. Structural changes in the economies of both Mexico and the United States also significantly affected this dynamic. Mexico's economic crisis of the 1980s propelled many married women with small children into the labor force, and with the maturation of transnational informational social networks—and especially the development of exclusive women's networks—it wasn't long before many Mexican women learned about U.S. employers eager to hire them in factories, in hotels, and in private homes.

Unlike Mexicans, Central Americans have relatively new roots in Los Angeles. The Salvadoran civil war (1979–92) and the even longer-running conflicts in Guatemala (military campaigns supported by U.S. government aid) drove hundreds of thousands of Central Americans to the United States during the 1980s. Almost overnight, Los Angeles became a second capital city for both Salvadorans and Guatemalans. Estimates of this population, many of whose members cannot speak English and remain undocumented (and hence officially undercounted), vary wildly. The 1990 census counted 159,000 Guatemalans and 302,000 Salvadorans in the Los Angeles region, but community leaders believe that by 1994, the number of Salvadorans in Los Angeles alone had reached 500,000. Central

Americans came to the United States fleeing war, political persecution, and deterio-rating economic conditions; and though the political violence had diminished by the mid-1990s, few were making plans to permanently return to their old homes. There have been numerous careful case studies of Central American communities in the United States; among their most stunning findings is that wherever Central American women have gone in the United States, including San Francisco, Long Island, Washington, D.C., Houston, and Los Angeles, they predominate in private domestic jobs.

The growing concentration of Central American and Mexican immigrant women in Los Angeles and their entry into domestic service came on the heels of local African American women's exodus from domestic work. The supply of new immigrant workers has helped fuel a demand that, as noted above, was already growing. That is, the increasing number of Latina immigrants searching for work in California, particularly in Los Angeles, has pushed down wages and made modestly priced domestic services more widely available. This process is not lost on the women who do the work. Today, Latina domestic workers routinely complain to one another that newly arrived women from Mexico and Central America are undercut-ting the rates for cleaning and child care.

As a result, demand is no longer confined to elite enclaves but instead spans a wider range of class and geography in Southern California. While most employers of paid domestic workers in Los Angeles are white, college-educated, middle-class or upper-middle-class suburban residents with some connection to the professions or the business world, employers now also include apartment dwellers with modest incomes, single mothers, college students, and elderly people living on fixed incomes. They live in tiny bungalows and condominiums, not just sprawling houses. They include immigrant entrepreneurs and even immigrant workers. In contempo-rary Los Angeles, factory workers living in the Latino working-class neighborhoods can and do hire Latino gardeners to mow their lawns, and a few also sometimes hire in-home nanny/housekeepers as well. In fact, some Latina nanny/housekeepers pay other Latina immigrants—usually much older or much younger, newly arrived women—to do in-home child care, cooking, and cleaning, while they themselves go off to care for the children and homes of the more wealthy.

Domestic Work Versus Employment

Paid domestic work is distinctive not in being the worst job of all but in being regarded as something other than employment. Its peculiar status is revealed in many occupational practices . . . and in off-the-cuff statements made by both employers and employees. "Maria was with me for eight years," a retired teacher told me, "and then she left and got a real job." Similarly, many women who do this work remain reluctant to embrace it *as* work because of the stigma associated with it. This is especially true of women who previously held higher social status. One Mexican woman, formerly a secretary in a Mexican embassy, referred to her five-day-a-week nanny/housekeeper job as her "hobby."

As the sociologist Mary Romero and others who have studied paid domestic work have noted, this occupation is often not recognized as employment because it takes place in a private home. Unlike factories or offices, the home serves as the site of family and leisure activities, seen as by their nature antithetical to work. Moreover, the tasks that domestic workers do—cleaning, cooking, and caring for children— are associated with women's "natural" expressions of love for their families. Although Catharine E. Beecher and Harriet Beecher Stowe in the late nineteenth century, like feminist scholars more recently, sought to valorize these domestic activities (in both their paid and unpaid forms) as "real work," these efforts past and present have had little effect in the larger culture. House-cleaning is typically only visible when it is not performed. The work of wives and mothers is not seen as real work; and when it becomes paid, it is accorded even less regard and respect.

Another important factor that prevents paid domestic work from being recognized as real work is its personal, idiosyncratic nature, especially when it involves the daily care of children or the elderly. Drawing on her examination of elder care workers, the public policy analyst Deborah Stone argues that caring work is inherently relational, involving not only routine bodily care, such as bathing and feeding, but also attachment, affiliation, intimate knowledge, patience, and even favoritism. Talking and listening, Stone shows, are instrumental to effective care. Her observation certainly applies to private child care work, as parents want someone who will really "care about" and show preference for their children; yet such personal engagement remains antithetical to how we think about much employment, which, as Stone reminds us, we tend to view on the model of manufacturing. Standardization, and frameworks of efficiency and productivity that rely on simplistic notions of labor inputs and product outputs, simply is irrelevant to paid domestic work, especially when the job encompasses taking care of children as well as cleaning. Since we are accustomed to defining employment as that which does *not* involve emotions and demonstrations of affective preference, the work of nannies and baby-sitters never quite gains legitimacy.

In part because of the idiosyncratic and emotional nature of caring work, and in part because of the contradictory nature of American culture, employers are equally reluctant to view themselves as employers. This, I believe, has very serious consequences for the occupation. When well-meaning employers, who wish to voice their gratitude, say, "She's not just an employee, she's like one of the family," they are in effect absolving themselves of their responsibilities—not for any nefarious reason but because they themselves are confused by domestic work arrangements. Even as they enjoy the attendant privilege and status, many Americans remain profoundly ambivalent about positioning themselves as employers of domestic workers. These arrangements, after all, are often likened to master-servant relations drawn out of premodern feudalism and slavery, making for a certain amount of tension with the strong U.S. rhetoric of democracy and egalitarianism. Consequently, some employers feel embarrassed, uncomfortable, even guilty.

Maternalism, once so widely observed among female employers of private domestic workers, is now largely absent from the occupation; its remnants can be found primarily among older homemakers. When employers give used clothing and household items to their employees, or offer them unsolicited advice, help, or guidance, they may be acting, many observers have noted, manipulatively. Such gestures encourage the domestic employees to work harder and longer, and simultaneously allow employers to experience personal recognition and validation of themselves as kind, superior, and altruistic. Maternalism is thus an important mechanism of employer power.

Today, however, a new sterility prevails in employer-employee relations in paid domestic work. For various reasons—including the pace of life that harries women with both career and family responsibilities, as well as their general discomfort with domestic servitude—most employers do not act maternalistically toward their domestic workers. In fact, many of them go to great lengths to minimize personal interactions with their nanny/housekeeper and housecleaners. At the same time, the Latina immigrants who work for them—especially the women who look after their employers' children—crave personal contact. They *want* social recognition and appreciation for who they are and what they do, but they don't often get it from their employers. I argue that while maternalism serves as a mechanism of power that reinscribes some of the more distressing aspects of racial and class inequality between and among women, the distant employer-employee relations prevalent today do more to exacerbate inequality by denying domestic workers even modest forms of social recognition, dignity, and emotional sustenance. As we will see, personalism, achieved by exchanging private confidences and by recognizing domestic workers as individuals with their own concerns outside of their jobs, partially addresses the problem of social annihilation experienced by Latina domestic workers, offering a tenuous, discursive amelioration of these glaring inequalities.

Ironically, many employers are enormously appreciative of what their Latina domestic workers do for them, but they are more likely to declare these feelings to others than to the women who actually do the work. In informal conversation, they often gush enthusiastically about Latina nanny/housekeepers who care for homes and children, expressing a deep appreciation (or a rationalization?) that one almost never hears from someone speaking about his or her spouse. You might hear someone say, "I don't know what I would do without her," "She's perfect!" or "She's far better with the kids than I am!"; but such sentiments are rarely communicated directly to the employees.

The employers I interviewed did not dwell too much on their status as employers of nanny/housekeepers or housecleaners. They usually identified first and foremost with their occupations and families, with their positions as accountants or teachers, wives or mothers. Like the privilege of whiteness in U.S. society, the privilege of employing a domestic worker is barely noticed by those who have it. While they obviously did not deny that they pay someone to clean their home and care for their children, they tended to approach these arrangements not as employers, with a particular set of obligations and responsibilities, but as consumers.

For their part, the women who do the work are well aware of the low status and stigma attached to paid domestic work. None of the Latina immigrants I interviewed had aspired to the job, none want their daughters to do it, and the younger ones hope to leave the occupation altogether in a few years. They do take pride in their work, and they are extremely proud of what their earnings enable them to accomplish for their families. Yet they are not proud to be domestic workers, and this self-distancing from their occupational status makes it more difficult to see paid domestic work as a real job.

Moreover, scarcely anyone, employer or employee, knows that labor regulations govern paid domestic work. Lawyers that I interviewed told me that even adjudicators and judges in the California Labor Commissioner's Office, where one might go to settle wage disputes, had expressed surprise when informed that labor laws protected housecleaners or nanny/housekeepers working in private homes. This problem of paid domestic work not being accepted as employment is compounded by the subordination by race and immigrant status of the women who do the job.

Globalization, Immigration, and the Racialization of Paid Domestic Work

Particular regional formations have historically characterized the racialization of paid domestic work in the United States. Relationships between domestic employees and employers have always been imbued with racial meanings: White "masters and mistresses" have been cast as pure and superior, and "maids and servants," drawn from specific racial-ethnic groups (varying by region), have been cast as dirty and socially inferior. The occupational racialization we see now in Los Angeles or New York City continues this American legacy, but it also draws to a much greater extent on globalization and immigration.

In the United States today, immigrant women from a few non-European nations are established as paid domestic workers. These women—who hail primarily from Mexico, Central America, and the Caribbean and who are perceived as "nonwhite" in Anglo-American contexts—hold various legal statuses. Some are legal permanent residents or naturalized U.S. citizens, many as beneficiaries of the 1986 Immigration Reform and Control Act's amnesty-legalization program. Central American women, most of whom entered the United States after the 1982 cutoff date for amnesty, did not qualify for legalization, so in the 1990s they generally either remained undocumented or held a series of temporary work permits, granted to delay their return to war-ravaged countries. Domestic workers who are working without papers clearly face extra burdens and risks: criminalization of employment, denial of social entitlements, and status as outlaws anywhere in the nation. If they complain about their jobs, they may be threatened with deportation. Undocumented immigrant workers, however, are not the only vulnerable ones. In the 1990s, even legal permanent residents and naturalized citizens saw their rights and privileges diminish, as campaigns against illegal immigration metastasized into more generalized xenophobic attacks on all immigrants, including those here with legal authorization. Immigration status has clearly become an important axis of inequality, one interwoven with relations of race, class, and gender, and it facilitates the exploitation of immigrant domestic workers.

Yet race and immigration are interacting in an important new way, which Latina immigrant domestic workers exemplify: Their position as "foreigners" and "immigrants" allows employers, and the society at large, to perceive them as outsiders and thereby overlook the contemporary racialization of the occupation. Immigration does not trump race but, combined with the dominant ideology of a "colorblind" society, manages to shroud it.

With few exceptions, domestic work has always been reserved for poor women, for immigrant women, and for women of color; but over the last century, paid domestic workers have become more homogenous, reflecting the subordinations of both race and nationality/immigration status. In the late nineteenth century, this occupation was the most likely source of employment for U.S.-born women. In 1870, according to the historian David M. Katzman, two-thirds of all nonagricultural female wage earners worked as domestics in private homes. The proportion steadily declined to a little over one-third by 1900, and to one-fifth by 1930. Alternative employment opportunities for women expanded in the mid- and late twentieth century, so by 1990, fewer than 1 percent of employed American women were engaged in domestic work. Census figures, of course, are notoriously unreliable in documenting this increasingly undocumentable, "under-the-table" occupation, but the trend is clear: Paid domestic work has gone from being *either* an immigrant woman's job *or* a minority woman's job to one that is now filled by women who, as Latina and Caribbean immigrants, embody subordinate status both racially and as immigrants.

Regional racializations of the occupation were already deeply marked in the late nineteenth and early twentieth centuries, as the occupation recruited women from subordinate racial-ethnic groups. In northeastern and midwestern cities of the late nineteenth century, single young Irish, German, and Scandinavian immigrants and women who had migrated from the country to the city typically worked as live-in "domestic help," often leaving the occupation when they married. During this period, the Irish were the main target of xenophobic vilification. With the onset of World War I, European immigration declined and job opportunities in manufacturing opened up for whites, and black migration from the South enabled white employers to recruit black women for domestic jobs in the Northeast. Black women had always predominated as a servant caste in the South, whether in slavery or after, and by 1920 they constituted the single largest group in paid domestic work in both the South and the Northeast. Unlike European immigrant women, black women experienced neither individual nor intergenerational mobility out of the occupation, but they succeeded in transforming the occupation from one characterized by live-in arrangements, with no separation between work and social life, to live-out "day work"—a transformation aided by urbanization, new interurban transportation systems, and smaller urban residences.

In the Southwest and the West of the late nineteenth and early twentieth centuries, the occupation was filled with Mexican American and Mexican immigrant women, as well as Asian, African American, and Native American women and, briefly, Asian men. Asian immigrant men were among the first recruits for domestic work in the West. California exceptionalism—its Anglo-American conquest from Mexico in 1848, its ensuing rapid development and overnight influx of Anglo settlers and miners, and its scarcity of women—initially created many domestic jobs in the northern part of the territory for Chinese "houseboys," laundrymen, and cooks, and later for Japanese men, followed by Japanese immigrant women and their U.S.-born daughters, the nisei, who remained in domestic work until World War II. Asian American women's experiences, as Berkeley sociologist Evelyn Nakano Glenn has demonstrated, provide an intermediate case of intergenerational mobility out of domestic work between that of black and Chicana women who found themselves, generation after generation, stuck in the occupational ghetto of domestic work and that of European immigrant women of the early twentieth century who quickly moved up the mobility ladder.

For Mexican American women and their daughters, domestic work became a dead-end job. From the 1880s until World War II, it provided the largest source of nonagricultural employment for Mexican and Chicana women throughout the Southwest. During this period, domestic vocational training schools, teaching manuals, and Americanization efforts deliberately channeled them into domestic jobs. Continuing well into the 1970s throughout the Southwest, and up to the present in particular regions, U.S.-born Mexican American women have worked as domestics. Over that time, the job has changed. Much as black women helped transform the domestic occupation from live-in to live-out work in the early twentieth century, Chicanas in the Southwest increasingly preferred contractual housecleaning work—what Romero has called "job work"—to live-in or daily live-out domestic work.

While black women dominated the occupation throughout the nation during the 1950s and 1960s, there is strong evidence that many left it during the late 1960s. The 1970 census marked the first time that domestic work did not account for the largest segment of employed black women; and the proportion of black women in domestic work continued to drop dramatically in the 1970s and 1980s, falling from 16.4 percent in 1972 to 7.4 percent in 1980, then to 3.5 percent by the end of the 1980s. By opening up public-sector jobs to black women, the Civil Rights Act of 1964 made it possible for them to leave private domestic service. Consequently, both African American and Mexican American women moved into jobs from which they had been previously barred, as secretaries, sales clerks, and public-sector employees, and into the expanding number of relatively low-paid service jobs in convalescent homes, hospitals, cafeterias, and hotels.

These occupational adjustments and opportunities did not go unnoticed. In a 1973 *Los Angles Times* article, a manager with thirty years of experience in domestic employment agencies reported, "Our Mexican girls are nice, but the blacks are hostile." Speaking very candidly about her contrasting perceptions of Latina immigrant and African American women domestic workers, she said of black women, "you can feel their anger. They would rather work at Grant's for $1.65 an hour than do housework. To them it denotes a lowering of self." By the 1970s black women in the occupation were growing older, and their daughters were refusing to take jobs imbued with servitude and racial subordination. Domestic work, with its historical legacy in slavery, was roundly rejected. Not only expanding job opportunities but also the black power movement, with its emphasis on self-determination and pride, dissuaded younger generations of African American women from entering domestic work.

It was at this moment that newspaper reports, census data, and anecdotal accounts first register the occupation's demographic shift toward Latina immigrants, a change especially pronounced in areas with high levels of Latino immigration. In Los Angeles, for example, the percentage of African American women working as domestics in private households fell from 35 percent to 4 percent from 1970 to 1990, while foreign-born Latinas increased their representation from 9 percent to 68 percent. Again, since census counts routinely underestimate the poor and those who speak limited or no English, the women in this group may represent an even larger proportion of private domestic workers.

Ethnographic case studies conducted not only in Los Angeles but also in Washington, D.C., San Francisco, San Diego, Houston, El Paso, suburban areas of Long Island, and New York City provide many details about the experiences of Mexican, Caribbean, and Central American women who now predominate in these metropolitan centers as nanny/housekeepers and housecleaners. Like the black women who migrated from the rural South to northern cities in the early twentieth century, Latina immigrant women newly arrived in U.S. cities and suburbs in the 1970s, 1980s, and 1990s often started as live-ins, sometimes first performing unpaid household work for kin before taking on very low paying live-in jobs for other families. Live-in jobs, shunned by better-established immigrant women, appeal to new arrivals who want to minimize their living costs and begin sending their earnings home. Vibrant social networks channel Latina immigrants into these jobs, where the long hours and the social isolation can be overwhelming. As time passes, many of the women seek live-out domestic jobs. Despite the decline in live-in employment arrangements at the century's midpoint, the twentieth century ended in the United States much as it began, with a resurgence of live-in jobs filled by women of color—now Latina immigrants.

Two factors of the late twentieth century were especially important in creating this scenario. First, as many observers have noted, globalization has promoted higher rates of immigration. The expansion of U.S. private investment and trade; the opening of U.S. multinational assembly plants (employing mostly women) along the U.S.-Mexico border and in Caribbean and Central American nations, facilitated by government legislative efforts such as the Border Industrialization Program, the North American Free Trade Agreement, and the Caribbean Basin Initiative; the spreading influence of U.S. mass media; and U.S. military aid in Central America have all helped rearrange local economies and stimulate U.S.-bound migration from the Caribbean, Mexico, and Central America. Women from these countries have entered the United States at a propitious time for families looking to employ housecleaners and nannies.

Second, increased immigration led to the racialized xenophobia of the 1990s. The rhetoric of these campaigns shifted focus, from attacking immigrants for lowering wages and competing for jobs to seeking to bar immigrants's access to social entitlements and welfare. In the 1990s, legislation codified this racialized nativism, in large part taking aim at women and children. In 1994 California's Proposition 187, targeting Latina immigrants and their children, won at the polls; and although its denial of all public education and of publicly funded health care was ruled unconstitutional by the courts, the vote helped usher in new federal legislation. In 1996 federal welfare reform, particularly the Immigration Reform Act and Individual Responsibility Act (IRAIRA), codified the legal and social disenfranchisement of legal permanent residents and undocumented immigrants. At the same time, language—and in particular the Spanish language—was becoming racialized; virulent "English Only" and anti–bilingual education campaigns and ballot initiatives spread.

Because Latina immigrants are disenfranchised as immigrants and foreigners, Americans can overlook the current racialization of the job. On the one hand, racial hostilities and fears may be lessened as increasing numbers of Latina and Caribbean nannies care for towheaded children. As Sau-ling C. Wong suggests in an analysis of recent films, "in a society undergoing radical demographic and economic changes, the figure of the person of color patiently mothering white folks serves to allay racial anxieties." Stereotypical images of Latinas as innately warm, loving, and caring certainly round out this picture. Yet on the other hand, the status of these Latinas as immigrants today serves to legitimize their social, economic, and political subordination and their disproportionate concentration in paid domestic work.

Such legitimation makes it possible to ignore American racism and discrimination. Thus the abuses that Latina domestic workers suffer in domestic jobs can be explained away because the women themselves are foreign and unassimilable. If they fail to realize the American Dream, according to this distorted narrative, it is because they are lazy and unmotivated or simply because they are "illegal" and do not merit equal opportunities with U.S.-born American citizens. Contemporary paid domestic work in the United States remains a job performed by women of color, by black and brown women from the Caribbean, Central America, and Mexico. This racialization of domestic work is masked by the ideology of "a color-blind society" and by the focus on immigrant "foreignness."

Global Trends in Paid Domestic Work

Just as paid domestic work has expanded in the United States, so too it appears to have grown in many other postindustrial societies—in Canada and in parts of Europe—in the "newly industrialized countries" (NICs) of Asia, and in the oil-rich nations of the Middle East. Around the globe Caribbean, Mexican, Central American, Peruvian, Sri Lankan, Indonesian, Eastern European, and Filipina women—the latter in disproportionately great numbers—predominate in these jobs. Worldwide, paid domestic work continues its long legacy as a racialized and gendered occupation, but today divisions of nation and citizenship are increasingly salient. Rhacel Parreñas, who has studied Filipina domestic workers, refers to this development as the "international division of reproductive labor," and Anthony Richmond has called it part of a broad, new "global apartheid."

In the preceding section, I highlighted the inequalities of race and immigration in the United States, but we must remember that the inequality of nations is a key factor in the globalization of contemporary paid domestic work. This inequality has had three results. First, around the globe, paid domestic work is increasingly performed by women who leave their own nations, their communities, and often their families of origin to do it. Second, the occupation draws not only women from the poor socioeconomic classes but also women of relatively high status in their own countries—countries that colonialism made much poorer than those countries where they go to do domestic work. Thus it is not unusual to find middle-class, college-educated women working in other nations as private domestic workers. Third, the development of service-based economies in postindustrial nations favors the international migration of women laborers. Unlike in earlier industrial eras, today the demand for gendered labor favors migrant women's services.

Nations use vastly different methods to "import" domestic workers from other countries. Some countries have developed highly regulated, government-operated, contract labor programs that have institutionalized both the recruitment and working conditions of migrant domestic workers. Canada and Hong Kong exemplify this approach. Since 1981 the Canadian federal government has formally recruited thousands of women to work as live-in nanny/housekeepers for Canadian families. Most come from third world countries, the majority in the 1980s from the Caribbean and in the 1990s from the Philippines; and once in Canada, they must remain in live-in domestic service for two years, until they obtain their landed immigrant status, the equivalent of the U.S. "green card." During this period, they must work in conditions reminiscent of formal indentured servitude and they may not quit their jobs or collectively organize to improve job conditions.

Similarly, since 1973 Hong Kong has relied on the formal recruitment of domestic workers, mostly Filipinas, to work on a full-time, live-in basis for Chinese families. Of the 150,000 foreign domestic workers in Hong Kong in 1995, 130,000 hailed from the Philippines, with smaller numbers drawn from Thailand, Indonesia, India, Sri Lanka, and Nepal. Just as it is now rare to find African American women employed in private domestic work in Los Angeles, so too have Chinese women vanished from the occupation in Hong Kong. As Nicole Constable reveals in her detailed study, Filipina domestic workers in Hong Kong are controlled and disciplined by official employment agencies, employers, and strict government policies. Filipinas and other foreign domestic workers recruited to Hong Kong find themselves working primarily in live-in jobs and under two-year contracts that stipulate job rules, regulations for bodily display and discipline (no lipstick, nail polish, or long hair; submission to pregnancy tests; etc.), task timetables, and the policing of personal privacy.

In the larger global context, the United States remains distinctive, as it follows a more laissez-faire approach to incorporating immigrant women into paid domestic work. Unlike in Hong Kong and Canada, here there is no formal government system or policy to legally contract with foreign domestic workers. In the past, private employers in the United States were able to "sponsor" individual immigrant women working as domestics for their green cards, sometimes personally recruiting them while they were vacationing or working in foreign countries, but this route is unusual in Los Angeles today. For such labor certification, the sponsor must document that there is a shortage of labor able to perform a particular, specialized job— and in Los Angeles and many other parts of the country, demonstrating a shortage of domestic workers has become increasingly difficult. And it is apparently unnecessary, as the significant demand for domestic workers in the United States is largely filled not through formal channels but through informal recruitment from the growing number of Caribbean and Latina immigrant women who are already living (legally or illegally) in the United States. The Immigration and Naturalization Service, the federal agency charged with stopping illegal migration, has historically served the interest of domestic employers and winked at the hiring of undocumented immigrant women in private homes.

As we compare the hyperregulated employment systems in Hong Kong and Canada with the U.S. approach to domestic work, we must distinguish between the regulation of labor and the regulation of foreign domestic workers. As Sedef Arat-Koc puts it in discussing the labor conditions of Filipina and Caribbean domestic workers in Canada, "while their conditions of work have been under-regulated, domestic workers themselves, especially those from the 'least desirable' backgrounds, have become over-regulated." Here, the United States is again an exception. U.S. labor regulations *do* cover private domestic work—but no one knows about them. Domestic workers' wages and hours are governed by state and federal law, and special regulations cover such details as limits on permissible deductions for breakage and for boarding costs of live-in workers. These regulations did not fall from the sky: They are the result of several important, historic campaigns organized by and for paid domestic workers. Most U.S. employers now know, after the Zoë Baird incident, about their obligations for employment taxes—though these obligations are still widely ignored—but few employers and perhaps fewer employees know about the labor laws pertaining to private domestic work. It's almost as though these regulations did not exist. At the same time, the United States does not maintain separate immigration policies for domestic workers, of the sort that mandate live-in exployment or decree instant deportation if workers quit their jobs.

This duality has two consequences. On the one hand, both the absence of hyper-regulation of domestic workers and the ignorance about existing labor laws further reinforce the belief that paid domestic work is not a real job. Domestic work remains an arrangement that is thought of as private: It remains informal, "in the shadows," and outside the purview of the state and other regulating agencies. On the other hand, the absence of state monitoring of domestic job contracts and of domestic workers' personal movement, privacy, and bodily adornment suggests an opening to upgrade domestic jobs in the United States. Unlike in Hong Kong and Canada, for example, where state regulations prevent Filipina domestic workers from quitting jobs that they find unsatisfactory or abusive, in Los Angeles, Latina immigrant domestic workers can quit their jobs. Certainly they face limited options when they seek jobs outside of private homes, but it is important to note that they are not yoked by law to the same boss and the same job.

The absence of a neocolonialist, state-operated, contractual system for domestic work thus represents an opportunity to seek better job conditions. The chance of success might be improved if existing labor regulations were strengthened, if domestic workers were to work at collective organizing, and if informational and educational outreach to the domestic workers were undertaken. But to be effective, these efforts must occur in tandem with a new recognition that the relationships in paid domestic work are relations of employment.

Social Reproduction and New Regimes of Inequality: Transnational Motherhood

Sometimes it is necessary to state the obvious. In employer households, women are almost exclusively in charge of seeking and hiring domestic workers. This social fact speaks to the extent to which feminist, egalitarian goals of sharing household cleaning and care work remain unachieved. Even among wealthy white women born and raised in the United States in the late twentieth century, few escape the fetters of unpaid social reproductive labor. As many observers have noted, their reliance on housecleaners and nannies allows well-to-do women to act, in effect, as contractors.

By subcontracting to private domestic workers, these women purchase release from their gender subordination in the home, effectively transferring their domestic responsibilities to other women who are distinct and subordinate by race and class, and now also made subordinate through language, nationality, and citizenship status. The work performed by Latina, Caribbean, and Filipina immigrant women today subsidizes the work of more privileged women, freeing the latter to join the productive labor force by taking jobs in business and the professions, or perhaps enabling wealthier women to become more active consumers and volunteers and to spend more time culturally grooming their children and orchestrating family recreation. Consequently, male privilege within homes and families remains uncontested and intact, and new inequalities are formed.

Some feminist theorists, especially those influenced by Marxist thought, have used the term "social reproduction" or "reproductive labor" to refer to the myriad of activities, tasks, and resources expended in the daily upkeep of homes and people. Taking care of ourselves, raising the next generation, and caring for the sick and elderly are projects requiring constant vigilance and dedication. As the sociologists Barbara Laslett and Joanna Brenner put it, "renewing life is a form of work, a kind of production, as fundamental to the perpetuation of society as the production of things." More recently, feminist scholars influenced by feminist Scandinavian research on social welfare have shifted their focus to "caring" and "care work." Regardless of specific theoretical underpinnings, two important points must be emphasized.

First, the way we socially organize reproductive labor has varied historically, and across culture and class. Different arrangements bring about different social consequences and different forms of inequality. Second, our definitions of what are appropriate forms and goals of social reproduction also vary. What passes today as a clean house or proper meal? What behavioral or educational expectations do we hold for our children? The proliferation of fast, frozen, and already prepared foods, and of women's magazines that promise to reveal how to make family meals in ten minutes, suggests that standards for what constitutes a proper American middle-class meal have dropped. (Meal preparation is a task rarely assigned to contemporary domestic workers; perhaps convenience foods have made it trivial, or perhaps meal preparation remains too symbolic of family life to assign to an outsider.) Simultaneously, standards of hygiene and home cleanliness, like the size of the average American home, have increased throughout the twentieth century. And perhaps nowhere has the bar been raised more than regarding what constitutes proper child rearing, especially among middle-class professionals. Parents (mostly mothers) study books and attend classes on how to provide babies and toddlers with appropriate developmental stimulation, and middle-class children today are generally expected to perform grueling amounts of homework, participate in a variety of organized sports and social clubs, take music lessons, and exhibit prescribed stages of emotional literacy and sensitivity. In any society, raising children is work that requires tremendous expenditures of manual, mental, spiritual, and emotional energy, but enormous amounts of money and work are now invested in developing middle-class and upper-class children, presumably so that they can assume or better their parents' social status. Paid domestic work, especially the work of nanny/housekeepers, occurs in this context of diminished expectations for preparing meals and heightened standards for keeping homes clean and rearing children.

Inequalities of race, class, and gender have long characterized private, paid domestic work, and as we have seen, globalization is creating new regimes of inequality. We must remember that the immigrant women who are performing other people's private reproductive work are women who were themselves socially reproduced in other societies. The costs of their own social reproduction— everything that it took to raise them from infants to working adults—were shouldered by families, governments, and communities in Mexico and in Central American and Caribbean nations. For this reason, their employment as domestic workers represents a bargain for American families and American society. The inequalities of social reproduction in these Latinas' contemporary family and work lives, however, are even more glaringly apparent when we consider their own children.

Today, many of these domestic workers care for the homes and children of American families while their children remain "back home" in their societies of origin. This latter arrangement, which I call transnational motherhood, signals new international inequalities of social reproduction. A continuing strain of contemporary xenophobia in California protests the publicly funded schooling for the children of Mexican undocumented immigrants (e.g., Proposition 187 in 1994 and the 1999 attempt by the Anaheim School Board to "bill" the Mexican federal government for the schooling of Mexican children in Orange County), but this same logic might be used to promote an alternative view, one emphasizing that the human investment and reaping of benefits occurs in precisely the opposite direction. Though the children (themselves U.S. citizens) of undocumented immigrants are later likely, as adults, to work and reside in the same society in which they were raised (the United States), Central American and Mexican immigrant women enter U.S. domestic jobs as adults, already having been raised, reared, and educated in another society. Women raised in another nation are using their own adult capacities to fulfill the reproductive work of more privileged American women, subsidizing the careers and social opportunities of their employers. Yet the really stinging injury is this: They themselves are denied sufficient resources to live with and raise their own children.

Since the early 1980s, thousands of Central American women and Mexican women in increasing numbers have left their children behind with grandmothers, with other female kin, with the children's fathers, and sometimes with paid caregivers while they themselves migrate to work in the United States. The subsequent separations of time and distance are substantial; ten or fifteen years may elapse before the women are reunited with their children. Feminist scholarship has shown us that isolationist, privatized mothering, glorified and exalted though it has been, is just one historically and culturally specific variant among many; but this model of motherhood continues to inform many women's family ideals. In order to earn wages by providing child care and cleaning for others, many Latina immigrant women must transgress deeply ingrained and gender-specific spatial and temporal boundaries of work and family.

One precursor to these arrangements is the mid-twentieth-century Bracero Program, discussed above. This long-standing arrangement of Mexican "absentee fathers" coming to work in the United States as contracted agricultural laborers is still in force today, though the program has ended. When these men come north and leave their families in Mexico, they are fulfilling masculine obligations defined as breadwinning for the family. When women do so, they are entering not only another country but also a radical, gender-transformative odyssey. As their separations of space and time from their communities of origin, homes, children, and sometimes husbands begin, they must cope with stigma, guilt, and others' criticism.

The ambivalent feelings and new ideological stances accompanying these new arrangements are still in flux, but tensions are evident. As they wrestle with the contradictions of their lives and beliefs, and as they leave behind their own children to care for the children of strangers in a foreign land, these Latina domestic workers devise new rhetorical and emotional strategies. Some nanny/housekeepers develop very strong ties of affection with the children in their care during their long workweeks, and even more grow critical of their employers. Not all nanny/housekeepers bond tightly with their employers' children (and they do so selectively among the children), but most of them sharply criticize what they perceive as their employers' neglectful parenting—typically, they blame the biological mothers. They indulge in the rhetoric of comparative mothering, highlighting the sacrifices that they themselves make as poor, legally disenfranchised, racially subordinate working mothers and setting them in contrast to the substandard mothering provided by their multiply privileged employers.

Notions of childhood and motherhood are intimately bound together, and when the contrasting worlds of domestic employers and employees overlap, different meanings and gauges of motherhood emerge. In some ways, the Latina transnational mothers who work as nanny/housekeepers sentimentalize their employers' children more than their own. This strategy enables them to critique their employers, especially the homemakers who neither leave the house to work nor care for their children every day. The Latina nannies can endorse motherhood as a full-time vocation for those able to afford it, while for those suffering financial hardships they advocate more elastic definitions of motherhood—including forms of transnational motherhood that may force long separations of space and time on a mother and her children. Under these circumstances, and when they have left suitable adults in charge, they tell themselves that "the kids are all right."

These arrangements provoke new debates among the women. Because there is no universal or even widely shared agreement about what constitutes "good mothering," transnational mothers must work hard to defend their choices. Some Latina nannies who have their children with them in the United States condemn transnational mothers as "bad women." In response, transnational mothers construct new measures to gauge the quality of mothering. By setting themselves against the negative models of mothering that they see in others—especially the models that they can closely scrutinize in their employers' homes—transnational mothers redefine the standards of good mothering. At the same time, selectively developing motherlike ties with other people's children allows them to enjoy the affectionate, face-to-face interactions that they cannot experience on a daily basis with their own children.

Social reproduction is not simply the secondary outcome of markets or modes of production. In our global economy, its organization among privileged families in rich nations has tremendous repercussions for families, economies, and societies around the world. The emergence of transnational motherhood underscores this point, and shows as well how new inequalities and new meanings of family life are formed through contemporary global arrangements in paid domestic work.

Point of Departure

As we have seen, no single cause explains the recent expansion of paid domestic work. Several factors are at work, including growing income inequality; women's participation in the labor force, especially in professional and managerial jobs; the relatively underdeveloped nature of day care in the United States—as well as middle-class prejudices against using day care; and the mass immigration of women from Central America, the Caribbean, and Mexico. We have also examined the cultural and social perceptions that prevent paid domestic work from being seen and treated as employment, and have observed how contemporary racialization and immigration affect the job. Yet simply understanding the conditions that have fostered the occupation's growth, the widely held perceptions of the job, or even the important history of the occupation's racialization tells us little about what is actually happening in these jobs today. How are they organized, and how do employers and employees experience them?

Jobs in offices, in factories, or at McDonald's are covered by multiple regulations provided by government legislation, by corporate, managerial strategies, by employee handbooks, and sometimes by labor unions; but paid domestic work lacks any such formal, institutionalized guides. It is done in the private sphere and its jobs are usually negotiated, as Judith Rollins puts it, "between women." More broadly, I argue, paid domestic work is governed by the parallel and interacting networks of women of different classes, ethnicities, and citizenship statuses who meet at multiple work sites in isolated pairs. While employer and employee individually negotiate the job, their tactics are informed by their respective social networks. Today, many employers in Los Angeles and many Latina immigrants are, generationally speaking, new to the occupation. Rather than relying on information passed down from their mothers, both employers and employees draw on information exchanged within their own respective networks of friends, kin, and acquaintances and, increasingly, on lessons learned from their own experiences to establish the terms of private, paid domestic work (hiring practices, pay scales, hours, job tasks, etc.). That employers rarely identify themselves as employers, just as many employees hesitate to embrace their social status as domestic workers, means that the job is not always regarded as a job, leading to problematic relations and terms of employment.

Although there are regularities and patterns to the job, contemporary paid domestic work is not monolithic. I distinguish three common types of jobs: (1) *Live-in nanny/housekeeper*. The live-in employee works for and lives with one family, and her responsibilities generally include caring for the children and the household. (2) *Live-out nanny/housekeeper*. The employee works five or six days a week for one family, tending to the children and the household, but returns to her apartment, her own community, and sometimes her own family at night. (3) *Housecleaner.* The employee cleans houses, working for several different employers on a contractual basis, and usually does not take care of children as part of her job. Housecleaners, as Mary Romero's research emphasizes, work shorter hours and receive higher pay than do other domestic workers, enjoying far greater job flexibility and autonomy; and because they have multiple jobs, they retain more negotiating power with their employers.

Questions for Study and Review

1. The number of women employed as household domestics has varied dramatically over the last one hundred years. What factors influence these fluctuations?

2. What is novel about this most recent wave of immigration? Do you see parallels between turn-of-the-century objections to immigration and the current backlash?

3. How is the American need for household domestic labor changing communities in other parts of the world, and how are American domestic arrangements being shaped by globalization?

4. What lessons could contemporary immigrant workers draw from earlier organizing drives among immigrants? For instance, what advice might Pauline Newman, Rose Schneiderman, Fannia Cohn, and Clara Lemlich offer to a Latina union organizer today? And if they noted that earlier immigrants had drawn on the sympathy of more affluent women to bolster their organizing efforts, how might current immigrant domestic workers respond?

Suggested Readings and Web Sites

Barbara Ehrenreich and Arlie Russell Hochschild, eds., *Global Woman: Nannies, Maids, and Sex Workers in the New Economy* (2003)

Miriam Ching Yoon Louie, *Sweatshop Warriors: Immigrant Women Workers Take on the Global Factory* (2001)

Ruth Milkman, *L.A. Story: Immigrant Workers and the Future of the U.S. Labor Movement* (2006)

Rhacel Salazar Parreñas, *Servants of Globalization: Women, Migration and Domestic Work* (2001)

A Mother's Effort to Reunite with Her Children
    http://www.nppa.org/competitions/best_of_still_photojournalism/2005/photography/winners/egress.cfm?cat=DNS&place=HM3&img=99851

National Immigration Forum
    http://www.immigrationforum.org

United Methodist Women's Division
    http://gbgm-umc.org/umw/action_labor.html

Campaign for Migrant Domestic Workers Rights
    http://www.ips-dc.org/campaign/index.htm

The shape of American families has changed with increasing speed since the 1960s. In the 1940s, 75 percent of American households included a married couple; by the end of the century, only one-quarter of households did so. In the twenty-first century, women wait longer than ever to wed—the average age of first marriage is now twenty-five—and they rarely end their lives with their first spouse since half of all marriages end in divorce. While those who do divorce usually remarry, many women are deciding to never marry at all. At the same time, more unmarried women are becoming mothers; one-third of all children are born to mothers who are not married.

Even so-called traditional marriages look different today. Most include two wage earners; the male breadwinner has become increasingly obsolete as the median income of young husbands dropped by one-fourth in the last quarter of the twentieth century. Mothers with young children are more likely than ever to be working for wages. In Chapter Thirteen, Hondagneu-Sotelo illustrates that many couples with high combined incomes now hire nannies and maids to care for their children and perform their household duties. In sum, very few American households fit dominant stereotypes of a conventional nuclear family: children under eighteen supported by a breadwinner father and nurtured by a homemaker mother. Yet this domestic ideal popularized during the 1950s continues to hold powerful sway on the national imagination and has fueled a backlash determined to re-establish this "traditional" family at the center of American life.

Of all the alternative family forms to emerge in this period, the most novel and controversial have been those created by gays and lesbians. Statistically, this trend is difficult to enumerate; one analysis of the 2000 census indicates that there were 5.5 million same-sex couples in the United States. The same sources reveal that one-third of those households were raising children. Lesbian couples all over the world are creating families by birthing and adopting children, a practice that began garnering media attention in the 1980s. Books providing parenting advice, how-to films for those considering motherhood, and newspaper articles in the lesbian press all encouraged lesbians seeking to become parents. Queer activists pioneered new slogans that incorporated their identity as mothers: "We're here and we're gay and we're in the PTA" chanted one group of women in the 1988 San Francisco Gay Pride parade. In the last twenty-five years, lesbian mothers have written books, started playgroups, founded summer camps, and formed support groups to help them build a sense of community for themselves and their children.

These new families owe their existence to the convergence of powerful political and medical developments. They are rooted, at least in part, in the Stonewall Rebellion, which signaled the beginning of a more broad-based movement for gay liberation. In 1969, a police raid on a working-class gay bar called the Stonewall Inn sparked a series of riots in New York that quickly escalated into a full-blown national movement for gay liberation. Activists demanded that private homosexual acts between consenting adults be recognized as a legitimate form of sexual desire. They also began the struggle to ensure civil rights for those who identified as homosexuals. Lesbians and gays demanded full equality and citizenship and challenged conservative campaigns that stigmatized them as "dangerously deviant." They also asserted their right to avoid discrimination in employment and family law. This last issue—discrimination in family law—was especially important for gay men faced with the HIV/AIDS epidemic in the 1980s and 1990s. Laws that assigned medical guardianship to next of kin often left longtime homosexual partners without any authority over critical health-care decisions.

As the gay liberation movement grew, many lesbians were simultaneously inspired by the audacity of gay liberation and angered by the misogyny of gay men. They responded with the creation of women-only institutions that were inspired by lesbian feminism. This philosophy emerged from women's liberation and was reshaping the worldview of longtime lesbians while also encouraging a new generation of female activists to forge intimate partnerships with other women. Lesbianism, for the women who embraced this way of life, was a conscious political choice driven by the conviction that sexual relationships with men would always be exploitative. A sexual desire for other women was not innate, according to these women. Instead, it was a possibility for all women interested in escaping the brutal effects of patriarchy and the cycle of female exploitation. These activists viewed lesbianism as a way for women to engage in intimate relationships without collaborating with the individuals most responsible for their oppression.

Initially many gay liberation advocates defined family life as incompatible with gay existence. The AIDS epidemic changed the minds of some gay men as they sought to cope with chronic illness and death. At the same time, many lesbians who desired children began to challenge gay attitudes toward family life as well. A new generation of lesbian mothers had witnessed the devastating custody battles of older women forced to fight for the custody of children conceived in heterosexual relationships, once they came out as lesbians. These younger lesbians were determined to have children without the threat of future legal entanglements. Like the families described by Maureen Sullivan in this chapter, they chose to build their families through the use of new reproductive technologies that allow the separation of sexuality and procreation. In some cities, sperm banks sprang up to cater to lesbians seeking motherhood. By screening sperm for potential pathogens and standing as a legal shield between donors and would-be mothers, these organizations provide vital services for women determined to create families without men.

The women profiled by Sullivan are trying, in many cases, to realize the feminist dream of a family constructed to meet the needs and desires of women. They view their decision to raise children in this kind of environment as a political act. These families have gained heightened visibility, however, not only due to the demands of lesbian mothers. Conservative activists have focused on lesbian and gay parents as another sign of moral decay in America. Under pressure from New Right political groups and evangelical churches, many states have codified definitions of family that reject alternative kinship arrangements among same-sex partners. By 2003, thirty-seven states had banned gay marriage, denying same-sex partners legal protections in the areas of insurance, health care, family finances, immigration, and child custody that heterosexual-parent families take for granted. Far fewer states have legally recognized gay marriage or same-sex civil unions. Only three—Vermont, Massachusetts, and New Jersey—have done so as this book goes to press. The challenges faced by these brave new families will continue to define the activist agenda in the United States for years to come.

Lesbian Mothers and Baby Making in the Age of Assisted Procreation: The Transformation of American Families at the End of the Twentieth Century

Maureen Sullivan

On a clear day from midway up Mount Tamalpais, with its popular hiking trails and fragrant eucalyptus trees, one can usually see three of the five bridges connecting the various landforms that make up the larger San Francisco Bay Area. Most days the City of Lights itself is nestled in a bed of fog and is known for its chilly summers requiring several layers of cotton, heavy sweaters, and often leather. Many of the denizens of the San Francisco metropolis, however, require neither weather conditions nor fashion trends to display, proudly, their membership in a community that sports and supports an affinity for leather. For here, in the Gay Capital of the United States, as *Life* magazine famously dubbed it in 1964, reside hundreds of thousands of people who have something in common but also diverse racial-ethnic identifications, nationalities, masculinities and femininities, ages, religious affiliations, class statuses, and cultural styles—including those who are in fact quite indifferent to leather. What they have in common concerns the people they choose to love, those they desire, and now, those with whom they choose to raise children.

Lesbian mothers are among the most controversial faces of the new American family. Lesbians began to challenge the assumption that family life was incompatible with gay existence in the mid-1980s. In the intervening years, queer families have gained visibility but not necessarily widespread acceptance among Americans. Indeed, Americans across the political spectrum fear that the disintegration of the 1950s 'traditional' family carries grave consequences for national life.

The San Francisco Bay Area, along with its surrounding counties, is by all accounts one of the regions of the United States most densely populated by citizens who identify with or claim membership in communities of gay, lesbian, bisexual, and transgender people. The city is home to the Gay and Lesbian Historical Society of Northern California, which holds one of the nation's most comprehensive archives of material related to the "history of homosexuality." Over the years the Bay Area has been home to some of the most significant figures and organizations not only in regional gay culture and politics but in national and international literary circles and political, economic, and social movements. The modernist literary figure Gertrude Stein and her life partner, Alice B. Toklas, both had roots in the Bay Area. Harry Hay, radicalized by his participation in the massive San Francisco General Strike of 1934, extended his Marxist analysis to the oppression suffered by gay people and founded the country's first "homophile" organization, the Mattachine Society.

Like the rest of California and the nation, the Bay Area has had cycles of economic boom and bust with continuous movement toward deindustrialization—marked importantly by the 1998 announced departure from San Francisco to Third World production sites of Levi-Strauss & Co., one of the last holdouts of domestic brand-name clothing fabrication and rated by gay employees as one of the best companies to work for. The Silicon Valley still operates some electronics assembly facilities, but more common are the corporate complexes that function as brain trusts for research and development. Like most dense urban centers in the United States and elsewhere in the early to mid-1990s, the Bay Area went digital, and gay groups with names like Digital Queers have assisted various political and service organizations with their conversions to cyberspace. Today, despite the collapse of the dot-com "new" economy, service and information organizations still make up important economic sectors that both serve and employ members of gay and lesbian communities in the Bay Area, including organizations that facilitate gay family creation.

The thirty-four families who are the subjects of this scholarship reside in the larger Bay Area corridor. In the city itself, they live in the gritty Mission District with its savory taquerias; Bernal Heights, a well-known lesbian neighborhood; and the upscale Twin Peaks area with its panoramic views. In the South Bay they live in Daly City, Palo Alto, and even Felton, a small community nestled in the mountains just east of Santa Cruz. They live in the heart of Silicon Valley—San Jose and its suburbs. To the east they live in Oakland, Berkeley, and Richmond; to the north they have put down roots in the more sedate Sonoma and Napa Counties, the lush coastal region known simply as wine country.

In mid-January of 1994, I drove my aging Honda to the East Bay home of Eliza Cohen, Gretchen Zindosa, and their eleven-month-old daughter, Rayna. As I approached the house, which I was later to learn they rented, I saw a stroller parked at the bottom of the steps and some of Rayna's toys at the top, and it occurred to me that, in meeting these families, I was going to be around young children again for the first time in about twenty years—a long hiatus from my babysitting days. I realized I had forgotten completely what it was like to be with children. When I rang the doorbell, a tall, slim woman with large brown eyes and dark hair pulled back in a ponytail greeted me with "Hi, I'm Eliza," and, pointing to a strawberry-blond-haired toddler, said, "and this is Rayna. Come on in." Rayna was dressed in a one-piece outfit that looked like pajamas. She held a blue plastic block in one hand and then suddenly, letting out a couple of squeals, started waving it. Eliza introduced me to Gretchen, who also had long, thick dark hair. When I saw the two mothers together with their child, the thought crossed my mind that the way in which Rayna had been brought into the world, and the family in which she was being raised, were profoundly unique.

It seems fitting to begin an exploration of a relatively new family form "at the beginning," the point at which a desire for children and family of one's own becomes a practical plan and consequent reality. Like other prospective parents using assisted-procreation services, lesbian would-be mothers such as Eliza and Gretchen may justifiably claim that every child brought into the world under their auspices is not just wanted but wanted in a big way. Prospective lesbian parents want children so much that they undertake even more than the considerable financial, emotional, and practical planning that many prospective parents do when they start families. Just to get to the starting gate of family planning, they must decide how they are going to get pregnant and whose sperm will be used to do it.

Their problem is the opposite of that of millions of women using contraceptives to avoid pregnancy and is at once similar to and different from that of the growing numbers of heterosexual women and couples seeking infertility "treatment" and medically assisted procreation. For lesbian couples seeking to become parents using procreative assistance, their process differs in that their first task is to locate a sperm donor (or broker); they must procure what neither partner is able to supply from her own body. The lesbian mothers I spoke with had different names for it, like "baby juice" and "liquid gold." But for many of the Bay Area couples, even before the gold rush began, there was some deliberation about adopting versus birthing a child. Their rationales for having biological children are revealing of their views about biogenetic relatedness and kinship and the demands of assisted-procreation procedures.

Getting Pregnant, Part I: Whose Ova, Whose Sperm?

Most of the Bay Area mothers said that they decided not to adopt because it was their impression that getting pregnant was easier. Nina Taringetti, a labor lawyer and birth mother, reasoned: "The concept of adopting is fine except that it takes a lot of time and you have to go through lots of hoops and so on, and it just seemed a lot faster to just get pregnant and do it, you know." This assumption was borne out for some couples, like Nina and her partner Emily Trindall, who got pregnant on the first try, but for others, difficulty in becoming pregnant proved emotionally and economically draining, especially as anxiety set in after months of trying, months of hopes dashed as pregnancy tests reported negative results and menstruation cycles continued uninterrupted.

Most other rationales offered for getting pregnant rather than adopting had to do with the desirability of biogenetic relatedness. But this assumption led to a different set of concerns for many couples. Perhaps one of the most interesting and culturally revealing versions of the biogenetic rationale was provided by Cathy Lotti and Katrina Smith. Cathy and Katrina were one of the most methodical, planning-oriented couples of those with whom I became acquainted. At thirty-four, with a master's degree in health services, Cathy was well on her way to realizing her career goals as a hospital administrator, with a roomy $80K salary to match. Earning roughly a third less than Cathy, thirty-six-year-old Katrina Smith worked for the same university hospital as a budget analyst, though at one time during their relationship she had seriously toyed with the idea of returning to school and doing art restoration, a divergent path from her undergraduate business degree and budget work. Their thinking on the subject of adopting versus birthing a child revealed them to be not only "goal oriented" and "planners," as they declared to me with some pride, but also quite sensitive to discourses of biological determinism and the ways in which biogenetic connection with a child would automatically trump other forms of relationship and attachment. The concept of a self-evident correspondence between biogenetic and ontological relatedness—that is, a correspondence by which relatedness by blood and genes defines human connection—permeated their thought as their considerations moved from adoption, to one partner giving birth, to acceptance by families of origin, to determining a donor, as illustrated in the following dialogue:

KATRINA: We thought first that the only way to feel like equal parents was to adopt, do an independent adoption. I think we were completely convinced of that and that was what we planned on doing.

M: Why would adopting help you feel like equal parents?

KATRINA: Well, now we don't see it that way, but I think it was just sort of, it would be hard not to be the birth parent.

CATHY: But I think another part of it was our families, that we were thinking, like, Katrina's family might not be able to give *equal credence* to the child I bore and my family might not, you know . . . like somehow they might not *buy in* as much as they would if there were a totally *neutral* baby that was adopted. I don't know, this is how we felt then. It's hard to remember why.

KATRINA: Right. We came a long way from there so it's kind of hard to even think about it.

CATHY: So we started there and then went to . . .

KATRINA: Then we realized, wait a minute, why don't we, we could at least have *one of us in our children, rather than have none of us in our children.*

CATHY: And at that point we were focused on, *let's get the other half* from somebody on the other side of the family. You know, like one of Katrina's brothers. We talked about that, we never approached anybody and decided that that was really weird.

KATRINA: We just thought that it would never work. Thanksgiving dinner would be . . .

CATHY: Right. You know, "Here's your uncle and your father!" It was just too weird. Plus we were worried about somebody wanting to have custody in some way. So we [had] made this shift [from adoption] to we were going to have the baby. And then, that we, there was nobody in our lives that we would use as a donor. I mean it would have to be an exceptional situation to even think of it, because of our not wanting interference. 'Cause we didn't want to do a third-party arrangement. We wanted to be the parents, period. We didn't want anybody potentially to have custody.

Cathy and Katrina's conceptualization of biogenetic relatedness as an agent of legitimation providing "credence" winds its way through their thinking in the preceding sequence. They implicitly recognize the social and cultural power of biogenetic connection as a credential of ontological connection. In their earlier thinking, an adopted child would be "neutral" because it would lack the cachet of shared DNA, the genealogical assurance of a shared bloodline with either parent's family. And a baby "neutralized" by virtue of having no DNA or blood in common with either parent would provide the basis for their being equal parents. Despite this, the possibility of a biogenetic connection was alluring, so that they could next speak of "having one of us" rather than "none of us in our children," and "getting the other half" from the nonbirth parent's "side of the family." Remarkably, although these thought experiments assign primacy to biogenetic relatedness over and above other ways of construing human being and relationship, by envisioning how they might play out in concrete social situations (the Thanksgiving scenario resulting from having gotten "the other half" from "the other side") Cathy and Katrina inadvertently reveal the social constructedness of a putative biogenetic relationship. Finally, and somewhat paradoxically, the biogenetic credential that would play so well with the family of whoever became the birth mother could in fact be turned against them should a donor wish to pursue a custody claim. Thus it would be better to "get the other half" from an anonymous donor and to secure the nonbirth mother's parental status though legal means.

Cathy and Katrina's reflections shed some light on how resilient and protean the power of biogenetic determinism is. It never loses its grip on their thinking, and it exerts its influence in a way that requires them to employ the kind of strategic thinking one uses in chess, projecting scenarios or moves into the future.

For lesbian couples, starting families via pregnancy launches them into the world of techno-procreation and its metaphysical ramifications, where even the most seemingly practical considerations require contemplation of questions, such as the nature of being, that would ordinarily be the province of philosophers. They must grapple with conceptions of being and relationship, ontological status and connection, that arise from both the unconventional, technologically assisted method of procreation and the social fact of their being same-sex parents. One could argue that these concerns are present for heterosexual couples using procreative technologies as well, but in practice, the metaphysical issues are already resolved by the structural requirements of heteropatriarchy. That is, to sustain its dominance, heteropatriarchy requires a mystified reproductive process that starts with (hetero) sexual intercourse (although this is less and less the case), creates a sexual differentiation of bodies, and leads to a division of parenting based on the presumed naturalness of that sexual differentiation. Thus, even for heterosexual prospective parents who do not contribute genetic material "equally," or who engage a gestational surrogate, the couple, because they are heterosexual, almost always retain parental rights in contested custody cases and play out their gendered mother/father roles accordingly.

The Biological/Nonbiological Mother Decision

When lesbian couples thinking of starting families have ruled out adoption for their first child, as did all the Bay Area couples, the next decision they face is who will become pregnant if they plan on having only one child, or who will become pregnant first if they plan on having more than one and both partners wish to be birth mothers. Among the group of thirty-four Bay Area couples, only one, Kelly Kronenberg and Diane Chaucer, had biological children borne by each partner. For Kelly and Diane and other couples, the decisions concerning who would become pregnant, or who would become pregnant first, almost always revolved around three primary factors: age, desire, and work; extended-family considerations such as those discussed by Cathy and Katrina were cited less often, but with some frequency, as an important consideration.

Since couples in which only one partner wished to be a birth parent represented half of all the couples, those seventeen whose decisions about maternity concerned both partners cited age or work (or unpreparedness) as reasons why one partner tried to become pregnant first. For the four couples citing age considerations, there existed an age gap between partners that they perceived as significant enough to warrant the older partner's trying first. About thirteen couples—three-quarters of the couples in which both partners wished to be biological mothers—cited as a reason the nonbirth parent's work or career situation, stating that it seemed incompatible with the demands of pregnancy and childbirth at the time. These work and career issues also seemed to involve feelings of "not being ready" for maternity.

But since nonbiological mothers in half of the couples did not wish to become pregnant or give birth, desire played the most substantial role in couples' decisions concerning maternity. Jill Collins, whose partner, Nora Duncan, gave birth to their son Danny, had never wanted to give birth to a child but had always wanted to parent, a typical explanation given by these nonbirth mothers. Jill expressed this preference in her inimitable jovial style: "I'm not opposed to getting pregnant, it's just that I don't . . . You know when people talk about their biological clocks ticking and stuff, I don't have any feelings like that. Like I wanted to have a kid, but I'd be perfectly happy to get it from someplace else (laughs). Find it on the street! A knock on the front door, 'Oh, here's your little package.' That would be fine!"

Decisions concerning which partner becomes pregnant and in what order once again highlight the amount of planning, reflection, research, and rehearsal that lesbian prospective parents undertake in making their desire for families materialize. After deciding whose body will bear the challenges and joys of pregnancy and childbirth, whose ovaries will provide the DNA, whose blood will nourish the child in the womb, couples must locate a sperm donor, a task made considerably easier by the increased prevalence of sperm banks and fertility and insemination clinics that serve lesbians. But the logistics of locating a sperm donor flow from the type of donor couples want, and this decision, as we learned from Cathy Lotti and Katrina Smith's protracted deliberations, involves careful consideration of the social relationships that shape and are shaped by it.

The Donor Decision

In the Bay Area in the late 1980s, the open adoption movement began in an atmosphere of heated dispute. Public debates and forums in San Francisco and the East Bay, especially among lesbians considering parenthood, took up the issue of whether it was better for adopted children to know or have access to biological parents. The discussions grew strident, and, according to mothers I spoke with, a "correct" recommendation emerged for lesbian prospective parents: Choose a known donor so that your children will be spared the pain of a potentially protracted or unsuccessful search later in life and the insecurity of not knowing "where they came from." Kelly Kronenberg and Diane Chaucer described the tense, emotionally charged atmosphere at the time:

KELLY: There was this whole big controversy in the lesbian community about women who had been adopted. [They] felt very strongly that lesbians should not use anonymous donors because it would deprive the child of its biological roots. I mean it was this very, I mean, emotional issue to people. I had thought that that was . . . that it had sort of turned people away from the anonymous donor, to some extent.

DIANE: People were really being harassed. People were, I mean, you know, I just felt sorry for everybody I knew who had kids with an anonymous donor. I mean people were just saying it's criminal, it's horrible. There was really this vitriol.

KELLY: And you kind of felt like, "Oh I'm really glad I did this with a known donor."

DIANE: You know, it was scary. I mean, there were like big community forums and it was a big deal. I feel really strongly that women should be able to have, do what they think is best for their families, but um, I don't know . . .

As is clear from Diane's and Kelly's recollections of these debates, and from Cathy's and Katrina's worries about where they would "get the other half," the donor decision is fraught with emotional, social, political, and philosophical concerns. What has changed for many lesbian parents and couples considering parenthood since the late 1980s, however, is that now numerous "how to" books, support groups, and parenting classes organize the variables that must be reckoned with when couples begin thinking about creating families.

For example, in her popular 1993 resource book, *The Lesbian and Gay Parenting Handbook*, the psychologist April Martin combines practical advice with anecdotes from both her own experience in forming a lesbian-coparent family and the experience of the gay male and lesbian families she interviewed. Her work typifies the practical assistance and information gay and lesbian parents seek and use in making decisions about creating and sustaining families. As such, it has become part of the common stock of knowledge and has taken on the authority and normative character of rules. Martin's advice concerning the donor selection recognizes the continuing importance of this decision for the lives of children and parents. She writes that couples "must decide who the sperm donor or biological father will be, whether he will be known to the child, and whether he will assume a parenting role. In short, they have to define the family. The family unit has to be defined." Whereas an infertile heterosexual couple may choose a sperm donor with the knowledge that the husband's social paternity will stand in for his lack of biological paternity, so that there is little in the way of actively "defining the family unit," prospective lesbian parents cannot avoid making these decisions: Each step of the way, they engage in definitional acts involving biological elements that they must reckon with.

Among the Bay Area couples, only five had selected known donors; the remaining twenty-nine had anonymous donors, selected from the offerings of the bank or clinic whose services they had employed for this purpose. Of the twenty-nine anonymous donors, twenty-eight were "yes" donors, meaning that they had agreed to release their identity to a child when that child would reach majority age. The twenty-ninth donor would remain anonymous permanently. In an already logistically challenging method of procreation, the "yes" donor option offered by the fertility and insemination organizations has provided a welcome solution to a vexing decision. The Bay Area mothers' recollections of their donor decision are instructive for illustrating how the known and anonymous options can play out.

The Known-Donor Choice

When a couple opt for a donor who will be known to them and to their children, they transform a hidden, socially insignificant biological event—a conveyance of genetic material—into a durable social relationship. This is a moment in which culture organizes and shapes nature. From the decision to select a known donor stems another decision about the character of the donor's relationship to the couple and the children. Three different types of relationship appear to result: The donor may be a symbolic father; a flexibly defined male figure with whom the child has a relationship but to whom no parental status is imputed; or, finally, an active, practicing parent with all the rights and responsibilities implied by that coparent status but without legal custody.

In the first type of relationship, that of symbolic father, the child will have a live human being to whom the sign "father" is attached but of whom no one has parental expectations. The sign may be something else, like "daddy," or even "seed daddy," to indicate the procreative rather than the parental function of the donor. A known donor who is a symbolic father is simply someone the family can hang the label "dad" on—an embodied human referent that the child may identify as his or her progenitor. But it is a purely sign-driven, semiotic arrangement, because the sign *pater* pervades our culture as an entity independent of embodied referents, thus compelling the need for flesh-and-blood daddies even in cases in which they were not part of the original plan. Known donors who function as symbolic fathers are fathers in name only but in the person of the donor.

Kelly Kronenberg told a story of how this worked for her six-year-old, Noam, and Noam's friend Jake, who also has two mothers. Noam and Jake were having a disagreement about family structures, and Kelly overheard Noam saying, "I don't have a dad and neither do you, Jake, so don't talk about that." Jake said, "I do too, I have a seed daddy," to which Noam replied, "Well, I have that too."

It appears to be important for the mothers and children with these known donors who are primarily if not exclusively symbolic fathers that *daddy, dad, father,* or some other conventional signifier of paternity be included in the term they use to refer to him. The term *donor* or *sperm donor* defeats the purpose of having a symbolic father, as Cathy Lotti indicated:

> We went to family night and one of the other guests who came, a woman with her daughter, told a funny story about her daughter on the playground. I think the story went like: One little girl was upset because her parents were getting divorced, and the daughter of the lesbian came over and said, "Oh, don't feel sad, I don't have a father either, I just have a sperm." Which was very funny but which was also like, "Oh my God!" That's not quite what we would want our children to have in their mind, that they don't have a father, first of all, cause they do. But . . . "I have a sperm," I mean, that was just bizarre.

The advantages of having a symbolic father in the embodied person of the known donor are that children can have a living human referent whom they may regard as a real figure in their lives in a society that still views heterosexually created kinship as the rule, even though increasing numbers of children are actually raised in mother-only families. It should be noted here that there is no necessary or "naturally" logical relationship between donating sperm and fulfilling the role of symbolic father. The relationship is brought about entirely by a couple's having chosen a sperm donor who, in addition to providing genetic material, agreed to this symbolic role. In other words, the choice of a known donor fuses, in one individual, a biological event and a semiotic function that could have been fulfilled by two different individuals.

Some couples with known donors want their children to know and have a relationship with the donor but do not emphasize the symbolic role. Parents with this second type of arrangement refer to the donor by his first name, as do their children. They downplay his semiotic function as *pater* unless children ask. The point of his being known to them is purely pragmatic: Children can know him as being related to them, connected to them. Though they do not relate to him as "Dad," they can know that they have *a* dad with whom they may pursue a relationship at any time as they mature and as their understanding of their family structure changes. Mothers themselves can contact him at any time should the need arise, for example, in the event they want a second child by him. There is a built-in flexibility when the known-donor relationship is defined in this way. Indeed the very definition can evolve according to the needs and desires of all parties. Olena Porzak and Resa Frank recalled a situation in which this flexibility proved helpful:

RESA: We have been very careful to never ever say [to daughter Sarah], "You don't have a dad," because we felt like, well, she does. We didn't use a[n unknown] donor, we purposely picked a friend. We wanted them to be able to have a relationship. But she doesn't call him Dad; she calls him Rick Ricky.

OLENA: So, a while ago, Sarah started saying, "I don't have a dad." But Resa said, "Yeah, you do have a dad, Rick." And Sarah said, "Rick? He's not my dad, he helped make me grow as a little tiny baby." So she had a way of making sense of where he fit into our family. She has once since actually called him "Dad." It was just so out of the ordinary that it struck us. She was sitting here and looked up and said, "Can I call my dad, Mom?" [on the telephone]. So we said "Sure." And then she got distracted and never called him.

RESA: She was just trying it out.

OLENA: Yeah, I think she was just trying it out.

Of the five families who chose known donors, all but one have donors who are either symbolic fathers or nonfather figures whose relationship with the family is continually and flexibly defined.

The remaining couple with a known donor has a quasi-multiparenting arrangement with the donor. Donors involved in this type of relationship fulfill a symbolic role as "father" and, in practice, become active, involved parents. This construction of the donor thus fuses the biological, semiotic, and social or parental elements in one person. The only aspect missing is de jure paternity, or legal custody, which is where mothers draw a very important line in their family definitions. I know of no families with two mothers in which the donor is also a legal parent, guardian, or custodian.

In general, a known-donor choice represents a decisive moment in the path to family formation for lesbian couples insofar as it sets one of the boundaries signifying immediate family status beyond the couple-child unit to include at least one additional adult, usually as a symbolic father or flexibly defined father/male figure but occasionally as a fully active, involved one. There is no disavowing this relationship once it has been established, most importantly because the act of establishment institutes and socially legitimates a biological occurrence that itself, as a cultural symbol, wields great authority. At a more practical level, lesbian couples who choose the known-donor option and wish to retain the status of primary parents generally do so confidently—that is, with the foreknowledge that they can (and do) successfully negotiate the donor's nonactive role as a function of choosing a particular donor. Thus most lesbian couples whose children have known donors who are also fathers in name are still regarded by all involved as the parents.

The Anonymous-Donor Choice

The alternative to a known donor is an anonymous one. Anonymity may be achieved through the use of an intermediary, or someone known to the couple and entrusted with the task of finding them a donor and the duty of keeping secret his identity from them and theirs from him. Because this method is precarious in terms of the intermediary's capacity both for suppressing information and for screening the donor, the most secure, most depersonalized, and thus most preferred avenue for transacting with an anonymous donor is by way of a sperm bank or physician. Eighty-five percent or twenty-nine of the Bay Area couples chose this option, even those who were not recruited from the clinic database.

More important than the means of achieving anonymity is the question of what is achieved with anonymity. The choice of an anonymous donor means that couples trade knowledge of biological connection for protection from claims of kinship. Their not knowing is exchanged for protection from potential kinship claims and from the very basis of such claims: paternity. Kinship claims, such as those involving custody of children, are rarely pursued without evidence of biological consanguinity. When a third party such as a sperm bank controls the evidence, bilateral ignorance of paternity among donors and recipients prohibits any pursuit of such claims. The whole configuration is a social mechanism for suppressing the symbolic power of biology. In one sense, ignorance, or not knowing, trumps and therefore gains greater value than knowledge in this social game that gets played around biology. For lesbian couples who choose anonymous donors, this protection from kinship claims—and coincidental erasure of paternity—is manifested pragmatically on the child's initial birth certificate where "the father" is listed as unknown. (Later, when a second-parent adoption is successfully undertaken by the nonbirth mother, her name is listed as a second, legal parent.)

Lesbian parents who choose an anonymous donor via a sperm bank or fertility facility have yet another option when choosing anonymity. They may choose lifetime anonymity, or they may choose a "yes" donor, as mentioned earlier, where the "yes" indicates the donor's agreement to allow children to learn of his identity when they reach eighteen and to contact him if they desire. Of the twenty-nine couples who chose anonymity, all but one opted for a "yes" donor. Indeed, this provision was the most frequently cited criterion for donor selection. This provision in a sense offers the best of both worlds: Couples are protected during the child-raising years from external threats to their family sovereignty, and once they reach majority, children may pursue the officially suppressed knowledge of the identity of their progenitor if they so desire.

Getting Pregnant, Part II: The Vicissitudes of Sperm Management and the Comother's Role

Sperm Management

The mothers I spoke with talked about the trials and tribulations of getting pregnant when careful charting of ovulation patterns and coordination with the insemination clinic often failed to produce a pregnancy or, perhaps worse, began to take over their lives to the extent that the emotional stakes became very high indeed. A primary reproductive task becomes sperm management: The prospective parents must decide whether to use frozen or fresh sperm (fresh is highly desirable but far more difficult to coordinate with the donor at the right time) and whether to inseminate at home, where partners can make insemination attempts ceremonial and thereby satisfy the social need of creating meaning and memory of a life-changing event, or in the clinic, where partners can meet the practical need of ensuring that the procedure is most efficient.

Mothers spoke variedly and candidly about how mundane and "clinical" the procedure was; about the economic exploitation they experienced as lesbian couples who needed medically screened, potent, and anonymous-donor sperm in order to conceive; and about their attitudes toward creating meaning from the procedure versus ensuring efficiency. Birth mother Shannon Cavner, whose working-class background may account for some of the cynicism with which she viewed both the procedure and the institutional arrangements necessary for her to become pregnant, described the process, with her partner Marian Gould-Whitmer, as at once mundane and manipulative:

SHANNON: Well, I mean, it's just very clinical. I mean, you go in, you know, you lay there, they put sperm in you, you lay there some more. A lot of people [inseminate] at home. I'm glad that I didn't do it that way the first time because the donor actually had a sperm problem, a low sperm count problem. Which is not something you would obviously be able to detect if you were doing it at home. And because they were doing it in the office, when they unfroze it they saw [the problem] so they double dosed it in the office. So, but it's a lot of money to pay for a problem like that because I know there are a lot of people, there were other people using the donor who didn't get pregnant, or who had a hard time getting pregnant. You certainly have to wonder if that's the reason for it, or if they were just having . . . you can't ever say for sure. But in this particular case I was glad that I did it that way. When you get inseminated you really have to sort of lay there, you know, upside down more or less, you know, while the sperm works its way up and you know that wasn't an option necessarily because they had all these people coming in and out [of the clinic]. That actually really irritated me. The second time I did it I told them I wasn't leaving. (Marian laughing). Forget it, "I'm staying here, upside down," you know? It's too much money, it really is, and to them it's a business. It's not really, it's not that they're mean or anything like that, but it's still a business and they treat it like a business. We're just people to make money off of. No matter how nice anybody is or what their best of intentions are, you are still someone to be made money off of. And that's really how I feel about it after going through it. I mean it's like, heterosexual people boink and they get a baby. All right. It costs nothing, they do nothing. No, to me, I see that and I see the whole [second-parent] adoption process too, and I mean it's just a way to make money off of gay people. Really it is, because it's a lot of money for not a lot. But, that aside, it's still just a clinical procedure. That's how I feel about it. You know, if you do it at home, it's still a clinical procedure but at least you're at home. (Marian laughing). It's just something. . . I mean it's just the means to the end. That's sort of how I look at it.

MARIAN: There's nothing really romantic about it; I mean, you can make something romantic out of it.

SHANNON: Even if you do it at home, I mean, you know, you're still shoving sperm up there and you know, to me that's not overly romantic (laughs). It's like I said, it's just the means to the end. The faster, the sooner, the better.

The average cost to recipients of donor semen, just the semen, runs about $100 per vial, and this is not covered by insurance. When couples inseminate at home using frozen semen that they have thawed, that is their cost per insemination attempt. Costs begin to increase if the insemination is done in the clinic, if couples do "double dosing" as Shannon mentioned, if intrauterine insemination is done, and especially when unsuccessful attempts begin to add up. The average length of time it takes to conceive has been widely cited at six months. Thus most couples can expect that, at a minimum, their semen costs alone will amount to $600. The costs involved with second-parent adoptions, depending on the county in which they are undertaken, can run anywhere from $500 to $3,000, which mostly covers the cost of the home study, in which a social service worker comes into the home and effectively collects and reports data on the home environment and on the nonbirth mother's background and perceived fitness to be a parent. In terms of the second-parent adoption expense, since this money flows into local government treasuries, Shannon's perception of the economic exploitation involved is not unfounded, as the state is effectively extorting money from a class of citizens whom it denies the right to marry, which would automatically confer parental status on the non-birth-giving spouse.

Shannon and Marian were fortunate in that Shannon became pregnant on the second attempt, which makes her observations of the process even more remarkable for the sense of antigay, economic injustice they reveal, as though she had been involved in the process much longer. Like Shannon and Marian, Belinda Tarpin and Caitlin Simonds expressed unsentimental views about the logistics and meaning of becoming pregnant via alternative insemination:

BELINDA: I don't know. We didn't really have a need to do a whole ritual. I mean, I have a spiritual perspective and that, but my perspective was not that this little soul was waiting to come in and it was ready. And it didn't matter really if the candles and, you know, all that stuff.

CAITLIN: (chuckling) We just split the cost of the sperm 50–50, half of it went on my credit card and half of it went on hers!

Shannon and Marian and Belinda and Caitlin were not the only mothers to express concern over the costs involved in becoming pregnant via donor insemination. Other low-income couples expressed their frustration with the expenses, often with a weariness or even matter-of-factness that betrays a lifetime of struggling to make ends meet, as Clara Mueller, the comother of eight-year-old Andrea and three-year-old Ethan, complained: "It's expensive. Each kid cost about a thousand dollars each. We wanted the donor to be anonymous so that there could be no legal claims made in the future. We paid about a thousand dollars for the vials of sperm per kid. And that is not covered by insurance." Clara explained that it took six months for her partner Madeline Lovadas to become pregnant with each child, making their monthly conception costs about $165 per attempt. Jill Collins and Nora Duncan mentioned the expense as well:

NORA: If you hold onto the sperm and do it [inseminate] yourself, it's cheaper; when they do it for you, it's really expensive. One hundred sixty-five dollars each time.

JILL: No insurance will pay for this. They'll cover some of the other tests, but they won't cover this.

And Pat Keating proclaimed about the expense of conceiving the son her partner Sarah Alton had given birth to: "This was not a cheap child! To hell with his college, he wasn't cheap getting here!"

But it wasn't just lower-income couples who complained of the cost, as Cathy Lotti, the hospital administrator, attested:

> But buying the sperm is not covered, or any of the procedures. Now had I gotten to an infertility point, then it would have been covered by my insurance, the infertility part of it, but not the artificial insemination part of it. Yeah, it adds up. I mean every month, it's probably, it was probably $375 between purchasing the ovulation kits and buying the stuff and the pregnancy tests and, I mean it's an interesting thing that lesbians have to go through just to get pregnant. The cost is tremendous. Now, even the fact that we've purchased some sperm that's in deep freeze, we have to pay rent! We have to pay storage fees on the sperm that's reserved for future attempts!

Nor was it strictly lower-income prospective parents who took an unromantic view of the procedure. Marilyn Weiss also described her partner Brenda Jacobsen's and her perspective in terms of means and ends and money: "Oh yeah, I could have inseminated [at home] for the weekend, but we sort of felt for that kind of money maybe we should have a professional do it, you know, we don't need to light candles and be all romantic and everything." One professional, socially active couple, Serena Walby and Carrie Johnson, described the logistical hazards of sperm management in a story about packing and transporting their frozen "baby juice" on a trip that happened to overlap with Serena's peak time to inseminate:

SERENA: It's comical now. One time, the fourth time [insemination attempt], we dragged this stuff [frozen semen] all over Vancouver. I was in the Gay Olympics. We dragged it to Seattle and then to Vancouver for two weeks and kept it perfectly, with the dry ice. And then one day we found a dry ice company in Vancouver and Carrie said . . .

CARRIE: He said, "Shall I fill it up?" I said, "Great." So he took it [cooler] into the back and came back with it all filled and I thought it was fine but then two days later when I started looking for it realized the specimen was gone! Apparently he had just dumped out the old ice. Put in the new!

SERENA: So there's $254 when you think of all the costs.

Despite the costs and logistical difficulties of inseminating, some couples were quite interested in the romantic or ceremonial aspect, as Angeline Bowen and Dana Engels described:

ANGELINE: It felt really important [for me] to be inseminating her, to really be having a role from the very beginning. I mean, I'm real glad that I did, even though that feels like maybe it shouldn't be that important, it felt really good.

DANA: Yeah, we know people who weren't able to have that [partner inseminating at home], who needed to be inseminated at the clinic. But it was nice . . .

ANGELINE: Yeah, it was, it felt important that I inseminated her.

Angeline related the importance of inseminating Dana in the comfort and privacy of their home to how it would make her feel more involved, more included from the very beginning, as a coparent to a child with whom she would not share the culturally defined, all-important biogenetic link. For many comothers lacking the bio-ontological credential, other means of creating the meaning and feeling of connection to the child become paramount. At what point prospective parents undertake this social-symbolic work varies depending upon how they view their needs in relation to economic exigency, logistical convenience, and philosophical outlook.

"Tying in" the Nonbirth Mother

Angeline and Dana's approach to the insemination process and pregnancy as equally involved prospective parents illustrates that becoming a parent is a social process, or rather, the result of social practice. In Angeline's words, "I'll be a coparent as much as I feel that I am one." Implicit here and in the views presented by most of the Bay Area couples is the understanding that the degree to which one feels and acts like a parent (or prospective parent) is related to what one does to make that happen. Partners recognized both implicitly and explicitly the power of the bio-ontological credential the birth mother would possess, a type of unfair advantage in the construction of parental status, so, paradoxically, they both compensated for this while simultaneously acknowledging that it—the biological credential—is itself socially, culturally, and legally determined and not given by the biological facts of pregnancy, parturition, and breast-feeding. Thus all of the prospective-parent couples actively thought about or pursued opportunities for "tying in" the nonbirth parent, to use a popular expression of the mothers.

Tying in the nonbirth mother can take many forms: giving the child her last name exclusively or in hyphenated form with the birth mother's; putting the child on her health insurance policy if possible; securing the second-parent adoption, perhaps the most socially and legally important step lesbian parents attempt toward ratifying the parental status of the nonbirth mother; and providing for the total and equal involvement of nonbirth mothers from the very beginning, as Angeline and Dana endeavored to do.

The equal involvement of both prospective parents among the Bay Area couples over the course of the birth mother's becoming and being pregnant reached levels mostly unheard of among heterosexual couples. Cathy Lotti and Katrina Smith had this to say about their equal involvement and those "unfortunate" women who do not have this level of support during their pregnancies:

KATRINA: I actually wanted to be part of everything, absolutely everything. I went to every appointment. I may have missed one, but I really felt part of things by being at every appointment and hearing every question, hearing every response and every decision along the way.

CATHY: Well you had to be there. We wouldn't have done it any other way. I mean the first time you hear the heartbeat and all those things. I mean how could you. . . . I don't know how women, so many women, do all that part alone. I don't know how they do it. I couldn't stand it.

If the insemination process reflects the inequities of being gay in heteronormative society and exacts economic and social penalties, the penalties appear to be mitigated somewhat by the potential rewards from not following the identity rules that straight society has created for heterosexual couples. Without overstating the case, since a great many heterosexual men have consciously or unconsciously begun to think of themselves more as their wives' and girlfriends' partners, and to support them more than have previous generations, it is still striking that nonbirth partners in lesbian-parent couples, unlike heterosexual male partners, not only earnestly and enthusiastically engage in a personal and interpersonal process of becoming parents but do so with both a sense of matter-of-factness and self-conscious practice. Their level of attentiveness simultaneously betrays a kind of "but of course" attitude *and* an intentional praxis involving "tying in" the nonbirth mother, as Pat Keating described, comparing her earlier experiences of being an unsupported heterosexual wife and mother and her current situation as lesbian comother to baby Seth, to whom her partner Sarah Alton had given birth:

PAT: This has been a team thing that we work together at raising him. I always felt terribly alone before [as a heterosexual mother]. Like this childbirth thing. You know it's supposed to be this wonderful pride thing for the fathers, but for me it wasn't. That's not what I saw from them [former husbands]. You know, this

10TH ANNIVERSARY EDITION

HEATHER HAS TWO MOMMIES

WRITTEN BY LESLÉA NEWMAN   ILLUSTRATED BY DIANA SOUZA

The children's book *Heather Has Two Mommies* reflects both the increasing prevalence of lesbian mothers and the related campaign to win broader social acceptance for queer families. The book–first published in 1989–sought to provide the children of gay and lesbian parents with reading material that reflected the realities of their lives. It quickly gained notoriety beyond the lesbian community, earning the ire of social conservatives who argue that it normalizes deviant sexual relations for impressionable children. *Heather Has Two Mommies* is one of the most frequently banned books in the United States.

was something that was my job, my responsibility, and I was supposed to take care of the baby and go out to work and still take care of the house and do all this crap. And it was like, bullshit! That's not right. So a lot of what I come into this [lesbian family] with was, I want to make it different. I want to do it the way I thought it should have been done. And that's that you're supported.

SARAH: I think that that's why my pregnancy was so, was so positive, is because she was always there. She was there to say, "Did you take your vitamins? Why not?" Or "Don't eat that, don't take that." Or "This is good for you, take this." And just really, really supportive.

Pat and Sarah attributed this supportive mutuality in their expectations and experience of Sarah's pregnancy to the fact that they were "two women doing this," an argument in line with the thesis that gender socialization both prepares women for mothering and orients their behavior toward relationality. But as Pat's account of her decision to support Sarah attests, along with other accounts of nonbirth mothers who made clear they had no desire to physically bear a child, it is not given in nature or in some primary socially acquired gender identity that women *as* women will automatically or necessarily mother, nurture, or support loved ones who do. Rather, mothering and gender are reproduced (or not) in a particular interpersonal and sociohistorical context.

Questions for Study and Review

1. Have changes in the American family been positive for women, and how have these transformations altered the shape of American communities?

2. Do you see lesbian families as a challenge to or an affirmation of the traditional family? Why and how?

3. Family has been a central trope for many of the activists analyzed in this volume. How do you think earlier activists like the Goldwater Girls or Women's Advocates would have responded to the lesbian families analyzed by Sullivan?

4. How have new assisted reproductive technologies changed the form and function of families in recent decades? What are the consequences for women, for families, and for communities of disconnecting sex from reproduction?

Suggested Readings and Web Sites

Mary Bernstein and Renate Reimann, *Queer Families, Queer Politics: Challenging Culture and the State* (2001)
Lisa Duggan and Nan D. Hunter, eds., *Sex Wars: Sexual Dissent and Political Culture* (1995)
Lillian Faderman and Stuart Timmons, *Gay L.A.: A History of Sexual Outlaws, Power Politics and Lipstick Lesbians* (2006)
Kath Weston, *Families We Choose: Lesbians, Gays and Kinship* (1997)
History of the Family
    http://www.digitalhistory.uh.edu/historyonline/famhist_biblio.cfm#4

A Statistical Portrait

RUTH MILKMAN
VANESSA V. TINSLEY

To recapture the historical experience of women, scholars have pursued a host of new methods and turned to a variety of sources. Some famous or elite women left letters, diaries, and family papers, which historians have used to re-create these women's relations with their fathers and husbands as well as with female kin and friends. These documents also provide information about women's activities in churches, schools, and voluntary organizations as well as intimations of their attitudes toward children. A smaller number of poor, working-class, and minority women also wrote about their lives or had their spoken testimony transcribed by others. Yet uncovering and understanding the daily lives and thoughts of these nonelite and less well-known women, and their male kin and neighbors, requires investigation of more than the conventional literary sources. Examinations of physical artifacts such as housing or dress, the use of visual and aural documents in the form of photographs or recordings, the gathering of oral histories, and the analysis of quantitative data all provide new means of illuminating the past.

The use of statistical information is especially important for reconstructing the objective boundaries of people's lives. Such data might include the relative numbers of women and men in a community, the average number of children borne by an adult woman, the likelihood of a woman working for wages, the types of jobs she might hold and her average earnings, the life expectancy of women and men, and how each of these varied by region, race, class, and ethnic background as well as over time.

For most women, the size and makeup of their household, the amount and type of domestic labor they performed, and their access to paid employment set the framework of their lives. These factors shaped their relationships with relatives, neighbors, and the larger community and powerfully affected the opportunities open to them for education, recreation, and participation in public activities or institutions. For most of our nation's history, women of all regions, races, classes, and ethnic backgrounds shared certain experiences. More than 90 percent of all women did housework, were married, or lived in marriage-like relations, and bore children at some point in their lives. Yet more often it was not these broad similarities but rather the differences among women that were important in shaping the contours of individual, family, and community history. Thus, it is critical to locate women in place as well as in time and to chart change over time both for women as women and in relation to men.

Since the late nineteenth century, several new factors have emerged as significant in shaping the lives of women and men. Before this time, it was the death of one of the partners that ended most marriages. But with the dramatic increase in life expectancy after 1900, more and more marriages were ended by separation and divorce. This, in turn, created new types of households and placed different demands on women and men in terms of providing for themselves and their children. Over the same period, women's fertility rate declined, though more slowly for some groups than for others. The size of the average household shrank, and more women graduated from high school and college and entered the paid labor force. At the same time, women were still relegated to certain types of jobs, and black and immigrant women faced an even narrower range of choices than native-born white women. The gap between men's and women's wages remained remarkably consistent, although the gap between the wages of blacks and whites, especially for women, closed significantly after World War II.

In the tables, figures, and graphs that follow, Ruth Milkman and Vanessa V. Tinsley provide quantitative portraits of women from a range of families and communities and across the expanse of American history. Though limited by the amount, types, and quality of data collected in past centuries, these statistical snapshots allow us to view our ancestors with a new clarity and to compare their experiences—their life expectancy, the size of their families, the racial and sexual balance in their communities, their opportunities for paid work, and their participation in various occupations—with our own.

The articles in this volume describe women in specific times and places and engaged in a variety of activities—childbirth and childrearing, factory work, shopping and fashion, wartime service, or political or religious pursuits. Consulting the graphs and tables provided here as you read the articles will help you place the women you read about within the larger context of the American experience. The statistical information will help you grasp better the different relationships between native-born white and immigrant women and men in early twentieth-century families. You will see, for example, that in the first group, there were roughly equal numbers of women and men, but in the second, there were substantially more men than women. You can perceive the importance of bearing children, rearing children, and earning wages for both white and black women, as well as how these experiences differed between the two groups. Fertility rates (the average number of births per woman) declined much more quickly for white than African American women in the twentieth century, yet the percentage of black women in the paid labor force was much higher than that for whites until 1970.

You can begin to imagine what dramatic changes in individual and family life occurred as the average woman bore fewer and fewer children over the course of the century, with a woman of the 1970s bearing only half the number of children borne by her turn-of-the-century grandmother. And that granddaughter, born in the "baby boom" of 1946–1964, had a much better chance than any of her foremothers of attending high school or college, working for wages at some time in her life, and joining a union. She was also likelier, however, to get a divorce, become head of a household, or live alone for some part of her life. These changes in family and work life give us a new perspective on what a political movement like feminism might mean to different generations of women, or to African American women, who by the 1960s had long been in the paid labor force in large numbers, versus white women, who were just entering paid labor in large numbers.

These statistical portraits throw into sharp relief the outlines of women's lives across the last century of our nation's history. Tracing the common as well as the quite different experiences of women of various ethnic backgrounds, classes, and races across both time and place, the charts, graphs, and tables included here set the contours of our own lives in a larger context and help us understand the conditions and the constraints under which earlier Americans carved out their individual, familial, communal, and national identities.

Suggested Readings and Web Sites

Sandra Opdycke, *The Routledge Historical Atlas of Women in America* (2000)

U.S. Bureau of the Census, *Negro Population, 1790–1915* (1918)

U.S. Department of Labor Bureau of Labor Statistics, *Women in the Labor Force: A Databook* (2006)

Lynn Weiner, *From Working Girl to Working Mother: The Female Labor Force in the United States,1820–1980* (1985)

Women's Action Coalition, *WAC Stats: The Facts About Women* (1993)

Center for American Women and Politics
   http://www.cawp.rutgers.edu/

United States Historical Census Data Browser
   http://fisher.lib.virginia.edu/collections/stats/histcensus

Equal Pay site of the AFL-CIO
   http://www. aflcio.org/issues/jobseconomy/women/equalpay/index.cfm

Women's Data Center, Institute for Women's Policy Research
   http://www.iwpr.org/femstats/index.htm

Women Working Website, 1800–1930
   http://ocp.hul.harvard.edu/ww/

Over the last century, life expectancy has increased dramatically for the entire U.S. population. However, women's longevity has increased substantially more than men's, among both whites and blacks. Whites of both sexes had significantly higher life expectancies at the beginning of the twentieth century. The life expectancies of black females born in the mid-1960s, however, began to exceed those of white males born in the same year and continues to be slightly higher for those born at the beginning of the twenty-first century. Figure A.1 shows the rise in life expectancy by gender and race from 1900 to 2003.

FIGURE A.1 LIFE EXPECTANCY (IN YEARS) AT BIRTH, BY GENDER AND RACE, 1900–2003

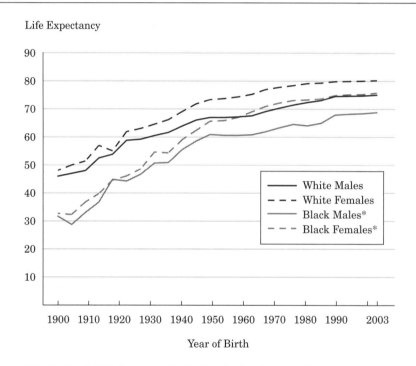

Life Expectancy

Year of Birth

For 1980 and 1985, figures are for blacks only; for prior years, figures are for "Negro and other."

SOURCE: U.S. Bureau of the Census, *Historical Statistics of the United States, Colonial Times to 1970* (Washington: GPO, 1975), 55; U.S. Bureau of the Census, *Statistical Abstract of the United States: 2006* (Washington: GPO, 2006, 125th ed.), 76.

Fertility rates (the average number of births per woman) have fluctuated significantly in the past century. They fell gradually in the period from 1890 to the Great Depression of the 1930s, revived during World War II and in the "baby boom" of the postwar period, and fell again to reach new lows in the 1970s before climbing upward to around 2.0 in the 1990s for whites. Fertility rates were consistently higher for blacks and other minorities than for whites until 2002, when fertility rates for blacks dipped below that of whites for the first time; in general, the trends over time are similar in direction for both groups. Figure A.2 shows the fluctuation in births per woman for whites from 1890 to 2002 and for blacks and others from 1940 to 2002. Data are not available for fertility rates for blacks and others from 1890 to 1939.

FIGURE A.2 FERTILITY RATES (BIRTHS PER WOMAN) FOR WOMEN IN THE UNITED STATES, BY RACE, 1890–2002.

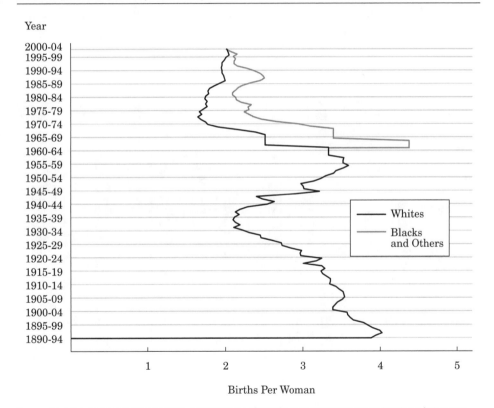

SOURCE: Ansley J. Coale and Melvin Zelnik, *New Estimates of Fertility and Population in the United States* (Princeton: Princeton University Press, 1963), 36; U.S. Bureau of the Census, *Statistical Abstract of the United States: 2006* (Washington: GPO, 2006, 125th ed.), 67.

A major source of population growth in the period before World War I and in the period from the 1960s to the present has been immigration. (See Figure A.3.) However, the two waves of mass immigration differ in important ways. In the pre–World War I era, men outnumbered women among immigrants, whereas more recently, the opposite has been true. Sex ratios have shifted in favor of women in the U.S. population as a whole in the course of the last century (due largely to the relatively greater increase in female longevity). The shift has been most pronounced among the foreign-born, reflecting the disproportionate growth of female immigration. By 2004, however, foreign-born women were outnumbered by foreign-born men in the population. A second difference between the two waves of immigration is that in the pre–World War I era, the vast majority of immigrants were Europeans; in the recent period, immigrants have come predominantly from Asia and Latin America.

FIGURE A.3 SEX RATIOS IN U.S. POPULATION, FOREIGN-BORN AND TOTAL, 1890–2004

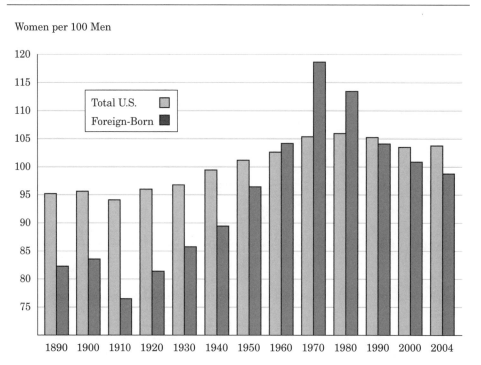

Women per 100 Men

SOURCE: U.S. Bureau of the Census, *Historical Statistics of the United States. Colonial Times to 1970* (Washington: GPO, 1975) 14; U.S. Bureau of the Census, "Historical Census Statistics of the United States on the Foreign-born Population of the United States: 1850–2000," Population Division Working Paper No. 81 (Washington, DC 2006) 48–52; U.S. Bureau of the Census, *Statistical Abstract of the United States: 2006* (Washington: GPO, 2006, 125th ed.), 13, 46.

Note that the graphs shown in Figure A.3 and A.4 are for the *foreign-born population* rather than for *immigrants* entering the United States in a given year. This creates a time lag effect: The sex composition of immigrants changed sooner than that of the foreign-born population shown in Figure A.3; similarly, the change in the representation of immigrants of various national origins occurred sooner than the data in Figure A.4 might appear to suggest. We use the figures for the foreign-born here, however, because they are much more reliable than those for immigration itself for the recent period, due to the difficulty in counting the large numbers of undocumented or illegal immigrants. In addition, figures for the foreign-born are more meaningful in the long run because there is substantial re-migration back to the home country among many groups. However, although they are better than the available figures for immigrants entering the nation, the census data that these tables are based on are widely believed to have undercounted recent immigrants. Thus, these figures should be interpreted with caution.

FIGURE A.4 U.S. FOREIGN-BORN POPULATION, BY REGION OF BIRTH, 1890–2000

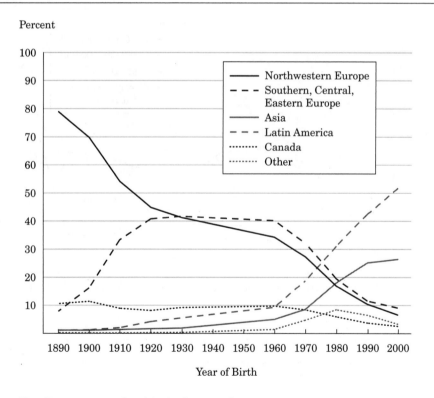

Note: Percentages are of total foreign-born population.

SOURCE: U.S. Bureau of the Census, "Historical Census Statistics of the United States on the Foreign-born Population of the United States: 1850–2000," Population Division Working Paper No. 81 (Washington, DC 2006) 109–110.

Another characteristic of the twentieth-century United States was enormous internal migration, especially the movement of population from rural to urban areas. Here there were no significant differences in the behavior by sex, but the implications of urbanization were nonetheless profound for women. Figure A.5 shows the pattern of urbanization from 1890 to 2000, which mainly involved shifts from rural to small- and medium-sized urban settlements (including suburbs, which grew dramatically in the post–World War II years). The huge shift in population in 2000 from smaller cities to very large ones is artificially inflated because of a change in how the 2000 Census defined urban areas.[*] The smaller cities were actually suburbs of larger metropolitan areas and were reclassified as such in 2000.

FIGURE A.5 PERCENT OF U.S. POPULATION LIVING IN RURAL AND URBAN AREAS, BY SIZE OF URBAN TERRITORY, 1890–2000

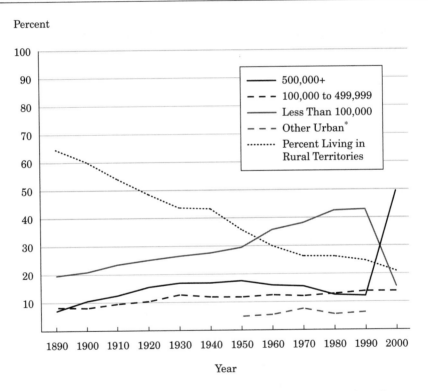

This category was introduced in the 1950 census; hence, no figures appear for earlier years.

SOURCE: U.S. Bureau of the Census, 2000 Census of Population and Housing, Population and Housing Unit Counts PHC-3-1, United States Summary (Washington: GPO, 2004), 9,12.

---

[*]The number of people living in urban/rural places changed significantly in the 2000 Census as the current urban definition ignored place boundaries entirely when defining urban areas, while the 1950–1990 urban definition used whole places in defining urban areas. Essentially, the smaller suburbs (<100,000) around a metropolitan area in 1950–1990 became part of a larger urban area (1,000,000+) in 2000.

The average size of households in the United States was nearly twice as large a century ago as it is today, as Figure A.6 shows. This trend reflects not only lower fertility but also the increasing diversity of household types. Many more people live outside of traditional families today than in the past. The U.S. government refers to such people as "primary individuals," a group that includes people living alone as well as those living in households whose members are unrelated by kinship or marriage. In addition, there are more single-parent households today than in the past—most of them headed by women. Figure A.7 summarizes the changes in the distribution of household types from 1940 to 2004.

FIGURE A.6 AVERAGE HOUSEHOLD SIZE, 1890–2004

Number of Persons

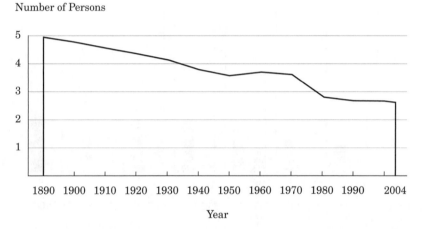

Year

SOURCE: U.S. Bureau of the Census, *Historical Statistics of the United States, Colonial Times to 1970* (Washington: GPO, 1975), 41; U.S. Bureau of the Census, *Statistical Abstract of the United States: 2006* (Washington: GPO, 2006, 125th ed.), 51.

FIGURE A.7 DISTRIBUTION OF HOUSEHOLD TYPES, 1940–2004

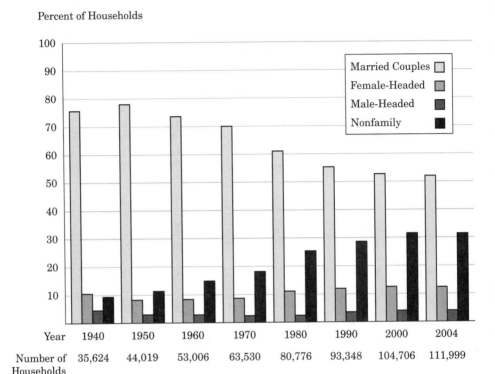

Percent of Households

Year	1940	1950	1960	1970	1980	1990	2000	2004
Number of Households (Thousands)	35,624	44,019	53,006	63,530	80,776	93,348	104,706	111,999

SOURCE: U.S. Bureau of the Census, *Historical Statistics of the United States, Colonial Times to 1970* (Washington: GPO, 1975), 41; U.S. Bureau of the Census, *Statistical Abstract of the United States: 2006* (Washington: GPO, 2006, 125th ed.), 51.

A major factor contributing to the declining proportion of traditional husband-wife households is the dramatic rise in the divorce rate. Figure A.8 shows the rates of marriage and divorce for selected years between 1920 and 1990.[*] Both rates rose sharply immediately after both world wars and both declined during the early 1930s, as a result of the Great Depression. In the late 1960s, the divorce rate rose sharply until it stabilized in the 1980s. Marriage rates have been falling steadily since 1970.

---

[*]Collection of detailed data on marriage and divorce rates was suspended in 1996 because of limitations in the information collected by the states as well as budgetary considerations. Rates are now commonly reported as marriages or divorces per 1,000 persons rather than unmarried/married women.

FIGURE A.8 MARRIAGE AND DIVORCE RATES, 1920–1990

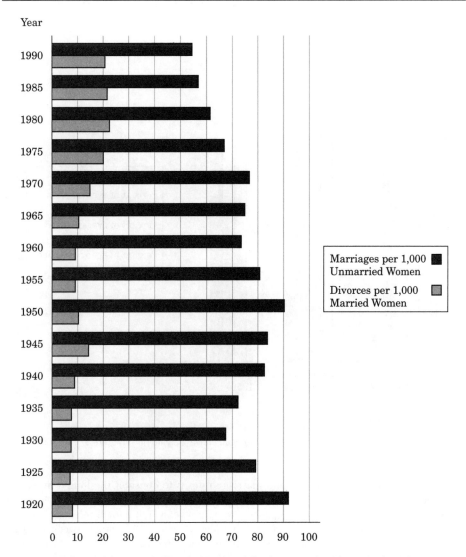

Year

SOURCE: U.S. Bureau of the Census, *Historical Statistics of the United States. Colonial Times to 1970* (Washington: GPO, 1975) 64; National Center for Health Statistics, Vital Statistics of the United States, 1988, Vol III, Marriage and Divorce (Washington: Public Health Service 1996) Section 1, p. 2, Section 2, p. 1; Clarke, Sally C. "Advance Report of Final Marriage Statistics, 1989–1990," Vol 43 No. 12, Supplement. (Hyattsville, MD: National Center for Health Statistics 1995) 7; Clarke, Sally C. "Advance Report of Final Divorce Statistics: 1989–1990," Vol 43 No. 8, Supplement. (Hyattsville, MD: National Center for Health Statistics 1995) 9.

FIGURE A.9 PERCENTAGE EVER MARRYING, DIVORCING, REMARRYING, AND REDIVORCING FOR WOMEN BORN BETWEEN 1910–14, 1930–34, AND 1950–54

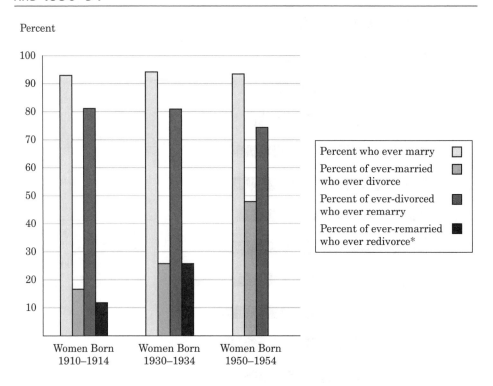

*Data for 1950–54 not available.

SOURCE: Andrew J. Cherlin, *Marriage, Divorce, Remarriage* (Cambridge: Harvard University Press, 1981), 122–23.

Another way to look at divorce and marriage rates is to consider the long-term experiences of individuals, rather than the annual rates of marriage and divorce. Figure A.9 shows the frequency of marrying, divorcing, remarrying, and redivorcing for three generations of women: those born between 1910 and 1914, between 1930 and 1934, and between 1950 and 1954. The figures vividly illustrate how much more common divorce became in the twentieth century, as well as the fact that while most people who divorce do eventually remarry, many of them later redivorce.

Perhaps the single most dramatic change for women in the twentieth century was the increased extent of their involvement in the paid labor force, especially since World War II. While in 1890 only 18 percent of women were employed outside the home, by 2000 almost 60 percent were so employed. Meanwhile, male labor force participation rates declined significantly over the same period. (See Figure A.10.)

FIGURE A.10 LABOR FORCE PARTICIPATION OF WOMEN AND MEN, 1890–2005

Women Workers (Millions)

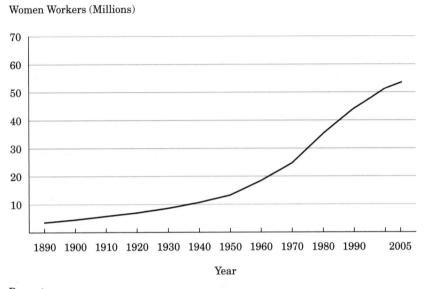

Year

Percent

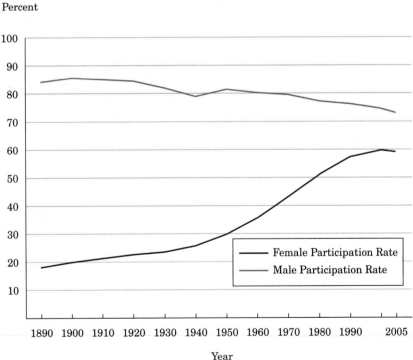

Year

SOURCE: U.S. Bureau of the Census, *Historical Statistics of the United States, Colonial Times to 1970* (Washington: GPO, 1975), 131–32; U.S. Bureau of the Census, *Statistical Abstract of the United States:* 2006 (Washington: GPO, 2006, 125th ed.), 365. For 1890–1950 this table uses government data from the decennial census; for 1960–1987, the source is the Current Population Survey. These two sources use slightly different enumeration methods; thus, the two sets of figures are not strictly comparable.

The feminization of the workforce has been accompanied by feminization of labor union membership. (See Figure A.11.) However, since the mid-1950s, while labor union membership has become increasingly feminized, unionization levels in the U.S. workforce as a whole have declined. With few exceptions, the absolute number of women union members increased steadily over the course of the twentieth century. From 77,000 female union members in 1910, the number grew to 260,000 in 1930; 800,000 in 1940; 3,000,000 in 1944 (at the height of women's wartime employment); 3,304,000 in 1960; and 7,191,000 in 1980. Since 1980, the actual number of female unionists has grown slowly to 7,626,000 in 2005; as union

FIGURE A.11 FEMINIZATION OF U.S. LABOR UNION MEMBERSHIP, 1910–2005

^{a}*Union*

^{b}*Unions and emloyee associations*

^{c}*Represented by unions and employee associations (including nonmembers covered by contracts)*

SOURCE: U.S. Bureau of the Census, *Historical Statistics of the United States. Colonial Times to 1970* (Washington: GPO, 1975) 131; Gladys Dickason, "Women in Labor Unions," *The Annals of the American Academy of Political and Social Science*, 251 (May 1947), 70–71; U.S. Department of Labor, Women's Bureau, Bulletin 298, *Time of Change: 1983 Handbook on Women Workers* (Washington: GOS, 1983), 49; Leo Troy and Neil Shelfin, *U.S. Union Sourcebook* (West Orange, NJ: Industrial Relations and Information Services, 1985), A-1, A-2; U.S. Department of Labor, Bureau of Labor Statistics, *Women in the Labor Force: A Databook* (Washington 2006) 79.

membership has generally decreased, the proportion of union workers who are women has risen markedly to comprise 44 percent of all union members.

Black women had much higher rates of labor force participation than white women during most of the previous century, but in recent years the gap has been nearly eliminated. (See Figure A.12.) Similarly, foreign-born white women had higher participation rates than their native-born counterparts in the pre–World War II years, although by 1950 the difference was insignificant.

FIGURE A.12 WOMEN'S LABOR FORCE PARTICIPATION BY RACE AND NATIONAL ORIGIN

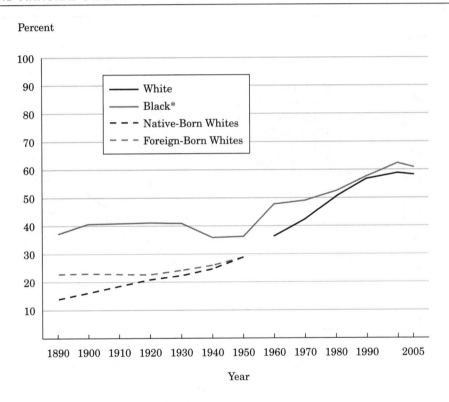

Percent

Year

*Figures for 1980 and 1986 are for blacks only; figures for earlier years are for "nonwhites" or "Negro and other." Data for 1910 are not available.

SOURCE: U.S. Bureau of the Census, *Historical Statistics of the United States. Colonial Times to 1970* (Washington: GPO, 1975) 133; U.S. Bureau of the Census, *Statistical Abstract of the United States: 2006* (Washington: GPO, 2006, 125th ed.), 387; Clarence D. Long, *The Labor Force under Changing Income and Employment* (Princeton: Princeton University Press 1958), Table A-4; U.S. Department of Labor, Bureau of Labor Statistics, *Women in the Labor Force: A Databook* (Washington 2006) 10–11.

There has been a dramatic change in the pattern of female employment over the life cycle as large numbers of married women and mothers have begun working outside the home in the postwar era (see Figure A.13.). In 1940 only 15 percent of married women with husbands were present in the paid labor force; by 2005, over 60 percent of this group of women worked outside the home. While single (never married) women are still more likely to be employed than married women, the gap has narrowed considerably over time. And since the late 1960s, widows and divorced women actually have had a lower labor force participation rate than married women, reversing the previous pattern.

FIGURE A.13 WOMEN'S LABOR FORCE PARTICIPATION, BY MARITAL STATUS, 1890–2005

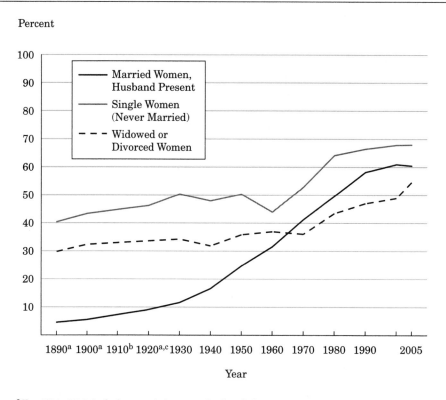

[a]*For 1890–1930, includes married women, husband absent.*
[b]*Data for 1910 are not available.*
[c]*For 1920, widowed and divorced women are included with single women.*

SOURCE: U.S. Bureau of the Census, *Historical Statistics of the United States. Colonial Times to 1970* (Washington: GPO, 1975) 133; U.S. Bureau of the Census, *Statistical Abstract of the United States: 2006* (Washington: GPO, 2006, 125th ed.), 392; U.S. Department of Labor, Bureau of Labor Statistics, *Women in the Labor Force: A Databook* (Washington 2006) 12.

FIGURE A.14 LABOR FORCE PARTICIPATION RATES OF MARRIED WOMEN, HUSBAND PRESENT, BY PRESENCE AND AGE OF OWN CHILDREN, 1950–1987

Percent in the Labor Force

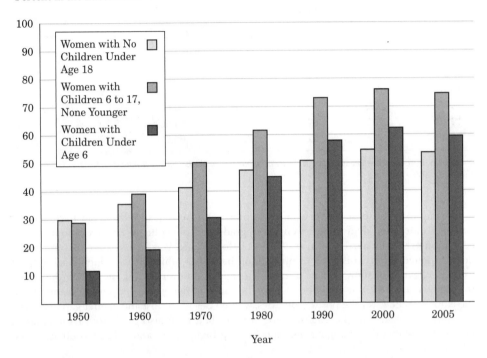

Year

SOURCE: U.S. Department of Labor, Women's Bureau, Bulletin 298, *Times of Change: 1983 Handbook on Women Workers* (Washington: GPO, 1983) 20; Bureau of Labor Statistics, unpublished data from the March supplement of the Current Population Survey 1948–2004; U.S. Bureau of the Census, *Statistical Abstract of the United States: 2007* (Washington: GPO, 2007, 126th ed.), 380; U.S. Department of Labor, Bureau of Labor Statistics, *Women in the Labor Force: A Databook* (Washington 2006) 16.

The labor force participation rate of married mothers has increased dramatically since World War II, especially since 1970: (See Figure A.14.) A majority of married women with children under age 6 are now employed, and today married mothers of children aged 6 to 17 are more likely to be employed than married women with no children. As recently as 1950, married women without children were more likely to work outside the home than married mothers. Table A.1 provides further details about the labor force participation of married mothers, showing that the majority of those with very young children (1 year old or younger) are now employed outside the home and that black married mothers have much higher labor force participation rates than white married mothers, whose rates are themselves high. These figures do not include single mothers, who also frequently work when their children are young.

TABLE A.1 LABOR FORCE PARTICIPATION RATES OF MARRIED WOMEN, HUSBAND PRESENT, BY AGE OF YOUNGEST CHILD AND BY RACE, 1975–1987

	WHITE MARRIED WOMEN YOUNGEST CHILD AGED:			BLACK MARRIED WOMEN YOUNGEST CHILD AGED:		
	1 YEAR OR LESS	*3–5 YEARS*	*6–13 YEARS*	*1 YEAR OR LESS*	*3–5 YEARS*	*6–13 YEARS*
1987	51.2	59.3	69.6	70.3	77.9	80.7
1980	37.7	49.4	61.4	52.9	72.3	71.8
1975	29.2	40.3	50.8	50.0	61.7	64.9
1990	53.3	62.5	72.6	64.4	80.4	77.6
2005	55.5	62.1	72.8	65.5	77.7	78.7

Source: U.S. Bureau of the Census, *Statistical Abstract of the United States: 2007* (Washington: GPO, 2007, 126th ed.), 380.

Throughout the past century, more women than men graduated from high school, although more men than women went on to graduate from college. The sex ratio in higher education gradually narrowed in the period before World War II, but after the war it suddenly widened again. This was a result both of the GI bill, which provided financial support for the college education of many returning soldiers (an overwhelmingly male group), and the fact that after the war, higher education became an increasingly important credential in the labor market. Over the postwar decades, women began to close the gender gap in college education rates and in the 1990s, more women than men also graduated from college. Figure A.15 shows the changing sex ratios among high school and college graduates from 1890 to 2004.

FIGURE A.15 SEX RATIOS OF HIGH SCHOOL AND COLLEGE GRADUATES IN THE UNITED STATES, 1890–2004

Women per 100 Men

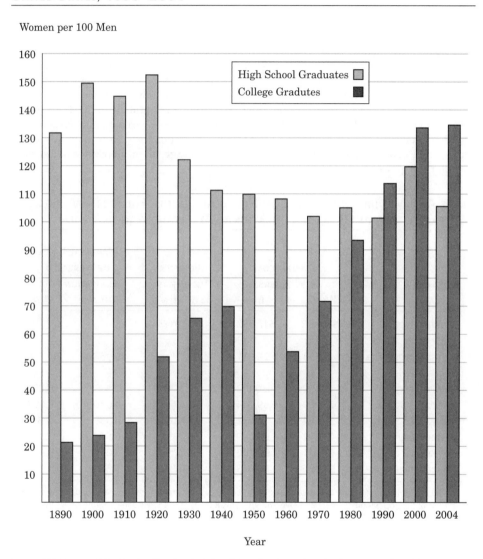

Year

SOURCE: U.S. Bureau of the Census, *Historical Statistics of the United States, Colonial Times to 1970* (Washingon: GPO, 1975), 379, 385–86; U.S Bureau of the Census, *Statistical Abstract of the United States:* 2006 (Washington: GPO, 2006; 125th ed.), 174, 186.

Figure A.15 shows the educational attainment of the entire adult population. For the smaller adult population that was in the labor force, the historical pattern of gender differences in education is fairly similar, except that the gap between women and men closed sooner. (See Table A.2.) In 1940, women workers had completed a median of 11 years of education, compared to 8.6 years for men workers; by 1962, women workers had a median of 12.3 years, compared to 12.1 for their male counterparts.[*] However, Table A.2 makes clear, the experience of four decades of women achieving equal or greater educational attainment is not reflected in the earnings of male and female workers in 2004. At all educational levels, full-time, year-round women workers had earnings of no more than 70 percent of men with the same educational attainment in 2004. Full-time, year-round women workers who had completed an associate's degree earned less, on average, than men who had completed high school; and full-time, year-round women workers who earned professional degrees earned less, on average, than men who had earned bachelor's degrees.

TABLE A.2 MEDIAN INCOME IN 2004 OF YEAR-ROUND, FULL-TIME WORKERS 25 YEARS OLD AND OVER, BY EDUCATIONAL ATTAINMENT AND GENDER

LEVEL OF EDUCATION	MEDIAN INCOME OF WORKERS: WOMEN	MEN	WOMEN'S INCOME AS % OF MEN'S	MARGINAL VALUE OF INCREASED EDUCATION FOR: WOMEN	MEN
Less than high school diploma	$10,198	$17,552	58.10%		
High school diploma (incl. GED)	16,164	29,331	55.11%	$5,966	$11,779
Some college	21,159	36,162	58.51%	4,995	6,831
Associate's degree	25,199	39,764	63.37%	4,040	3,602
Bachelor's degree	31,584	51,081	61.83%	6,385	11,317
Master's degree	42,242	63,259	66.78%	10,658	12,178
Professional degree	50,311	90,209	55.77%	8,069	26,950
Doctoral degree	55,996	80,033	69.97%	5,685	⁻10,176

Source: Bureau of Labor Statistics, Current Population Survey, CPS 2005, Table 8, "Income in 2004 by Educational Attainment of the Population 18 Years and Over, by Age, Sex, Race Alone, and Hispanic Origin: 2005," Internet Release Date: October 26, 2006.

---

[*]Figures for 1940 are from U.S. Bureau of the Census, *Historical Statistics of the United States, Colonial Times to 1957* (Washington: GPO, 1960), 214; and for 1962 from U.S. Bureau of Labor Statistics, Bulletin 2217, *Handbook of Labor Statistics* (Washington: GPO, June 1985), 164.

From 1955 to 1985, women's earnings fluctuated between 60 and 65 percent of men's earnings, despite the dramatic increase in female labor force participation and the passage in the 1960s of national legislation prohibiting sex and race discrimination in employment. After 1985, however, women's earnings, relative to men's, began to rise so that in 2005, women earned almost 80 percent of what men earned. (See Figure A.16.)

FIGURE A.16 MEDIAN EARNINGS OF YEAR-ROUND, FULL-TIME WORKERS, BY SEX, 1955–2005

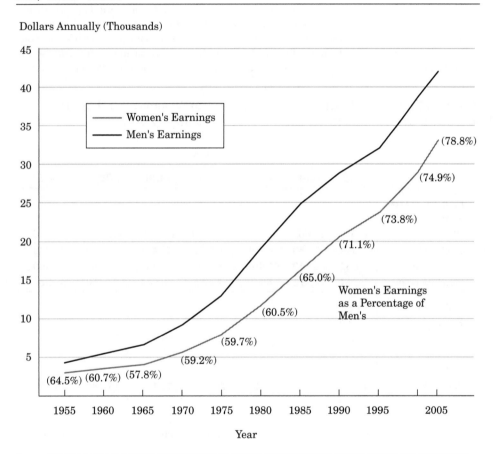

Dollars Annually (Thousands)

SOURCE: U.S. Census Bureau; "Table P 36 Full-Time, Year-Round All Workers by Median Income and Sex: 1955 to 2005," last modified Nov. 29, 2006; http://www.census.gov/hhes/www/income/histinc/p36ar.html.

Statistics were compiled on average hourly earnings, by sex, for production workers in 25 manufacturing industries between 1914 and 1948. Manufacturing jobs generally paid better than such traditionally female occupations as domestic service or clerical or sales work, but even in manufacturing, women were paid far less than men. In 1914 a woman factory worker earned 62¢ for every $1 earned by a man; in 1935 the rate was 70¢ to $1; and in 1948 it was 73¢ to $1 (U.S. Bureau of the Census, *Historical Statistics of the United States, Colonial Times to 1970* [Washington: GPO, 1975], 172).

The earnings gap between black and white workers has narrowed significantly over time. Black women workers continue to earn less than their white counterparts, but the race gap in earnings among men has been even more resistant to change. All the figures in Figure A.16 and Table A.3 are for full-time, year-round workers only. If part-time or part-year workers were included, the disparity in earnings by sex would be far greater, since many women work part time.

The primary reason for the large disparity between the sexes in earnings is not sex discrimination in wages for men and women doing the same jobs. Although this does occur, much

TABLE A.3 MEDIAN WAGE OR SALARY INCOME OF YEAR-ROUND, FULL-TIME WORKERS, BY SEX AND RACE, SELECTED YEARS, 1939–2005

	YEAR						
	1939	**1960**	**1970**	**1980**	**1990**	**2000**	**2005**
MEDIAN ANNUAL EARNINGS:							
White Men	$1,419	$5,662	$9,373	$19,720	$30,081	$40,253	$43,696
Black* Men	639	3,789	6,598	13,875	21,481	30,489	34,233
White Women	863	3,410	5,490	11,703	20,839	29,951	34,100
Black* Women	327	2,372	4,674	10,915	18,544	25,750	30,363
EARNINGS RATIOS:							
White Women as % of White Men	60.8%	60.2%	58.6%	59.3%	69.3%	74.4%	78.0%
Black* Men as % of White Men	45.0%	66.9%	70.4%	70.3%	71.4%	75.7%	78.3%
Black* Women as % of Black* Men	51.2%	62.6%	70.8%	78.7%	86.3%	84.5%	88.7%
Black* Women as % of White Women	37.9%	69.6%	85.1%	93.3%	89.0%	86.0%	89.0%

*Blacks only for 1980–2005, blacks and other minorities for earlier years.

Note: After 2001, respondents to the Current Population Surveys were allowed to report more than one race. The figures reported here are for respondents who reported only a single race.

Source: U.S. Census Bureau; "Table P 36 Full-Time, Year-Round White Workers by Median Income and Sex: 1955 to 2005," last modified Nov. 29, 2006; http://www.census.gov/hhes/www/income/histinc/p36w.html.

more significant is the fact that women and men are segregated into distinct occupations, and those occupations that are primarily female have lower pay rates than those that are predominantly male. Even in classifications of workers by major occupational group, the concentration of women in certain types of jobs, and of men in other types, is quite apparent. An even greater degree of segregation is evident in more detailed classifications. For example, the category "professional, technical, and kindred workers" groups such predominantly female occupations as nursing, teaching, and social work with occupations that primarily employ men, such as engineering and dentistry.

Table A.4 shows the distribution of women and men workers across major occupational categories in 1900, 1930, 1960, and 1990.

TABLE A.4 Occupational Distribution of U.S. Workers, by Sex, 1900, 1930, 1960, and 1990

| | YEAR | | | | | | | |
| | 1900 | | 1930 | | 1960 | | 1990 | |
INDUSTRY GROUP	MEN	WOMEN	MEN	WOMEN	MEN	WOMEN	MEN	WOMEN
Professional, Technical, and Kindred Workers	3.4%	8.2%	4.8%	13.8%	10.4%	13.3%	14.9%	18.6%
Managers, Officials, and Proprietors	6.8	1.4	8.8	2.7	10.8	3.8	13.6%	11.0%
Clerical and Kindred Workers	2.8	4.0	5.5	20.9	7.2	30.9	5.9%	27.8%
Salesworkers	4.6	4.3	6.1	6.8	7.0	8.3	11.1%	13.1%
Craftsmen, Foremen, and Kindred Workers	12.6	1.4	16.2	1.0	20.6	1.3	19.3%	2.2%
Operatives, Laborers, and Kindred Workers	25.0	26.3	29.0	18.9	29.0	17.8	20.7%	8.5%
Private Household Workers	–*	28.7	–	17.8	–	8.4	0.0%	1.4%
Other Service Workers	2.9	6.7	4.6	9.7	6.3	14.4	9.9%	16.4%
Farmworkers	41.7	19.0	24.8	8.4	8.5	1.9	4.5%	1.0%

Note: Figures may not total 100 percent because of rounding.

*– = less than 1 percent.

Source: U.S. Bureau of the Census, *Historical Statistics of the United States. Colonial Times to 1970* (Washington: GPO, 1975) 139–140. Bureau of Labor Statistics, Current Population Survey. Contact the BLS Division of Labor Force Statistics for data at (202) 691–6378 or e-mail cpsinfo@bls.gov.

Figure A.17 shows the occupational distribution for men and women in 2005. Although the categories are somewhat different in the 2005 count, the general pattern of employment by sex and the ways in which it has changed over time can be observed. In 1900, over one-fourth of all women workers worked as private household workers. By 2005, about one-fifth of all women workers were still in service occupations but very few (about 1 percent of all women workers) were employed as private household workers. Another fourth of the female labor force in 1900 was made up of factory workers—operatives and laborers; in 2005 less than 5

FIGURE A.17   OCCUPATIONAL DISTRIBUTION OF U.S. WORKERS, BY SEX, 2005

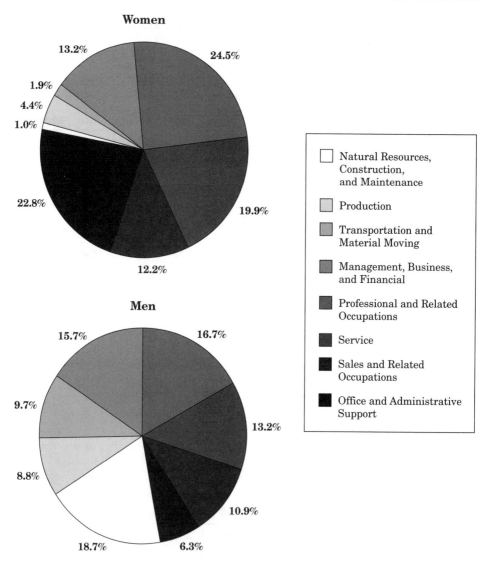

SOURCE: U.S. Department of Labor, Bureau of Labor Statistics, *Women in the Labor Force: A Databook* (Washington 2006), 26–27.

percent of women workers were so employed. Farmworkers made up about one-fifth of all women workers in 1900 but accounted for less, about 1 percent, of women workers in 2005, one of many jobs included in the *natural resources, construction and maintenance* category. Conversely, the occupations employing the bulk of the female workforce today—professional, clerical, service, and sales—were relatively insignificant in 1900. Changes in the overall occupational structure have also been responsible for changes in the distribution of men's occupations. Most interestingly, however, is that while particular occupations for both men and women have changed over time, occupational segregation by sex has persisted intact.

In addition to segregation by sex, segregation by race, ethnicity, and nativity has also characterized the U.S. labor force. Table A.5 shows the occupational distribution of women by

TABLE A.5 OCCUPATIONAL DISTRIBUTION OF U.S. WOMEN WORKERS 15 YEARS AND OLDER, BY RACE AND NATIVITY, 1900

	NATIVE WHITE		FOREIGN-BORN	
OCCUPATIONAL GROUP	BOTH PARENTS NATIVE-BORN	ONE OR BOTH PARENTS FOREIGN-BORN	WHITE	BLACK
Agricultural Laborers*	5.0%	0.6%	0.6%	33.5%
Farmers and Other Agricultural Pursuits†	9.9	1.7	4.3	6.3
Professional Service	15.1	9.9	3.0	1.3
Manufacturing and Mechanical Pursuits	27.0	40.1	31.4	2.8
Laundresses	2.3	2.6	5.0	18.6
Servants and Waitresses	17.7	20.9	38.0	27.8
Other Domestic and Personal Service	10.4	6.5	10.6	9.4
Saleswomen	3.4	3.9	2.0	–
Clerks, Stenographers, and Typewriters	4.8	5.9	1.6	–
Other	4.3	7.8	3.6	0.2

(Figures may not total 100 percent because of rounding.)

*Wage earners performing agricultural work
†Farm owners and supervisory personnel

Source: U.S. Bureau of the Census, *Statistics of Women at Work* (Washington, GPO, 1907), 159, 161.

FIGURE A.18   OCCUPATIONAL DISTRIBUTION OF U.S. WOMEN WORKERS 16 YEARS AND OLDER, BY RACE AND HISPANIC ORIGIN, 2002

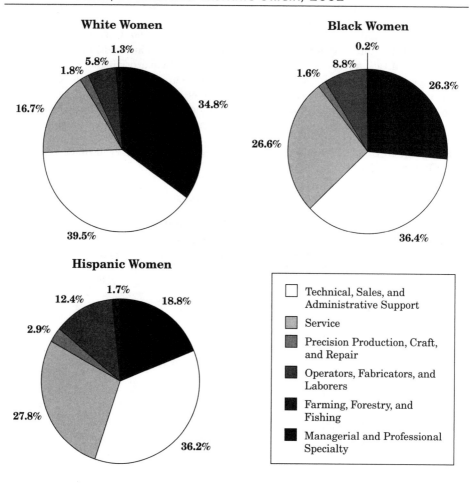

Note: Detail for the race and Hispanic-ethnicity group will not sum to totals because data for all race groups are not presented. Hispanics may be of any race and, therefore, are also included in the race groups.

SOURCE: Current Population Survey, Bureau of Labor Statistics.

race and nativity in 1900; Figure A.18 shows the occupational distribution by race and Hispanic origin for 2002. Racial segregation was extremely pronounced in 1900, with black women virtually excluded from both factory work and the emerging white-collar occupations and confined almost entirely to agricultural labor, laundry work, and domestic service. Racial segregation decreased throughout the previous century but has by no means disappeared. Relative to white women, black women today are overrepresented in service and factory jobs and underrepresented in managerial and professional jobs.

The segregation of foreign-born women workers was less extreme than that of black women in 1900, but virtually all immigrant white women workers were confined to domestic service and factory jobs at that time, while native-born white women were distributed over a somewhat greater range of occupations. Even among native-born women, those with one foreign-born parent were much more likely to be employed in manufacturing and much less likely to be employed in professional service or farmwork than their counterparts with two native-born parents.

Comparisons to the present foreign-born workers are difficult because of limitations on available data. The presence of large numbers of undocumented immigrant workers in the populations today—many of whom are not included in these statistics—make comparisons particularly treacherous. The pie chart presents 2002 data for "Hispanics" rather than immigrants (and many Hispanics today are not immigrants). The occupational distribution of Hispanic women is quite different from that of both white and black women. A higher proportion of Hispanic women work in factory jobs while a much lower proportion work in managerial and professional jobs relative to white and black women. Like black women, Hispanic women are overrepresented in service jobs relative to white women. Of course, some Hispanics are white while others are black, so these categories are not mutually exclusive.

Women finally won the right to vote with the ratification of the Nineteenth Amendment to the Constitution in 1920. Since then, women have increasingly entered political life at the local, state, and federal levels. Table A.6 shows the number of female members of the U.S. Congress rising steadily in the House of Representatives since 1920 to a total of 81 in the 109th Congress. The number of women who have been elected to the Senate, however, has been relatively small and did not increase in significant numbers until the 1990s. In the last two congressional elections in 2002 and 2004, fourteen women were elected as U.S. Senators. Women in Congress are much more likely to belong to the Democratic Party rather than the Republican Party.

TABLE A.6 NUMBER OF FEMALE MEMBERS OF CONGRESS

| | | SENATE | | HOUSE OF REPRESENTATIVES | |
CONGRESS	YEARS	DEMOCRAT	REPUBLICAN	DEMOCRAT	REPUBLICAN
1st–64th	1789–1917	0	0	0	0
65th	1917–1919	0	0	1	0
66th	1919–1921	0	0	0	0
67th	1921–1923	1	0	0	3
68th	1923–1925	0	0	0	1
69th	1925–1927	0	0	1	2
70th	1927–1929	0	0	2	3
71st	1929–1931	0	0	5	4
72nd	1931–1933	1	0	5	2
73rd	1933–1935	1	0	4	3
74th	1935–1937	2	0	4	2
75th	1937–1939	2	1	5	1
76th	1939–1941	1	0	4	4
77th	1941–1943	1	0	4	5
78th	1943–1945	1	0	2	6
79th	1945–1947	0	0	6	5
80th	1947–1949	0	1	3	4

(continued)

TABLE A.6 CONTINUED

CONGRESS	YEARS	SENATE DEMOCRAT	SENATE REPUBLICAN	HOUSE OF REPRESENTATIVES DEMOCRAT	HOUSE OF REPRESENTATIVES REPUBLICAN
81st	1949–1951	0	1	5	4
82nd	1951–1953	0	1	4	6
83rd	1953–1955	0	2	5	7
84th	1955–1957	0	1	9	8
85th	1957–1959	0	1	9	6
86th	1959–1961	1	1	9	8
87th	1961–1963	1	1	11	7
88th	1963–1965	1	1	6	6
89th	1965–1967	1	1	7	4
90th	1967–1969	0	1	6	5
91st	1969–1971	0	1	6	4
92nd	1971–1973	1	1	10	3
93rd	1973–1975	0	0	14	2
94th	1975–1977	0	0	14	5
95th	1977–1979	2	0	13	5
96th	1979–1981	0	1	11	5
97th	1981–1983	0	2	11	10
98th	1983–1985	0	2	13	11
99th	1985–1987	0	2	12	11
100th	1987–1989	1	1	12	11
101st	1989–1991	1	1	16	13
102nd	1991–1993	3	1	20	9
103rd	1993–1995	5	2	36	12
104th	1995–1997	5	4	32	17
105th	1997–1999	6	3	36	17
106th	1999–2001	6	3	41	14
107th	2001–2003	10	3	43	18
108th	2003–2005	9	5	42	21
109th	2005–2007	9	5	46	25

Source: Sandra Opdycke, *The Routledge Historical Atlas of Women in America* (New York: 2000), 278; Mildred Amer, CRS Report RS22007, *Membership of the 109th Congress: A Profile*, 5; Mildred Amer, CRS Report RS21379, *Membership of the 108th Congress: A Profile*, 5; Mildred Amer, CRS Report RS20760, *Membership of the 107th Congress: A Profile*, 5; Mildred Amer, CRS Report RS20013, *Membership of the 106th Congress: A Profile*, 5.

Text credits Appendix, "A Statistical Portrait" by Ruth Milkman, copyright 1989 by Ruth Milkman. Reprinted by permission of the author. Updated by Vanessa V. Tinsley.

Photo Credits Page xv Baby Huestis and Nurse, 1871. Valentine Richmond History Center; Part I Opener, **page 2** Lewis Hine, Library of Congress; **page 11** The Granger Collection, NY; **page 34** Jane Addams Memorial Collection, Richard J. Daley Library, University of Illinois Library, Chicago; **page 50** Lewis Hine, Library of Congress; **page 64** UNITE Archives, Kheel Center, Cornell University, Ithaca, NY.

Part II Opener, **page 66** A'Lelia Bundles/Walker Family Collection/madamcjwalker.com; **page 74** Division Street, Photo: Wurts Brothers, June 29, 1910. Museum of the City of New York. Print Archive; **page 86** The New York Public Library/Art Resource, NY; **page 93, page 109** A'Lelia Bundles/Walker Family Collection/madamcjwalker.com; **page 114** Special Collections, Bracken Library, Ball State University.

Part III Opener, **page 126** Dorothea Lange, Library of Congress; **page 139** San Antonio Light Collection, UTSA's Institute of Texan Cultures, #L-1822-B, Courtesy of the Hearst Corporation; **page 151** John Philip Falter, artist/Library of Congress; **page 167** Recruiting Publicity Bureau, United States Army, Minnesota Historical Society; **page 172** Photofest.

Part IV Opener, **page 186** AP Images; **page 194** Courtesy of *The Famuan*, the Florida A&M University student newspaper, May, 1959; **page 215** Jane Crosby Collection, UCLA; **page 230** all buttons: From the button archive of the CWLU Herstory Project and Jo Freeman; **page 246** all posters: Copyright Chicago Women's Graphics Collective, www.cwluherstory.org.

Part V Opener, **page 248** Jeff Greenberg/PhotoEditInc.; **page 256** Pamela Duffy; **page 278** Tom and Dee Ann McCarthy/Corbis; **page 293** Cover Illustration by Diana Souza, *Heather Has Two Mommies* © 1989, 2000 Leslea Newman Alyson Publications, Los Angles California/London England.